The Economics of Labour Markets and Management

The Economics of Labour Markets and Management

TONY MALLIER and
TONY SHAFTO

HUTCHINSON

London   Sydney   Auckland   Johannesburg

Hutchinson Education

An imprint of Century Hutchinson Ltd
62–65 Chandos Place
London WC2N 4NW

Century Hutchinson Australia Pty Ltd
89–91 Albion Street, Surry Hills,
New South Wales 2010, Australia

Century Hutchinson New Zealand Limited
PO Box 40–086, Glenfield, Auckland 10,
New Zealand

Century Hutchinson South Africa (Pty) Ltd
PO Box 337, Bergvlei, 2012 South Africa

First published 1989

Typeset by Hope Services (Abingdon) Ltd,
Printed and bound in Great Britain by
Scotprint Ltd, Musselburgh

British Library Cataloguing in Publication Data

Shafto, T.A.C. (Thomas Anthony Cheshire), *1929–*
    The economics of labour markets and management.
    1. Labour markets
    I. Title II. Mallier, A.T., *1931–*
    331.12

ISBN 0–09–173166–6

Contents

Preface

Almost all of us at one time or another for part of our lives and most of us for most of our lives participate in and form part of the labour market. The small segment of the total labour market that we see may not always appear to function too well and we may suspect that other bits are not much better. The difficulty with our perception of the market may be that we do not always appreciate that jobs, careers, promotions, redundancies, and unemployment are the consequences of labour market operations. Our ancestors who put mops in their caps and went to local fairs to advertise that their work was for hire might possibly have had a better understanding of how labour markets worked than some of us today.

In this book we seek to explain the underlying forces of labour markets and why these forces do not always function effectively in practice. Our starting point is the neo-classical model, but we acknowledge the limitations of this approach in modern economies. We also recognise the segmentation of contemporary markets and the consequences of this for attempts to manage an economy through the manipulation of aggregates.

The book is intended to make a significant contribution to the development of modern studies by linking the analysis of markets to the problems faced by business management in planning a labour force, in recruitment, and in constructing and operating a wages structure. Job evaluation procedures are explained and discussed.

Throughout all discussions the constant theme is that of change. The reader is encouraged to think about contemporary trends, such as increased labour mobility, and probable future developments. For individuals and labour managers, decisions made today bear their fruits tomorrow. The young school or college leaver must always look to the future. Too often the advice they receive from amateur career advisers is based on the past. This is always dangerous, but in a period of such fundamental change as today it can lead to personal tragedy and a general waste of scarce and valuable economic resources.

This is a working textbook containing over 200 questions for discussion and about 80 suggestions for written assignments. Many of the discussion questions are also suitable for written, individual or team, projects or assignments.

Our sincere hope is that this book will encourage the serious study of labour markets in business courses so that the question of human resource allocation can share a position of equality with traditional studies of the capital and financial markets. Effective labour management is as crucial to the modern business as financial management. Indeed, managing finance without the former can be wasteful and expensive. Labour is the ultimate economic resource, but workers are also human beings, members of social as well as economic structures. If this book contributes to a better understanding of the issues involved in labour management it will have been well worth while.

1
The Changing Pattern of Work

The Meaning of Work

What do we mean by 'work'? This is a question that has long puzzled and fascinated sociologists. You may have heard the story of the daily help who greeted a casual caller to her employer's house with, 'Come in. You're not likely to disturb the professor because he's not working—only reading a book.'

The professor, perhaps, might have liked to relax from his studies with a game of tennis and he, in his turn, might have found it difficult to accept the fact that a growing number of people work and make their living from playing tennis.

If one person's leisure is another's work how, then, do we define work? Clearly we cannot define it by the nature of an activity pursued. The economist might be tempted to define it in terms of an activity which provides satisfaction or utility for which individuals or groups in the community are prepared to pay some of their own resources, usually money. However, most of us have some hobby or leisure activity on which we spend money and which gives us satisfaction but which we do not regard as work. On the contrary, many of us regard our 'work' as little more than the means of providing us with the money to pursue activities in which we are really interested. Any attempt to define work in terms of the results of the activity is going to present problems. Is the local amateur drama group working when it presents its winter productions? Are the local Guides and Scouts working when they arrange sponsored activities in aid of handicapped children? Is Grandma working when she knits a sweater for a favoured grandchild?

In fact, the economist accepts a much more limited definition of work in terms chiefly of the motive for working. An activity becomes work when it is pursued in anticipation of receiving a financial gain or reward. The reward may be in the form of wage, salary, fee, prize money, profit or any other inducement devised to meet the literal requirements of the Inland Revenue or sporting management authorities. It is, therefore, the financial implications that distinguish work from leisure. This, however, does not rule out the possibility that work may be undertaken to secure rewards in addition to money or which the individual regards as being more desirable than money, but 'work' as here defined always involves a financial reward.

In contrast, a leisure activity is pursued wholly or chiefly for personal satisfaction and any financial return is subsidiary to this main purpose. So Grandma's knitting, the local drama productions and the professor's tennis are leisure, but the actor in the latest TV 'soap' series, and the journalist who watches it in order to write his or her weekly column are working as, too is the professor reading his book in preparation for tomorrow's lecture.

Of course, as with any other attempt to put human activities into neat classifications, there are always grey areas. There will always be many people who train hard at sports in the hope that they can reach a standard that makes earning a living at the sport a possibility, just as there are many others who pursue a hobby partly for self-fulfilment and partly to gain some extra income.

Question for Discussion and Review

1 Do people work only for money? If not, what other motives can you suggest would still distinguish 'work' from 'leisure'?

The Changing Pattern of Work

The economist is interested in all forms of work and leisure and is particularly interested in trends and attitudes which bring about changes in the pattern and structure of work.

The path of technology and its effect on production and work is clearly marked. First, it provides people with machines that allow them to produce more. The machines replace many of the people who formerly did the work and also change the nature of the work of those who remain. The pattern of work and life styles change and new needs are created, and the machines make possible their satisfaction.

Rising levels of technology produce a clear path of development. First, it is the pattern of food production that is changed. Producing food ceases to occupy the time of the vast majority of people. A much smaller proportion of people produce much more food and more is imported from other, favoured food-producing countries by virtue of improved transport systems.

Figure 1.1 shows the change in the proportion of the civilian labour force employed in agriculture in a number of countries between 1970/71 and 1985. Notice that British figures alter relatively little over this period because Britain's working population had moved out of farming many years previously.

The people displaced from the land—or, in most cases, their children, for it is generally the young who leave the old places and styles of work to seek new opportunities—moved during the main period of change to the industrial factories. The population became urban rather than rural. By the second half of the present century, however, further advances in technology were producing very similar changes in manufacturing employment to those earlier experienced in agriculture. Fewer and fewer people were using increasingly advanced technology and manufacturing 'know how' was making it possible for a declining work force to produce more and more goods.

This trend became very clear by the 1970s, and Figure 1.2 shows the decline in industrial employment between the years 1974 and 1986. In this period the number of workers employed in the production and construction industries fell from 9 895 000 to 6 766 000, a reduction of 31.6%. Nevertheless, in 1986 total output of these industries (at constant factor cost, i.e. allowing for price changes) was over 10% higher.

These broad totals hide a number of significant details. For example, between 1976 and 1986 the volume of oil and gas extracted in fields within the United Kingdom expanded ninefold while the number of people employed in this sector grew only fourfold and actually fell between 1985 and 1986 even though production continued to rise.

While employment in farming and industry was falling, more and more people were moving to the service sector. The trend in some representative European countries is shown clearly in Figure 1.3. A more detailed breakdown of the British figures is shown in Figure 1.4 which clearly illustrates the growth of the financial services.

These trends are expected to continue. A report commissioned by the Occupations Study

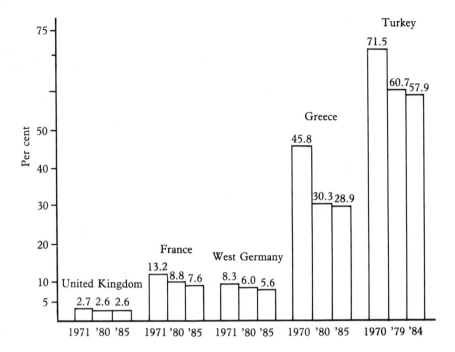

Figure 1.1 *Percentage of the civilian labour force employed in agriculture in five European nations, various years*
Note: Figures for 1970/71 include unemployed
Source: Statistics of the Community (Eurostat), various years

Group and prepared by the Institute of Manpower Studies, 'UK Occupation and Employment Trends to 1990', edited by Rajan and Pearson, and based on information supplied by a large sample of employers, forecast that the main rises in employment in the late 1980s would be in the distributive, finance and business services and other services.

Questions for Discussion and Review

2 How would you expect the composition of the service sector in Turkey to differ from that of the service sector in the United Kingdom?

3 In the 19th century there was a major shift of employment from agriculture to manufacturing industry. In the 20th century there has been another major shift from manufacturing to services. What movement, if any, would you expect in the 21st century?

The Organisation of Work

The Changing Employer

These trends have implications for the kind of employing organisation providing employment. The twentieth century has seen the growth of the very large business firm which has dominated employment in the advanced industrial countries and which, in particular, has swallowed up a very high proportion of the most able and highly qualified entrants to the work force.

In the late 1980s large firms still retained their dominance but there were signs of emerging change. The complex network of highly specialised services was already giving opportunities for individual, technologically gifted entrepreneurs. Only large firms had the resources to produce computers sophisticated enough to meet the demands of modern business, and these generally still employed teams of software engineers to produce the 'driving mechanism' for the computers. However, to modify standard software packages to meet individual needs, and to 'de-bug' programs so that they can stand up to the rigours of daily use—and mis-use—often requires the work of a talented individual. Such individuals tend to operate as freelance entrepreneurs.

The communication and leisure industries also use the services of individual specialists, often valued for a particular talent. A multinational group of hotels, seeking to offer leisure services to guests, will employ individual sports instructors under contracts that enable these people to pursue careers of their own and to work for more than one employer.

There are other trends supporting an increase in self-employment. Within the distributive trades there has been a huge expansion of franchising, a practice that enables a person to operate his or her own business to a design formulated, partly marketed, and often partly controlled by a national or international organisation. The franchise holder receives some of the benefits of belonging to a large-scale undertaking while having opportunities to use his or her own initiative and energy to generate personal profits.

Between 1976 and 1986, the UK total employed labour force fell slightly from about 24.8 million to 24.5 million. In the same period, however, the number of self-employed people rose by more than 34.5%, from 1.9 million to over 2.6 million. This, of course, is still a tiny fraction

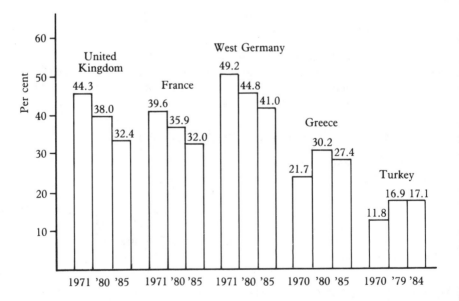

Figure 1.2 *Percentage of civilian labour force employed in the industrial sectors in five European nations, various years*
Note: Figures for 1970/71 include unemployed
Source: Statistics for the Community (Eurostat), various years

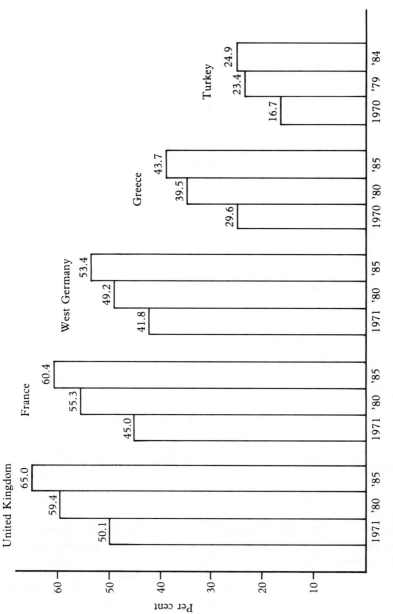

Figure 1.3 *Percentage of civilian labour force employed in service sectors in five European nations, various years*
Note: Figures for 1970/71 include unemployed
Source: Statistics of the Community (Eurostat), various years

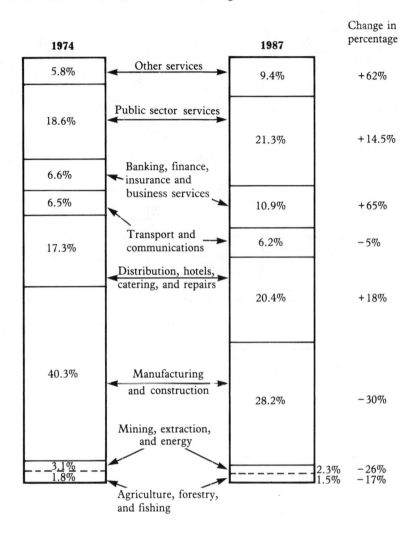

Figure 1.4 *Percentage distribution of employment by sector for United Kingdom, 1974 and 1987*
Source: 'United Kingdom National Accounts', HMSO, London, 1985 and 1988

of the total workforce and it would be foolish to think that all or most self-employed people are highly skilled specialists, but the trend is interesting and in some respects there is even a return to pre-industrial society work patterns when actual production was carried out in people's homes using their own tools and equipment, though it was often organised, financed, and marketed by merchants operating on a large scale.

These individual merchant 'entrepreneurs' (risk-taking organisers of production) were mostly swept away by the structured firm of the factory system which provided the power, machinery, discipline, and management needed for mass production to be successful. Structured firms are not going to disappear and may well continue to grow in power and influence, but they are already being joined by organisers of production operating in sectors such as computer software production, the provision of contract labour, the marketing of holiday cottages, and the provision of such personal services as the supply of people to look after homes and pets for those going on holiday. These organisers fulfil the essential market function of linking supply and demand. They are also entrepreneurs in that they play a large part in stimulating both demand and supply and in taking the risks of initiating business enterprise.

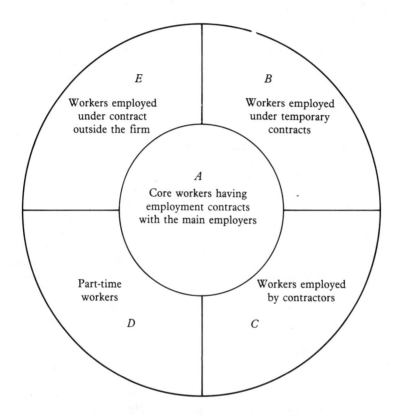

Figure 1.5 *The structure of a firm's labour force*
Typical examples of non-core workers:
B—Specialist consultants, designers, etc.
C—Cleaners, canteen workers
D—Word-processor operators, clerical staff
E—Printers, computer software writers

The Changing Technology of Work

Such changes in the structure of work are themselves partly the result of changes in the technology of work. In the eighteenth and nineteenth centuries, work moved from the home to the mill and factory because new machinery needed the power, first of water and later, of coal and steam, and because new production methods required a degree of conformity to set standards of quality and design that could only be guaranteed by direct personal supervision of work within a single place of work.

An increasing amount of modern production machinery requires only a power point to the electricity grid, or even no more than a mobile generator. The franchise holder who offers 'thief desisting' window lettering for motor cars can wheel a machine around a superstore car park and seek out customers rather than expect customers to drive to a factory or garage. The hairdresser can bring equipment to the customer's home rather than expect the customer to visit the salon. Growing numbers of people offer 'office services' from their own homes. A word processor is no more unsightly than a video recorder and television set, and rather less noisy than a carpet cleaner. Desk-top publishing with laser printing will probably soon be within the financial means of large numbers of people and will require no more space than a small spare room in the house. This development is likely to have as large an impact on the 'communication of news and views' as Caxton's introduction of the printing press to England.

The Hierarchy of Work

These and other developments in technology, e.g. telephone computer links, make possible the return of much work to the home, so that a smaller proportion of people actually need to 'go to work' in order to earn their livings or to work for a single employer. At the same time, technology is also transforming relationships between workers within the factory and office.

When work—whether making goods or carrying out office processes—was generally noisy, dirty, and smelly, the worker was banished to the workshop and the office worker to the 'general office' or 'typing pool'. The manager withdrew to more pleasant surroundings. The distance from production work to source of authority for that work measured the length of the hierarchy from 'top management' to worker and was a good indicator of the size of the firm.

Many of the benefits of the latest technology are lost if that distance between manager and managed is retained. With automated production, delays in dealing with a rogue machine or an electrical or program fault can cost the firm millions of pounds in spoilt production. Reactions to warning signals have to be prompt and decisive. The manager must be on the spot to override the automated system at the first sign of trouble. Socially, the manager finds it acceptable to live among dials, VDUs, and the other trappings of automation in a way that would have seemed unthinkable in the days of the heavy steel hammer. Similarly, the office manager has to work with and interpret the software which provides up-to-the-minute records of sales, profit breakdowns, market trends, and other information required for managerial decision making. Decisions have to be made swiftly. There is less time and opportunity for the preparation of bulky, typed reports discussed in leisurely conferences. The manager, secretary, and word processor operator tend to share the machinery and technology in ways that must bring about fundamental changes in the structure, i.e. the managerial hierarchy, of work.

Questions for Discussion and Review

4 In the past decade, the average number of people employed per working establishment has fallen. Does this mean that firms have been getting smaller?

5 In what ways do you think automation is changing the personal qualities required to become a successful business manager?

The Changing Workforce in Great Britain

Measuring Change

The subject matter of this book is people, and people are never static. By 31st December in any year, somewhere between 3 and 5% of those who were in employment on 1st January of that year will have left the labour force because of retirement, ill-health, or family or other personal reasons. At the same time an almost equal number will have entered (or re-entered) employment having completed a period of formal education or family formation. Those entering the labour force each year are likely to do so with rather different skills than those who leave. Many of the leavers will have had upwards of 50 years in employment. Nor do those who enter employment necessarily come into the industries which those who retired have left.

This aspect of labour economics relating to the deployment of the labour force can be analysed with the help of employment statistics. These permit either a cross-sectional analysis of the labour force's industrial and occupational development on a specific date (for example, 1st January 1989), or alternatively make possible a time series analysis showing how the deployment of the labour force has changed over a period such as, say, the end of the Second World War to the present day. Before undertaking an examination of these changes in labour force deployment in the British economy over the twentieth century, it is appropriate to consider the economic reasons why the changes have taken place.

The Case of Coal and the Demand for Labour

The reasons for changes in the structure of employment may be identified by examining specific industries. Aggregate employment is the sum of employment in each individual industry and in each firm within the industry. In this study we examine the coal industry in Britain. In 1947 this became state-owned, with the integration of previously separate firms into a single nationalised organisation. Since that date the industry has had one management with near monopoly power over the production and distribution of one product, coal. Consequently, employment in the industry has been dependent upon the success, or otherwise, of that product. The first observation to be made from Table 1.1 relates to the industry's output rather than to employment. In 1947, the first year of public ownership, output was 200 million tonnes; forty years on, output had declined by approximately 50%. This decline in output reflected the fall in demand for coal and led to the reduction in employment in the industry. A more theoretical analysis of the relationship between the demand for a product and that for the labour

Table 1.1   Employment, output, and producing collieries in the British coal industry 1947 and 1986

	1 January 1947	27 December 1986
Number of employees[a]		
Total industrial employees	692 173	135 421
Total non-industrial employees	30 123	19 751
Number of producing collieries	970	113
	12 months to 31 December 1947	12 months to 27 December 1986
Output (million tonnes)		
Deep-mine	187.5	89.5
Opencast	10.4	12.9

[a] Figures include Coal Products and other subsidiaries
Source: British Coal data

involved in producing it is given in Chapters 4 and 5. At this stage attention is concentrated on certain practical implications.

There is no simple, single answer to the question of why the demand for coal should have fallen in this period. Some of the most important reasons appear to be:

(a) The discovery of more easily obtainable alternative energy sources which have acted as coal substitutes. For example, in 1947 households cooked with 'town gas' which was extracted from coal, but this has been substituted by the alternative 'natural gas', and coal is no longer used to produce gas. The continued discovery of oil has led to the replacement of coal by oil in many processes. Diesel locomotives, for example, have replaced steam trains on the railways.

(b) Advances in technology have resulted not only in more efficient ways of producing coal and other energy sources but also in developing methods of transforming coal into a more efficient and flexible energy source. As late as the 1940s large numbers of factories in Britain relied for their main power source on individual coal-powered steam engines. Today the main source of industrial power is electricity. Coal is used in electricity generation (and indeed, in Britain this is the main use for coal) but, because of continued improvements in the technology of electricity supply, the increase in demand for coal by electricity power stations is less than the decline in demand from the former direct users. Further developments, e.g. in nuclear and wind-powered energy, are continuing to reduce the dependence of the electricity supply industry on coal.

(c) In the 1940s there was a large demand by households which burned coal in open grates to heat individual rooms. Improved technology and rising incomes, encouraged by clean air legislation passed after a series of devastating winter 'smogs', led to the widespread replacement of open coal fires by central heating systems and the use of 'cleaner' and more easily managed fuels, including oil and natural gas. Household demand for coal fell almost as rapidly as industrial demand.

There appear, therefore, to be three main causes for the decline of coal: the development of substitute sources of power, advances in technology, and changes in community taste leading to the desire for a cleaner, smog-free environment and for homes that can be kept warmer, cleaner, and easier to manage. The same three basic causes—new substitutes, developing technology, and changing taste—closely associated with rising incomes, living standards, and expectations, lie at the heart of most of the major changes in labour demand in the past half century.

The Coal Industry and Changing Employment Patterns

The history of the coal industry provides a further lesson in relation to changes in the occupational structure. In 1947 the average output per 'industrial employee' was 286 tonnes. Forty years later this had risen to 756 tonnes. The decline in the demand for coal and competition with other fuels has resulted in the closure of the least productive coal mines. This provides part of the explanation for the increased output per miner, but a much more important reason has been the far-reaching technological development that has transformed the way coal is actually mined.

A high proportion of the 286 tonnes per man in 1947 resulted from miners using picks and shovels. By the mid-1980s miners were dependent upon complex machinery to cut, load, and transport coal underground. Physical strength alone was no longer sufficient. More important were electrical and engineering skills very similar to those found in other industries. The technology that has allowed output to increase requires an appropriately skilled labour force.

Not only has the number of 'industrial employees' declined by 80% but, equally significantly, those remaining require different occupational skills.

Another aspect, therefore, of the coal industry's changing labour force is the relative growth in the number of 'non-industrial employees'. In 1947 the ratio of non-industrial to industrial employees was 1:23; by 1986 this had become 1:7. The reasons for this change in the character of the labour force can be found in the increasing complexities of organising an industry which needs forward planning, skilled appraisal, and monitoring of investment in increasingly complex equipment and modern marketing techniques in what is now a highly competitive, international market. Thus, over a period of forty years not only has the size of the labour force changed in response to changed levels of product demand, but equally significantly the character of that labour force has changed with a relative increase in both skilled and professionally qualified workers.

Questions for Discussion and Review

6 In the light of this chapter's outline of changes in the coal industry, describe and discuss the nature and the causes of changes that have taken place in the steel industry.

7 Changing technology destroys jobs but expands employment. Explain and discuss this paradox.

Changes in the Employment Structure of Great Britain

The broad pattern of changes in employment that are associated with economic and technological change were outlined in an earlier section of this chapter. Here we detail the main structural changes that have taken place in the workforce of Britain.

During the course of the twentieth century, employment in Britain has risen from 16.3 million in 1901 to 24.5 million in 1986. More significant however, than this 50% increase in total employment are the changes in the distribution of employment between differing industries.

The 'Primary Sector' of the economy—agriculture, forestry, fishing, mining, and quarrying—has throughout the period declined in both absolute and relative significance. As a source of employment, in relative terms, these sectors have declined by 75% in the period to the 1980s. The decline in the relative significance of agriculture has been a long-term trend reflecting a combination of the factors discussed in this chapter. They include the development of new sources of supply, increasing output arising from scientific and technical developments, and changing consumer tastes. At the same time the changing employment levels in British agriculture have to be viewed against the wider international economy. The same is true of many of the other older industrial sectors. For example, while a proportion of the decline in employment in the Textile and Clothing sectors can be attributed to new technology and the development of artificial fibres, much is also due to growing competition from the newly industrialised nations. As one of the world's principal trading nations Britain benefits considerably from its exports, but the pattern of imports and exports has also changed significantly and this has helped to change the structure of British employment.

Britain now imports goods that once were exported. Table 1.2 shows that in 1901 nearly 15% of British employment was concentrated in Textiles and Clothing. The relative decline of Textiles was matched by a proportional increase in employment, also to nearly 15% by 1981, in the Metal Industries, which were also important suppliers of exports. There were equally

Table 1.2 Percentage employment in Britain by industrial sector for various years

	1901	1951	1971	1981
Primary industries	(14.0)	(8.9)	(4.3)	(3.4)
Agriculture	8.5	5.1	2.7	1.8
Mining	5.5	3.8	1.6	1.6
Productive industries	(39.4)	(44.2)	(42.8)	(34.8)
Metals	9.4	16.7	17.8	14.5
Textiles & clothing	14.7	7.9	4.7	2.9
Other manufacturing and public utilities	7.6	13.3	13.3	12.2
Construction	7.7	6.3	7.0	5.2
Service industries	(39.4)	(46.9)	(53.1)	(61.9)
Transport and communications	8.1	7.7	6.6	6.7
Public and local administration	2.5	7.7	6.6	7.2
Other services	28.8	31.5	39.9	48.0
Not classified	7.0	—	—	—

Source: Census of Population, various years

significant changes within these industries: while shipbuilding declined, vehicle manufacturing expanded together with electrical engineering.

The basic causes of change—new materials, technology, and changing tastes associated with rising living standards—continued to produce changing employment patterns throughout the century.

The relative increase in the significance of 'Productive Industry' employment, which had begun a century earlier, continued through the first half of the twentieth century. By the mid-1960s, however, British industry began to experience the effects of foreign competition. Initially this came from other advanced industrial nations, but later it also came from developing nations, many (but not all) of which are located in the Far East. While employment in Productive Industry had fallen slightly to 42.8% of total employment by 1971 compared with 44.2% in 1951, the major employment changes took place in the 1970s and 1980s. In 1981 these sectors continued to provide employment for over a million more workers than at the beginning of the century, but their relative significance as a proportion of total employment was less than in 1901. This relative decline in manufacturing employment and in the productive industries generally, a process sometimes termed de-industrialisation, is discussed by Singh (1977) and Thirwell (1982).

In 1901 the Productive Sector and Service Sector were of roughly equal proportional size. For most of the first half of the twentieth century both grew at the expense of employment in the Primary Sector. By 1971, however, their paths had diverged. Productive Industry was beginning to decline relatively while the growth of the Service Sector had reached the stage where it was employing about half the workforce. In the following decade employment continued to decline in the Productive Sector, but there was a compensating growth in the Service Sector. This trend had about it an element of inevitability, having been anticipated by Clark (1960), and others, who recognised that the application of technology to manufacturing processes would create wealth and greater leisure and lead to consumers demanding an increasing variety of services.

Nevertheless, it would be incorrect to suggest that the Service Sector has developed only to provide services for individual consumers to use and enjoy. Although such activities as retail distribution, hotels and catering, and many other services are clearly consumer services this is not the whole story. In a modern economy numerous Service Sector activities such as banking, computer software design, and industrial catering are activities primarily undertaken to support the operation of Productive Industry in ways already outlined. Indeed, one of the features of the post-1971 de-industrialisation era has been the willingness of Productive Industry' to sub-contract to the 'Service Sector' activities previously undertaken in-house. This partial shift of certain types of employment from the Productive to the Service Sector of the economy has taken place without any significant change either in the actual work undertaken or in the nature of the end-user. Such a trend is a useful reminder that statistical data relating to employment may not necessarily be a perfect guide to the development of either the economy or the structure of employment.

Questions for Discussion and Review

8 Discuss the effects of so-called 'de-industrialisation' on international trade. In what ways can services be exported?

9 Developments in technology, especially those in electronics, have changed the structure of employment in the manufacturing industries. They are increasingly likely to have an impact on the service sectors. How might these developments change employment in the financial services?

Changes in the Nature of Work

Analysing the Structure of Work

An alternative approach to studying labour-force deployment is to consider the nature of work undertaken by those in employment, i.e. investigate the occupational structure. The long-term changes in distribution of the labour force between different industries do not necessarily reflect what has been happening in the pattern of working occupations. There are many occupations which are common to virtually every industry. These include, for example, managers, office secretaries, and clerical workers. While one industrial sector declines another is likely to be growing so that those employees who follow occupations that are common to many industries may switch from one industry to another. It is also necessary to take into account that, over time, certain occupations may die away while new ones emerge. In 1901 there were numerous skilled blacksmiths but few motor mechanics: by 1981 the situation had been reversed.

In the 1981 Census of Population in Britain the economically active population was classified into 163 clearly defined occupations. However, changes in occupational content during the twentieth century make it impossible to relate many of these to earlier occupations with a similar name. For example, the term 'van driver' described a very different occupation in 1981 to that implied by the same term at the beginning of the century. Because of the changes within occupations, the information presented in Table 1.3 relating to the occupational distribution of employment has been classified into eight broad categories.

Changes in Manual Occupations

These eight occupational groupings may be further sub-divided into manual and non-manual occupations. Both industrial and technical changes in the twentieth century have helped to

Table 1.3   Percentage employment in Britain by occupational classification for various years

	1911	1951	1971	1981
Non-manual				
Professional				
(i) Higher	1.00	1.93	3.29	4.72
(ii) Lower	3.05	4.70	7.78	9.83
Employers, administrators, and managers	3.43	5.53	8.21	15.61
Clerical	4.84	10.68	13.90	15.96
Foremen, inspectors, and supervisors	1.29	2.62	3.87	3.78
Manual				
Skilled	30.56	24.95	21.56	16.19
Semi-skilled	39.48	32.60	25.23	25.71
Unskilled	9.63	12.03	11.94	8.19

Source: Census of Population 1981; derived from Routh (1980) pp. 221–5 for 1911, 1951, and 1971

bring about a continuous decline in the proportion of the labour force employed in manual occupations relying wholly or mainly on physical skills of strength and dexterity. On the basis of the estimates by Routh (1980), 80% of the gainfully employed labour force in 1911 were engaged in manual occupations and over the period to 1951 this fell to 70%. Analysis of the 1981 Census of Population Data suggests the proportion of the labour force in manual occupations had further declined to about 50%.

Not only are there now fewer manual workers but some of the old manual occupations have disappeared while others have emerged. Many others have changed in content. For example, a telephone engineer in 1911 needed to know little beyond a basic knowledge of electrical circuits but his 1981 counterpart increasingly requires a knowledge of computer engineering.

Over the long term the proportion of the labour force classified as 'manual unskilled' has fluctuated and was, by 1981, marginally below the figure of 70 years earlier. Of more significance are the changes, and timing, of the proportion engaged in manual semi-skilled and skilled occupations. While both categories have declined relatively, the former appears to have stabilised in recent years while the proportion of skilled workers has continued to decline. This is because many of the old skills based on early apprenticeship and long periods of practical experience have now been destroyed by modern electronics. In pre-automated steel making, for instance, the quality of a batch of steel depended on the skill of the man who could tell by the colour of the liquid just when to pour the molten metal. Modern production depends on precise computer calculations and carefully regulated and timed production processes. The skills employed in production are now those of the scientists and engineers who devise, plan, and programme the production method and machinery on which it depends. The relatively few people needed to operate the process equipment are likely to be watching dials ready to report any unplanned variations in readings to more senior supporting staff.

Growth of Non-manual Work

This illustration helps to explain another trend that has been evident during the recent period of major technological change. Although modern production requires far fewer people to work manually on the actual production line, these depend on a growing army of supporting non-manual workers. Each of the recognised non-manual classifications has grown during the twentieth century. The increase in the relative, and absolute, numbers of employees in non-manual occupations was examined by Elliot (1977) who identified two differing but complementary processes. These reflect the increasing complexity of business and industry in the modern international economy and the changing technological basis of employment. Consequently, there has been a significant increase in the proportion of workers described as 'employers, administrators, and managers' and an increase also in the various categories of 'clerical' workers.

Questions for Discussion and Review

10 Talk to parents and older friends and find out what changes have taken place in the nature and extent of manual work in your local industry. Discuss the consequences of these changes for local job opportunities.

11 Identify and discuss the changes that have taken place in office work since about 1960. What office skills have changed and what skills have remained unchanged?

The Importance of Technology for Employment Changes

This chapter has identified changes in the level of employment, in the industries where people are employed, and in the work tasks undertaken. All result from a complex series of interactions, but if there is to be identified one key consideration in the twentieth century which has brought these changes about then it would be the change in technology. The impact of technical change upon employment occurs at different levels and in different ways, but underlying the process three types of change may be identified.

New Product Development

Changes in technology may create entirely new types of product which may replace existing products. For example, the development of quartz watches had a devastating effect upon more traditional watch-making employment. Changed technology may also bring about entirely new products which by their nature create an entirely new consumer demand. Obvious examples include the development of television and, of course, the computer.

New Production Methods

Radical new methods of production have resulted from modern technology. Although Henry Ford is largely credited with the development of mass production of motor vehicles, the skills required on his moving production line were little different to those previously needed in manufacturing. More recent technological developments of computer-aided manufacture and the use of robots has revolutionised both the skills required and the numbers offered employment in the motor industry.

New Types of Raw Materials and Industrial Components

Examples of new raw materials that have had major effects on the demand for labour and the structure of work include plastics and artificial fibres. New components include transistors, which replaced valves in radio communication, and silicon chips, which made possible the desk-top computer. In some cases the new developments have replaced existing products to reduce employment in some industries to the benefit of others. The substitution of plastics for metal has clearly had this effect. In other cases entirely new goods and services have been developed. One example of this would be the introduction of cash dispensers providing a 24 hour cash dispensing service outside banks.

It should be noted that the effect of such developments on employment is not always entirely one way. Cash dispensers, for example, reduced the demand for bank cashiers and clerical staff in the short run but, by making bank services more useful and accessible to the public they have encouraged wider acceptance of payment of wages through bank accounts and thus, in the long term they have contributed to the expansion of the banking and financial sector and helped to expand employment in that sector.

General Effect of Technology on Employment

To understand the impact of technical change upon employment, therefore, it is necessary to take into account each of the three main effects and to understand the way they are likely to interact with each other in the long run.

The history of radio provides an interesting example. In many countries the post-1945 era is often regarded as the high point of the radio industry. During this period a large radio and radio components manufacturing industry grew up in the older industrial countries, providing employment to large numbers of skilled and semi-skilled workers. When radio gave way to television in the 1950s the same companies, using very similar technology, were involved and employment within the industry actually grew. However, the costs and unreliability of early television sets stimulated technical research, and further technical advances, especially the introduction of transistors to replace the old glass valves, transformed both television and radio manufacturing. Manufacturing systems have become highly mechanised and factory locations have mostly moved to the Pacific region where assembly is carried out by relatively low-cost labour supported by a small, highly qualified and paid, expatriate technical and managerial staff.

Not all developments in technology lead to such radical changes. Shops and warehouses around the world contain many technically advanced products for which it has subsequently been discovered there is no consumer demand, and the employment consequences have been small. Similarly, in research establishments there are countless files detailing new raw materials and/or components and new production methods. The failure of business firms to take advantage of these developments arises from their possible impact upon costs. If new materials and/or production methods are thought to lead to higher unit costs then business managers stay with established technology and the employment consequences of such developments will be virtually nil. The way the unit cost will be affected is often the result of changing the capital:labour ratio. The introduction of new production methods or materials is likely to increase expenditure on capital and to increase expectations of the output that can be produced from that capital. More theoretical aspects of this kind of change in the productivity of capital and labour are examined in a later chapter; at this stage it is sufficient to note that firms facing increased capital costs will probably try to justify and finance these by making corresponding savings in their labour costs. This they may seek to do by employing fewer workers with different skills or by employing the same number of workers but with reduced skill and wage levels. Each advance in technology, therefore, must be examined from the point of view of its effects on the demand for consumer products and on the cost of production. Only those changes that have a significant impact on either of these are likely to have important consequences for employment.

Question for Discussion and Review

12 Use the analytical framework outlined in this chapter to discuss the impact on employment, if any, of the following developments in technology: satellite communications; home video equipment; desk-top publishing; laser scanning; wind-powered electricity generation.

Suggestions for Written Assignments

1 With the help of your tutor, establish suitable boundaries of a local area or region. Using the most recent available Census of Population reports and other available sources, construct suitable tables and diagrams to show the occupational structure of the working population within your chosen area. Identify and explain the main differences between this structure and the occupational structure of the country as a whole. What changes do you anticipate in the local occupational structure in the next decade?

2 Choose one local firm or industry. To what extent is automated machinery used in this firm or industry? What changes to the structure of work can be attributed to automation in the past decade? What further changes are expected in the future?

3 Using any appropriate investigative method, examine the extent and nature of home-based work in your local area. Try to include at least one actual case study in your survey.

Suggestions for Further Reading

The changes in the character of occupational opportunities which are currently taking place in Britain and other nations are discussed by Gershuny (1978). The employment consequences of these changes and the evolution of the 'flexible firm' are considered in an Institute of Manpower Studies (1986) Report and by Hakim (1987). The changes in the content of occupations and in the character of the employment relationship are not necessarily achieved without conflict, and while such conflict is not the subject of this book its existence should be noted. Meredeen (1988) has produced a most useful set of case studies on conflicts of interests and their resolution.

2
The Workforce

Some Problems of Analysis

In Britain, the workforce as officially defined includes the self-employed, the unemployed, and people engaged in work-related government training programmes in addition to those in paid employment. The distribution of the workforce in these categories for 1977 and 1987 is shown in Figure 2.1.

The size of the workforce is influenced by numerous considerations, not all of which are economic. To take a contemporary example, one of the significant changes in the British working population during the past quarter of a century has been the increase in the number of married women successfully seeking employment. That this should have occurred is partly a reflection of changing economic circumstances leading to an increased demand for female workers. At the same time, as shown later in this chapter, this increased employment has also been encouraged by a range of demographic, social, and legal changes all interacting to produce this major shift in the structure of the working population.

Although it is not always possible to identify the precise causes and effects of any major shift in trends, it is possible to state in general terms that the size of the working population in any country is influenced by the interaction of economic and non-economic factors and is determined by:

(a) the size and age structure of the total population, and
(b) the proportion of the total population which claims to form part of the working population.

The Size of the Total Population

The Population of Great Britain

The 1981 Census of Population suggests that the total population of Great Britain in 1981 was 53.55 million (Table 2.1), an increase of 10% of the 1951 figure. During the course of the twentieth century the population of Britain has increased by nearly 50%, but this increase has been relatively slow compared with the estimated rise of 250% in the British population from 1801 to 1901. The recent increase in Britain, as in most other countries of Western Europe, has been much smaller than that experienced in most of Africa and Asia, as can be seen from Table 2.2.

Changes in the size of the total population in developed countries are not likely to be immediately reflected by similar changes in the size of the workforce because this excludes

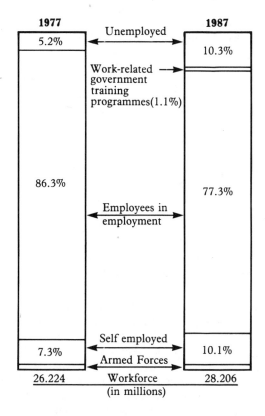

Figure 2.1 *Percentage distribution of the United Kingdom workforce by activity, 1977 and 1987*
Source: 'UK National Accounts' (CSO Blue Book), HMSO, London, 1988

Table 2.1   Population (usually resident) of Great Britain by selected age groups in April 1981 (in millions)

	Male	*Female*	*Total*
0–15 years	6.09	5.80	11.90
16–59 years	—	15.40	32.20
16–64 years	16.81	—	
over 60 years	—	6.30	9.45
over 65 years	3.15	—	
All ages	26.05	27.50	53.55

Source: Census of Population 1981

Table 2.2   Mid-year estimates of population for selected countries 1950 and 1980 (in millions)

	1950	1980	Percentage increase 1950 to 1980
Australia	8.19	14.69	79
Brazil	52.12	121.29	133
Egypt	20.44	42.29	107
France	41.94	53.71	28
Great Britain	49.24	54.77	11
India	358.00	663.60	85
Italy	46.28	57.07	23
Kenya	5.56	16.67	200
Philippines	19.87	48.09	142
USA	151.69	227.70	50

Source: 'United Nations Demographic Year Book', 1952 and 1983

young people required by law to attend school. In Great Britain the minimum school leaving age is 16, and there are strict legal controls over the employment of children below that age.

At the other end of the age range the workforce is not usually held to include people over the 'normal' age of retirement. In Great Britain this is 65 for men and 60 for women, although there is pressure, including that from the European Community, to end this form of sex discrimination. Official statistics suggest that the number of people who retire before the 'normal' ages is roughly balanced by the number remaining in employment after those ages. However, it must be admitted that many older people are employed on a part-time and casual basis and there are powerful financial incentives for both employers and workers to keep such employment concealed from the authorities; hence the true extent of post-retirement employment is not known with any accuracy.

If we retain the convention of excluding from the workforce those below compulsory school leaving age and those above normal retirement age then a little over 60% of the population of Great Britain can be considered to be 'of working age'.

The Age Structure of the Population

Figure 2.2 reveals the trends over the twentieth century for Great Britain. The total population did not grow at a steady rate throughout the period. Variations reflect changes in the birth, death, and migration rates during the century. Changes in these rates affect the age structure of the population and consequently the size of the population of working age. Figure 2.2 indicates that the proportion of the population aged between 15 and 65 has varied from a low of 62.8% in 1901 and 1971 to a high of 68.4% in 1931. This difference of 5.6% may seem fairly small, but as a proportion of a total population of about 53.5 million it represents about 3 million people of working age. Even the relatively small increase of 2.2% between 1971 and 1981 meant that there were an additional 1 350 000 people of an age to seek employment.

Current projections to 2025 for the population of Britain imply a modest 5% increase in the total population, but simultaneously forecast a reduction in the proportion within the age range 15–65 to 62–62.5%, i.e. a fall in the population of working age. This possibility of a decline in the size of the population of working age would represent a situation that has previously not been experienced in Britain, and the consequences of this are discussed by Reddaway (1977)

However, it must be stressed that past population predictions have been notoriously inaccurate!

Although the majority of the population in advanced nations falls into the 15–65 year age group, it is important to take account of the trends for both the young and the old (see Figure 2.3). The proportion of those aged 14 and below in the total population has declined continuously throughout the twentieth century. The birth rate, defined here as the number of children born per 1000 of the population in any one year, has halved during this century. In 1901 nearly one in three of the population was aged 15 years or under. At that time the minimum school leaving age was 12 and truancy from school was widespread and often encouraged by parents who expected their children to contribute to the family income. Thus

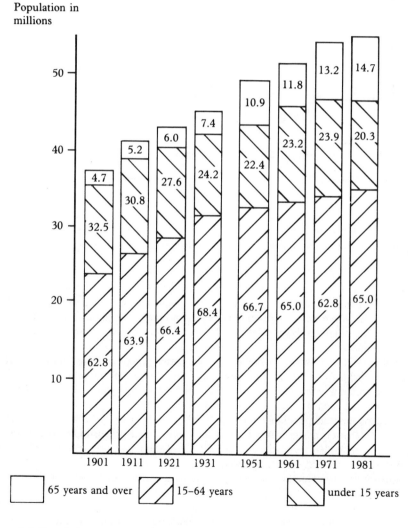

Figure 2.2 *Population of Great Britain by selected age groups, census years 1901–1981*
Source: Census of population, various years

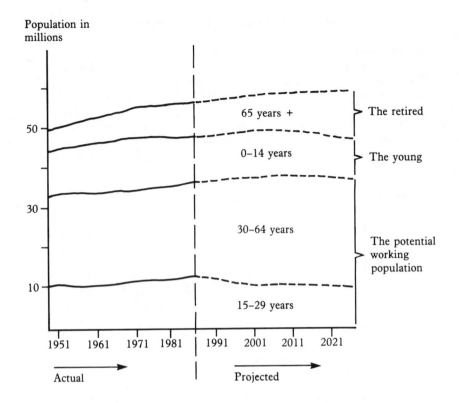

Figure 2.3 *Population structure by specified age groups: actual, 1951–1986; projected, 1986–2025*
Source: Based on 'Social Trends No. 18', 18th edn, HMSO, London, 1988

large numbers of children aged 13 and 14 were in full-time employment, including many in the armed forces. In contrast, barely one in five of the population was aged under 15 in 1981 so that, by this year, there were a million fewer young people in the population than in 1901.

However, while there has been a decline in the numbers and proportion of the young there has been a significant rise in the proportion of people aged 65 years and over. This change has been brought about by improved medical services, better general hygiene and diet, and safer and healthier working conditions. The death rate, defined here as the number of people per thousand of population who die in any one year, has declined by a third, and in particular, the death rate for those aged 0–4 years has fallen by 95%.

Consequently, the total population has continued to rise in spite of the falling birth rate. On average, the population has grown older and the number and proportion of people over the normal retirement age has risen sharply. In 1901 5% of the population was aged 65 or above; this proportion had trebled to 15% by 1981.

For comparative purposes, the size and age structure of a population is often illustrated in the form of a 'pyramid', with males on one side, females on the other. The two pyramids in Figures 2.4 and 2.5 show the age structure of the population of Great Britain in 1901 and 1981, respectively. Their shapes are very different. The 1901 pyramid indicates a high proportion of adults aged 15–65 years. It also suggests a decreasing birth rate, the numerical size of the age groups up to 15 years being almost equal to those in the groups 15–24 years.

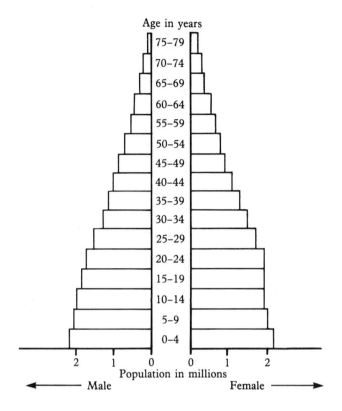

Figure 2.4 *Population age pyramid for Great Britain, 1901*
Source: Census of Population, 1961

The 1901 pyramid is one which, as Goetschin (1987) observed, occurs when economic growth, often linked with the adoption of new scientific developments, is taking place.

The shape of the 1981 pyramid is of the kind associated with an ageing or elderly population. The decreases in birth rate suggest that those retiring from the workforce will not be fully replaced by the young, with the consequence that the number of the elderly in the population will continue to rise. If it is assumed that young people tend to be more inventive and innovative than their elders, then this pyramid implies a slowing down of technical innovation and hence of economic growth. The numerical size of the workforce will also decline.

While the population pyramids for Great Britain have changed over the twentieth century as the economy has matured and the population has aged, elsewhere in the world the position is often quite different.

Some International Comparisons of Population Structures

Figure 2.6 shows the 1984 age structure of the Philippines, a nation with a total population similar to that of Great Britain in 1981. In spite of their similar size, the age structures of the two countries are very different (as can be seen by reference to Figures 2.5 and 2.6). In 1984 nearly 40% of the Philippines' population was aged under 15 years, twice the equivalent British proportion. Only 3% of the people of the Philippines were aged over 65 years.

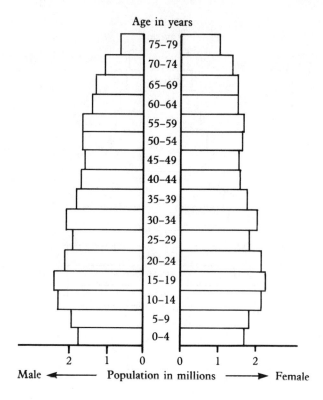

Figure 2.5 *Population age pyramid for Great Britain, 1981*
Source: Census of Population, 1981

Despite recent strides in economic development, the Philippines remains a nation with high birth and mortality rates. The relatively small proportion of adults in the total population may be a barrier to economic growth although there are other factors, including political instability, that also hinder economic progress. Nevertheless, the Philippines is already moving along the road to economic development, even though maintaining this requires a substantial amount of external financial and technical aid from countries such as the USA.

By contrast, in countries such as Bangladesh the development process has hardly begun. The entire economy of Bangladesh is devoted to sustaining a population of which almost 50% is under the age of 15 (see Figure 2.7).

Compared with both Bangladesh and the Philippines, Britain has a higher proportion of its total population in the age range 15–65 years, but unlike those two nations it has a considerably smaller proportion of the very young. Although it is useful to make comparisons between countries as different as Britain, the Philippines, and Bangladesh, we must remember that we are looking at very different economic systems. The Philippines and Bangladesh, though changing, are still predominantly agrarian, subsistence societies in which the distinction between 'working' and 'non-working' sectors of the population is not really valid. All but the extremely young and weak are expected to assist in the struggle for daily survival. In a subsistence society unemployment, as understood in industrial economies, does not exist but there is very widespread 'underemployment', with everyone in a large family struggling to make a living from a small plot of land or trading stall barely capable of supporting one or two people. Consequently, large numbers of young people flock to the towns hoping to find better conditions but in reality only helping to swell the numbers of the genuinely unemployed and of the urban poor and aggravating the massive social, economic, and political problems of modern urban life.

Questions for Discussion and Review

1 In some predominantly agrarian communities such as Turkey, the normal retiring age in the early 1980s for many occupations was much lower than in Western Europe. Suggest reasons for this.

2 How and for what reasons would you expect the size and structure of the populations of the West African countries to change in the next 25 years? Contrast these changes with those anticipated in the developed Western European countries.

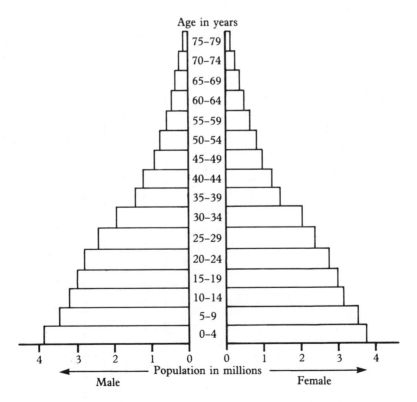

Figure 2.6 *Population age pyramid for the Philippines, 1980*
Source: United Nations Demographic Year Book

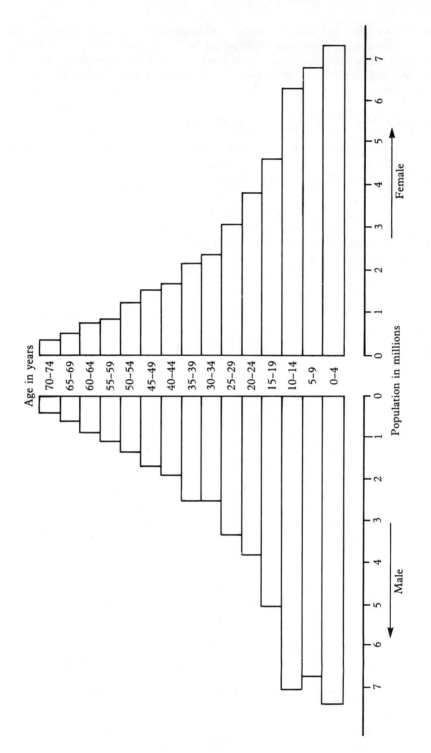

Figure 2.7 *Population age pyramid for Bangladesh, 1981*
Source: United Nations Demographic Year Book

The Economically Active Population

Trends in the Size and Structure of the Workforce

The term 'economically active' is another way of describing those who choose to work or to seek work, i.e. to join the 'workforce' as defined at the beginning of this chapter. Remember we are here concerned with work as it is defined by the economist and excluding unpaid work such as that of the voluntary services (e.g. the Red Cross) and of housewives and mothers.

In the mid-1980s the British workforce was estimated to be about 61 per cent of the total population above the minimum school leaving age of 16. During the twentieth century it might have been anticipated that this proportion would decline as the British economy entered a period sometimes described as that of 'economic maturity', during which

(a) there would be a rise in the proportion of the population choosing to remain in full-time education after the minimum school leaving age, and
(b) there would be an increase in the proportion of the population aged 65 and over with a consequent rise in the proportion of people who have retired from paid work.

Both of these developments have indeed taken place. There has been a considerable increase in the numbers of young people spending several years in further and higher education before starting a career, and we have already noted the rise in the proportion of elderly people. An increasing number of people have also chosen to retire before the 'normal' ages of 60 and 65. Nevertheless, Figure 2.8 indicates that for the sixty years since 1921 (for which reliable figures are available) the proportion of the population over the school leaving age in the workforce has stayed remarkably stable at about 60%.

Such consistency in the face of apparently contrary economic, social, and demographic influences needs to be explained. If, however, we separate the workforce into male and female sectors the explanation becomes clear.

The trends just outlined have indeed operated as anticipated on the economically active male sector in Britain and in other countries, as Parsons (1980) explains. The proportion of British males over school leaving age who were in the workforce fell from nearly 90% in 1921 to 77% in 1981. In the same period, however, there was an increase in the total male population so that the actual number of males in the 1981 workforce was little changed from the 1921 total.

If the proportion of males of working age who are economically active has fallen while the total workforce has kept proportionally steady there must have been an increase in the proportion of women choosing to work. In fact, the proportion of females over school leaving age who choose to enter the workforce has increased by 50%. In 1921 one woman in three was economically active. By 1981 this ratio had risen to nearly 1 in 2. The number of women recorded as being economically active in 1981 was 10 million, an increase of more than 75% over the 5.7 million in, or seeking, paid employment in 1921. Within this total there has been a significant change in the number of married women in the workforce. In 1921 only 700 000 (or fewer than 10%) of married women were regarded as being economically active. By 1981 this number had risen to over 6 million, representing almost half of all the married women aged 16–60.

The Economic Activity Rate

In the above paragraphs comparisons have been made of the actual numbers economically active, or the relative proportions who are economically active. The practice in Labour

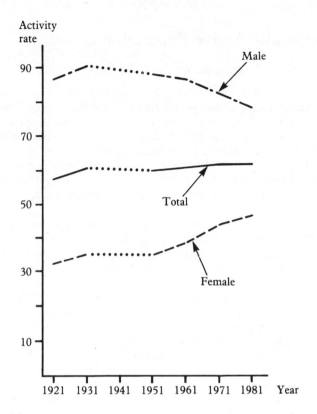

Figure 2.8 *Trends in economic activity rate for Great Britain, census years 1921–1981*
Source: Census of Population, various years

Economics is to try and standardise such comparisons largely through the use of a measure known as the economic activity rate.

The economic activity rate (EAR) can be defined as the proportion of people of working age who are officially recorded as being in gainful employment or as seeking work. Using the terms employed in the United Kingdom official statistics it is calculated as shown below:

$$\text{EAR} = \frac{\text{the working population}}{\text{the population of working age}} \times 100$$

The workforce has earlier been defined as consisting of those in employment, the self-employed, and those officially recorded as unemployed. The population of working age consists of those over the minimum school leaving age and below the 'normal ages of retirement'—the ages when national insurance pensions normally become payable.

In practice this formula is not always strictly followed, particularly when figures are prepared in the expectation that they will be used in international comparisons. The most common variation is to ignore the retirement ages so that the population of working age, also often termed the population 'at risk' of working, is made up of all those over the minimum school leaving age. An arbitrary minimum age may also be chosen.

When making international comparisons it is necessary to remember that school leaving ages, retirement ages, and methods of measuring unemployment all vary considerably from country to country as, of course, does the reliability of the statistics recorded.

In Table 2.3 the EAR has been estimated from the 1981 Census data for Britain using the definitions of the above formula. When adequate information is available it is possible to calculate economic activity rates for any number of sub-divisions of the population. For example, Figure 2.9 shows the 1981 economic activity rates for males, non-married females (single women, divorcees, and widows), and married women.

Table 2.3 Economic activity rate (EAR) for specified populations aged 16 years and over for Great Britain for 1981

$$\text{Total population EAR} = \frac{25.405}{41.662} \times 100 = 60.98$$

$$\text{Male population EAR} = \frac{15.537}{19.962} \times 100 = 77.83$$

$$\text{Female population EAR} = \frac{9.879}{21.700} \times 100 = 45.53$$

Source: Census of Population 1981

Questions for Discussion and Review

3 Many students in full-time higher education are in fact preparing for a definite career. They include students on medical, dentistry, teacher training, engineering, and many other courses.

Discuss the view that all full-time students above the school leaving age should be regarded as forming part of the workforce. What would be the implications for financing such students?

4 Should non-working mothers of young children also be regarded as belonging to the workforce?

British Economic Activity Rates, 1981

Rates for Men and Women

The EAR for males (see Figure 2.9) rises from the age of 16 until it reaches over 90 per cent for those in their early twenties, by which time most males will have completed their full-time education. For males the EAR remains over 90 per cent until the 60–64 age range when it begins to fall as early retirement is taken. Above 65 years, the formal age of retirement, there is a sharp decline.

For the non-married female a life-time pattern of economic activity can be identified, the peak level being reached in the early twenties. The pattern for non-married women differs from

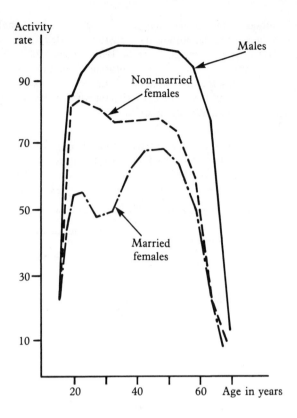

Figure 2.9 *Economic activity rates for Great Britain by age and sex, 1981*
Source: Census of population 1981

that of males. The level of economic activity for this group of women, while high, is, for most age groups, about three-quarters that of the corresponding male level. There is a modest decline in the EAR in the late twenties, which is likely to be associated with family formation and its consequences. Notice that economic activity begins to decline at an earlier age for women than for men. This reflects different retirement patterns.

However, the economic activity curve for non-married women exhibits a greater similarity to the male curve than the one for married females, a feature noted by Greenhalgh (1979). This may now imply that for the majority of non-married women the choice of whether or not to work is affected by factors similar to those influencing males.

Greenhalgh (1980*a*) suggested that for married women the pattern of economic activity was quite different from that for the other two groups. The EAR of young married women is significantly lower than that for non-married women, reflecting their withdrawal from employment for family formation. The family clearly remains the dominating influence for married women. The proportion of women in their early twenties—the most common ages for family formation—who choose paid work falls, but at higher ages it rises, at first slowly but then more rapidly at the ages when children are likely to be entering the school system. The pattern of re-entry to the workforce as family commitments become less restricting had become well established by 1981.

Regional Economic Activity Rates

Another approach is to study economic activity rates for geographical areas, and in Table 2.4 these are shown for the standard regions in Britain.

Table 2.4 indicates that there are significant differences between regions. These were particularly evident in 1971. The largest difference for males was between the West Midlands and the South West. In the latter region the economic activity rate was nearly 9% lower than it was in the former. In the same year the proportion of the female population of Wales which was economically active was 10% less than the equivalent proportion for women in the West Midlands. These differences, though still significant, were much reduced in 1981, to nearly 4.5% and over 6%, respectively.

Table 2.4 Economic activity rates by standard regions for Great Britain for 1971 and 1981

	Males		Females	
	1971	1981	1971	1981
South East	81.7	77.4	45.2	48.1
East Anglia	77.0	77.9	38.7	46.8
South West	75.9	73.6	37.6	43.9
West Midlands	84.7	78.0	45.6	48.5
East Midlands	82.0	77.9	43.0	47.9
Yorkshire and Humberside	81.2	76.4	41.8	47.2
North West	82.5	77.1	44.7	48.5
North	81.0	76.6	40.4	45.9
Wales	78.8	73.9	35.9	42.1
Scotland	81.1	76.9	42.6	47.0

Source: Census of Population, 1971 and 1981

Such regional differences were the result of a number of factors. One explanation for the high male EAR in the West Midlands was that area's economic prosperity at the time. The resulting employment opportunities attracted many from other areas. Virtually all the male migrants to the region were economically active. When those migrants lost their jobs or retired they tended to move out of the Midlands back to their original homes or to more attractive retirement areas. In the South West, for example, a factor contributing to the relatively low level of male economic activity is the high proportion of males who retire to the region.

A second feature to note of the regional EARs is the differences between 1971 and 1981. In every region with the exception of East Anglia, male EARs declined. Simultaneously, in all regions the female EAR rose, although the increases varied. The changes in the regional EARs over the decade were not accidental but reflected fundamental changes in the structure and location of economic activity.

Question for Discussion and Review

5 In North East England, older 'heavy' manufacturing industries are being replaced by distribution, service, and light engineering firms. What effect would you expect this change to have on the pattern of economic activity rates in that region?

The Employment of Women in Industrial Societies

The reasons for the increasing numbers of women in the workforce have been the subject of extensive research including, for example, the work of Greenhalgh (1977) and Joshi, Layard, and Owen (1985). Although such research has identified numerous economic factors contributing to the increase in female EARs, it must be admitted that the causes of this very profound change are rather complex. However, it is not difficult to identify the more obvious economic explanations.

Economic Forces Encouraging Female Employment

(a) Changes in the structure of British industry have created more employment opportunities that attract women. This has been shown in a number of studies, including Mallier and Rosser (1987). The old manufacturing industries, which relied overwhelmingly on the physical strength of male workers, have declined both absolutely and relatively. Their place in the economy was taken first by light manufacturing industries, where dexterity, not physical strength, was the prerequisite for gaining employment. At the same time there has been a considerable growth in the service sector. It should not, of course, be forgotten that the major employment activity of women in the early part of the century was domestic service. This area of employment has declined, but the decline has been more than made good by other economic and technological changes which have created or expanded job opportunities that are intrinsically non-sexist. Communications, insurance, and education are just a few examples.

(b) There is evidence [for example, the work of Greenhalgh (1980a)] that female employment is positively related to the level of real incomes. Although it can be shown that an increase in the real wages of men tends to discourage some married women from seeking employment, this tendency is outweighed by the encouragement to female employment which arises from increases in the real wages of women. Thus even if the real wages of males and females had risen at the same rate there would have been an increase in the numbers of women seeking employment. In practice the real wages paid to women have risen more rapidly than those paid to men (women's average hourly earnings increased from just under two-thirds of men's in 1970 to nearly three-quarters in 1986), so this served to encourage more women to enter the workforce.

(c) The actual, negotiated, weekly hours of employment have fallen, especially since the Second World War. This has probably made it earlier for women to take paid jobs, but Robinson (1979) suggests that of greater significance has been the expansion of part-time employment. In 1951 just over 11% (some 600 000) of women in employment were employed part-time. By 1981 the figure was over 3.5 million. By 1987 rather more than one in three of all women and over half the number of married women in employment were employed on this basis.

(d) The evidence relating to the effect of unemployment on women's economic activity, which was an area of study at the beginning of the 1970s [for example, Corry and Roberts (1970 and 1974)], has possibly been overtaken by more recent economic events. The influence of unemployment levels on the willingness of females to seek employment has been shown to vary between geographical areas. In those areas where there were above-average levels of long-standing male unemployment the female economic activity rates were found to be relatively low. The existence of male unemployment appeared to discourage women from seeking employment. However, in the areas where male unemployment was thought to be either low or of recent origin, its existence appeared to have an encouraging effect on female employment leading to above-average female activity rates.

Socio-economic Influences on Female Employment

There are other significant considerations where economic and social factors interact.

(a) *The family.* During the twentieth century the proportion of women who marry has increased, and the age of first marriage has declined. Simultaneously, the number of children in the average family has fallen and family formation is completed at an earlier age. The increasing percentage of women marrying younger coincided with the post-1945 period of high employment, which may have encouraged employers to retain the services of newly married female employees, reversing the widespread pre-1939 practice, noted by Summerfield (1984), of dismissal upon marriage. Smaller family size and advances in the prevention of child illness have combined to reduce the period mothers require to devote to child care, facilitating their return to employment if they so wish. At the same time, developments in the technology of birth control have enabled women to gain greater control over family planning.

(b) *Expanding educational provision.* One aspect of this has been the expansion of higher education places open to women. This has enabled women to seek careers in the more highly paid occupations and has tended to make employment more attractive; it has also enabled families to afford the additional services such as child minding and domestic help needed when both marriage partners are in full-time employment. Moreover, women who have made sacrifices to obtain qualifications and gain satisfying careers are less inclined to give these up or more determined to make an early return to work as soon as family commitments permit.

The changes in education provision have had further effects. The average child now enters school earlier while legislation has established a higher school leaving age than in the 1930s. Earlier school entry by children permits an earlier re-entry to employment by the mother should this be desired. The rise in the school leaving age, and the increasing proportion of children remaining in full-time education, has deprived families of the income previously earned by teenage children and simultaneously created new demands on the family budget. In these circumstances married women may have returned to employment as substitute wage earners.

(c) *The home environment.* Modern homes tend to be better designed and easier to manage than those built earlier in the century. At the same time the range of durable household goods such as washing machines, vacuum cleaners, and microwave cookers has expanded and the real cost of these goods has fallen. These changes in household technology have been accompanied by the development of convenience foods, non-iron fabrics, and ready-to-wear clothes. Consequently, housework, cooking, and shopping need no longer be full-time occupations and all three are increasingly shared by males.

(d) *The opportunity to spend income.* Over the past quarter of a century opportunities to spend income have expanded beyond the dreams of most of our grandparents. New images of the minimum acceptable life style have generated a demand for a range of goods and services previously considered unnecessary or unobtainable and may have simultaneously encouraged re-entry to employment and incidently created new employment opportunities for women wishing to work.

Notice that the above list of influences implies that they have all encouraged female employment. It could equally well be argued, as mentioned at the beginning of this chapter, that these developments were all stimulated by the determination of women to seek fuller and more satisfying lives involving work and careers outside the home and to achieve a greater degree of equality with men. The image of the full-time housewife really only belongs to a particular class of women at a particular stage of economic development. Historically, women have always been extremely active economically. Even a brief visit to an agrarian society in a developing country will bring home the fact that in pre-industrial societies, and indeed in the early stages of industrialisation, women have usually borne more than their fair share of heavy manual work. In nineteenth-century Britain, pit ponies relieved women from the work of hauling coal in the coal mines. The relatively low economic activity rates recorded for Wales conceal the fact that many wives of hill farmers are not recorded as forming part of the workforce. This does not mean that they do not work!

To seek to predict the future is at best foolhardy. To endeavour to anticipate the future size of the workforce is equally risky. Shipiro and Shaw (1983) expressed the belief that it was unlikely that there would be any rapid reversal of the rising level of female economic activity rates. In the economic recession of the early 1980s, which produced the highest unemployment rates for fifty years, the concept of women fully participating in economic life has gone (largely) unchallenged. Women have become an essential, and significant, element in the workforce of Britain and other industrialised countries, and appear likely to remain so.

Questions for Discussion and Review

6 'Escape from drudgery' was a press headline above a report of a survey published by the Bird's Eye frozen food company which showed how the average time spent by women on housework had fallen from 14 hours a day in 1938 to under 7 hours in 1988.

Suggest ways in which this 7 hours may be further reduced in the future and discuss the implications of the trend for both male and female activity rates.

7 'As increasing numbers of women gain the freedom to choose whether or not to work in paid employment, the class divisions between the female rich and poor are bound to increase.' Discuss this view of the possible results of modern trends in female employment.

Measurement and Analysis of Changes in the Workforce

This chapter has identified a mixture of demographic and socio-economic influences on changing employment patterns. For a better understanding it is important to separate the effects of demographic changes from those of the other influences.

With the help of Table 2.5 we can establish some general principles for analysing changes in the workforce (which in Britain before 1988 was termed the 'working population').

To identify the relative effects of the demographic and activity rate changes occurring between two years, X and Y, we need to know the size of the population of working age in each of the years and the respective levels of economic activity. Analysis can now be made, taking the following steps.

(a) An estimate of the size of the workforce in year Y can be obtained by multiplying the population of working age in that year by the level of economic activity in year X. The resulting figure will not be the actual size of the workforce in year Y, but an estimate of the size if the EAR had remained constant between the two years.

Table 2.5   Identification of the demographic and activity rate effects on the changes in the size of the working population in Britain between 1971 and 1981 (in thousands)

Male age groups	Working population		Actual change	Demographic effect	Activity rate effect
	1971	1981			
15 years	104	0	− 104	+ 18	− 122
16–19	1051	1178	+ 127	+ 221	− 94
20–29	3581	3543	− 38	− 10	− 28
30–39	3108	3642	+ 534	+ 549	− 15
40–49	3264	2965	− 299	− 281	− 18
50–59	3011	2869	− 142	− 61	− 81
60–69	1625	1189	− 436	− 69	− 367
Total all ages	15744	15386	− 358	+ 367	− 725

Female age groups	Working population		Actual change	Demographic effect	Activity rate effect
	1971	1981			
15 years	101	0	− 101	+ 20	− 121
16–19	911	986	+ 75	+ 191	− 116
20–29	1979	2353	+ 374	− 13	+ 387
30–39	1537	2129	+ 592	+ 299	+ 293
40–49	2067	2071	+ 4	− 219	+ 223
50–59	1841	1832	− 9	− 93	+ 84
60–69	661	440	− 221	− 47	− 174
Total all ages	9097	9811	+ 714	+ 138	+ 576

Source: Census of Population, 1971 and 1981

(b) The demographic effect is now identifiable and may be obtained by subtracting from this estimated workforce in year Y the actual workforce in year X. Because the EAR has been held constant the resulting 'demographic effect' figure (see Table 2.5) will reflect only the changes in the size of the population of working age between years X and Y.

(c) The activity rate change is now identifiable (Table 2.5) and may be obtained by subtracting from the estimated workforce in year Y the actual workforce in that year. Because the population of working age is constant, the resulting figure will reflect only the changes in the level of economic activity between the two years X and Y.

The size of the workforce in 1971 was determined by the level of economic activity for each age group and the numbers in each of the population's age groups. The resulting economically active population figures are shown in Table 2.5, along with similar information relating to the workforce in 1981 and the actual changes in the workforce size.

Although the total workforce increased by 350 000, there was a contrasting pattern between the sexes. The female workforce grew by twice this figure and the male workforce declined. These are the aggregate figures. Table 2.5 also shows the estimated demographic and activity rate effects. If there had been no changes in the EAR between 1971 and 1981, then for demographic reasons the workforce would have increased by half a million, of whom approximately 75% would have been males. There were, however, simultaneous changes in the levels of economic activity. These changes resulted in there being nearly three-quarters of a million fewer males in the workforce than would have been predicted given the 1971 level of economic activity.

On the other hand, rising levels of female economic activity resulted in a net increase of nearly 600 000 in the numbers of females in the workforce. Observation suggests that certain influences on some of the changes in economic activity can be identified. Economic activity changes resulted in there being 450 000 fewer 15–19 year olds in the workforce in 1981 than would otherwise have occurred. Some 50% of this reduction was directly brought about by raising the school leaving age to 16: the other half reflects the increased participation by young people in an expanded system of educational provision.

Similarly, there were over half a million fewer individuals aged between 60–69 in the workforce in 1981 than would have been expected if there had been no changes in the levels of economic activity. It seems reasonable to suggest that this reduction may be attributed to earlier retirements.

When account has been taken of the young and the elderly, there remain those aged between 20 and 59 years. Amongst males, the downward trend in EARs led to fewer men being in the workforce in all age groups. However, the female EARs rose in all of these age groups, with the result that the workforce contained a million more women aged 20–59 in 1981 than in 1971.

Questions for Discussion and Review

8 Contrast the female economic activity rates for South East England and for Wales (Table 2.4). How much of this difference do you think can be attributed to economic factors and how much to social factors?

9 Contrast the male and female activity rates for South East and South West England. How much of the differences do you consider to arise from demographic factors and how much from economic and social factors?

Suggestions for Written Projects and Assignments

1 Refer to the most recent reports of the Population Census of Great Britain and write a report comparing the structure of the workforce and activity rates of your town or area with another town or area in Great Britain of similar size but different geographical region. In your report you should use tables or diagrams to illustrate the data, list possible causes for the differences/similarities you identify, and suggest possible future trends.

2 Prepare a survey of the proportions of males and females registered for the main courses of subjects offered by your own educational institution. Illustrate your findings with suitable tables and illustrations and discuss the implications for future trends in the occupational structure of the female workforce.

Suggestions for Further Reading

An extensive discussion on the growth of world population and the interaction of population growth and economic development can be found in Nixson (1988) which will enable you to place Britain's population trends in a wider context.

An early approach to the analysis of activity rates is to be found in Galambos (1967). However, the influences on the level of male activity rates is an under-researched area, though recent material can be found in Greenhalgh (1979) and Parsons (1982).

Weisseff (1972) provides a useful introduction to the place of women in the labour market, while Bowen and Finegan (1966) discuss the relationship between educational attainment and economic activity.

The relationship between the 'family' activities of women and their willingness to enter the paid labour force is discussed in Gramm (1974), Greenhalgh (1980b), and Layard et al. (1980).

The initial modern growth in female activity occurred in many nations in periods of full employment and economic prosperity. When economic conditions began to change, Werneke (1978) anticipated a decline in the significance of female employment. However, Joshi (1981) and Owen and Joshi (1987) have been rather less pessimistic about the consequences, although Blundell et al. (1987) examine the relationship of the 'new' unemployment and female labour supply.

3

The Quality of the Workforce

The Potential Efficiency of the Workforce

Influences on Human Efficiency

The economic capital of a nation which helps to determine the rate at which its economy can develop is not solely dependent upon its physical resources nor upon the size and age structure of its population. It is not only the quantity of labour that is significant, but also its quality, for the quality of the potential working population will partially determine the efficiency of those in employment and the uses they are able to make of the physical resources at their disposal.

The quality of the workforce can, and does, mean quite different things, all of which are important. The quality of the workforce, and hence its potential efficiency, may for example be influenced by:

(a) The general level of health and the average expected lifespan. Workers will not be particularly efficient if ill health prevents them from operating at their full potential.

(b) The general level of education. The modern industrial/service economy is increasingly dependent upon a formally educated working population. While subsistence farmers in Bangladesh do not require School Leaving Educational Certificates, the lack of certain formal qualifications could have serious implications in industrialised nations. Indeed, there are extensive statistical data showing a strong positive correlation between the proportion of a country's population which has participated in higher education and the rate of that nation's economic growth.

(c) The availability of training for those in or entering the working population. Specifically vocational skills can rarely be acquired in an educational environment separated from the actual place of work, and given the speed of change of modern technology these skills usually require constant development and modification.

These requirements interact with each other, and it might be anticipated that a healthier, better educated and trained workforce would be more efficient than one where any one, or all, of the above were missing.

Evidence Relating to Health

Regrettably, there are no extensive records relating to the rise in individual health standards. However, it is possible to identify a number of significant indicators of health improvement.

For example, over the twentieth century the average life expectancy for male babies has increased by twenty-five years: in 1901 the average life expectancy was 46 years; by the early 1980s this had risen to 71 years. Similarly, female babies at the start of the century had, on average, a life expectancy of 50 years; this has now risen to 77 years. The steady improvement in the general health of the developed countries and the elimination of many of the old killer diseases are the result of improved medical facilities, more informed and efficient public health, sanitation, and environmental care authorities, a better-educated population, and improvements in working and living conditions.

Table 3.1 provides further evidence of the changes which have occurred. If it is assumed that in 1910 most undergraduates were drawn from families in the upper strata of society, who spent their youth in superior surroundings and received a varied diet, then their physical characteristics provide an indication of what could be achieved at that period. In contrast, few of those joining the army between 1914 and 1918 would have had access to such advantageous conditions, and the consequences are observable in their physical characteristics. By the Second World War significant improvements were evident. Nevertheless, not until after that war did the average weight of young men equal that of the students forty years earlier, and there was a further thirty years delay before the height was equalled. The changes reflected in Table 3.1 owe much to improving medical provision, but account must also be taken of the trend to smaller families, improvements in housing provision, the availability of more nutritionus diets, opportunities for physical exercise in schools, and the availability of welfare services.

Table 3.1 Changing physical characteristics of young males in Britain for various years

	Average height Average weight	in metres
Oxford & Cambridge students, 1908–10	10 st. 4 lb.	1.75
Army intake, aged 18 years, 1914	8 st. 7 lb.	1.65
Army intake, aged 20 years, 1939	9 st. 10 lb.	1.71
Army intake, aged 20 years, 1951	10 st. 4 lb.	1.73
OPCS survey, aged 20 years, 1981	10 st. 13 lb.	1.76

Sources: Various

The available data do not provide a direct, identifiable link between improving health and the efficiency of those in employment. However, if the working population is physically stronger (measured by height and weight), and if life expectancy has increased by 50%, then it is not an unrealistic conclusion to assume that efficiency in the work place will also have improved.

Questions for Discussion and Review

1 In recent years some moves have been made towards reducing the extent of tobacco and cigarette smoking at work. Do you think this is justified in the interests of improving the health of the working population?

2 Discuss the case for legislation to reduce the consumption of alcohol during normal working hours.

Education and the Quality of the Workforce

Evidence Relating to Education

Industrial change, associated with economic development, leads to the reshaping of the employed labour force. Previously important industries decline and are replaced by more technically advanced ones. This is true for all countries as they experience economic development. In the Philippines, for example, mass-production clothing industries are replacing agriculture, while in many industrialised nations nuclear energy is replacing coal. One result of the changing character of industry is that each new advance in technology leads to new skills being required while older skills become relatively less important. One consequence of this process is that the educational levels of new entrants to the labour force also have to rise. The number of occupations which require specialised skills based upon initial educational achievement rather than, or in addition to, natural abilities has steadily increased. Each new stage of economic development depends upon a more advanced level of science-based technology.

A new technology, whether it is an early steam engine or the latest advance in computer engineering, involves the application of a higher level of knowledge than the older technology it replaced. The foundation for the required growth of knowledge is built during the educational process.

Over the last generation the statistical relationship between a nation's educational provision and its ability to generate wealth has been recognised. With the recognition of this relationship more attention has been paid to education quality. There remains, however, the fundamental difficulty of how to measure and improve educational quality. One approach has been to assume that the general expansion of educational provision, on either a compulsory or voluntary basis, will lead to improvements in quality. An alternative approach has assumed that changes in quality may only be determined by measuring the achievements of those who have completed their formal education. An examination of the records of industrialised nations over the past fifty years reveals that both processes have been at work. Young people are now educated over a longer period than was the case at the start of the Second World War and achieve higher levels of educational attainment than was previously the case.

In Britain, the right to a secondary education was established in the Education Act 1944. Until that legislation only a limited percentage of children experienced secondary education as it is now understood. The majority left their 'senior' schools at the age of 14. While the right to secondary education was established in 1944 there was a thirty year delay before the minimum school leaving age was raised to 16, thereby guaranteeing children twelve years of schooling. Nevertheless, during this period there was a continual growth in the number of young people who chose to extend their education beyond the legal minimum.

Estimates, for England and Wales alone (see Table 3.2), indicate that between 1951 and 1985 the proportion of the 15–19 age group who continued their full-time education beyond the minimum school leaving age doubled from 6.7 to 13.7%, although it has to be remembered that by 1985 the age of leaving school had risen to 16.

Other changes were taking place at the same time. There was a parallel growth in the number of young people taking vocationally orientated courses in colleges of further education in contrast to the more 'academic' courses offered in schools.

This general extension of education can be expected to ensure that more people entering the workforce are better equipped to acquire the new skills that they are likely to need. However, Britain exists not in isolation but in a highly competitive world, and it is instructive to compare its record in educational expansion with achievements in other countries.

Table 3.2 Pupils staying on at school beyond the school-leaving age in England and Wales for various years

	1950[a]	1970[a]	1980[b]	1985[b]
Pupils staying on over the school leaving age (in thousands)	178	211	293	312
Population at risk of staying on at school (in thousands)	2704	2498	2290	2282
Percentage remaining at school	6.7	8.4	12.8	13.7

[a] *Minimum school leaving age 15 years*
[b] *Minimum school leaving age 16 years*
Source: 'Annual Abstract of Statistics', HMSO, London and Department of Education and Science data, various years

Table 3.3 indicates that the provision, and take-up, of full-time education for the 16–18 year old age group is more extensive in other nations. Of course, care has to be exercised when making this type of comparison. This table does include information on part-time education, which is a more important part of the total provision in Britain than it is in many other countries. However, the figures do not take into account differences in the age of commencement of formal schooling and in the content of the educational courses provided. These aspects are likely to have just as much influence on the quality of education as the age when formal education is completed.

Table 3.3 Percentage participation in education by young people aged 16 to 18 years in selected countries for 1981

	Full-time		Part-time	Total
	School	Other		
United Kingdom	18	14	32	63
France	33	25	8	66
Germany (Federal Republic)	31	14	40	84
Italy	16	31	18	65
Japan	58	11	3	73
USA	65	14	—	79

Source: Based upon data in 'Social Trends No. 17' (17th edn), HMSO, London, 1987

Provision for Higher Education

A second approach to determining educational quality is to examine the higher education provision, and especially the output of first-degree graduates. Since the Second World War the provision for higher education has greatly increased in every nation, and even when account is taken of population increases the relative increase in the number of new graduates produced annually is impressive.

If the university sector only in Britain is considered, the number of students reading for first degrees rose by nearly 300% between 1951/2 and 1981/2, from 66 500 to over 260 000. Not surprisingly, there was a percentage increase of similar proportions in the annual number of university graduates with first degrees, the number increasing from under 18 000 to over 70 000. These are absolute figures and thus reflect a change in population size. Consequently, the first-degree graduate numbers for a year need to be compared with a standardised population age group, taken here as those aged between 18–21. The number of new British university graduates in 1981/2 expressed as a percentage of the total population aged 18–21 was 2.74%; the equivalent figure for 1951/2 was 0.96%. Over this period there developed in parallel with the British university expansion an alternative degree awarding system of higher education which in 1981/2 awarded 34 500 first degrees. When this number is combined with the university first degrees the proportion of the age group receiving degrees rises to 4.1%. By comparison, the higher education system in the USA awarded over one million degrees in 1981/2, representing 5.8% of a much larger population of 18–21 year olds.

The question of how Britain might compare in the provision, and output, of higher education with other nations is complex, depending not only upon the number of places available and the content of courses but also on the approach adopted by a nation towards education. In very few nations is the normal period of undergraduate study 3 years as it is in Britain, where this particular pattern reflects the nature of schooling before entry to higher education. Where the practice is to have 4 or 5 year undergraduate courses, the undergraduate population can be expected to be larger. In such circumstances comparisons of numbers give no indication of the quality of total higher education provision. Moreover, in some countries there are very few entry hurdles to university courses but only a restricted number of places on the second and subsequent years. It then becomes normal for students to make several attempts to pass their first- and second-year examinations and a scheduled 4 year course becomes 5 or 6 years for large numbers of students.

In certain countries limits are placed, as a matter of public policy, on which institutions award degrees. In West Germany, for example, there has developed a system of public sector higher education in the Fachhochschules similar to that in the British polytechnics. On the other hand, the German non-university institutions may not award degrees and the 4/5 years of study lead to the award of diplomas. Thus direct comparison between Britain and Germany may result in misleading conclusions.

The fairly general consensus that there is some relationship between knowledge and wealth generation has led to the belief that an expansion of higher education is a necessary condition for economic development. Consequently, most nations have, over the past fifty years, endeavoured to raise the educational standards of their potential labour force. There is less agreement concerning how this objective should be achieved and there is also a substantial body of opinion opposed to the idea that the primary purpose of education is to produce a productive workforce. Many would argue that education is a consumer good and, as such, one of the civilising benefits of economic growth rather than one of its causes.

Questions for Discussion and Review

3 The Education Act 1988 established the framework of a 'core curriculum' for secondary education. Explain what you understand by this term and discuss the relationship between this core curriculum and the expectations of employers seeking to recruit an educated workforce.

4 Discuss the case for and against a core curriculum in higher education.

Training and the Workforce

The Training Framework

Most modern states accept some degree of direct responsibility for the provision of education, although they may leave the detailed implementation of policies in the hands of reponsible bodies enjoying varying degrees of independence. This approach has developed during a period in which there has been a growing belief in the economic importance of education. Many governments also acknowledge the significance of training and re-training facilities, recognising the productive benefits of a workforce with up-to-date skills. However, in contrast to attitudes towards pre-work education few governments, except when they act as employers, are prepared to accept direct responsibility for worker training. Such responsibility is usually left to employers, although some assistance may be given towards its cost. One consequence of this is that training provision is often determined by the short-term requirements of employers at the expense of what may be desirable to meet needs in the longer-term future.

The Analysis of Training Provision

The analysis of training provision must taken account of the following.

(a) *The nature of the training provided.* The value of training will vary from one individual to another and between employers. The basic distinction, initially suggested by Becker (1975), between general and specific training provides a useful framework for examining both the provision and value of training.

General training refers to that training which is not employer-specific. The term refers to the training that individuals receive which is transferable between employers. The traditional practice of craft training for apprentices is an example of general training. Upon completion of an approved apprenticeship with any one employer the craftsman possessed occupational skills acceptable to other employers. Similarly, the training received by word-processor operators in a vocational college is a form of general training. General training will, therefore, raise the marginal product of a worker for all employers. It is of direct value to the individual worker and it leads to higher efficiency, higher productivity, and often higher wages. To the employer it is essential that workers receive general training, but the employer is not concerned as to which workers receive the training—only that some do.

In contrast it is recognised that even the most highly skilled worker needs some company-specific training if the firm is to gain the full value of the worker's skills. The specific training may be restricted just to company administrative procedures and methods, the subject content of induction training, or it may extend into additional training to enable a skilled employee to operate highly specialised equipment, such as particular machines or specially designed software.

The value to the individual worker of specific training is that it converts the previously acquired general skills into a package employers require. To the employer, specific training is the process whereby previously trained potential employees may be transformed into efficient and productive employees. Specific training will, therefore, increase the contribution which the worker can make to the production achieved by the firm which provides the training. A fuller discussion of the worker's contribution to production is contained in Chapter 4.

b) *The nature of the training provision.* By its nature any training provision will involve the use of resources which might otherwise be used for productive purposes. The reasoning behind an employer's use of resources for training is the anticipation that a trained labour force will be more efficient and productive. Training is regarded as a form of capital investment in which the cost of lost production in the current period is set against the expectation of increased output in subsequent periods.

The types of training discussed above are those which will be formally recognised by employer and employee alike. It would, however, be incorrect to ignore other, informal, types of training which occur continuously in the workplace. Whether intentionally or not, working individuals are exposed to tasks other than those directly related to their own work. In time they gain an understanding of other types of work and they may, on occasions, experiment by doing other work tasks. For most employees, though to differing degrees, informal training is a life-long process and may open up different employment possibilities.

Although governments have tended to stay aloof from the detailed provision of training at work, this attitude has been modified from time to time. One such period was that immediately following the Second World War. There are signs that another might be arising in the late 1980s as governments recognise the implications of contemporary advances in technology for the structure of employment. A number of member states within the European Community, for example, have taken steps to ensure that all young people under the age of 18 are either participating in education or receiving government-subsidised training with an employer.

Questions for Discussion and Review

5 In the 1960s there was a widespread view among educationalists that all vocational training courses should contain an element of 'liberal studies' in order to give a wider educational background to students taking these courses. Discuss the arguments for and against this view.

6 Discuss the economic case for stipulating that all vocational training courses should contain an element of physical and health education.

Suggestions for Written and Project Work

1 Prepare a report comparing the vocational education and training provisions in your own country with those available in one other country.

2 Identify and discuss the main changes that have taken place in the provision of secondary and higher education for females in your country since about 1930. Discuss the effects of these changes on female employment opportunities and identify any ways in which you believe that the educational facilities for females are still inferior to those for males.

For both these questions you will probably have to visit a good reference library, but you should also try to obtain suitable information from other institutions and sources.

Suggestions for Further Reading

Information relating to the elimination of certain diseases which had an adverse effect on the health of the labour force in the earlier part of the twentieth century is presented in chapter 8 of

Culyer (1980). This chapter also incorporates a review of the research relating to health as an investment.

The relationship between educational provision and/or achievement and economic growth was developed by Denison (1967) and Briggs (1987). Harbison (1973) placed his emphasis on the relationship between education and wealth creation.

The link between educational provision and training was examined by Baxter and McCormick (1984), while Hartley (1985) has reviewed aspects of youth training which are relevant to the discussion in this chapter. The effects and determinants of training were examined by Greenhalgh and Stewart (1987), and Sheldlake and Vickerstaff (1987) provide a survey of the development of industrial training in Britain. Additional information can be found in two articles by Johnson (1984*a* and 1984*b*) in which he examined training in some European countries.

4
The Demand for Labour

People cannot work unless they themselves are prepared to produce some good or service which others are prepared to pay for or unless another producer wishes to hire them to work in his or her production organisation. There must, therefore, be a demand for workers, and understanding how this demand is formed and operates constitutes an important part of the study of labour economics.

The Product of Work

Derived Demand

The economist's approach to the demand for labour is to regard it as an intermediate demand. An employer does not demand labour for its own sake, but rather wishes to employ labour for its ability, when mixed with other factors of production, especially capital, to produce goods and services which can be offered for sale on the market. The firm's demand for labour therefore, is often referred to as a 'derived' demand. Labour demand is assumed to be dependent upon the actual demand for goods and services. It follows from this that should the demand for goods and services change (for example, the decline in the demand for coal discussed in Chapter 1) then the derived demand for labour will also change.

The demand for labour is, therefore, a consequence of the firm's desire to produce goods and services which can be sold on the market. In Britain this normally implies an opportunity to increase an organization's profits from the sale of output made possible by any increase in employment. If this opportunity to increase profits from selling additional output does not exist then the firm will not increase production and there is no increase in the demand for labour. Initially, we assume that firms are motivated to raise output (and consequently employment) by a desire to increase profits to the maximum potentially possible under any given set of circumstances. The initial assumption, therefore, is that firms seek to maximise their profits.

The Margin

It is helpful here to introduce 'the margin', a technical concept commonly used by economists. The term 'marginal' refers to a very small change in one variable which is the result of a small change in another; the change in either variable can be an increase or a decrease. Marginal revenue, then, is the change in total revenue resulting from a very small (one unit) change in the total output produced.

This concept of the margin can be applied to labour:

(a) The marginal worker or unit of labour is the last worker employed. The unit of labour may be an individual worker but in some cases, as when a team of workers is needed to perform a task or operate a machine, the unit will be the smallest team that can be employed.
(b) The marginal cost of labour, MCL, is the change in total labour costs to the firm resulting from a change of one unit in the quantity of labour employed. This is not necessarily the same as the wage paid to the marginal worker. Some of the additional costs that an employer may have to face are outlined later in this chapter.
(c) The marginal physical product of labour, MPPL, is the change in total production that can be attributed to the employment of the marginal worker. This is not necessarily the same as the extra output of the last worker employed. This worker may help the rest to make more productive use of their time and the available machinery.
(d) The marginal revenue product of labour, MRPL, is the change in total revenue that can be attributed to the employment of the marginal worker.

Question for Discussion

1 What difficulties might arise when attempting to calculate the marginal physical product of the following workers: assembly line operator (motor manufacturing); storeman (light engineering); sales assistant (travel agency); fireman (National Fire Service)?

The Employer's Decision
Implications of Profit Maximisation

Starting from the assumption that the employer's objective in employing labour is to achieve the largest possible (i.e. the maximum) profit, then we can identify the considerations that will influence the decision whether or not to take on an additional worker. The employer will wish to know the following.

(a) The extra cost of employing that worker (or unit of labour if the unit is a team). This has been defined as the marginal cost including wages and further expenses of labour—the MCL. The employer must clearly have an understanding of the labour market as it affects the firm.
(b) The effect on the firm's production. This was identified as the marginal physical product, MPPL. The marginal physical product will itself be dependent upon a number of influences including:
   1 The amount of labour already employed in relation to the quantity of other productive resources held. It is not difficult to imagine instances where the extra production from each successive additional worker could start to fall. This is not because the quality of labour is falling. A extra worker might desire to work just as hard and conscientiously as the others but, with restricted space and access to equipment, might only be able to contribute a very small increase to total production. Our reasoning here is in line with one of the best known of economic 'laws', that of diminishing marginal physical product (known more widely as diminishing returns). This 'law' reminds us that if we continue to increase one production resource, known technically as a factor of production (here the factor being increased is labour), while other factors are held constant then there comes a time when each further increment yields a smaller increase in total production.
   2 The quality of the other production factors employed. A farm worker will produce more

corn on fertile than on barren land; an industrial worker more manufactured goods with efficient, technically advanced equipment than with unreliable and out-of-date machines.

3 The level of technical and managerial skill available. The most advanced equipment will not help labour to be highly productive unless it is skilfully managed and integrated into the full production process. The potential for increased production cannot be achieved unless the extra product can also be sold.

(c) The effect on the firm's profits. As long as the firm's marginal revenue product is greater than the marginal cost of labour, i.e. when MRPL > MCL, then employing additional workers will increase profits. To achieve the profit maximising level of employment the employer should seek to employ up to the level where the extra revenue attributable to the marginal worker, i.e. the marginal revenue product of labour, just equals the extra cost of employing that worker, i.e. the marginal cost of labour. To ensure that MRPL = MCL is not, of course, as easy as it sounds, especially at critical levels of output where employing more workers also involves acquiring more machines. Decisions at such critical levels of production can be very difficult. The wrong decision can quickly turn business success into expensive failure. The employer must have a sound understanding of the product market as well as of the labour market.

The employment decision, therefore, depends upon the interaction of a number of interrelated considerations. However, as long as we continue to assume that an employer's basic objective is to maximise profits the central consideration will be a comparison of costs and revenues at the level of the marginal worker.

The Combination of Labour and Capital

The theory of labour demand which is being presented at this stage can be described as the 'neo-classical theory'. This is because it rests on a number of assumptions that are part of what is termed the traditional or classical school of economic thought. This neo-classical theory, with its stress on marginal analysis, makes some important assumptions concerning the availability and character of the potential labour available. It is assumed that in the short run period there is no practical limit on the quantity of labour available, all of which is of the same specified quality, and that labour productivity is independent of the length of the working period.

When used by economists, the term 'short run' means the period during which at least one production factor is fixed. In the analysis of labour demand the 'fixed' factor is usually assumed to be capital. The long run, therefore, is that period during which all factors, including capital (machines), are variable in that they can be increased or decreased as output rises or falls.

If in the short run the quantities of either labour or capital, or both, are fixed, then the level of output which may be achieved will depend on the nature of the existing technology. In many cases the employer will have a choice of production methods and indeed of technologies, and will choose the one which is the most appropriate to a given situation. The choice is generally between fairly simple tools or machines generously supported by labour or more advanced machines with less labour.

This choice between different combinations of capital and labour is illustrated in Figure 4.1. The three lines A, B, and C represent three 'production rays' indicating different combinations of labour and capital that can be employed to produce a given product. For simplicity it is assumed, perhaps unrealistically, that the relative proportions of capital and labour in the combinations represented by each ray do not change as production levels increase.

Ray B shows a combination where an equal number of units of capital and labour are always used. Ray A represents the situation where three units of capital are always combined with one of labour and ray C is where three units of labour are always employed with each unit of capital, i.e. A represents the more capital intensive method and C the more labour intensive method.

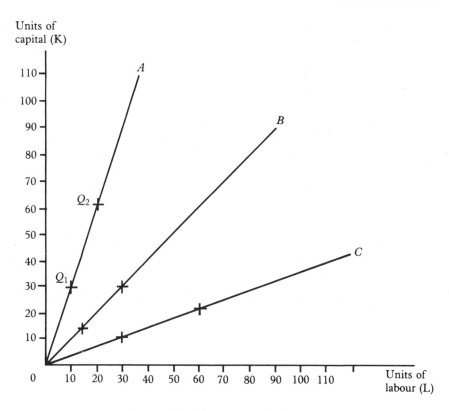

Figure 4.1 *Alternative production rays*

There is no suggestion here that one is better than the other. Each will be suitable under a given set of circumstances. Notice also that points further out along the ray from the point of origin (0) represent the higher levels of production. More can be produced at point Q_2 on ray A (representing 60 units of capital and 20 workers) than at point Q_1 (30 units of capital and 10 workers).

Suppose that, say, 200 units of a product could be produced in the same time period by using method A with 60 units of capital and 20 workers, or B with 30 units of each capital and labour, or C with 20 units of capital and 60 workers. Drawing a line to join each of the points on the rays representing these three combinations produces the dashed line Q in Figure 4.2, which represents the production level of 200 units. Such a line linking points of equal product or output level that can be produced by different combinations of production factors is called an **isoquant** or sometimes an **equal product curve**.

For simplicity Figure 4.2 continues to assume that production rises at a constant rate (constant returns to scale) so that, for example, doubling the quantities of labour and capital along any one ray will also double the quantity of production.

Isoquants may, therefore, be used to represent the different potential levels of production illustrated in Figure 4.3. This shows three possible production levels—100, 200, and 300 units of output—each of which can be achieved by using the different factor combinations represented by the rays A, B, and C.

Should the employer (for example, one operating a multiplant company) also have a choice between a number of different production processes which use different combinations of labour and capital, then a given level of output could be reached by combining the processes. For example the employer wishing to produce 300 units might produce 200 units by method *B* (point *X*) and a further 100 by method *A* (point *Y*). The total quantity of capital and labour used (60K and 40L) is indicated at point *Z* on the 300 unit isoquant. Notice that *Z*'s position on the segment of the 300 unit line between *A* and *B* reflects the proportions in which output is derived from each process. Two-thirds of the total output used process *B* and *Z* is two-thirds along the isoquant between *A* and *B*.

Economists use the isoquant as a convenient device to analyse the choices open to employers in their employment and output decisions. The number of possible capital–labour combinations, in practice, is usually limited by what are called indivisibilities—you cannot buy half a machine, though part-time or overtime working does make possible the employment of fractions of workers—so that a kinked shaped isoquant of the kind shown here is realistic. It indicates that production can only take place using the combinations and production processes represented by the separate production rays. A point such as *Z* can only be achieved if the employer is able to divide production between two or more of these different processes.

In practice, however, economists usually prefer to simplify this shape to a smooth curve for the purposes of analysis. This then implies that capital and labour are infinitely divisible and can be combined in any proportion. Analysis is simplified at some sacrifice in realism. It is, of course, possible to defend this simplification by pointing out that as the number of possible labour–capital combinations, and hence the number of separate production rays, increases the

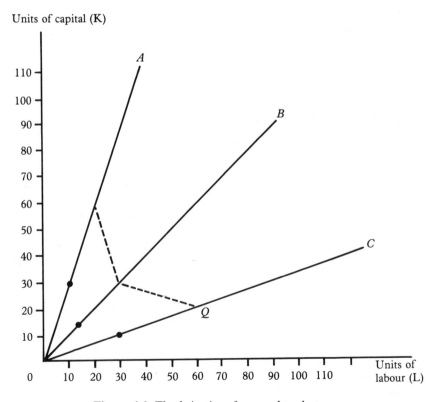

Figure 4.2 *The derivation of an equal product curve*

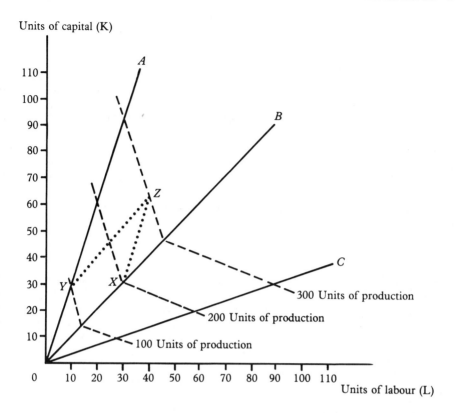

Figure 4.3 *Alternative output levels represented by different equal product curves*

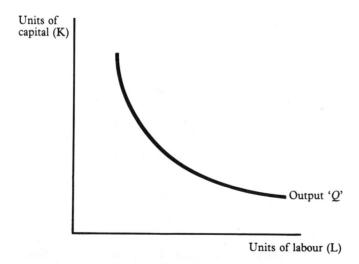

Figure 4.4

kinked isoquant will become smoother and start to approximate to the smooth curve shown in Figure 4.4.

Changes in Technology

The long run in production terms was earlier described as that period during which all factors of production could be varied. So far only labour and capital have been taken into account, and the level of technical knowledge has been assumed to be constant. The true long run period therefore, is that where technological developments are able to change the relationship between capital and labour. This is normally, of course, in the direction of replacing labour by capital so that higher levels of production can be achieved with the same input of capital and less labour, or the same levels of production can be maintained with less labour and often with less capital.

For example, a report in the journal *Economist* in April 1980 described a £200m. investment to produce the Austin Metro. This was designed to provide four multi-welding stations to pin car panels together ready for on-the-spot welding by two lines of fourteen robots. Each line needed just one supervisor. The new car body production plant required 38 workers in place of the 138 needed by old conventional methods.

In many cases there are certain levels of technology that are only open to firms able to sustain a high minimum level of production. Before the 'electronic revolution' a volume car production line was only really feasible for an annual potential production of a about a quarter of a million cars. For much of this century this kind of technology has tended to favour large firms which have then enjoyed cost advantages denied to smaller firms and which, consequently, have been able to offer employment conditions and rewards that enabled them to employ the best quality labour. A striking feature of the modern electronic revolution is that it has reduced both the cost and the operational complexity of advanced capital equipment to bring it within the range of the smaller firm. This development not only creates new opportunities for small firms but also increases the demand for those workers who have the knowledge and the imagination to exploit the possibilities opened up by new technology. Such people are now attractive to small and large firms and, of course, many may prefer, and are preferring, to start their own business operations.

Questions for Discussion and Review

2 In what ways might an employer reduce the effect of indivisibilities in (a) capital and (b) labour?

3 Although perfect profit maximisation would require the firm to operate a minimum cost, observation suggests that the majority of firms normally operate with spare capacity in both capital and labour. Suggest reasons for this.

4 Is it always more efficient to replace labour by machines?

The Firm's Demand for Labour

Demand in the Short Run

'Short run' is here used to denote the period during which both the quantity of capital and the level of technology available to the firm are fixed. The options open to the firm can be illustrated with the help of isoquants.

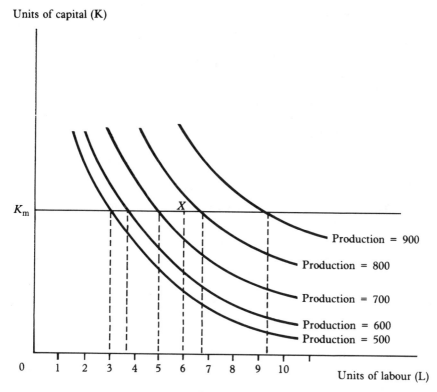

Units of capital (K)

K_m

Production = 900

Production = 800

Production = 700

Production = 600
Production = 500

0   1   2   3   4   5   6   7   8   9   10

Units of labour (L)

Figure 4.5 *Alternative levels of labour demand in the short-run*

Figure 4.5 shows various isoquants, each representing different levels of production and the different combinations of labour and capital that can produce those levels. Suppose the quantity of capital employed by the firm is fixed at K_m, i.e. in the short run the firm has available a certain number of machines represented by the quantity of capital, K_m. This constant level of capital is represented by the line at K_m drawn parallel to the horizontal axis. The intersections of this line with the production isoquants indicate the number of workers required to combine with K_m units of capital to produce each level of production. Notice that Figure 4.5 illustrates a number of features that employers frequently have to face in practice:

a) The intersections do not coincide exactly with a precise number of workers. For example, if the employer wishes to raise production from 500 to 600, one extra worker will be needed. However, at this level the workers are not fully employed, i.e. there is spare labour capacity. The employer has the choice of accepting this, employing part-time workers to obtain, in effect, fractions of workers, or adjusting production levels to try to keep all production factors fully employed. It may, for example, be possible to vary production at different times of the year and to store goods. This, however, may keep labour fully employed at the price of having spare machine (capital) capacity for some periods. The attempt to avoid factor shortages without creating spare capacity is one of the most common problems of business management.

b) The space between each successive isoquant gets larger with each successive 100 unit increment of production. This means that, with capital held constant, it requires successively more labour to reach each increased production level. This is the direct result of experiencing diminishing marginal product, as explained earlier in this chapter. The amount of additional product achieved by each additional worker employed is the marginal physical product of labour, as also explained earlier.

In Table 4.1 the additional product resulting from each extra worker (estimated from Figure 4.5) is given in the marginal physical product (MPP) column.

Table 4.1   Marginal physical product and marginal revenue product

Workers	Total product units	Marginal physical product (MPP)	Marginal revenue product (MRP) (MPP × MR for constant MR = £5)
3	500		
		117	585
4	617		
		75	375
5	692		
		64	320
6	756		
		54	270
7	810		
		45	225
8	855		
		30	150
9	885		

Suppose the employer is able to sell each and every unit of the output at a constant price of £5, then this £5 will be the additional or marginal revenue (MR) obtained for each additional unit of production achieved by the additional workers. Multiplying MPP by MR (in this case £5) will give the marginal revenue product (MRP) as defined at the beginning of this chapter.

If we accept the proposition that the profit-maximising employer wishes to employ labour up to the point where the marginal revenue product is just equal to the marginal cost of the last worker employed, i.e. where MRPL = MCL, then the MRP schedule which has been identified becomes the firm's demand for labour schedule. This can be represented graphically as in Figure 4.6. If, for simplicity, it is assumed that

(a) the marginal cost of labour is the wage paid, and
(b) all workers employed are paid the same rates,

then it is easy to deduce the quantity of labour that the firm would want to employ at a given range of possible wages.

Suppose the wage per worker is £300. The firm does not want to employ seven workers because the seventh (marginal) worker is only adding £270 to the firm's revenue, £30 less than cost. It is, however, worth employing six workers because the sixth is adding £20 more than the employment cost. If the firm only employed five workers it would lose the £20 extra net revenue available from one more worker.

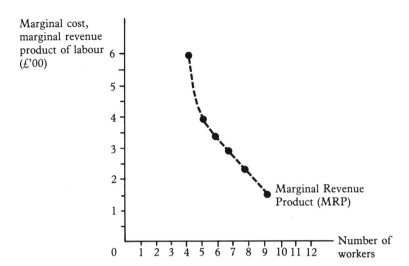

Figure 4.6 *The marginal revenue product curve*

These examples support the statement that the basis for the demand for labour curve for a firm seeking to maximise profits is its MRP schedule, because this determines the number of workers that it is profitable to employ at any given wage level.

If the firm employed six workers it could achieve a production level of about 750 units. This is shown in Figure 4.5 at point X where the vertical dotted line at six workers meets the capital level K_m. If the firm tried to produce more it would have to employ more labour and pay additional wages; if it produced less it would be operating with spare or unused capacity.

The Firm's Choice of Labour and Capital in the Long Run

If capital also becomes a variable factor together with labour, there arises the problem of choice of the most profitable production method. This usually hinges on the choice between different possible combinations of labour and capital.

This is more in the nature of a long-run choice which the firm has to make when it either replaces existing equipment or has to decide whether or not to increase its productive capacity. Although we are not here specifically concerned with the effect of technology changes, it should be remembered that the firm will also be concerned with this aspect when considering the various kinds of machinery and equipment available.

The underlying principle that is assumed to guide the firm's decision is the wish to minimise production costs at the desired level of production. The firm will not knowingly spend £2000 to make a given quantity of product when it can make the same quantity to the same quality standard for £1000. This is often considered to be a necessary implication of an assumption that the firm's objective is to maximise profits.

If we accept the objective of production cost minimisation and if we also assume knowledge of the options available, then the choice of the desired quantities of capital and labour becomes a comparatively simple matter of mathematical application. One possible method is to make use, once again, of isoquants or equal product curves which represent the various combinations of capital and labour that can produce the same level of total production. As the concern is now with cost, it is necessary to take into account the unit costs of both capital and labour and to introduce what is often termed a budget line to indicate the actual potential combinations of labour and capital that it is possible to acquire for a given total spending budget. This method is illustrated in Figure 4.7. The isoquant Q shows the different combinations of labour and capital that are capable of producing 1000 units of output. The firm plans to spend a total budget of £3600 on labour and capital over a given time period in order to produce this output level. The cost of labour is £4 per unit and that of capital £3.

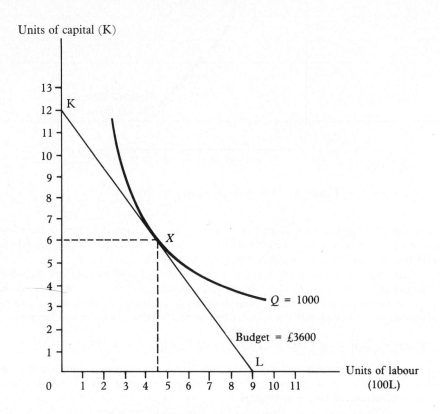

Figure 4.7 *The budget line constraint*
Price of capital (PK) = £3 per unit
Price of labour (PL) = £4 per unit
Total budget = £3,600
Total capital employed = 600 units; cost = £1800
Total labour employed = 450 units; cost = £1800
Total budget = £3600

Should the firm spend the whole £3600 on labour, it could acquire 900 units, at point L. At the other extreme, the whole budget spent on capital would acquire 1200 units, at point K. The line KL, drawn from 1200 on the capital axis to 900 on the labour axis, indicates all the combinations of capital and labour that can be acquired for £3600.

The line KL just touches (is tangential to) the isoquant Q at the point X, indicating 600 units of capital and 450 units of labour. No other combination of capital and labour that can be acquired for the sum available will reach the desired level of output, i.e. all the other points on KL are below the isoquant Q. The point X where isoquant Q is tangential to the budget line KL

thus represents the least cost combination for that production level. Other combinations of capital and labour costing a total of £3600 are possible but all fall below the 1000 unit (Q) production level.

An Examination of the Least Cost Combination of Capital and Labour

The isoquant Q in Figure 4.8 represents a constant output level achieved by different combinations of labour and capital which are assumed to be infinitely substitutable. Moving along the curve keeps output at the same level but results in the substitution of one factor for the other. For example, moving from A to B changes the amount of capital employed from 550 to 400 units and the amount of labour employed from 400 to 500 units. Thus the extra 100 units of labour are able to make good the production lost from 150 units of capital. This means that

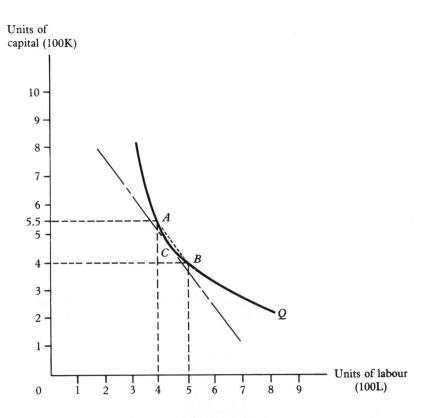

Figure 4.8 *The least cost combination of capital and labour. A reduction from 500 to 400 units of labour can be compensated for by raising capital from 400 to 550 units, with production remaining unchanged at Q. This implies that 150 units of capital produce the same change in product as 100 units of labour, i.e. that $150 \times MPPK = 100 \times MPPL$, so that $\frac{150}{100} = \frac{MPPL}{MPPK}$. However, $\frac{150}{100} =$ the tangent of the line AB joining the two points of change on the isoquant and therefore parallel to the tangent at C. As $\frac{150}{100} = \frac{MPPL}{MPPK}$, it follows that the tangent of the isoquant at any point is $= \frac{MPPL}{MPPK}$ at that point.*

the productive potential of 150 units of capital is equal to that of 100 units of labour. Putting this more formally we can say that 150 × the marginal physical product of a unit of capital = 100 × the marginal physical product of a unit of labour, or:

$$150 \times \text{MPPK} = 100 \times \text{MPPL}$$

Rearranging this equation gives:

$$\frac{150}{100} = \frac{\text{MPPL}}{\text{MPPK}}$$

Mathematicians will now recognise that the ratio 150/100 is the slope of the line joining the two points A and B. This line is parallel to the tangent of the isoquant at C. However, when capital and labour are combined so that the level of output Q is achieved at the lowest possible cost then the isoquant representing output Q is at a tangent to (just touches) the budget line. This means that the slope of the budget line must equal the ratio of the marginal productivities of capital and labour.

The implications of this are indicated in Figure 4.9. The budget line joins two points, A on the capital axis and B on the labour axis. If we use the symbol Bt to represent this budget, then the number of units of capital at A, $0A$, equals the amount Bt divided by the unit price of capital, PK. Similarly the total number of units of labour at B, $0B$, is Bt divided by the unit price of labour, PL. Since the slope of the budget line AB is $0A/0B$ and as $0A = $ Bt/PK and $0B = $ Bt/PL, then:

$$\frac{0A}{0B} = \frac{\text{Bt}}{\text{PK}} \div \frac{\text{Bt}}{\text{PL}}$$

Rearranging this equation gives:

$$\frac{0A}{0B} = \frac{\text{PL}}{\text{PK}}$$

However, the line AB, whose slope is represented by $0A/0B$, is tangential to the isoquant at the least cost capital–labour combination for output Q, at Z. The slope of AB was previously shown to be equal to:

$$\frac{\text{MPPL}}{\text{MPPK}}$$

Therefore

$$\frac{0A}{0B} = \frac{\text{MPPL}}{\text{MPPK}}$$

If we combine equations we obtain:

$$\frac{\text{MPPL}}{\text{MPPK}} = \frac{0A}{0B} = \frac{\text{PL}}{\text{PK}}$$

or

$$\frac{\text{MPPL}}{\text{MPPK}} = \frac{\text{PL}}{\text{PK}}$$

which is the same as:

$$\frac{MPPL}{PL} = \frac{MPPK}{PK}$$

This suggests an extremely important conclusion. When the firm is producing with the least cost combination of capital and labour for any given level of output, the ratio of the marginal productivities of labour and capital will be equal to the ratios of their unit prices. This also means that the ratios of each factor's marginal physical product to its unit price must also be equal.

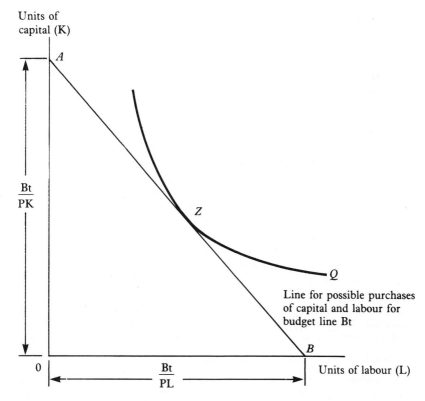

Figure 4.9

$0A = \dfrac{Bt}{PK}$ where $PK = $ *Unit price of capital*

$0B = \dfrac{Bt}{PL}$ where $PL = $ *Unit price of labour*

The tangent of line AB $= \dfrac{0A}{0B} = \dfrac{Bt}{PK} \div \dfrac{Bt}{PL} = \dfrac{PL}{PK}$

At Z the tangent of AB $=$ the tangent of Q, which has been shown to be $\dfrac{MPPL}{MPPK}$,

so $\dfrac{PL}{PK} = \dfrac{MPPL}{MPPK}$

Although non-mathematicians will have to accept this conclusion on trust, in practice all it really does is to state in formal, analytical terms the common-sense conclusion that the cost-minimising producer will seek to combine capital and labour in such a way that the last pound spent on capital achieves the same additional output as the last pound spent on labour. If, for example, an extra pound spent on capital achieved more output than the last pound spent on labour, then it would pay the producer to spend more on capital (machines) and less on labour. The formal model reinforces the common-sense deduction and makes possible the further analysis of long-run changes in factor prices and productivities.

A Note on the Marginal Cost of Labour

So far, the simplifying assumption has been made that the marginal cost of labour could be equated to the wage paid to the last worker, although it has been recognised that this may not be the case in reality. It is, therefore, desirable to recognise the various elements that can help to determine marginal cost, because changes in these are also likely to influence the demand for labour. Some of the elements arise out of market conditions, while others arise from outside, usually legislative, forces.

Market Conditions and Marginal Cost

The wage rate only equates to the firm's marginal wage cost if the labour market is perfectly competitive in that there is an unlimited supply of workers waiting to be employed at the market wage rate and this supply is not significantly reduced by any one employer's demand for labour. In practice, although this may be a reasonable assumption for many small firms such as small retail shops, it is an unlikely position for large firms, particularly in local labour markets, and especially markets for skilled workers. It is more probable that the large firm has to pay higher wages the more workers of any particular type it requires. If this is the case then the wage paid to the last or marginal worker will affect the expectations of workers of similar skills who are already employed by the firm. The worker currently employed for, say, £4 per hour, seeing a new recruit joining at £5 per hour is likely to conclude that it will be worthwhile to leave and join a rival employer at the higher rate. To prevent a local labour merry-go-round and to avoid ill feeling in the workforce the employer generally finds it desirable to increase the wages of existing workers if it is found that new workers can only be recruited by raising the existing wage rate. This means that the marginal cost of adding additional workers must include any costs of raising the wages of existing workers where this is necessary.

Non-market Influences on Labour Costs

When a firm employs a person, a number of costs are involved in addition to wages to meet statutory requirements and which may also be modified by agreements with unions or by the employer's desire to project an image of a 'caring employer'. The most common of these costs include contributions for national insurance, redundancy payment funds, retirement pensions, private health insurance, industrial training levies, and such costs as providing toilet, washing, and rest facilities as required by legislation such as the British Health and Safety at Work Act. Changes in any of these employment costs will affect the firm's demand for labour in much the same way as changes in wage rates, and they should be regarded as forming part of the price of labour (PL) in the model of employer's choice presented in this chapter.

Questions for Discussion and Review

5 Some employers have suggested that employment protection legislation of the 1970s and improved benefits for redundancy in the 1960s and 1970s all contributed to the rise in unemployment of the early 1980s. Can this argument be supported using models of the type introduced in this chapter?

6 Identify and discuss the conditions that have to be fulfilled for the firm's demand for labour to be based on the marginal revenue product of labour.

Changes in Factor Relationships

The previous section suggested that the producer's best combination of labour and capital depended on certain relationships between labour and capital prices and their marginal productivities. It follows, therefore, that any change in these must change the relative quantities of labour and capital that the producer will wish to employ. The effects of some possible changes are now examined.

Changes in Factor Prices

Suppose that with a total budget of £3600 the unit cost of labour falls from £4 to £3 per unit, while the budget provision and the unit cost of capital remain the same. The implications are illustrated in Figure 4.10. At this reduced labour cost the maximum amount of labour that can be acquired for £3600 rises to 1200 units. The new budget line moves outwards from the old, which is shown as a dashed line in Figure 4.10. This new line makes it possible to reach the higher isoquant representing the increased production level of 1100 units. The new combination of capital and labour that can achieve this output is 650 units of capital and 550 units of labour. (The assumption is made that the shape of the isoquant remains unchanged.)

If the firm wished to keep production at the old level of 1000 units the diagram can be used to estimate the revised quantities of capital and labour required. The revised combination can be found by drawing a line parallel to the new budget line but just touching the old (broken line) isoquant. This estimate suggests 580 units of capital and 480 units of labour. It might, of course, in the short run, not be possible to readjust the capital–labour combination so that the firm would have spare machine capacity if it did not wish to increase production. In the long run, however, the fall in wages is likely to lead to a more labour-intensive production process.

Figure 4.11 illustrates the possible consequences of a rise in the unit price of labour with the price of capital and marginal productivities of capital and labour remaining unchanged. It is also assumed that the budget for spending on production factors remains the same.

If the unit price of labour rises the same budget will buy a smaller quantity of labour if no capital is purchased so that the theoretical maximum quantity of labour falls from B to C. The budget line, therefore, shifts from AB to AC. Given that the marginal productivities of labour and capital have stayed the same, the firm has to produce a smaller quantity of output, represented by the isoquant Q_0 which is lower than the original Q_1.

In this model the rise in labour price results in a reduction in the quantity of labour and a small rise in the quantity of capital employed. If the producer wishes to maintain the original output level (Q_1) the budget must be increased, but the quantity of labour employed still falls.

Changes in Factor Productivities

Changes in technology and managerial skills are likely to change the marginal productivity of both capital and labour. The effect of an increase in the marginal productivity of labour is illustrated in Figure 4.12. A rise in the marginal productivity of labour means that a small change in the quantity of labour employed is needed to make good any potential loss of output brought about by a reduction in the employment of capital. If this happens the isoquant for any given level of output will become steeper. (If the reason for this is not clear, refer to Figure 4.9

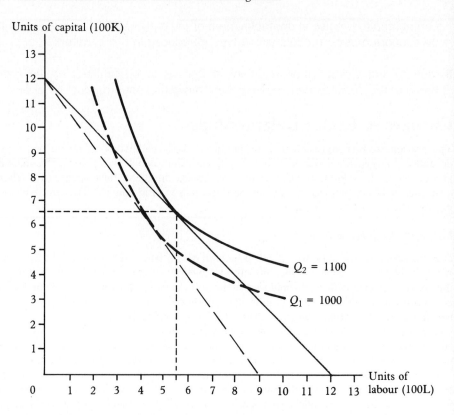

Figure 4.10 *The least cost combination of capital and labour with a reduction in the wage rate*
Price of capital (PK) = £3 per unit
Price of labour (PL) = £3 per unit (reduced from £4)
Total capital employed = 650 units; cost = £1950
Total labour employed = 550 units; cost = £1650
                    Total budget = £3600

and work out the effect on the isoquant if the ratio of MPPK to MPPL changes from 150/100 to, say, 150/50.)

In Figure 4.12 the increase in labour's marginal productivity changes the shape of the isoquant from Q_1 to Q_2. As factor prices are unchanged, the budget line stays unchanged at AB. The steeper isoquant Q_2 is tangential to AB at the higher level of labour employment $0l_1$ (instead of $0l$). In this model the increase in the employment of labour is accompanied by a reduction in the employment of capital. An example of this kind of change would be the acceptance by a workforce of flexible work practices, whereby certain jobs were no longer reserved for workers with certain approved skills. Output from a given number of workers would rise because there would be fewer delays and workers could be kept more fully employed.

In practice there are likely to be time lags between changes in factor prices or factor productivity and changes in the levels of factor employment. An employer's freedom to make changes can be restricted by previous investment decisions, trade union power, employment protection legislation, indivisibilities, and delays in acquiring new machines, but the models outlined in this section suggest tendencies that have important implications for the effects of wage bargaining and changes in technology.

Questions for Discussion and Review

7 What do you think will be the effect on the firm's demand for labour of the development of new technology that increases the productivity of both capital and labour?

8 There is evidence that in recent years many firms have tried to turn fixed costs into variable costs, e.g. by hiring, not buying, equipment and employing contractors rather than increasing the size of the workforce. Suggest reasons for this.

Suggestions for Written Assignments

1 Using the published accounts of three large public companies covering at least three years, estimate the changes in the productivity of capital and labour for these companies over the period covered by the accounts. Comment on any

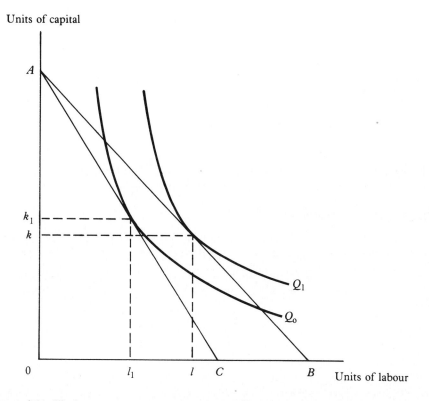

Figure 4.11 *The least cost combination of capital and labour with an increase in the wage rate*

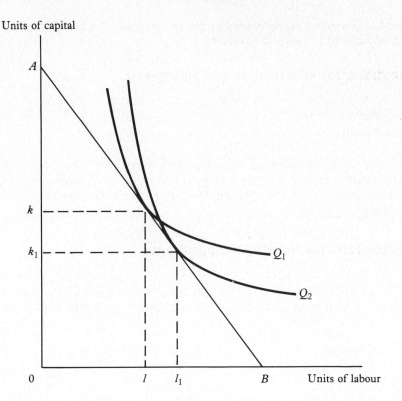

Figure 4.12 *The least cost combination of capital and labour with changes in labour productivity*

changes you observe in the ratio of capital to labour employed by these companies.

2 Explain and discuss the problem of 'indivisibilities' as they relate to labour and capital and show how firms try to overcome these.

Suggestions for Further Reading

Any good microeconomics textbook should provide further explanations of the concepts and analytical techniques employed in this chapter [for example, Blight and Shafto (1989)].

5
Wider Aspects of the Demand for Labour

The Wage Elasticity of Demand for Labour

Meaning of Wage Elasticity of Demand

Not all employers will react in precisely the same way or with the same speed to a given set of changes in labour costs. What is clearly needed is to have some measure of the strength of reactions to labour cost changes. At this stage the simplifying assumption that labour cost = the wage paid is maintained. A suitable measure of change is provided by adapting an economic measure of demand changes. This is the concept of demand elasticity.

Demand elasticity is used to measure the extent to which demand changes in response to a change in any of the influences that affect demand. One of the most important of these is, of course, price, and the *price elasticity of demand* for any given product is calculated using:

$$\frac{\text{the proportional change in the quantity demanded of the product}}{\text{the proportional change in the price of the product}}$$

This may be adapted to identify the response of firms' demands for labour following a change in the wages paid to a given group or class of workers, so that the *wage elasticity of demand* for any defined group of workers is:

$$\frac{\text{the proportional change in the number of workers which firms wish to employ}}{\text{the proportional change in the wage rate paid to that group of workers}}$$

When the resulting calculation gives a figure greater than unity, demand for labour is responding more than proportionally to the change in wages and labour demand is said to be wage elastic. When the result is less than unity demand is responding less than proportionally to the change in wages and the demand for labour is said to be wage inelastic.

As with price elasticity of demand, a rise in wages can be expected to lead to a fall in the quantity of labour demanded. Consequently, the wage elasticity of labour demand is normally a negative value.

For example, suppose a group of workers secured a wage rise of, say, 10% but then found that, in the following year employment in their industry fell by 15%, even though there did not appear to be a significant fall in demand for the product they were making. Because demand had fallen by 15% in response to the wage rise of 10% it was clearly wage elastic with an elasticity figure of $-15/10$, i.e. -1.5. If another group secured a similar 10% wage rise which, however, produced only a 7.5% fall in employment, the demand for this group's labour would be wage inelastic with a figure of $-7.5/10$, i.e. -0.75. This contrast is illustrated in Figure 5.1.

It is important to remember that elasticity depends on proportional or percentage changes.

Influences on Wage Elasticity of Labour Demand

Different groups of workers are likely to face different demand conditions. The preceding chapter explained how a change in labour cost would probably lead to a shift in the quantity of labour that an employer would seek to employ if that employer was trying to achieve a given production level at the lowest cost combination of capital and labour. The wage elasticity of demand for any given group of workers, therefore, will reflect the pressures on their employers to achieve and maintain their least cost capital–labour ratios. These pressures are likely to result from a number of other influences, including the following.

(a) *The price elasticity of demand for the product of labour.* Firms will seek to pass on wage increases to customers through price increases. If a given price rise resulting from an increase in labour costs produces a more than proportional fall in product demand then a wage increase is likely to lead to pressure to reduce the number of workers employed. Product price elasticity of demand is itself partly influenced by the competitive market pressures to which the employer is subject. For example, the wage elasticity of labour in public sector monopolies where product demand is price inelastic is generally much less elastic than in highly competitive private sector consumer product markets, such as food retailing.

(b) *The proportion of labour costs to total costs.* Where labour costs represent a small proportion of total costs (i.e. production is capital intensive), a wage increase is likely to have only a small impact on the product's price and hence on its demand.

(c) *The capacity of the group of workers to inflict financial damage on the employer.* If the cost of a wage increase is small in proportion to the potential cost of a labour stoppage or dispute, employers will tend to accept wage increases without too much challenge or reduction in employment. In this kind of situation the strength of a work group can itself depend on a number of factors, including:

   1 Their importance to the production process. Sometimes a small group of key workers has the power to disrupt a whole production line. Some chemical processes require continuous production and any stoppage can cause millions of pounds worth of damage to equipment.

   2 The strength of trade union organisation and its ability to inflict financial damage on an employer. Of course, trade union strength and wage elasticity of demand are to a large extent interdependent. It is easier to form a strong and active union in occupations and industries where labour demand is wage inelastic.

(d) *The substitutability of labour by capital or between different groups of workers.* Workers doing routine, mechanical jobs are always vulnerable to replacement, in the long run, by mechanical or electronic devices.

As with most forms of demand elasticity, the wage elasticity of demand for labour is likely to be greater in the long run than in the short run (when factors other than labour are considered to be fixed). Firms cannot speedily change production processes involving major capital investment without incurring considerable costs. In the short term it may be less expensive to suffer a wage increase than to make a major change in a production process. It may not even be possible to make such a change in the short term because specialised capital equipment may take a long time to supply.

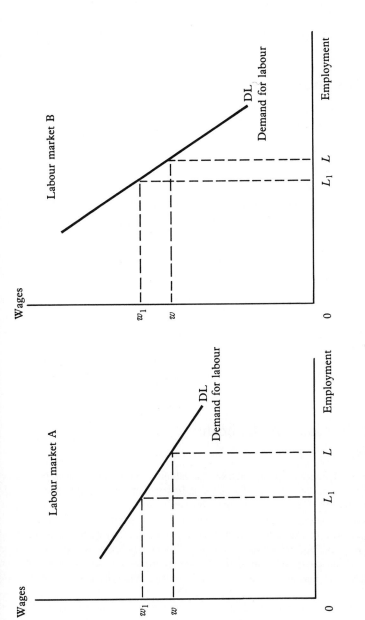

Figure 5.1 *Labour demand in differing product markets*

In market A a 20% increase in wages ($w_1 - w$) results in a 30% reduction in the quantity of labour demanded ($L - L_1$).
In market B a 20% increase in wages ($w_1 - w$) results in a 7.5% reduction in the quantity of labour demanded.
In market A the demand for labour is wage elastic; in market B the demand for labour is wage inelastic.

However, in the long term, technology and market changes may increase pressures on firms to respond to changes in labour costs. Past and anticipated future wage movements are taken into account when planning capital investment, and production processes may then be changed to reduce vulnerability to changes in labour costs. Firms can also, and do, make gradual adjustments to their employment levels by not replacing workers who leave or retire or by replacing full-time workers by part-timers; such tactics meet with less opposition than large-scale sackings or redundancies.

Questions for Discussion and Review

1 Discuss any differences likely to exist between the wage elasticity of demand for workers in the public sector in comparison with workers in the private sector of the economy.

2 Discuss the effects of modern advances in microelectronics on the wage elasticity of demand on the following groups of workers: computer software writers; office clerical workers; engineering lathe operators; print workers on newspapers; retail shop managers. What general points arise from your discussion concerning the effect of technology changes on the demand for labour?

3 Calculate the wage elasticity of demand in the following cases.
  (a) Wage increase from £8 to £9 per hour led to a reduction in employment of a group of workers from 1000 to 900.
  (b) An employer was able to secure a change in numbers employed so that a 10% rise in wages left the total wage bill unchanged.
  (c) A trade union leader warned union members that a 10% rise in wages could be expected to lead to a 15% fall in the numbers employed.
(Answers to Question 3 can be found at the end of this chapter.)

The Market Demand for Labour
Defining the market

It is not always easy to define the precise market for labour. The demand for a particular occupation, for example, is not always the same as the industry demand. In some cases the two may be regarded as being very similar. The demand for coal miners, for example, is limited to demand within the coal production industry. The demand for teachers arises from demand within the education service (or industry). Other workers, however, may be in demand across many industries. Most firms employ clerical staff, word-processor operators, motor vehicle drivers, and cleaners. Electricians and computer software engineers are required across many industries. An occupational market, therefore, may be rather different from an industrial market.

Another problem may be the geographical limits of a market area. Contrast the market for coal miners with, say, the market for machine tool setters. In the past, coal mining was an industry where there was a single industry dominated by a single large employer which also owned miners' houses. It was relatively easy, therefore, for a miner made redundant at one pit to be informed of a vacancy at another in a different part of the country and be moved to that area should he so wish.

Tool setters, on the other hand, work in the engineering industry where there are large numbers of employers of all sizes producing many different products. Firms employing tool setters are located in many different areas, sometimes where there is a heavy concentration of engineering manufacturing, sometimes where there is relatively little. It is often difficult for workers to find out about employment prospects and even wage levels in other areas. A worker moving from one firm to another in a different area may have to face substantial relocation costs and significant changes in living costs. Such workers may be very reluctant to move, and for them the realistic labour market is likely to be highly localised.

At another extreme, some markets can be international. When, for example, the Central Electricity Generating Board had a surplus of engineers in the early 1980s it was able to assist some of these to find employment at generating stations in Australia.

Market Demand and the Firm's Demand

It is tempting to think of the market demand for labour as being the sum of the demand curves of all the individual firms operating in that market, however it has been defined. This would not be correct because of the interrelationship between the price of labour and the price of the product. For example, suppose the wage rate for labour falls. Firms will wish to employ more labour and thus produce more of the product. This reaction is based on the reasonable assumption that if there is a fall in production costs, which include labour wages, firms are prepared to produce more. However, as all the firms in the industry seek to produce more the total supply of the product increases and if the demand for the product remains unchanged then its selling price is likely to fall. If the product price falls then the marginal revenue product of labour also falls. The firm's demand for labour, remember, is based on the marginal revenue product, so any fall in this will depress the demand for labour.

Consequently, the total increase in the market demand for labour following a fall in wage cost will be less than might be expected from a simple addition of each individual employer's demand.

Influences on the Market Demand

If it is remembered that the demand for labour is derived from the demand for the product of labour and that market demand for labour is dependent on the demand of individual firms operating in the market, then the main influences on labour demand can be related to three main types of economic change: changes in product and labour markets, cyclical changes in the economy, and changes in the structure of the national economy.

Changes in Product and Labour Markets

These can be further identified as:

(a) The demand for the product or products of the class of labour under consideration. The more widely dispersed are workers in different industries, the more closely is this demand likely to reflect the general level of economic activity in the country as a whole. If the labour is industry specific, e.g. coal miners, electricity supply engineers, or school teachers, then labour demand is likely to be tied to the fortunes of that particular industry.

(b) The price of the product or products of labour. If the product price rises while other market influences remain unchanged, then the quantity demanded of the product will fall and this will tend to reduce the demand for labour. On the other hand, a rise in product price is likely to increase the marginal revenue product of labour and so make labour more profitable. The net effect is likely to depend on the price elasticity of demand for the product.

(c) The marginal physical product of labour.

(d) The marginal productivity and price of capital where this is a substitute for labour.

(e) The cost of labour, i.e. the wage rate plus associated costs such as employers' national insurance or compulsory pension contributions.

(f) Government policies in so far as they affect wages, prices, and the process of wage bargaining.

Cyclical Changes in the Economy

These arise from a number of causes, including:

(a) The business cycle of periods of high consumer and business demand followed by periods of relatively depressed demand.

(b) Government policies intended to dampen down or stimulate consumer and business demand in attempts to avoid the extremes of price inflation and large-scale unemployment.

(c) Changes in other factor prices often resulting from events outside the country. These changes can affect total production costs and hence product prices. The steep rises in oil prices in the 1970s, for instance, contributed to the general reduction in economic activity by the late 1970s and early 1980s and, consequently, to the general fall in labour demand across most markets.

Changes in the Structure of the National Economy

These include:

(a) Changes in product development which bring about the decline of some product markets and the expansion of others. These changes may arise from shifts in consumer taste and attitudes or from technological developments that make new and improved products possible.

(b) Changes in production technology which change the nature, productivity, and price of capital and which also change the kind of labour skills required by employers, e.g. the requirement that office secretaries become skilled in word processing.

Question for Discussion and Review

4 During 1988 there were frequent press reports which commented on the difficulties experienced by hospitals, especially those in London, in recruiting nurses. Some world-famous hospitals were actively recruiting staff from outside Britain. Other reports pointed to the steep decline in the number of school leavers entering the workforce.

(a) List what you consider to be the main features in the demand for and supply of nurses in Britain.

(b) What would you expect to be the effect of the decline in school leavers
   (i) on the pay of young people, and
   (ii) on the demand for older workers?

The Theory of Labour Demand

Criticisms of the Theory

The theoretical model of the demand for labour developed in the previous chapter is based on a number of assumptions concerning the behaviour of employers, notably that employers are motivated by profit and, consequently, workers will be employed as long as their employment adds to profit. Not surprisingly, a theory resting on this foundation has produced a number of critics.

Observers have suggested that in reality the mechanisms which determine labour demand by a firm are more complex, and that even if the theory is a valid one, employers do not have the relevant knowledge to use it anyway.

In recent years there has amassed a substantial body of literature challenging the traditional theory of the firm with its basis of profit-maximising behaviour and presenting an alternative group of managerial theories of the firm having the common theme that the modern large business corporation is controlled by its professional managers and that business objectives are influenced, if not dominated, by managerial preferences among which profit remains a major, but not the only, consideration.

Managerial theories assume that managers pursue expansion at the expense of profit. It follows that they are likely to expand the firm's labour force beyond the level where the marginal cost of labour is equal to its marginal revenue product.

It must be stressed that there is no general consensus concerning these views. At least one writer, D.E. Williamson (1970), has argued that this employment preference is an imperfection that can and should be removed by organisational changes and checks within the firm. In the early 1980s there was an increased emphasis on profitability, but the return of economic growth from about 1986 has seen renewed take-over activity, suggesting that expansion remains a powerful driving force. The whole question of the profit-maximising assumption for business firms still remains open.

Some US research in the 1940s appeared to support the critics of profit-maximising models. A survey of US employers indicated that it was not the level of wages which determined how much labour they employed, but rather the level of demand for the products they produced. If the employers believed they could sell the product then they sought to employ labour to produce it, and questions of individual labour productivity and/or wage levels were not seriously considered.

Although the factual findings were not subsequently challenged, their interpretation has been questioned on two grounds.

(a) The immediate response of an employer who perceived that the market for his product was expanding would be to increase employment and output. Later, when the product market had stabilised, questions about the size and cost of the labour force would be raised.
(b) It was pointed out that the empirical findings themselves did not actually invalidate the theory. Employers were taking advantage of expanding markets. They would be aware of the prices they could charge for their goods, and they would also be aware of the additional (marginal) revenue arising from the sale of the extra output.

Further Defence of the Theory

There are, however, two other, less obvious, explanations which would suggest that the empirical findings do not necessarily invalidate the theory.

It is known that many firms use systems of 'cost-plus pricing' in which a specified percentage or 'mark up' is added to the production cost as a means of determining the price to be charged. Where this occurs, any increase in labour cost, which the theory suggests would lead to a reduction in labour demand, would be automatically passed to the customer, together with the additional percentage. Higher prices will normally imply a reduction in product demand. Employers, therefore, would be acting rationally by watching what happened to the demand for their products. As long as it held up, i.e. as long as product demand was price inelastic, they would employ more workers and/or pay higher wages, but once product demand fell they would reduce their labour demand.

Some criticisms may arise out of a misunderstanding of the theory and its implications. In a model whose function is to aid understanding of some of the most important features of an aspect of the real world, some simplifying assumptions have to be made so that the effect of each variable can be considered on the basis that other variables are held constant. When the models are developed to bring them closer to real-world conditions, there is no doubt that changes in the product market influence the firm's demand for production factors, including labour. The extension of the theory to market demand noted that changes in the product demand and price would influence marginal revenue product and hence the firm's least-cost production conditions. There does not seem, therefore, to be any fundamental conflict between the theory and the findings of the US research.

Special Features of Public Sector Services

At the same time it has to be acknowledged that in many modern economies, such as Britain's, not everyone in employment is working for private profit-seeking firms. Profit-maximising objectives are clearly not valid for those public sector services which provide social or community protection services, such as health, education, police, and fire-fighting services, to a level determined by the political machinery of the State. In these circumstances, the level of employment is determined by the level of funding accorded by political decisions to each separate activity. Both employment and wage levels will be the result of the interplay of political rather than of purely economic market forces. Nevertheless, public sector services may still be under pressure to combine labour and capital effectively, and economic markets cannot be totally ignored. In the mid-1980s, for example, pay for hospital nurses had fallen to a level that was not sufficient to attract and retain enough nurses to maintain the number of hospital beds considered necessary by government and public opinion. Some additional trained nursing staff was, however, being employed through private agencies at higher pay rates. However imperfectly, the economic market forces were operating in this sector of the labour market.

Further aspects of public sector pay are examined in Chapter 15.

The Effects of Technology

Our consideration of long-run conditions recognised that technology was likely to change and that this would influence the relative marginal productivities of capital and labour. In practice, a given level of technology may lead to what are often termed 'indivisibilities'. When a particular piece or set of machinery is acquired it is possible that this can only be operated effectively by a team of workers. Such teams can range from, say, three or four to about a hundred people depending on the nature of the process and scale of operations. Technical constraints of this kind, therefore, may cause the firm's, and sometimes the industry's, demand for labour to rise swiftly as certain critical levels of output are reached. Similarly, of course, a contraction in product demand can lead to an equally steep decline in demand for labour. If an entire production line is abandoned, several hundred workers may lose their jobs over a very short period.

Note that this technology constraint suggests that the realistic shape of the production isoquant is more likely to be that shown in Figure 4.3 in the preceding chapter than the smooth curve usually assumed for purposes of economic analysis.

Certain types of modern technology may actually determine labour requirements. Continuous production processes, as, for example, in the chemical industry, either operate 24 hours a day seven days a week, or not at all. Similar constraints apply in some very large-scale production processes. In a modern car assembly plant either the number of men required by the process are employed or it is not possible to operate. However, in this instance it is in fact possible to adjust labour demand in a different way. Suppose the car assembly track will only run if 1000 workers are employed, producing 1500 cars a week, but actual sales are for only 1000 cars a week. It is not technically possible to operate with only two-thirds of the labour force, but it is technically possible to operate the car track for two-thirds of the week. Thus, while employment continues at 1000, the actual labour demand, in terms of worker-hours during the week, is reduced by a third.

It should also be noted that among the consequences of the modern microelectronic revolution are:

(a) The number of people required to service the machines is reduced. One worker, for example, can 'nurse' a series of automated lathes or people carrying out routine movements can be replaced by automated robots.
(b) The cost of setting up some automated, continuous production processes has been much reduced so that they become possible for smaller scale operations, and the penalties for running at under capacity are reduced.

The Quasi-fixed Character of Labour

Finally, it has been suggested that the assumption that labour is a variable factor is no longer realistic. Employers in many countries are subject to employment protection legislation that either prevents them from hiring and firing workers according to fluctuations in product and labour markets or makes such practices very expensive through statutory compensation obligations. It has, therefore, been proposed that labour must be regarded as a quasi-fixed factor of production. This would recognise that certain labour costs, such as those of recruitment, selection, and training, are fixed, at least in the short run, although others, such as wages, may still be variable in accordance with hours worked. To avoid losing the benefit of past costs of recruiting and training workers when facing a downturn in product demand, employers may hoard labour and operate with excess labour capacity in the hope that this will be necessary only in the short term. They may also fear that essential skilled labour may be lost to competitors if not kept in continuous employment.

It may be argued that these considerations and adjustment costs account for the observed tendency for employers to avoid making rapid adjustments to their labour force following changes in product demand and price or in wage or productivity levels. They may prefer to make changes more slowly as workers leave and retire or wait until a general economic or industrial downturn makes their own labour shedding less conspicuous.

On the other hand, operating with spare labour capacity over a prolonged period is very expensive. Consequently, there has been increased dependence on part-time and contract workers, particularly for unskilled labour. This can be seen as a move towards restoring labour to its traditional status as a variable production factor.

The reservations, therefore, that we may have about the neo-classical model of labour demand do not mean that it is fundamentally wrong, but rather that it must be treated with caution in its application to the complexities of actual labour markets. Indeed, in recent studies Symonds and Layard (1984) concluded that, when allowance is made for price inflation and associated high interest rates, there is evidence that employment levels are determined by real factor prices. In his study of British manufacturing industry Symonds (1985) also concluded that the neo-classical labour demand theory provided an adequate explanation for the aggregate employment levels between 1961 and 1976.

It should be recognised that the fundamental truths of the theory are still very important, and attempts to ignore them in legislating for some socially desirable, idealistic labour market can sometimes aggravate the very problems that the legislation had sought to overcome.

Questions for Discussion and Review

5 If it is not possible to calculate the marginal revenue product of labour in a non-profit-seeking public sector service, how can management in that sector arrive at the most efficient combination of labour and capital?

6 In 1986 the British Government removed workers under the age of 21 from the minimum pay provisions which Wages Councils could apply to certain industries. Discuss the effect of this change on the demand for and supply of young workers and the employment prospects of workers as they reach the age of 21.

Suggestions for Written Assignments

1 Choose two occupations, one from Group A and one from Group B (below). Compare and contrast the demand influences which you think operate for each occupation.
Group A: airline pilot, company accountant, barrister at law, university lecturer, deep sea diver, technical expert in the oil industry.
Group B: word-processor operator, machinist (engineering), nursery nurse, medical secretary, heavy goods vehicle driver, merchant navy officer.

2 In the light of your reading of the book so far, explain and discuss the various ways in which the government can influence the demand for workers. What proportion of the workforce in your local area is directly employed in the public sector? What differences, if any, are there with the proportion of workers employed nationally in the public sector?

Suggestions for Further Reading

Chapters 4 and 5 have been largely based on what may be termed the neo-classical, marginal theory of labour demand. For an account of how this theoretical approach has developed over time and for a more detailed and analytical discussion of this theory, reference should be made to Cartter (1959). Hicks (1964) discussed the theory and examined how the concept of elasticity of demand could be applied to labour.

The initial questioning of the marginal revenue product/marginal wage concept was by Lester (1946). This produced an instant response by Machlup (1946). Machlup (1967) subsequently made a further examination of the significance of the economic assumptions in determining the influences on the demand for labour.

This aspect has been examined more recently by Simon (1979). The question of whether labour should be regarded as a fixed or variable factor is discussed by Oi (1962). A general discussion of managerial theories at an introductory level is provided in Old and Shafto (1989).

For an examination of the implications of treating labour as a fixed factor of production in contemporary Britain, see Bowers and Deaton (1982). Sleeper (1972) has provided an explanation of the different reasons why firms hoard labour.

Answers to Question 3

(a) −0.8; (b) −1; (c) −1.5

6
The Supply of Labour

The Individual's Decision to Work
The Nature of the Decision

It must always be remembered that the aggregate supply of labour and the supply of workers to particular occupations are the result of decisions made by thousands of individuals. It is therefore necessary to examine the various influences on these individual decisions about whether, where, and how long to work. Analysis in this area normally makes two basic assumptions:

(a) People are able to choose whether or not to work and how many hours to work subject, of course, to the obvious physical limitations.
(b) These choices are largely influenced by the wages offered in return for work.

In this approach to individual labour supply, the underlying assumption is that individuals will ultimately seek that combination of wage income and hours of leisure (here defined as non-working hours) which will afford them maximum satsifaction, as outlined in the following section.

Choice and Indifference Curves

Entering the labour force or increasing the time spent working normally involves some financial cost, e.g. to pay travel expenses and to provide the clothing needed for work. This cost, however, is usually small in relation to the income earned from working and it will not, therefore, be a major influence in the individual's decision whether to work or not. Financial costs may, of course, influence the decision whether to take one job or another. Some jobs or occupations, for example, may involve high entry costs. Usually, however, the financial costs are less important to the individual than the non-monetary sacrifices of time and effort required.

Theoretically, an individual has twenty-four potential leisure hours a day and each hour spent working involves an opportunity cost in terms of leisure sacrificed. The compensation for that sacrifice is the monetary income gained from working. In conventional neo-classical economics this income–leisure choice is frequently examined using the techniques of indifference curve analysis.

The indifference curve, which you may recognise as being very similar in principle to the isoquant used in the analysis of labour demand, represents the infinite combinations of income and leisure that are believed to offer the same level of total satisfaction to the individual. Thus at any given level of satisfaction a person is indifferent as to which particular combination is enjoyed. In graphical representations it is conventional to plot time on the horizontal axis as the independent variable and income on the vertical axis as the dependent variable. Income, at any given rate, normally depends on the time worked.

Figure 6.1 shows an indifference curve. The figures on the axes are there to aid understanding; they are not intended to be realistic for any actual person or period. The maximum number of hours in the week is 168 and this is the number that can be divided between work and leisure. The more hours of leisure that are chosen the lower is the income earned from work and vice versa. Assuming that the indifference curve I represents the total satisfaction that a hypothetical person gains from various possible combinations of income and leisure, this curve indicates that the same amount of satisfaction is gained from £200 income and 50 hours leisure (118 hours worked), or £100 income and 80 hours of leisure (88 hours worked), or £60 income and 130 hours of leisure (38 hours worked), or any other combination that can be read from the curve.

Notice that the shape of the curve, like the shape of the isoquant, is based on an assumption of diminishing marginal utility. If the person only earns £60 but enjoys 130 hours free from work, any additional income is valued highly in terms of the leisure that must be sacrificed to

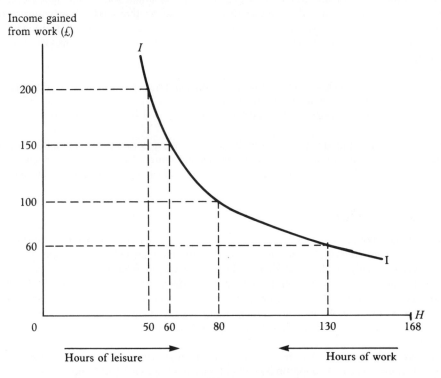

Figure 6.1 *The choice between hours of work and hours of leisure*
Note: The same level of satisfaction is gained from
    (a) £200 and 50 hours leisure, i.e. 118 hours worked
    (b) £100 and 80 hours leisure, i.e. 88 hours worked
    (c) £60 and 130 hours leisure, i.e. 38 hours worked

gain it. The person is willing to sacrifice 50 (130–80) hours of leisure to raise income from £60 to £100. Thus each hour of leisure is valued at £0.80 (£40/50). As leisure is lost it is valued more highly and to gain another £50 to raise income to £150 the indifference curve indicates that the person is only prepared to sacrifice 20 hours of leisure. Each hour of leisure is now valued at £2.50 (£50/20). An hour free from work is valued more highly when only 80 are being enjoyed than when 130 were available.

Of course, there are different levels of satisfaction. If it is possible to earn more from working any given number of hours then the indifference curve will move further from the point of origin of the graph. It is possible to imagine a map of curves all representing different levels of satisfaction depending on the attainable packages of leisure and income.

Figure 6.2 shows three indifference curves. Each represents a different series of income–leisure combinations offering different levels of total satisfaction. The individual has no preference for either of the combinations of income and leisure represented by points X and Y on curve II, i.e. he/she is indifferent between $0X$ hours of leisure with £x income and $0Y$ leisure with £y income, as both provide the same level of total satisfaction. Either of these is preferred to combination Z ($0X$ h leisure with £z income) on curve I, which is closer to the point of origin (0) and represents a lower level of satisfaction. On the other hand, both X and Y do not provide as much satisfaction as the combination A ($0Y$ h leisure with £a income) on the higher curve III. It is easy to see that X is preferred to Z because at X the worker enjoys the same amount of leisure with a higher income. For the same reason A is clearly preferable to Y.

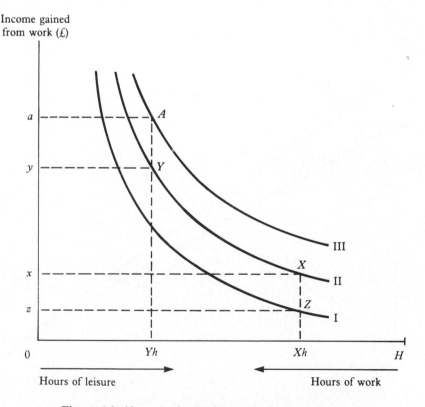

Figure 6.2 *Alternative levels of income–leisure combinations*

However, since an indifference curve joins points of equal total satisfaction, it should also be clear that any point on III is preferred to any point on II which in turn is preferred to any point on I.

Constraints on Choice: the Budget line

Economists generally believe that people make rational decisions. This implies that, given a choice between a higher and a lower level of total satisfaction, they will choose the higher and that they will try to maximise their satisfaction level subject to any existing constraints.

There are, of course, constraints on both leisure time and income. In any one day leisure cannot exceed twenty-four hours! Similarly, if overtime and shift premiums are excluded, it is not possible to earn more than twenty-four times the hourly rate of pay. This rate will vary for the individual according to that person's ability to achieve a particular wage payment.

These leisure and income constraints can be represented by a budget constraint, often called a budget or an income–leisure possibility line, which indicates the range of possible combinations of leisure and income that are available for any given hourly wage rate. Figure 6.3 shows two budget lines for two different pay rates: £2 and £2.50 per hour. The hourly rate in this analysis should be regarded as the rate actually received by the worker after unavoidable deductions such as those for income taxes or national insurance contributions.

If no work is chosen and the full 24 hours of the day taken in leisure then the pay rate is, of course, irrelevant and both lines start at the same point, H. If no leisure is taken the theoretical

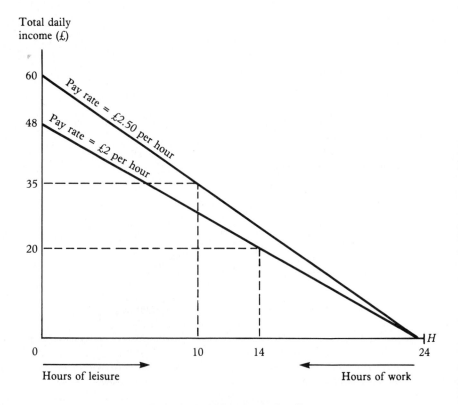

Figure 6.3 *Alternative budget lines*

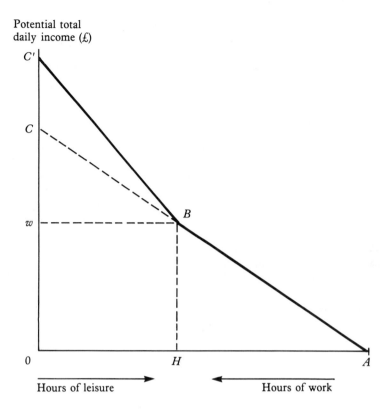

Potential total
daily income (£)

Hours of leisure   Hours of work

Figure 6.4 *A budget line with an overtime premium rate provision*

maximum income is 24 times the hourly rate (i.e. £48 at £2 and £60 at £2.50). The daily income for any given number of hours worked can be read from the budget line. At the £2 hourly rate 14 hours leisure (10 hours of work) provide an income of £20. At the £2.50 rate 10 hours leisure (14 hours of work) provide a daily income of £35.

Showing the budget constraint as a straight line (also known as a 'linear curve') makes the assumption that the hourly rate does not change however many hours are worked, i.e. that the income opportunity cost of leisure remains constant for all possible combinations of leisure and income from work. For purposes of analysis at this level of study, this assumption holds and linear budget lines are adopted unless there is a good reason to do otherwise. There are two common situations where straight lines are not acceptable and the budget line becomes kinked or curved (as shown in Figure 6.4 and 6.5). These are:

(a) *Payments at premium rates for overtime working.* When an individual works beyond the normal hours the common practice, particularly for manual workers, is to make a payment per hour which is greater than the rate applying to the normal hours. In Figure 6.4 the initial budget constraint for a standard hourly wage rate of C is AC. However, after AH hours are worked an overtime premium is paid, and this will change the gradient of the budget line beyond point B. Consequently there will be a new budget constraint operative, ABC'.

(b) *Taxation of income with stepped, progressive tax rates.* In such a tax system, income earned over a specified level is taxed at rates higher than the standard rate. These higher rates can rise as successive income level bands are exceeded. In Figure 6.5 the initial budget constraint for wage levels up to *C* is *AC*. However, once the income level *w* is reached, the rate of tax on subsequent income levels rises. The increase in tax at income level *w* produces a new budget constraint, *ABC'*.

The Optimum Income–Leisure Choice

The best possible choice for the individual worker can be illustrated with the help of indifference curves combined with budget lines. If the worker is rational, in the economic sense, the aim will be to seek the highest possible level of total satisfaction at any given wage rate. If it is imagined that there is a map of different indifference curves all representing different levels of total satisfaction from leisure and income from work, the highest curve that can possibly be attained is the one that the budget line is just able to touch at one point.

In Figure 6.6 the budget constraint *AB* is just able to touch, i.e. is tangential to, the indifference curve II at point *X*, which is the combination of 0*H* hours of leisure and an income of £*w* from work. The worker could choose any other combination on the line *AB*, for example, points *Y* and *Z* where the line cuts indifference curve I, but these all lie below curve II and are, therefore, regarded as inferior, i.e. represent lower levels of total satisfaction and so are rejected by the rational worker. Of course the worker would prefer to have a combination on curve III

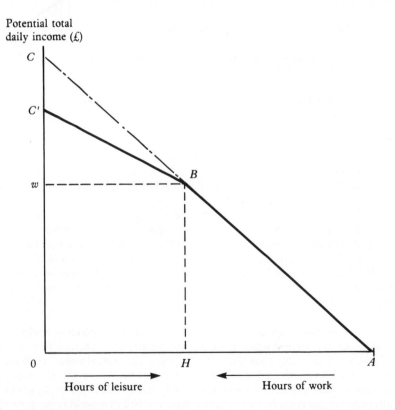

Figure 6.5 *A budget line with a progressive tax rate provision*

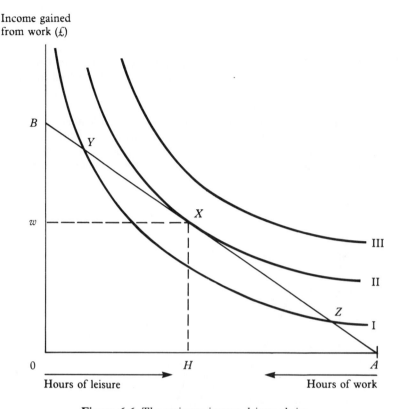

Income gained
from work (£)

Hours of leisure   Hours of work

Figure 6.6 *The optimum income–leisure choice*

but this lies above the constraint *AB* and none of these options are attainable by the worker at
the current wage rate.

The optimum daily combination of leisure and working income attainable within the wage
rate constraint is 0*H* hours of leisure and £*w* of income, derived from working *AH* hours per
day.

The Reality of Individual Choice

In explaining the decision to participate in the labour force by sacrificing leisure hours in favour
of time at work and the income this brings, it was assumed that the individual was able to make
a choice constrained only by the wage rate and the time available each day. In practice the
majority of workers may not appear to have such a choice. Employers have their own
preferences and offer employment in specified packages of, say, thirty-eight or forty hours a
week, these being specified in the employment contract.

For some workers the combination of hours and pay specified by the employer may coincide
with the choice they would have made given their own wage–leisure preferences. Nevertheless,
it is realistic to recognise that for most people the desired combination of monetary reward and
leisure hours would imply offering more, or less, hours than the number specified in the
employment contract.

Since the hours associated with particular jobs are likely to be strongly influenced by the
requirements of the job and by employer preferences, it seems probable that workers seeking to

change their hours of work will tend to change jobs. This conclusion is consistent with evidence provided in a series of detailed studies by Altonji and Paxson (1986). These showed that hours changes were significantly more variable across jobs than between jobs, and that this was true for both males and females and for both voluntary and non-voluntary job changes. This research also found that job changes which changed hours of work involved costs for workers.

A 40-hour week has been assumed in Figure 6.7, but the wage–leisure preference curves for two individuals 'X' and 'Y' indicate that they would respectively prefer to work more than 40 hours and so forego leisure to receive additional pay, and less than 40 hours, thereby increasing leisure time but accepting a reduction in pay. The requirement to work the specified forty hours, apparently with no choice, will reduce the satisfaction both X and Y could achieve if they could choose how many hours they work. X would prefer to work more hours per day, and Y fewer.

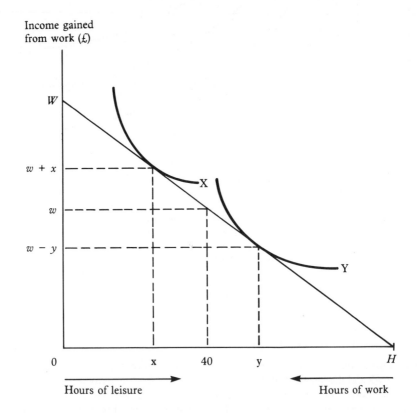

Figure 6.7 *The differing option income–leisure choices*

For X, whose preference is to work longer than the specified 40 hours, there are a number of possibilities. The existing employment may offer the opportunity of voluntary, paid overtime work. This would permit more flexibility in the choice between leisure and income. Alternatively, a somewhat similar solution may be achieved even where the employment (school teaching, for example) does not offer opportunities for paid overtime. There may be the possibility of seeking a second, part-time job. The worker might be able to 'moonlight'. A more radical solution would be a change of employment to an occupation or employer offering income–leisure options closer to the worker's preferences.

In our example Y faces the reverse problem. The desired choice is for fewer hours of work and less pay. Individuals may not be able to adjust hours downward on a weekly basis in a fashion similar to the upward adjustment permitted by overtime working but the possibility of reducing the average number of hours offered over a period does often exist and is utilised by many individuals. Surveys undertaken in British industry indicate that the average firm loses the equivalent of 5% of its potential number of working days each year through absenteeism.

Although it would be unrealistic to imagine that all workers are able to achieve their desired income–leisure preferences, close observation of actual work practices suggests that large numbers of people are able to exercise a significant measure of personal choice.

Questions for Discussion and Review

1 Use indifference curves to explain why some individuals will be indifferent as to whether or not they work overtime.

2 Use indifference curve analysis to show why an employer may have to pay premium rates for hours worked above the weekly norm in order to encourage workers to work overtime.

Choice and Unemployment

For most people of working age the question of whether or not to accept employment does not seem to warrant serious consideration. The monetary reward received from employment is a necessity of life. Yet, in many advanced countries the question is a serious one. For individuals previously employed but now unemployed there are likely to be state benefits available, and this may also apply to those leaving education for the first time. Individuals entitled to receive this type of benefit can sometimes choose between accepting it or taking employment.

This consideration may be incorporated into the model developed earlier, and is illustrated in Figure 6.8. In most cases the benefit is payable only if the person is unemployed, and it ceases or is replaced by other benefits if any paid work is undertaken. Consequently, the worker will not be willing to consider any package of leisure and income that produces an income lower than the benefit level.

Suppose the unemployment benefit is the equivalent of £15 per working day and the maximum number of hours per day that people will consider working is 14, leaving a minimum daily leisure time of 10 hours. Consider the position of the worker whose maximum earning rate is £1 per hour. The theoretical maximum income is thus £24 but the practical maximum is £14 for a 14-hour working day, which is below the level of unemployment benefit. A worker with this maximum earning potential will not be able to reach a point on an indifference curve that provides an income–leisure combination containing the required minimum of leisure and an income above the value of the unemployment benefit. A curve such as I is not, therefore, acceptable given the minimum income and leisure constraints. Accordingly the rational (in the economic sense) worker will chose total leisure and remain outside the employed labour force.

Acceptable combinations of income and leisure will only occur on sections of indifference curves which pass to the right of DD' and above VV'. Such sections are beyond the reach of a worker able to earn only £1 per hour but are attained by those able to secure a net wage of £2 per hour. Given the shape of curve III, the optimum achievable option for the latter worker is to work 10 hours and earn £20 per day.

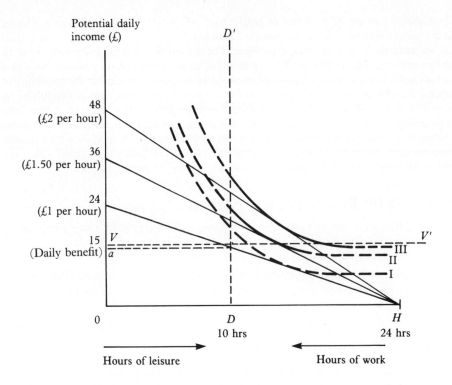

Figure 6.8 *The employment choice*
Note: Given the level of unemployment benefit, VV', and the minimum rest needs, DD', only the solid sections of the indifference curves offer acceptable combinations of leisure and income

The minimum wage rate required to bring a worker to the position where there is any degree of choice between income and leisure is the rate that would produce a budget (income possibility) line that just touches the indifference curve relevant to that worker's income–leisure preferences at the level of unemployment income. For a worker whose satisfaction from different income–leisure combinations is represented by curve II, this wage is an hourly rate of £1.50. In Figure 6.8 the budget line given by this rate is tangential to indifference curve II at the work income–leisure combination of £15 (the unemployment benefit rate) earned by 10 hours of work. This position where the budget line is tangential to the indifference curve just at the point of equality with the minimum income constraint is termed a corner solution.

The wage (in this hypothetical example, £1.50 per hour) that is just sufficient to persuade a person to switch from rejecting to accepting available work is termed the reservation wage.

Although the idea of a reservation wage is fairly easy to comprehend, it is not always easily measured for large groups of workers because a number of powerful non-economic attitudes and pressures are involved which vary considerably for different individuals, families, and groups. However, a research survey of unemployed 16 to 18-year-olds, carried out by Lynch (1983), provided an indication of their average reservation wage value. They would have been prepared to accept employment if it was available at two-thirds of the then average wage of those in their age group who were in employment. This weekly reservation wage was nevertheless twice the level of the benefits they received.

In the late 1960s, economists became increasingly interested in the willingness of those in receipt of benefits to accept or reject employment. [See, for example, Gujarat (1972), who first brought the problem to public attention.] For over twenty years unemployment in Britain had been low and of short duration, but in the second half of the 1960s it began to climb. This trend was particularly evident for males. Its beginnings were observed to coincide with two changes in labour law. The Redundancy Payments Act 1964 entitled employees in certain circumstances to a capital sum as compensation for the loss of their employment. Secondly, and almost simultaneously, wage-related unemployment benefits were introduced for the early period of unemployment, and these benefits were above the level of those paid previously. The effect of these measures was to increase the minimum non-wage income level and possibly to reduce the willingness of the unemployed to seek employment until the expiry of the period of entitlement to the higher benefits.

It is precisely because there is a choice between whether or not to seek employment that unemployment insurance schemes place an upper limit upon the level of benefit individuals may receive. For similar reasons it is common practice to deny benefit payments during the early weeks of unemployment to individuals considered to have become unemployed by their own actions. The British Government lengthened this period in 1988 in its efforts to discourage workers from becoming dependent on State unemployment benefits.

Questions for Discussion and Review

3 It has been the practice in many nations to pay monetary benefits to unemployed school leavers while at the same time offering the same monetary reward for participation in government-sponsored training schemes. Many young people have been unwilling to accept the offer of training. Why?

4 'Unemployment benefits encourage people to be idle and so increase the number of people choosing to remain unemployed.'
'It is necessary to pay unemployment benefits, preferably related to earnings, in order to maintain the purchasing power of the unemployed and so prevent other people from losing their jobs.'
Discuss these contrasting views of the desirability of paying unemployment benefits.

Influences on Income–Leisure Preference

The Effect of Non-wage Incomes

In the analytical approach adopted in this chapter, individuals not in receipt of unemployment benefits have been assumed to be dependent on work to gain monetary incomes. The decision concerning whether or how long to work thus depended on the wage rate that could be earned and the individual preference between income and leisure.

However, this assumption may not be correct for some potential participants in the labour market who may receive income from other sources (termed non-wage or non-market income).

If initially the individual has no non-market income, the income–leisure possibilities constraint HA in Figure 6.9 will be tangential to the wage–leisure indifference curve, I, at point X. This indicates that HM hours will be worked for an income of N. Suppose that the worker starts to receive a non-market income represented by the vertical line HB, forming a new income–leisure possibilities constraint BC parallel to HA (assuming an unchanged wage

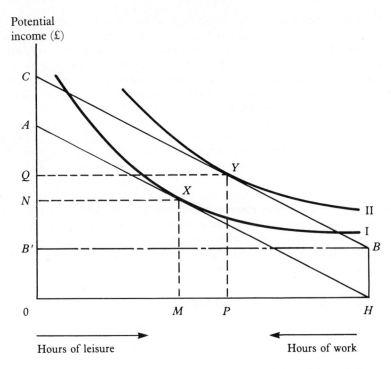

Figure 6.9 *Non-wage incomes and the optimum income–leisure choice*

rate). The distance *AC* represents the size of the non-market income flow. The new budget constraint *BC* is tangential to the higher wage–leisure preference curve II at point *Y*. This implies that receipt of the non-market income reduces the hours worked to *HP* and raises total income to *Q*.

There are two significant aspects of non-market incomes. In the first place the introduction of such an additional income enables the worker to achieve a higher level of total income–leisure satisfaction while reducing the amount of time spent at work. People receiving income from non-work sources may be expected to want to have time to enjoy that income. Possible exceptions where this income effect might increase the desire to work, especially for women, are examined later in this chapter.

A further consequence is that there is likely to be a level of non-market income where the preference for leisure rises to the point where no work is chosen and the individual leaves the workforce. This, of course, assumes that the sole reward sought from work is monetary income. There is ample evidence to suggest that this is not the case and that non-economic rewards such as companionship, the wish to exercise power, to pursue an interest, or perfect a skill, or even to pursue an activity perceived as being socially useful may all induce people to work even though the economic pressures to do so are very slight.

Changes in Wage Rates

However, once in the labour force an alternative possibility arises. The wage rate may increase. For the purpose of analysing the effect of a wage increase it is assumed that all other factors, including prices of goods and services, are held constant. This eliminates the difficulty of translating the changes in money wage rates into changes in real wages. Should the wage rate increase so that the theoretical maximum income rises from, say *A* to *B* in either Figure 6.10 or Figure 6.11, there are two possible effects.

The Worker May Work More Hours

This is illustrated in Figure 6.10. Before the wage rise the worker had reached the position where the last hour of leisure was perceived as having the same value as the income that would be gained from working an extra hour—so there was nothing in terms of extra satisfaction that the individual could gain from working an additional hour. The rise in wage rate, which shifts the budget line from *HA* to *HB*, raises the opportunity cost of not working. The income gained from working more is now greater than the value lost from the leisure sacrificed, so more time is worked. In Figure 6.10 the wage rate change allows the worker to rise from indifference curve I to II and gain an income rise *X'* to *Y'*, and encourages an increase in working time (sacrifice of leisure) from *Hx* to *Hy*.

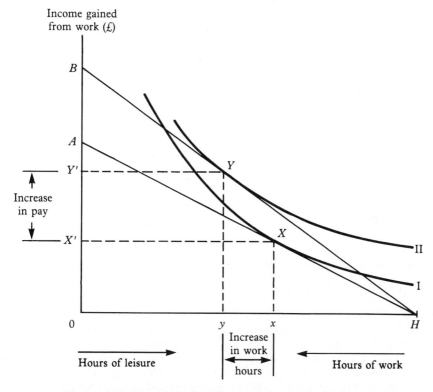

Figure 6.10 *The substitution effect of an increase in the wage rate*

The Worker May Work Fewer Hours

This is illustrated in Figure 6.11. In this example the wage rate change again shifts the budget line *HA* to *HB* and again allows the worker to move on to a higher level of total satisfaction from indifference curve I to II. However, this higher indifference curve has changed its shape to reflect an increased preference for leisure. It is steeper, indicating that an hour of leisure is

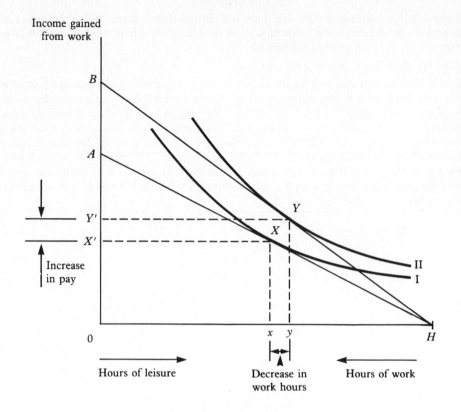

Figure 6.11 *The income effect of an increase in the wage rate*

considered to be equal to a greater amount of income. In this case the wage rate increase allows the worker to enjoy both more income and more leisure, and fewer hours are worked.

Income and Substitution Effects

In order to understand how such different outcomes are possible from the same change it is necessary to look more closely at the processes operating when wage rates change.

In Figure 6.12 the worker is able to earn an increased wage rate so that his budget or income–leisure possibility line moves from HA to HB. Maximum leisure, of course, remains unchanged at H but maximum income rises from A to B. This enables the worker to achieve a higher level of total income–leisure satisfaction on the indifference curve II. The line HB just touches II at Y, at which point $0y$ hours of leisure are enjoyed and yH hours are worked. Before the wage rate increase the worker enjoyed $0x$ hours of leisure, the line HA being tangential to curve I at X.

If we analyse this change more closely we can see that it contains two distinct elements. Part of the change is the result of the altered opportunity cost of leisure and part the result of the worker's ability to achieve a given income level with fewer hours of work, or to achieve a higher income from the same time spent working.

It is possible to separate these two aspects of the change. The change in income earning ability can be removed by imagining that the worker is content to stay on the same level of total satisfaction, i.e. on curve I. This is achieved by drawing the broken line $H'B$ exactly parallel to the new income–leisure possibility curve *HB*, but positioned so that it is tangential to the original indifference curve I. This point of tangency is *Z*. The movement from *X* to *Z* represents the effect of the change in gradient of the income–leisure possibility line which reflects the changed opportunity cost of leisure. The price of each additional hour of leisure rises as the wage value of an extra hour worked rises. This increased cost of leisure leads to a tendency to give up some leisure and spend more time working. At point *Z* the worker's leisure time would be reduced from 0*x* to 0*z* and working hours would increase by *xz*. This change, brought about purely by the changed relative cost of leisure and work, is termed the substitution effect of the wage rate alteration. Notice that the rise in the wage rate produces a reduction in leisure time and consequently an increase in working time. The substitution effect of a wage rate change on time at work is thus positive: they both rise (or both fall).

However, the substitution effect is only one element. The wage rise enabled the worker to move to a higher income level and so to a higher level of satisfaction, to curve II, and the movement from *Z* to *Y* is, therefore, the income effect. In this example the shift attributable to this income effect is in the reverse direction and is powerful enough to outweigh the substitution effect. As already noted, the point *Y* indicates increased leisure and a reduction in working time.

The income effect need not always reverse the substitution effect. A rather different result is shown in Figure 6.13. This represents the same rise in wage rate, the same movement in the

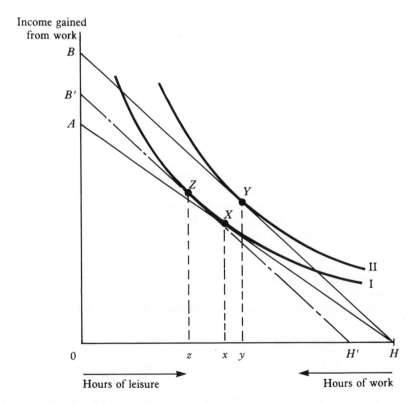

Figure 6.12 *The interaction of a substitution and an income effect of an increase in the wage rate, leading to a reduction in working hours*

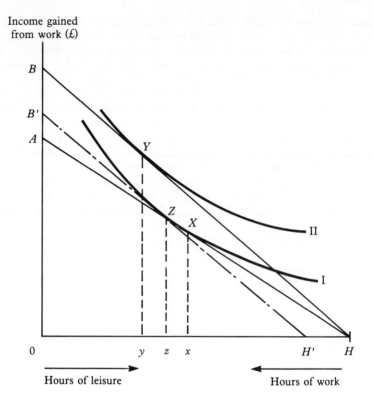

Figure 6.13 *The interaction of a substitution and an income effect of an increase in the wage rate leading to an increase in working hours*

income–leisure possibility line from *HA* to *HB*, and the same movement from point *X* on curve I to point *Y* on curve II. This movement again contains both substitution and income effects. The substitution effect is a similar tendency to increase working time shown by the shift from *x* to *z*, but in this model the income effect *ZY* produces a further sacrifice of leisure and increases the tendency to spend time at work from *Hz* to *Hy*.

The lesson suggested by these two models, and which can be proved by more detailed analysis, is that:

(a) the substitution effect always involves a positive relationship between wage rate and time at work, and
(b) the income effect relationship between wage rate and time at work can be either positive or negative.

Notice that the different results for Figures 6.12 and 6.13 arise from the different shapes of the indifference curves. In Figure 6.12 the higher curve is steeper than the lower, indicating that a greater value is placed on leisure as income rises. In Figure 6.13 the higher curve is flatter, indicating an increased desire for income.

This means that we cannot use indifference curve analysis to *prove* that any given result will follow from a change in wage rate. It can only be used to illustrate various possible results. We must, then, rely on observation of the real world to suggest possibilities. So far it has to be admitted that research results are far from conclusive.

Questions for Discussion and Review

5 There are occasions when governments reduce the level of taxation levied upon employment incomes in the belief that this will provide an incentive for those in employment to offer more work. Do you consider governments to be justified in this belief?

6 The practice has evolved in many nations for individuals in low-paid employment to receive supplements to their wage income in the form of either monetary or non-monetary benefits funded by the state, the value of the benefits being related to both the family circumstances and wage level. When family circumstances are held constant, what will be the consequences of this practice upon the willingness of individuals in low-paid employment either to accept alternative high-paid employment or to work overtime?

Evidence on Income Changes and Working Hours

While it would be unwise to suggest how any one individual will react to a wage increase, the empirical evidence appears to suggest that, in aggregate, increases in income result in the reduction of the work hours offered.

Empirical evidence of this within specific companies does exist. One example comes from the multinational oil company Esso's refinery at Fawley. In 1959 the management of this British refinery noted that the hours worked at Fawley, 18% of which were paid at overtime rates, were high compared with corresponding refineries elsewhere in the world. The company offered their employees the opportunity of a 35% wage increase over a 3-year period if the high level of overtime working could be eliminated. Within 2 years the employees had received the 35% wage increase and there was a simultaneous 15% reduction in the total number of weekly hours worked at the refinery.

In this particular case a negative income effect in relation to work seems to have been more powerful than the positive substitution effect. The position here follows the pattern illustrated in Figure 6.12.

Over a rather longer period, 1966–85, the income effect does in most years appear to have predominated for male manual workers employed in the British economy. This has produced an overall decline in working hours. In Figure 6.14 the changes in the level of average gross income, after allowing for the changes in prices, recorded in the government's retail price index, have been plotted against the changes in the average hours worked. This latter figure takes into account both short-time and overtime work. Over this particular twenty-year period the average hours worked by male manual employees fell by 6% while the estimated real wage before deduction of income tax and social security insurance contributions rose by nearly 40%.

When analysing influences on the supply of labour it is often helpful to make use of a measure, the wage elasticity of supply of labour; this is found by much the same method as the wage elasticity of demand, as explained in Chapter 5.

The wage elasticity of supply is found from:

$$\frac{\text{the proportional change in hours of work supplied by a group of workers}}{\text{the proportional change in the wages earned by that group}}$$

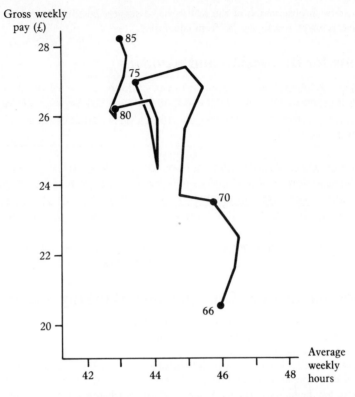

Figure 6.14 *Average weekly hours versus gross weekly pay in real terms, all manual workers for all industries and services, 1966–1985*
Note: Gross pay for 1966 = 100, for subsequent years the gross pay is corrected for changes in retail prices
Source: Employment Gazette, HMSO, London, various years

In the instance cited above, therefore, the supply curve for hours of work appears to be negatively sloped. The rise in gross income has led to fewer hours being offered. On the basis of this example, the labour wage supply elasticity of male manual workers is − 0.15. A 10% increase in wages produced a 1.5% reduction in hours worked. Rather more detailed studies in the USA, reviewed by Keeley (1981), suggest a consensus estimate of labour wage elasticity of supply for males of −0.1, although this overall figure contained considerable variations in the results of the studies Keeley used. The 'crude' estimate made here for British male manual workers appears to lie within the expected range. However, Keeley and others have drawn attention to the contrast between the wage elasticity of labour supply for males and that for females. For males, the research evidence appears to suggest that it is both relatively small and negative. In contrast to this, however, studies of the wage elasticity of labour supply for females show it to be positive and significantly larger. This suggests that increasing wages for females leads to an increase in the hours of work offered. These findings may reflect the traditional role of males, who have expected to work normal weekly hours throughout their working lives. They may feel that a rise in wage levels offers an opportunity to reduce the hours worked and gain extra leisure for which they have a relatively high marginal preference, so that the negative income effect is greater than the positive substitution effect.

Many married females, on the other hand, have withdrawn from paid employment to bring up families. Increasing wage levels may lead to a reassessment of the time spent on unpaid work in the home and result in the substitution of paid employment outside the home. The increase in wages available to females produces an income effect which supports the substitution effect as illustrated in Figure 6.13.

Over the longer period it is difficult to obtain realistic figures of the movement of real incomes. Information on wage levels are often available but without detailed information on price movements, changes in tax levels, and other deductions from pay, satisfactory estimates of real income levels cannot be undertaken. When only money income figures are available these may give a misleading picture. In the example above for 1966–85 the estimated change in income, after allowing for price changes, was 40%. In the same period the money wage rose from £20.30 to £172.50, a 750% increase.

The normal, negotiated, weekly hours for all manual workers over a fifty-year period, 1920–70, are shown in Figure 6.15, and two characteristics are worthy of note.

(a) Over this long period there was a trend for the normal number of hours worked per week to decline, from approximately 48 hours in the 1920s to 40 hours in 1970. This represents a one-sixth decline at a time when it is widely considered there were improvements in real living standards. To consider average weekly hours in isolation may provide a misleading impression. Between 1920 and 1970, not only were hours worked per week reduced, but the number of days per year worked also declined, reflecting a growth in the number of days holiday each individual was allowed. In 1920, the average holiday period for manual workers appears to have been a week plus a similar number of days of public holidays. This suggests an average working year of some 2400 hours. By 1970 the holiday period had been extended to an average of five weeks if public holidays are included. This implies an average

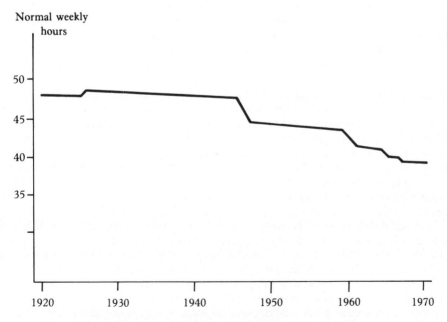

Figure 6.15 *Normal weekly hours for all manual workers in all industries and services, 1920–1970*
Source: Employment Gazette, HMSO, London, various years

working year of approximately 1900 hours. The reduction in working hours per year has, therefore, been a little over 20%.

(b) Over long periods the length of the normal working week has been stable. There was virtually no change during the first twenty-five years to 1945. Then, after three years of reductions, there was a further decade of stability. However, there were no correspondingly long periods of real income stability when price level changes are taken into account. The mechanism may be that, as real incomes rise, the initial, and continuous, adjustment in hours worked is through the level of overtime working. Normal hours are only modified when there is no longer an opportunity of achieving further adjustments through overtime working.

Questions for Discussion and Review

7 There are more days of public holiday in France than there are in Britain. Does this mean that French workers have a greater preference for leisure compared with workers in Britain? What information would you need to have in order to answer this question?

8 There is evidence to suggest that the more highly paid Japanese workers are beginning to value leisure more highly as part of rising living standards. If this trend continues, what changes would you expect in the structure of the Japanese economy and labour market?

The Decision to Work Part-time

One of the major innovations in the pattern of employment over the last generation in industrialised countries has been the expansion of part-time employment. In Britain, for example, between a quarter and a fifth of all those in employment are employed part-time. The actual definition of a 'part-time employee' does vary between nations, but is assumed here to refer to those who are employed for less than the normal conventional work period.

There are significant differences between nations in the character of their part-time labour forces. In the USA, where most students have to pay their way through higher education without the benefit of State grants, the data indicate that a majority of the part-time labour force consists of young people who are simultaneously in higher education. Part-time employment is regarded as a means whereby individuals can work their way through college. In other nations, including Britain, where grants to finance higher education are more widely available, few students normally take continuous part-time employment. Part-time employees are, therefore, drawn from different population groups. Many are married women who are either seeking a partial re-entry to the labour force after a period of absence, or who are facing increased home commitments but do not wish to give up their jobs completely and so seek to stay in part-time work.

These social differences in the origins of part-time employment are significant. Where the part-time labour force consists of relatively young people in higher education who have few job skills, the choice is whether to work a few hours weekly, as part-time employees, or not to work at all. The appropriate explanation for their decision is that outlined in Figure 6.8. However, for the potential employee with extensive previous work experience and job skills there is another option, whether or not to return to full-time employment. Married women who opt for part-time in preference to full-time employment often accept jobs which require lower skill levels than they had acquired in their previous employment. Consequently they receive lower rates of pay.

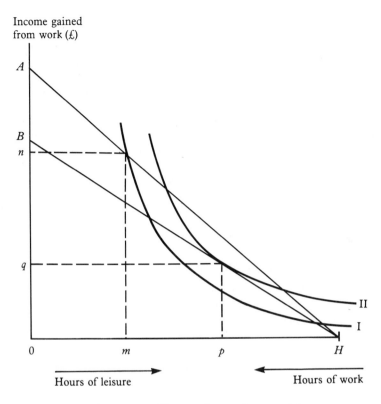

Income gained
from work (£)

Hours of leisure →

← Hours of work

Figure 6.16 *The part-time employment choice*

This may be explained in terms of the wage–leisure indifference curves. In Figure 6.16 a decision to opt for full-time employment requiring 35–40 hours (point *m* on the horizontal axis) and paying a wage rate represented by the budget or income–leisure possibilities line *HA* would involve a sacrifice of *mH* hours of leisure to gain an income of *n*. However, the opportunity cost of this employment to a married woman would be the 'leisure' time needed to meet her desire to fulfil family reponsibilities. Undertaking the full-time job might also involve substantial additional expenses in employing someone to look after the house and children. The married woman may feel that a more attractive alternative is to take part-time employment where the wage received puts her on a less favourable income–leisure possibility line *HB* but enables her to reach a higher level of total satisfaction represented by the higher indifference curve II. The income resulting from this choice is *q*, considerably less than the full-time income (*n*) but allowing much more non-working time, 0*p* as against the 0*m* gained when working full-time. At a certain stage in the growth of the family the part-time job is likely to be chosen. At another stage, or if a rather higher wage rate becomes available, sufficient to justify the employment of others to share in household and family duties, the preference might well move to full-time work.

The widespread development of part-time employment suggests that it does have attractions for potential employees. It provides a chance to re-enter the labour market when the full-time option is not considered to be practicable. At the same time, part-time workers provide a valuable source of labour for employers.

Nevertheless, there are differences in the character of the employer's labour demands and consequently in the types of part-time employment offered. The employer may have a demand for eight hours of labour a day, while the potential part-time employee is prepared to offer only four hours. In these circumstances the employer may be prepared to 'workshare', employing two part-time employees to undertake a normal full day's work. Blyton and Hill (1981) consider this approach to have advantages for both the employer and the potential employees. There is, however, another possibility. The employer may require an employee for a peak period when there is a heavy volume of work. In the absence of a pool of available part-time workers the employer would have to employ an individual full-time although in reality there was not a full-time job to do. If part-time staff can be employed the employer is still able to cover the work peak but saves a proportion of wage costs. Both employer and employee benefit from this arrangement. In some parts of the country there is a long tradition of part-time work—often provided by former employees prepared to return to their old employer during periods of seasonal peak working. The extension of part-time work nationally indicates that the advantages are being realised by a wider range of firms and industries.

Questions for Discussion and Review

9 Part-time work has been traditionally appealing to married women. Discuss the case for encouraging more men, especially those nearing retirement age, to work part-time. What barriers are there to this approach?

10 In Chapter 1 it was noted that there was a growing trend towards working from home. How does this affect the traditional view of the length of the normal working day?

The Household Labour Supply

The analysis presented so far has been in terms of leisure or work, but in reality there are other options in the use of time, and for many the choice will not be solely determined by an individual, but by an individual within a family unit.

The above sections have really been considering the choice not so much between work and leisure but rather between work and other possible uses of time. These, of course, include leisure, but they also include work in the home and looking after young children or old people. For young people the alternative to work is often the continuation of full-time education. Most individuals, in fact, have a range of possible uses of time other than work and leisure.

The majority of people live in families. The family is an economic as well as a social unit, and the decision whether to work and the level of rewards to be sought will be taken in a family context. It is increasingly being appreciated that labour supply is often dependent on family decisions concerning the allocation of time.

When the conceptual framework of income–leisure preference was developed it was usual for the majority of males to leave full-time education at the earliest possible age and then to work for the rest of their lives. Similarly, females would leave school and work until marriage when their roles were assumed to change to being full-time housewives and mothers. For very many people that pattern has now changed. A high proportion of children do not automatically leave school at the earliest possible date but remain in full-time education, and a growing proportion of married women pursue careers.

These decisions are often taken by families as groups rather than just by individuals. They are taken in the context of the available opportunities of family members for employment and their opportunity cost in terms of, say, household duties, education, and leisure activities. If the theory applied to individuals was correct in its assumption that people seek to achieve the highest attainable level of satisfaction from the possible combinations of income and leisure, then the same assumptions can be applied to the analysis of family choices. The family is simply a different economic unit.

It has become increasingly necessary to recognise and examine the interrelationship of individuals' decisions within the family. Earlier it was suggested that certain patterns of income–leisure preferences, reflected in the shapes of the relevant indifference curves, could produce an income effect capable of reducing the number of working hours supplied. Within the family, however, the effect may be a little different. A rise in the father's wage rate may not lead to a reduction in his working hours but to a child staying in education rather than leaving school for employment. The wage rate offered to a woman for part-time employment may be less than the wage rate her husband could receive for overtime work, but the family decision may be for the woman to work at the lower wage while her husband is also at work, and for both jointly to enjoy the higher family income in the same leisure period. Included in the husband's 'leisure' will be a proportion of the housework previously undertaken by his wife.

Nor should the non-economic aspects of such decisions be entirely ignored. The wife may well prefer to have income that is her own and which she can spend as she chooses instead of feeling dependent on her husband. Some income may be traded for self-respect.

Taxation must also be taken into account. The British taxation system applying before the important changes announced in the Budget proposals of 1988 ensured that two separate incomes of, say, £15 000 were taxed considerably less heavily than a single income of £30 000. For lower-income families, a wife's part-time earnings of, say, £40 per week would not be taxed at all whereas the husband's overtime earnings of a similar amount would be taxed, before 1988, at a rate of at least 27 per cent and possibly more.

As with the analysis of individual decisions, it is not always entirely clear what the consequences of a rise in wage rates will be. On the one hand, an increase in a husband's wage rate may encourage a woman to withdraw from the labour force because her previous contribution to the family budget is no longer required. On the other hand, a rise in wage rates for women may induce the housewife to re-enter the labour force and take the employment she was unprepared to accept at the lower wage, perhaps because she can now afford to pay for help in the home or in looking after children. Some possibilities can be examined through the following model.

It is initially assumed that the earnings received by the full-time worker (which, for simplicity, is assumed to be the husband) will represent a non-labour income to his wife. Consequently, this income may affect her decision whether or not to seek employment. The wife's decision is then determined by her own wage–leisure preference curves. However, should the wife obtain employment it is assumed that her income will have no effect on her husband's decision to work. Thus, as shown in Figure 6.17, the wife receives an initial non-labour income of M, and with a corner solution is on the wage–leisure preference curve I. In these circumstances the wife prefers to take employment with a potential wage income of MQ, the budget line being $M'Q$, and be on wage–leisure curve II and offer work hours HP for an earned income of Mq. Her total income is the non-labour income, OM, plus her own earnings, Mq. Should her husband's income now rise, and be transferred to the wife as non-labour income, $M'M''$ she can immediately achieve the wage–leisure preference curve III, which represents a superior, and preferred, combination, and consequently may now withdraw her own work hours HP. This particular approach to explaining the decision of a wife to enter the labour force has been the subject of criticism owing to the underlying 'sexist' nature of the assumptions made. Economists, however, as social scientists, are concerned with behaviour as

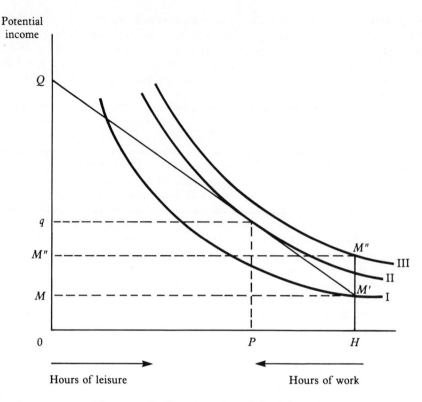

Figure 6.17 *The 'partners' employment choice*

it exists in practice and not with particular views of what behaviour ought to be. As people and as members of families they can have their own personal value judgements.

The inter-relationships between family members in determining work hours offered and the various possible uses of time are therefore complex matters, and it is by no means certain what the effects of various income changes are likely to be. Decisions are also influenced by prevailing social attitudes which, in the 1980s, have been undergoing profound, if unevenly distributed, changes.

Questions for Discussion and Review

11 Discuss the possible effects of the following on family decisions concerning work.
   (a) The further extension of private medical insurance financed by individually paid premiums.
   (b) The introduction of student loans and a reduction in the scope of grants to students in higher education.
   (c) An increase in the birth rate.

12 How would you expect the shape of individuals' income–leisure indifference curves to change as incomes and living standards rise?

Suggestions for Projects and Written Assignments

1 Use indifference curve analysis to examine the possible effects of reductions in income tax on the decision to work made by individuals at various income levels. How far are your findings supported by published data relating to average hours worked? Suggest reasons why published data of this kind may not be an accurate reflection of the true position.

2 Obtain up-to-date details concerning the amount of unemployment and other State benefits payable to the unemployed in your country. Identify the main factors likely to influence the amount payable to individuals. Compare these amounts with average incomes earned by unskilled and skilled manual workers. Discuss the probable level of the reserve wage likely to induce job acceptance for each group and compare this with average earnings.

Suggestions for Further Reading

A number of the issues discussed in this chapter are the subject of a study by Perlman (1969, Part 1), who provided a further exposition of the theoretical concepts involved. An extended essay by Killingsworth (1981) made a detailed analysis of labour supply models, with an appendix by McElroy (1981) which examined the labour supply decisions of husbands and wives. Killingsworth (1983) extended this work. A more limited number of 'wage–leisure' examples are to be found in Addison and Siebert (1979, Chapter 3), who developed a quantitative approach to their analysis. Research on questions of male and female labour supply was reviewed by Pencavel (1986) and Killingsworth and Heckman (1986).

In this chapter the underlying assumption has been the existence of a choice between leisure and its sacrifice for work and the monetary rewards that work brings. Atrostic (1982), however, acknowledged the existence of non-pecuniary rewards which can make work an attractive alternative to leisure.

The question of a fixed number of contract hours and its relationship to individuals' desired patterns of working time has been of considerable interest to economists in the USA: for example, Perlman (1960), Ehrenberg (1970), and Shishko and Rostker (1976). While these economists have sought to explain the implications of choice around the fixed number of contract hours, other economists have examined the implications of a reduction in contract hours. These include Bronfenbrenner and Mossin (1967) and Whitley and Wilson (1986).

The effects upon the willingness to work of unemployment insurance has been examined further in Hamermesh (1980) and Maki and Spindler (1975).

The emerging pattern whereby husband and wife are simultaneously employed is considered further by Gramm (1974) and Wales and Woodland (1976).

7
The Individual's Choice of Work

Aspects of Individual Decisions Concerning the Choice of Work

The individual has to choose not only whether to work or not but also which occupation to follow and which industry or sector of activity to enter. At the same time it has to be recognised that the choices open to any worker at a given point in his or her working life are affected by earlier decisions made by that worker concerning:

(a) the choice of occupation to be followed,
(b) the amount of time, energy, and other personal resources invested in actually searching for work, and
(c) the amount of time and personal resources invested in obtaining education and training.

Each of these decisions involves using economic resources and each has important economic implications. This is still true even when the decision appears relatively automatic and straightforward. For example, if you decide to take the first job offered instead of continuing to search and evaluate other possible options the cost of accepting the first job will be the benefits you could have received from other available jobs.

Question for Discussion and Review

1 What do you think are the main considerations that account for the fact that fewer people qualify each year as doctors than as nurses, or as barristers rather than as solicitors?

Occupational Choice
Definition of Occupation

Most government labour departments try to classify the various occupations within a national economy. Classifications are usually based on the collection of skills which are thought to be unique to each particular occupation. Any one skill, for example, the ability to type, may be required for several different occupations (secretary, journalist, telex operator, etc.), but when combined with a number of other skills such as the ability to take notes, organise office work, use a range of office equipment, and act as a personal assistant to a manager, then it is possible to recognise the combination that is usually associated with the work of the office secretary.

Defining each occupation in terms of the unique collection of skills and tasks associated with it makes it possible to identify those occupations, such as office secretary, common to quite different industrial sectors. These can be distinguished from those occupations, such as cut glass engraving, which are specific to only one industrial sector.

The total number of individuals who enter an occupation in any one period is determined by two interacting considerations. The first is the desire of individuals to pursue that line of work: not everyone is equally attracted to every occupation. A second consideration is the availability and cost of facilities to acquire the skills needed in that occupation.

Constraints on Choice

At first glance individuals may seem to have an immense number of job choices open to them. In Britain, for example, the number of specific occupations, identified under the CODOT method of classification, exceeds 20 000. Each individual could in theory choose any one of these. In reality, the practical choice is likely to be considerably more limited for some or all of the following reasons.

(a) The relatively poor communications existing in the markets for work ensure that few individuals can be aware of more than a small proportion of the total job opportunities available. Lack of knowledge of all the possibilities is thought to be the greatest single constraint to occupational choice.

(b) The limitations of individual abilities and inherent characteristics set further constraints on choice. Many occupations require a very special combination of physical and/or mental qualities that considerably reduces the number of successful entrants. Besides the more obvious examples of deep sea diver, Royal Marine Commando, steeplejack, and brain surgeon, there are others whose demands often surprise and disappoint the intended recruit.

(c) In spite of the breakdown of many old class distinctions and wealth differentials, it is still true that socio-economic status may make it difficult for an individual to enter certain occupations. The way individual socio-economic status is thought to restrict entry to certain occupations is through the educational system. In the latter years of schooling, education acts as a filter which partially determines subsequent occupational choice. Failure to choose certain subjects, often as early as the third year at secondary school, may virtually preclude later entry to many occupations. Schools vary greatly in their ability to provide career advice, obtain examination successes, and assist students to gain entry to higher education. When selecting recruits for management training it is clear that some large multinational companies look for personal qualities that are most likely to be cultivated by the top public schools and/or the older universities.

(d) There have always existed, and will always exist, barriers to entry to certain occupations. In the past it was not unusual for preferential treatment to be given to the children of skilled artisans in the allocation of apprenticeships to the detriment of other well-qualified and motivated potential entrants. Some 'professional' occupations now seek to restrict entry to graduates, when a generation ago anyone with a grammar school education 'up to school certificate level' was welcome.

For practical purposes, therefore, most new entrants to the labour market have to choose one occupation from a limited number of those that are known, available, and for which they are qualified.

Individual choice is also affected by personal preferences, objectives, ambitions, and dislikes. People often appear to reject occupations for which they appear well qualified for reasons that to others may seem trivial but are clearly important to them. It has to be acknowledged that many final choices of occupation are determined largely by various non-economic considerations [which have been examined by White (1968)] and that economic factors may take only second place.

Questions for Discussion and Review

2 Discuss the view that education serves more as a restrictive barrier to the entry of many careers rather than as a means of providing the skills and qualities needed to achieve competence in those careers.

3 Conduct a survey among your fellow students to identify:
(a) how many have firmly decided on a realistic future career, and
(b) of those who have made a clear career decision, which were the main influences determining that decision.

The Costs of Choosing an Occupation

The economic considerations involved in occupational choice relate both to the benefits which may arise from the choice and the costs incurred in making any particular choice. The individual can be expected to try to balance costs against the anticipated potential benefits of the chosen work. One difficulty is that the costs have to be met at the present time, while the potential benefits will be recovered over a longer period in the future. The benefits are also uncertain, and the degree of uncertainty increases with time. This, of course, is the typical problem of any form of investment, and in choosing a job the individual is, in effect, investing available resources in the expectation that benefits will be obtained in the future.

The Costs of Choosing an Occupation

Choice costs are likely to include the following.

Obtaining Information about Available Occupations
For those entering the labour force for the first time the monetary costs involved are often borne by public authorities; for a discussion of the significance of these activities see Maizels (1965). Those wishing to make a more extensive search than that carried out by the usual public services are likely to find that the cost is substantial, and this may restrict the search to a limited number of options.

Travel and Relocation Costs
This type of cost is usually borne by the individual and is more likely to arise for those leaving higher education than for those leaving school at the minimum age. In all cases they can prove a limiting factor.

Entry Fees
In a limited number of occupations there may exist a fee or premium which is required as a condition of entry. In earlier periods those wishing to become an apprentice or a 'pupil' in a professional occupation were required to pay for the privilege of doing so. These practices, at least in Britain, have largely disappeared and indeed the opposite may now occur. Some employers are willing to assist recruits with any entry costs they may have incurred.

Training Costs

There remains though a major cost for all occupations involving a skill and/or qualification, and that is the cost of the required training and/or education. While those who pursue higher education as a pre-requisite to entry to an occupation may be entitled to a financial grant, and those who undertake an apprenticeship receive a wage, the grant or wage will be below the level of earnings which might otherwise be obtained from other occupations. Choice may, therefore, be influenced by the cost, reflected in earnings forgone, of acquiring the required education and/or skills.

The Anticipated Benefits from Choosing an Occupation

It is often difficult to identify and measure the costs of exercising choice though for many, consciously or unconsciously, they are likely to represent a restricting influence. Nevertheless, a rational exercise of choice requires that the costs should be set against the benefits that may be anticipated from the various available occupations. These benefits appear in the form of rewards offered by the occupation, and these rewards require some examination.

The Current Wage Level for the Chosen Occupation

It is usually not too difficult to obtain information concerning current pay levels, but this can sometimes be a deceptive guide to longer-term expectations. The current wage reflects the current demand and supply conditions for differing occupations. An occupation which offers a high wage reward may do so because there has been an unwillingness to enter that occupation in the previous period and/or because those previously following the occupation have left it. Thus, a high wage may exist to compensate for other features that are disadvantageous and it may not, therefore, represent a sound reason for entry.

Potential Life-long Earnings

Another way to view the wage offered is to consider it in terms of potential life-long earnings. This involves an evaluation of the stability of employment in the occupation being chosen. In the present period of rapid and far-reaching technological change, many of the old 'certainties' can no longer be assumed and such an evaluation can be extremely difficult and potentially misleading.

Fringe Benefits

The reward package associated with any occupation extends beyond the wage offered into the area of fringe benefits. These range from subsidised sports facilities to pension arrangements and company cars. The results of extensive social legislation over the past quarter of a century combined with company/trade union agreements upon the harmonisation of benefits has reduced, but by no means eliminated, the fringe benefit differences between occupations. More than a quarter of a century of high income tax rates, particularly for the higher-income groups, has tended to increase the number and ingenuity of employers prepared to reward key employees with untaxed benefits. If the reductions in income tax achieved in the 1980s are maintained and continued it is likely that the importance of fringe benefits will decline in Britain.

The process of occupational choice is one where economic decision making might be expected, especially in view of the costs involved and the practical difficulties of changing occupations should a bad choice be made. Making the correct choice is clearly important for the individual whose economic and personal life depends on its outcome, but it is also extremely important for the economy as a whole. Decisions being made by individuals today will determine the pattern of labour supply to occupations for a long time in the future.

In spite of this importance, the available evidence suggests that people do not generally base their choices on careful and rational comparisons of costs and benefits associated with the various occupations available. In reality they appear to rely on the limited and imperfect information supplied by close family and friends and to be heavily influenced by current wage rates. For example, from his studies relating to staying on at school and entry to higher education, Pissarides (1981, 1982a) deduced that the present values of manual workers and university graduates were significant influencing factors. As a result, most new entrants to the workforce are probably not aware of the full range of choices open to them and are likely to be ignorant of occupations that could be the most appropriate for their particular circumstances.

Question for Discussion and Review

4 Choose two of the following occupations and prepare a report giving the following information: earnings rates; qualifications for entry; methods of obtaining the necessary qualifications and institutions where these qualifications may be obtained; expectations for and availability of post-entry training and qualifications; age at which a decision to enter the occupation is normally required.

Choices: veterinary surgeon; computer programmer; journalist; retail shop manager (major multiple store); solicitor; chartered engineer; electronics engineer; secondary school teacher (science subjects).

Present your report to your student group and discuss its findings.

The Theory of Human Capital in Labour Markets

The Concept of Human Capital

In most cases when economists refer to investment in human capital they mean the process whereby individuals forgo current earnings in anticipation of improving their ability to earn more in the future. This usually involves undergoing a period of further education and/or training during which the costs identified above are likely to be incurred.

For the individual this investment decision is a fairly straightforward matter of comparing known cost with anticipated future gains. This is much the same as any other business investment project, although in the individual case, particularly for older people, there are likely to be non-economic, personal considerations, such as the effects on other members of the family, that significantly influence the decision. However, investment in human capital also has important implications for the economy as a whole. When individuals withdraw for a time from the working population in order to gain further knowledge and skills, society as a whole is making a sacrifice of current production in anticipation of improving the productivity of labour in the future. The economy as a whole loses the work of the individuals during their period of education or training but it gains more productive people when they return to the active workforce. Of course, the balance of cost and benefit depends to some extent on current economic conditions. In a period of rapid technological change and high structural unemployment the costs to the community are likely to be low relative to the potential benefits of this kind of individual investment in human capital. It is important to stress that the rewards to the individual and benefits to the economy arise from the increased productivity of labour and not from the education and training in themselves, though these may bring significant non-economic social benefits, for example, in the form of increased personal satisfaction from work.

Paying the Cost of Human Capital Investment

Capital goods investment has been the subject of economic analysis for a long time, but the examination of the similar practice of investment in human beings, through education and training, is a relatively recent deveopment arising from the initial work by Schultz (1961) and Becker (1962 and 1975). The concept, however, is as old as the study of economics. Adam Smith, in Chapter 10 of 'The Wealth of Nations' (1961 edition), identified the desire to recover during a working lifetime the 'cost of learning a trade' as one reason for the existence of wage differences.

For an employer there are differences between investing in plant and machinery and investing in human capital. When a firm invests in machinery, ownership of the machine(s) passes to the firm. The employer may invest in human capital by financing a training scheme but, in non-slave societies, no ownership rights may be claimed over the trained worker.

Partly as a consequence of this, an employer investing in human capital is unable to make the kind of estimates of anticipated future increases in revenue resulting from the cost of investment that form the basis of rational capital budgeting for projected purchases of physical capital. No employer can predict with certainty the future productivity of any individual employee nor how long that employee will remain in the firm's employment.

There are clearly risks to the employer arising out of human capital expenditure. Consequently, firms will try to pass this cost on to others where possible: to the taxpayer through the agency of public sector educational services, or to the workers themselves through reduced wages during training or requirements that some costs of training should be paid by the recipients.

It was largely to try and overcome these reservations of employers concerning training costs that the British Government established Industrial Training Boards in the 1960s. The idea was that all or most firms in an industry should share training costs through a training levy and that the firms which undertook training should be reimbursed from the fund created by the levy. This development did not prove very successful and received some academic criticism. Lees and Chiplin (1970) expressed the view that there was no economic logic in the approach. There were major differences of opinion between firms and the Boards set up to organise training as to the nature and content of training courses, and firms resented what they regarded as high costs of administration by the Boards and their own lack of control over the way levies were used. In November 1981 the Secretary of State for Employment announced his decision to abolish all but 7 of the 27 Boards that had been created by the Industrial Training Act of 1964.

It has been argued that as society as a whole obtains benefits from human capital investment, the whole or the major burden of the cost should be borne by society through taxation administered by the government. However, if a government accepts all or part of the responsibility for financing education and training it engages in a non-market reallocation of income between families and generations. This is a major economic and social redistribution with political implications that are beyond the scope of this book.

It can, of course, also be argued that because the major share of the benefits from education and training are received by the individual and the individual's family it is the family that should pay the cost or at least a significant part of that cost. This is an argument that is considered later in this chapter, but at this stage it should be recognised that the investment does represent a reallocation of income between different generations of the family. When a parent, or grandparent, sacrifices a part of current income or savings to pay for the training of a child or grandchild it is in anticipation that this expenditure will result in improvements in income-earning potential and living standards of the children and future generations.

The Human Capital Investment Decision

The basic principles of human capital investment in education and training are simple. Whoever decides to make the investment expects that future benefits will be greater than the anticipated costs of the investment. Consequently, the decision is influenced by:

(a) the cost of the proposed investment,
(b) the expected level of return on investment, and
(c) the rate of return on alternative investment.

It is assumed that should the investment not be estimated to produce a return greater than that which could otherwise be obtained it will not be undertaken. The investment in education and/or training will continue until the point where the expected increase in earnings equals the additional costs of further training. This is simply an application of the basic economic principle that maximising the profit from an activity requires that the activity be continued until its marginal costs equal its marginal return in revenue. However, there is the difficulty that costs are incurred now or in the immediate future whereas the benefits are obtained as a stream of additional payments at a longer period in the future.

Any model of human capital must, therefore, recognise that a pound today is not the same as a pound tomorrow because today's pound can earn interest while waiting for tomorrow. Similarly, the parent who pays the cost of a child's training course is sacrificing not only the amount paid but also the income that amount could have earned if invested in, say, a bank investment account. The model must discount the future stream of benefits so that they are comparable with the more immediate payment of the costs.

To simplify the model and to make it more easily comparable with the standard models of physical capital appraisal on which it is based, it is convenient to assume that the cost is payable as a single sum immediately. This basic, simple model can be readily modified to bring it closer to reality. In its simplest form the model states that investment in further education or training will be worthwhile provided that its cost is less than or equal to the present value of the stream of additional income that can be expected from that investment. This can be expressed in the form:

$$C = PV = \frac{R(1)}{(1 + i)} + \frac{R(2)}{(1 + i)^2} + \frac{R(3)}{(1 + i)^3} + \ldots + \frac{R(n)}{(1 + i)^n}$$

where:

C = the present cost of the proposed investment in human capital;
PV = the present value of a stream of payments due in the future and discounted at a rate of discount i;
R = the anticipated additional income in each future year, $R(1)$ representing the first year when the increase is received, $R(2)$ the second year, and so on;
i = the chosen rate of discount, expressed as a decimal fraction and based on the market rate of interest which has been sacrificed by forgoing alternative forms of investment.

When $C = PV$ the rate of discount i is also the internal rate of return on the investment cost, i.e. the rate of annual interest that would be required from an investment in financial securities to give an equivalent return to the additional net income from improved job prospects after the further training. It is clear from this model that the higher the anticipated future earnings and the longer the period over which they can be expected to be earned, the higher the investment expenditure that can be justified. More young people aged 25–35 can be expected to attend graduate business school than 'mature' managers in their fifties.

There are some further interesting implications of this model arising from the effects of time and the rate of discount. To take some simple examples, a present cost of £1000 would be justified if this resulted in a single additional payment of £1277 received 5 years hence at a discount rate of 5%. The amount of future single payment needed to justify this cost rises to £1629 if the appropriate rate of discount is 12%. If the time gap between incurring the cost and receiving the additional payment is increased to 10 years then the amounts needed to justify payment of £1000 rise to £1763 for a 5% rate of discount and £3106 for a 12% discount rate.

It is evident from these simple illustrations that the higher the opportunity cost of investment expenditure, the greater will be the tendency to look for training that offers early prospects of increased income, and the higher will be the anticipated income gain needed to justify the training cost.

Questions for Discussion and Review

5 Discuss the view that all the costs of education and training above the national minimum should be borne by the individual receiving the benefits of that education and training or his or her family.

6 To what extent do you think the average earnings of the following occupational groups support the human capital theory of income differences outlined in this chapter?
Chartered accountant; hospital doctor; oil rig worker; farm worker; secondary school teacher; computer salesperson.

Some Applications of Human Capital Theory
The Value of a Degree

The acquisition of educational qualifications may be regarded as an investment for the future and requires sacrifice in the current period. A student, who is assumed to have the potential ability to gain a degree, is required to decide whether the current sacrifice will be balanced by anticipated returns in the future. Consider the following:

At the end of the first year of study a student is given the following choice:

(a) undertake ONE further year of study for a diploma before entering the labour market, or
(b) undertake TWO further years of study for a degree before entering the labour market.

The student is aware that for each year of study a grant of £2000 will be received, and that with a diploma a starting salary of £7000 will be obtainable. If, therefore, the decision is to study for a degree, the earnings forgone in the third year will be £5000. Note that the existence of the maintenance grant paid to students will reduce the level of earnings forgone, and hence the subsequent potential return. Secondly, the student is aware that the current market rate of interest is 10%. This information will enable an estimate of the minimum earnings increment, R', required to make an additional year of study a financially viable proposition.

The appraisal model outlined previously suggests that the degree will be a worthwhile investment if the present value of increased future earnings discounted at 10% is greater than or equal to £5000. To find the income increase that will satisfy this condition means finding values of R that satisfy the equation

$$5000 = \frac{R(1)}{(1+i)} + \frac{R(2)}{(1+i)^2} + \frac{R(3)}{(1+i)^3} + \dots + \frac{R(n)}{(1+i)^n}$$

The combinations of values for R spread over a large number of years are clearly almost limitless, so for practical purposes some simplifying assumptions are necessary. The most important of these is to assume that R is constant (or can be averaged) over the period of investigation. It is also necessary to make an assumption regarding the number of years for which an increased income can be anticipated. Here there are two possible arguments:

(a) It may be argued that possession of a degree opens up career prospects that are likely to affect the income earnings potential for the whole working life of the graduate. In this case the value of n is likely to be about 40, which in terms of mathematical progressions of the kind presented by the investment appraisal model is said to be 'very large' ($n \to \infty$). The result of applying the mathematical limit of this progression is to enable the equation to be very much simplified to:

$$C = R/i$$

As the value of C has been given as £5000 and i is 0.1, the value of R that satisfies the equation is £500. On this basis, therefore, the degree course is financially worthwhile if the annual additional earnings which it produces amount to at least £500 per year.

(b) It can, however, be argued that the earnings value of a degree diminishes rapidly. It enables a graduate to enter careers that might otherwise be denied, but progress in that career usually depends on a range of personal qualities and on work performance, and these are not directly related to the degree qualification. In this case it might be suggested that the degree only influences earnings for a maximum of, say, 10 years. The value of n in the equation thus becomes ten. The limit of the mathematical progression remains as before $(1 - r^n)/(1 - r)$, where $r = 1/1 + i$, but as n can no longer be considered to be 'very large' the equation cannot be simplified in the way that was possible for $n = 40$. In fact, the effect of $n = 10$ is to raise the value of R to £868, which is what is to be expected. If a short-term view is taken of the value of an additional qualification, the increase in earnings must be greater in order to justify the expense of gaining it.

When using this kind of appraisal technique it is commonly assumed by observers such as Ziderman (1973) that the expectation of financial reward is the only incentive for further education. In practice other, non-financial considerations are likely to influence decisions. There is a consumer attraction in the experience of college life and even in the educational experience itself.

Although this example has been based on the choice of pursuing a degree course, it has to be recognised that similar appraisal techniques are relevant to all forms of further education [see Selby Smith (1970)] and to the growing range of postgraduate and 'professional' or 'semi-professional' qualifications. For example, the Master of Business Administration (MBA) courses are 'sold' by higher education establishments largely on their value in increasing earnings potential. Most entrants to this course will be making a financial sacrifice and a growing number are likely to be borrowing money in order to gain the qualification. Nor are financial considerations limited to higher educational courses.

Further Investment and Return Possibilities

The above example illustrates the principles involved in determining whether or not an investment in human capital should be undertaken. The same principle is shown diagramatically in Figure 7.1. Here it is assumed that there is no income flow between the ages of 18 and 20 because the student is studying for either a degree or a diploma. In the third year, a degree student who is still studying forgoes the sum *A*. This area represents the earnings of a diploma holder. However, after graduation, the lifetime earnings of the graduate are increased by the sum represented by the area *B*.

In this example a simplifying assumption was made in that the only cost to the student in the extra years of study, after allowing for financial assistance from an external agency, would be the earnings forgone. Although this is a useful assumption it does not necessarily reflect the reality for those wishing to study in higher education. For example, schooling beyond the normal compulsory period is often a prerequisite for entry to higher education. Although the direct cost of providing this schooling is often met by a public agency the indirect costs, including food and clothing and out of pocket expenses, will be met by the student's family. In practice, therefore, not only are earnings forgone, but costs are also incurred. This aspect has been taken into account in Figure 7.2. Here the comparison is between those who leave school

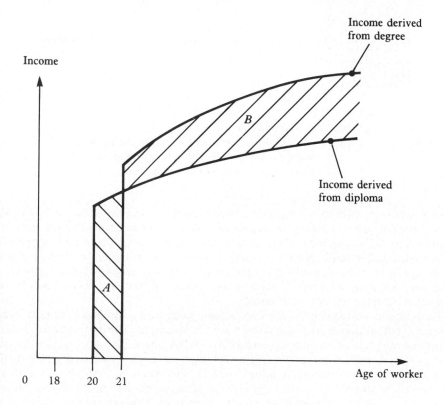

Figure 7.1 *Cost and return on a further year of study*
Note: A represents net income LOSS of additional year's study
B represents net income GAIN of additional year's study

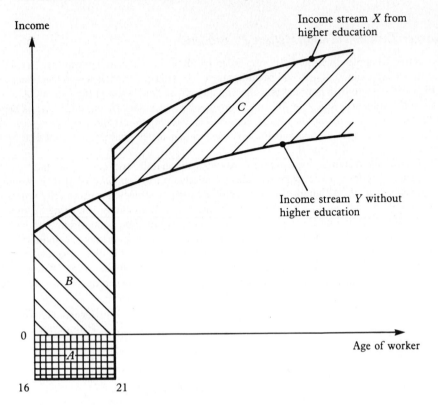

Figure 7.2 *Alternative income streams*
Note: A represents cost of maintenance, tuition, books, etc.
B represents net income LOSS arising from study
C represents net income GAIN arising from study

when compulsory education is complete and immediately begin to earn a wage and those who remain at school and then enter college to read for a degree. For the latter group the cost of the degree consists of two elements. These are illustrated by area A, representing the costs incurred by the individual, or family, and which would not have arisen if schooling had been terminated at the age of 16 years, and area B, representing the earnings forgone as a consequence of continuing into higher education. Thus the investment cost of the degree will be A plus B. The investment return is represented by area C.

The principles of analysing human capital investment have been examined in terms of higher education, but the majority of young people leave school once the compulsory element has been completed, and some then enter apprenticeships. When this occurs the principles outlined above still apply and are illustrated in Figure 7.3. In this diagram forgone earnings during the apprenticeship are represented by areas A and D. The return on investing in a skill are represented by area B. However, the practice of paying apprentices during training raises a different issue. In the early stages of training the value of the apprentice's product is zero. Indeed, the product value is likely to be negative because facilities and staff have to be deployed for the purpose of training. Nevertheless, it is the practice to pay a wage to apprentices. On the other hand, during the later stages of an apprenticeship, a product with a positive value greater than the apprentice wage is generated and this is retained by the employer to compensate for the earlier payments made. This aspect of the financing of apprenticeships is illustrated in Figure 7.3. The shaded area *C* represents the advance wage payments paid during the unproductive early stages of apprenticeship. The area *D* represents the difference in value between the apprentice's wages and the revenue from output retained by the employer.

The principles in the allocation of costs during apprentice training are applicable to other instances where general training takes place. In the later stages of the training period an employer pays a wage below the value of output in order to recover the costs of training.

Questions for Discussion and Review

7 Estimate the opportunity cost of the course on which you are currently studying. Use the techniques outlined in this chapter to estimate the approximate additional annual income resulting from the course to make it

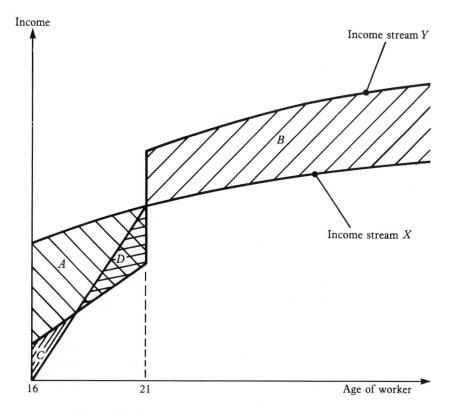

Figure 7.3 *Cost and return of an apprenticeship*
Note: *A + D   represents net income LOSS of apprenticeship*
      B   represents net income GAIN of apprenticeship
      C   represents advance wage payments by employer
      D   represents recovery of wages payments by employer

worthwhile as an economic investment. Discuss your findings and the relevance of this approach to your own and your friends' motives for studying.

8 If higher education in Britain were to receive less support from taxation, e.g. if students were to be expected to finance themselves to a greater extent, if necessary through loans, what effect do you think this would have on the nature and duration of higher education courses in Britain? Bear in mind that many courses are already being actively 'sold' to foreign students who pay full fees.

Identifying the Returns on Human Capital Investment

Evidence of Income Differences

The analysis of labour market data does suggest that earnings levels support the view that human capital investment in education and/or training produces a return in higher incomes. Earnings data for six different occupations, each requiring a different education and training input, are shown in Table 7.1. The following points should be considered.

(a) Two basic occupations, refuse collectors and office cleaners, are included. These occupations require no education or general training beyond the basic level. There may be a requirement for a modest specific training element and that issue is discussed below. It is, therefore, assumed that the median wage for these occupations incorporates no return for human capital investment.

(b) A secretary without additional schooling is likely to receive two years of education and training in a vocational college. The human capital investment cost will be two years' forgone earnings plus other expenditure incurred by the potential secretary or family. The return on this investment is a median wage 50% above that for the office cleaners.

(c) An apprenticeship is a prerequisite to becoming a toolmaker. For four or five years the apprentice wage is below that received by a refuse collector of similar age. The sum of the differences in wage levels represents the cost to the apprentice of the human capital investment. Subsequently, the median wage of a toolmaker is 40% above that received by the refuse collector.

(d) A secondary school teacher spends two additional years at school and four years in higher education. No earnings are received during these six years of extra education but there may

Table 7.1 Gross weekly pay for selected occupations for April 1986 (in £s)

	Lowest decile	Median	Highest decile
Accountant (male)	144.6	257.0	407.0
Secondary teacher (female)	151.6	197.3	259.9
Toolmaker/toolfitter (male)	140.1	187.5	266.0
Secretary (female)	95.5	134.1	195.3
Refuse collector (male)	118.2	134.2	196.4
Office cleaner (female)	68.7	92.0	137.6

Source: 'New Earnings Survey 1986', HMSO, London

be a modest income flow from education grants. The apparent return to the secondary school teacher for this investment is a median wage twice that of an office cleaner.

(e) The graduate accountant undergoes a different eduction/training programme. Two years of extended schooling is a prerequisite to three years of academic study before three years of professional training. During the period of education no earnings are received beyond, possibly, a small income from education grants. During the professional training period salary payments are normally received and these generally increase as the trainee progresses through the various levels of the required professional examinations. The return for this extended period of human capital investment is a median wage 90% higher than the refuse collector.

It is not suggested that the differences in the median wages for these occupations are attributable solely to differing levels of return on human capital investment. The economic influences leading to occupational income differentials are complex, and are discussed in a later chapter. Although these examples indicate that differing levels of human capital investment may exert an influence upon wage differences, they do not actually prove it. Precisely because of the significance of other economic influences and of the differing nature of the training provided for occupations, few empirical studies have been undertaken to estimate the human capital investment return attributable to training.

Nevertheless, there have been numerous studies to estimate the returns, in subsequent higher wage levels, of education provided beyond the basic level that all young people are expected to receive. For example, Carnoy and Marenbach (1975) examined the returns attributable to education in the USA and similar studies have been undertaken in Britain by Psacharopoulos and Layard (1979) and by Adamson and Reid (1980). The consensus of these, and other, studies is that individuals who extend their basic education and/or study in higher education receive positive financial returns. This is, perhaps, a fortunate conclusion for the career prospects of academic researchers and teachers!

Further Aspects of General and Specific Training

Post-compulsory school and higher education are not specific to the requirements of a single employer and consequently are similar in character and objective to general training. Similarly, the content of most higher and further education courses is of a generalised character. Some courses, such as those for medicine, dentistry, social work, and teacher training, do lead to clearly defined occupations. Nevertheless, those pursuing such courses have a choice of potential employer and may use their acquired skills and knowledge in occupations other than those for which they have been specifically prepared. A consequence of the general nature of education is that few employers pay a wage to those receiving it. The human capital investment costs associated with education tend to fall upon public authorities, who provide facilities at below or nil cost, and on students or their families.

Because employers do not contribute directly to the costs of post-compulsory education, the question of their receiving a return on the investment does not arise. Instead, the return is received by the individual in whom the investment has been made while an indirect return, the social return, is received by the public authorities. The requirement for a social return arises because the social costs of education exceed the private costs involved. Although educational provision is largely free to the individual, there are costs to society in providing education and in subsidising student users with grants.

The social returns of the community's investment in higher education, unlike the private returns, are difficult to evaluate, but they can be assumed to be reflected in the higher taxes paid by those receiving higher wage rates and, more widely, by the larger National Product arising from the more efficient workforce.

The acquisition of the underlying skills and knowledge associated with occupations is a further example of general training. While the training for the accountant and the toolmaker may occur on an employer's premises, the knowledge and skills are transferable to other employers. There are few financial incentives for an employer to undertake general training, for although the costs, which Oatey (1970) believes may not be fully recognised, fall upon the employer, it is the individual employees who gain the benefits of increased market value and mobility between employers.

In some industries and/or countries it is the practice for relevant employers and/or the government to contribute to a financial pool which is used to subsidise those employers who provide general training. The British experiment with Industrial Training Boards was described earlier in this chapter. However, even where this type of arrangement exists for general training it seldom covers the full cost either to employers or to individuals. The normal practice is to assume that the individual trainee wille eventually benefit from the investment through the receipt of higher pay. Consequently, the trainee is expected to contribute to the training cost through a wage rate below the level of marginal revenue product earned for the employer.

There remains, however, an element of the training received by an individual which is specific to the employer providing the training. For example, any induction training provided to new employees represents specific training to the firm providing it. General, and easily transferable, skills are required to operate plant and machinery but the application of those skills differs between employers and specific training is required to make the employee familiar with the employer's requirements. The skills required in cash handling, for instance, are general, but their application in any one financial institution is likely to be quite specific and not transferable. The further human capital investment involved in this specific training is assumed to be of little value to other employers. In these circumstances logic would suggest that the costs should be borne by the employer providing the specific training because no other employer may expect to benefit from it. In practice an employer will endeavour to pass a proportion of the specific training costs to individual employees by offering a lower wage rate during a 'six months trial period' of employment, or by incremental payment scales within which wage rates rise after the completion of specific training. Many British employers also sought to share these costs with other firms in the industry through industrial training schemes established under the Industrial Training Act of 1964. Although employers may seek to pass a proportion of specific training costs to the employee through an initial period of low wages, the opportunity to do this may be limited by the availability of other jobs offering higher pay.

Question for Discussion and Review

9 Discuss the difficulties of identifying the extent to which income differences can be explained by the human capital theory discussed in this chapter.

The Unanswered Questions Relating to Human Capital

Some doubts have been expressed concerning the validity of research findings on the evaluation of human capital.

Failure to Invest in Human Capital

The assumption throughout is that those who have received an extended education and/or general training will receive a higher level of earnings to compensate for the forgone income, and that these earnings are attributable to human capital investment.

Why, then, does not everyone seek education and/or training as a means of increasing earnings?

Ignoring the obvious conclusion that should everyone have a degree no individual would qualify for the premium payments, the reason is that not everyone has the academic ability to do so. Nor do all individuals necessarily have the ability to train as watch-makers or in other skilled crafts. Only those individuals who have the initially required attributes may be given the opportunity to receive the education or the training. The question, therefore, arises as to whether the higher wage rates of those who have experienced additional education and/or training receive them as a consequence of the human capital investment or as a reward for their natural ability. In a US study designed to resolve this question Taubman (1976) sought to compare the earnings potentials of identical twins who had received differing educational and training experiences. The assumption underlying this study is that as identical twins are genetically the same their natural abilities will also be identical. Consequently, any identifiable differences in earnings must be attributable to differences in the level of human capital investment. The study was restricted by the limited population available for the survey. Nevertheless, the findings did indicate that education and training did result in some increased income.

Measuring the Results of Education

A second question relates to how precisely the results of education are to be measured. For example, not only does the ability of undergraduates vary, but so does the quality of the education offered, not only between educational institutions but within institutions. An approach which suggests that any graduate in engineering may expect to receive lifetime earnings 50% greater than a non-graduate has the attraction of simplicity, but the very simplicity ignores the differing quality of engineering degrees and the different level of achievement by the students. To suggest that human capital accumulation may be measured solely in terms of a degree obtained after three years at university may be too crude a measure to be relevant.

Measuring the Returns from Education

Measurement of the returns gained from the investment is a further area fraught with difficulty. Simply to compare different occupational wage rates or median income levels ignores the fact that many occupations are rewarded, at least in part, on the basis of performance. This occurs not only for the machine operator who is partly paid by results but also for the managing director whose reward may be related to profit levels. An alternative approach could be to compare earnings levels over a specified period, but these may be distorted by opportunities for and willingness to work additional hours.

Variations within Occupations

Table 7.1 indicated that there are significant variations in earnings within occupations. Examples from this table show that:

a) An accountant in the highest decile earns nearly three times more than an accountant in the lowest decile, who, incidentally, earns only 75% of the income of a refuse collector in the highest decile.
b) Secretaries and office cleaners in the highest decile earn double that received by those following the identical occupations whose pay is in the lowest decile.

Consequently, the relative value of the return on human capital investment appears to differ according to which wage levels are being compared.

The Validity of Human Capital Theory

Although it remains difficult to provide definitive answers to many of the questions relating to the influences upon human capital accumulation and on its returns, the underlying principle of the theory that differing productivity levels provide a link between education and/or training and subsequent earnings is now widely accepted. Arrow (1973) and Thurlow (1975), however, while accepting that there is an identifiable statistical relationship between the level of education attained and subsequent earnings, offered an alternative explanation. In Thurlow's job competition model it is not education but the occupational skills learned after employment has started that result in the differing levels of earnings. The significance of education is that employers use it as a screening device during recruitment. The suggestion, therefore, is that education, as such, increases neither individual efficiency nor productivity. The employer simply uses education as an indicator of people likely to be suitable candidates for training. For their part, those desiring occupational training also need to have some indication of their own capacity to be trained successfully. The educational qualifications they are able to achieve are looked upon as an indication of this, and education may thus be regarded as a screening device. This view is supported by the work of Shah (1985).

The logic of this approach is that education should not be regarded as a form of capital investment but rather as a means of identifying and filtering those who are to be offered the investment opportunity afforded by occupational training.

Whatever the processes involved, it does seem clear that people will only make sacrifices to undergo prolonged, voluntary periods of education and training if they anticipate that these will lead to improved future living standards for themselves and their families. Income can be seen as a major, though not the only, ingredient in a family's standard of living.

It must also be recognised that this issue is not purely academic, nor is it just a matter for personal opinion. The growth of business-related qualifications, such as the MBA mentioned earlier, means that an increasing number of people have to make the decision whether or not to borrow money to invest in further education, and more and more bank managers are likely to be faced with the decision whether or not to grant them loans. The British Government is also reported to be considering loan schemes to replace all or part of the increasingly expensive grant system for higher education. Loans are already an established part of higher education finance in many countries, including the USA.

It appears that education beyond the minimum prescribed by the State is increasingly being seen as a form of both private and public investment and as a matter of concern to financial institutions. We can expect, therefore, more study of and learning about the relationship between education and income.

Question for Discussion and Review

10 Should a factory or office supervisor receive specific supervisory training outside the firm, or is experience within the firm sufficient? If you think that 'outside' training is desirable, outline what you think should be its content.

Suggestions for Projects and Written Assignments

1 Write a report on the provisions available in your country for entry to higher education for a person aged, say, between 30 and 45 who has left school at the minimum school leaving age with minimum educational qualifications.

2 Suppose a person aged about 35 and in the category described in question 1 was offered an opportunity to enter higher education. Discuss as fully as possible the considerations likely to influence that person's decision whether or not to take up this opportunity.

3 Explain the assumptions underlying the human capital theory as an explanation of income differences and discuss its adequacy in explaining any differences you observe between the incomes of members of the financial professions and those employed in manufacturing production.

Suggestions for Further Reading

For different perspectives on the subject matter of this chapter see the contribution of Lindley (1982) in Creedy and Thomas and Chapter 3 in Hamermesh and Rees (1984). This later work drew upon the experience and practices of the USA.

Paradoxically, while most of us are required to choose an occupation, this subject has been largely unexplored by economists. An attempt to fill part of this gap was made by Williams (1974).

Siebert (1985) in Carline *et al.* provided a comprehensive survey of the literature relating to the theory of human capital and its implications. A similar approach, providing a comprehensive review of American studies, was provided by Rosen (1977).

Articles by Thomas *et al.* (1969) and Woodhall (1974) developed frameworks for the evaluation of costs and benefits associated with employment training related to employment. While their discussion of the consequences of the Industrial Training Act has been overtaken by events, the economic framework these writers developed retains its relevance.

Finally, Ziderman (1978) examined the contribution the British Government can make and has made to training.

8
Labour Markets in Theory and Practice

Basic Features of the Labour Market
Problems of Definition

The term 'labour market' is an expression used by economists to describe a clearly defined condition. The term, however, has entered into the everyday language of politicians, employers, and working people, although all of these groups tend to interpret it in ways different from the approach taken by economists.

This approach has been to use the labour market as a conceptual framework for the examination of the demand for and supply of labour. Within that framework, and when certain simplifying assumptions are made, it is possible to identify the conditions under which labour demand is equated with labour supply and then to estimate the relevant levels of employment and wages. When the labour market is analysed in this way it takes on a degree of precision which is not normally observed in practice.

One of the primary functions of any market is to provide a means whereby price is determined. In a market economy, price is the main mechanism for determining the production and allocation of the market 'good'. The price of the 'good'—labour—is referred to generally as the wage. The analysis of labour markets, therefore, is closely linked to the analysis of wage determination.

While the recognition of the labour market as a mechanism for distributing jobs is retained, non-economists and a growing number of economists often attribute to the labour market a set of boundaries relating to geographical areas and/or occupations. They thus depart from the concept of the labour market as a unitary whole, embracing all the forces operating on the demand for and supply of labour, in favour of a segmented market with separate and virtually independent sectors with little provision for interaction between them.

These differing interpretations of what constitutes the labour market caused Professor Clark Kerr (1950) to suggest that the term had developed a double life. On one hand, the concept of the labour market was used to examine the interaction of wage levels and movements in the demand and supply of labour. In this context, Kerr considered that the quantity of labour supplied and demanded should be regarded as aggregates, i.e. total quantities in the national market. On the other hand, in its alternative 'life' he saw the concept of the labour market as applicable to an employment area, a term employed to describe not only a geographical locality but also an occupation or industry. This conflicting use of the same term, therefore, makes it desirable for us to examine first the way in which the unitary market can be expected to operate before looking at the actual operation of particular modern markets.

Questions for Discussion and Review

1 Suggest reasons why distinct geographical markets for labour may have developed over the past 25 years.

2 If it were desired to reduce these distinctions, i.e. for labour to become more mobile geographically, what social and economic changes might be suggested by the reasons which you have identified in question 1?

Theoretical Models of the Labour Market

The Underlying Assumptions

In developing a simple theoretical model capable of providing a framework for making realistic predictions, some assumptions have to be made. As the model is developed and brought closer to reality, some of these assumptions can be modified or abandoned. Initially, however, the following assumptions are made.

(a) The demand for labour by employers increases as the level of wages falls. This is consistent with the discussion in Chapter 4. It occurs either because existing employers wish to employ more workers as the wage rate falls and/or new employers seek to offer employment at the lower level of wages. The demand curve for labour, which is derived from the marginal revenue product curve, can be expected to be downward sloping, as represented by the curve *DD* in Figure 8.1.

(b) The supply of labour by existing and potential employees will increase as the level of wages rises. This is consistent with the discussion in Chapter 6. The supply curve of labour can therefore be expected to be upward sloping, as illustrated in Figure 8.2.

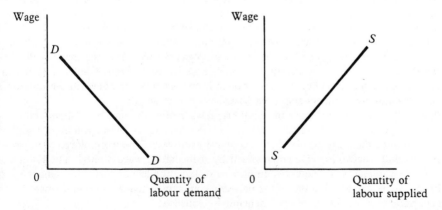

Figure 8.1 *The demand curve for labour*   **Figure 8.2** *The supply curve for labour*

(c) The labour market under consideration contains a large number of employers seeking workers and a large number of potential workers seeking employment.

(d) No single employer or group of employers operating together are powerful enough, by their actions alone, to influence either the wage level or the total number of workers employed.

(e) Potential workers act as individuals within the labour market and do not act collectively through organisations such as trade unions to influence wages or the total number of workers employed.

(f) Potential employees may be regarded as similar in both skills and ability. Employers, therefore, are indifferent as to which worker they employ. This rule of full homogeneity (uniformity) can be modified if workers can be classified by measurable degrees of skill and if employers are indifferent in their employment of workers within a clearly definable class.

(g) All employers and workers are fully aware of each other's actions within the labour market, i.e. that all participants have perfect knowledge of market conditions.

(h) There are no restrictions on employers and employees entering or leaving the labour market, nor of employees changing employers if they should wish to do so, i.e. there is perfect mobility within the market for all participants.

(i) Employees and employers are motivated solely by 'economic considerations', i.e. employers are seeking to employ workers only because of their contribution to production, and workers work only for a money wage. Considerations of social duty or obligation or the desire for social or political power and prestige are not perceived as 'economic'.

If you have studied any microeconomics you will recognise that these assumptions apply to the labour market the conditions necessary for any market to be 'perfectly competitive' in an economic sense. This does not mean that the market is socially or morally desirable but that it is one where the economic forces of supply and demand can interact freely without any hindrance or distortion from any market imperfection such as monopoly power or control from outside forces.

Equilibrium in Perfectly Competitive Labour Markets

It has been proposed earlier that within the labour market the employers' demands for labour and the individual's willingness to supply labour interact to determine both the quantity of labour employed and the appropriate wage level. This is shown for a perfectly competitive labour market in Figure 8.3. The varying quantities of the employers' total, or aggregate, demand for labour, at different wage levels, is signified by the labour demand curve DD. The varying quantities of labour which workers and potential workers are willing to supply at the different wage levels is signified by the labour supply curve SS. Given the shape of these two curves there is only one set of quantity and price levels where the desired demand for labour is equal to supply intentions. These levels, at point E on the graph, are known as the equilibrium levels of quantity or numbers employed (l) and price or wage (w).

Should the wage level be above the equilibrium wage, then the supply of labour will exceed the demand; if the wage offered is below w then the demand for labour will exceed supply.

If, therefore, the wage being offered is above w there will be unemployed workers and employers will react to increase employment by reducing the wage offered. The lower wage level may encourage some potential employees to leave the labour force, i.e. labour supply contracts. Given the assumptions of the perfectly competitive market, this adjustment process can continue until labour supply and demand are equalised.

If the wage being offered is below £w then employers would not be able to recruit all the labour they require. Consequently, employers would raise the offered wage to encourage workers to join them. This rise in wage levels can be expected to encourage an increase in the number of potential workers but will also cause some employers who cannot afford the extra wage cost to drop out of business or operate with fewer workers. Again, this process of adjustment will continue until labour supply and demand are equalised. Only at the point E, the equilibrium, will all employers wishing to employ labour and all those wishing to work be

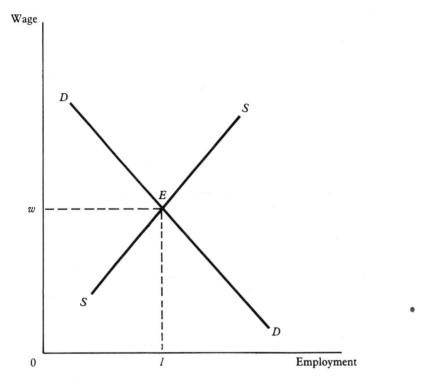

Figure 8.3 *Equilibrium in the competitive labour market*

satisfied. At this point, in the absence of any change in the economic environment within which the market operates, there is no desire by either employers or workers to change the wage level. To do so would introduce disequilibrium with resulting labour shortages or surpluses.

The equilibrium wage in the labour market, shown in Figure 8.3, represents that level of wage which will clear the market, i.e. it is the level of wage, established by the interaction of total market supply and demand, at which all employers wishing to hire labour are able to do so and all workers wishing to work can do so. Thus the equilibrium wage may be termed the 'going wage' that all employers and individuals wishing to work must accept and which, as individuals, they are powerless to alter. The consequence of this for an individual firm is illustrated in Figure 8.4. There is a large number of potential workers, all of whom have to accept the market equilibrium wage w. Thus, for any one firm labour supply, shown by the labour supply curve SS, is totally elastic at the wage w, any one firm being able to employ as many or as few workers as it wishes at the going wage. The actual level of employment by any one firm will of course be determined by the interaction of the firm's demand for labour and the labour supply curves. In this example the firm will employ l workers.

Changes in Market Equilibrium

The establishment of the equilibrium position provides a starting point for an analysis of the labour market. The equilibrium wage and quantity levels will change if there are any changes in demand or supply. The conditions determining either of these forces can, of course, change. The causes of changes vary, but it is possible to identify certain main causes. It must be

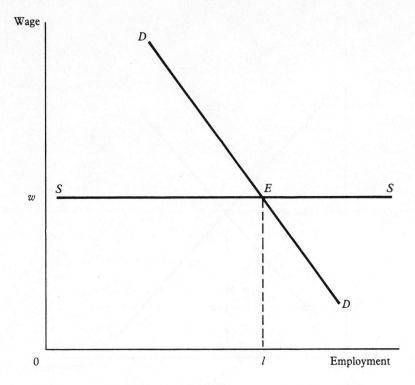

Figure 8.4 *Equilibrium for a firm in a competitive labour market*

remembered that we are here referring to influences that change employers' and workers' intentions at a range of possible wage levels, i.e. influences that produce a shift in the whole demand or supply curve. This is distinct from a movement along the curves which arises solely from a change in wage level.

Demand curves can shift because of the changes detailed in Chapters 4 and 5. The most important of these may be summarised as changes in:

(a) The marginal productivity of labour, i.e. the amount of extra product that can be expected from an increase in the number of workers employed.
(b) The marginal productivity of capital, bearing in mind that capital and labour are substitutes in many production processes.
(c) The demand for the product and the market price of the product. In our model of the labour market, labour demand depends on the marginal revenue product curve and this, in turn, changes if either (a) or (b) change.

The supply of labour in the labour market as a whole depends on influences that were explained in Chapters 6 and 7. These can be summarised as changes in any of the following.

(a) The demographic structure of the population.
(b) The normal age of entry to the workforce.
(c) The normal age of retiring from the workforce.
(d) The activity rates of men and women of normal working age.

At this stage our analysis continues to rely on the assumptions of the neo-classical approach as explained in Chapters 4–7. These, we must remember, rely heavily on models of marginal productivity, wage–leisure preference, and human capital.

Increase in Labour Demand and Market Equilibrium

As is normal in economic analysis of market changes, we examine one change at a time on the assumption that all the other influences remain constant. This is often referred to as the 'comparative static approach' and remains a useful starting point in spite of the increasing use of computers to aid analysis. If employers desire to employ more workers at each wage level within a given range, then the labour demand curve shifts to the right. This is illustrated in Figure 8.5 by introducing a new labour demand curve, D_1D_1, to the right of the original labour demand curve DD. For each wage level, the curve D_1D_1 indicates that more labour will be demanded than was signified by the original curve DD.

Figure 8.5 suggests that after the shift in demand, payment of the old wage w would result in disequilibrium between demand and supply. At the wage w the demand for workers rises to l_1 but the supply remains at l, leaving a shortfall in supply of $l_1 - l$. To close this gap and to induce more workers to enter employment, the wage offered by employers has to rise. At the same time this causes some employers to lower their demand for labour. As more workers are induced to offer their labour in return for a higher wage there is a movement along the labour

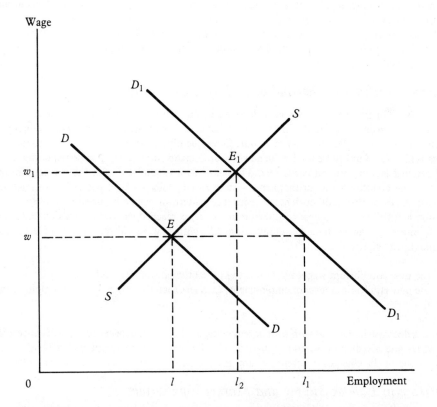

Figure 8.5 *Increase in labour demand and the competitive labour market equilibrium*

supply curve SS. Each 'step up' represents a marginal increase in the number of potential employees offering their services arising from the marginal rise in the wage paid. There is a corresponding movement along the new labour demand curve D_1D_1, with labour demand declining as the offered wage rises. These movements along the labour demand curve D_1D_1 and labour supply curve SS continue until a new equilibrium emerges, shown here at point E_1.

It is important to appreciate the process stages. These are:

(a) The changed conditions of labour demand lead to a shift in the labour demand curve to the right, from DD to D_1D_1, but that shift creates a disequilibrium between supply and demand at the old wage level.

(b) After a time, adjustments take place in the wage level and these lead to movements along both the demand and supply curves to produce a new equilibrium level of wages and number of workers employed. These correspond to the new equilibrium point E_1 where the new labour demand curve D_1D_1 intersects with the labour supply curve SS.

(c) The new equilibrium wage (w_1) is higher than the old (w) and the new equilibrium employment level (l_2) is also greater than the old (l).

When, therefore, there is an increase in labour demand, with labour supply conditions remaining unchanged, we can expect increases in both the equilibrium level of employment and the equilibrium wage. The size of these increases depends on the extent of the shift in employers' intentions, i.e. how far the curve moves, and on the relative elasticities of labour demand and supply at the relevant wage range. The responsiveness of labour demand and supply to changes in wages is roughly represented in simple graphical models by curves of differing slopes, although it is important to remember that the slopes (gradients) of both demand and supply curves are unreliable indicators of precise measures of elasticity should these be needed.

Decrease in Labour Demand and Market Equilibrium

Figure 8.6 illustrates the results of a decrease in the demand for labour with other market conditions remaining constant. This indicates that at each wage within a given range employers wish to employ a smaller quantity of labour. Consequently, the demand curve shifts to the left. This is illustrated in Figure 8.6 by the new labour demand curve D_aD_a, positioned to the left of the original labour demand curve DD. This shows, for example, that at the old equilibrium wage w the quantity of labour that firms wish to employ falls to $0l_b$. If you follow through the consequences of this shift in demand using the pattern of events outlined in the preceding section you will see that a new equilibrium point, E_a is reached where the new demand curve D_aD_a intersects the unchanged supply curve SS, with new equilibrium levels of wage and employment. Notice that:

(a) the new equilibrium wage, w_a, is less than the original wage w, and

(b) the new equilibrium level of employment, l_a, is less than the original level of employment, l.

Thus, a decrease in demand with supply remaining unchanged can be expected to produce a fall in wages and a reduction in employment levels. The extent of the shifts will depend on the magnitude of the changes in intentions and relative supply and demand elasticities as before.

Increase in Labour Supply and Market Equilibrium

In contrast to the two previous examples where supply, represented by the curve SS, was held

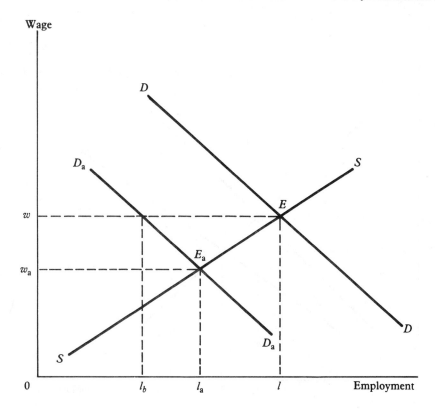

Figure 8.6 *Decrease in labour demand and the competitive labour market equilibrium*

constant and demand (and demand curves) shifted, we now examine the result of a shift in supply and the supply curve with demand held constant (Figure 8.7).

An increase in supply where the supply curve shifts to the right indicates that at each wage level within a given range workers seek to supply more labour. Again this should be contrasted with a movement along the supply curve showing changes in quantity of labour supplied following changes in wage level.

Once again a shift in the curve over time is depicted by drawing a new curve, S_aS_a. Because this is to the right of the original curve SS, the shift indicates that more labour is offered at each wage level.

This new curve S_aS_a produces a new equilibrium point, E_a, where it intersects with the unchanged demand curve DD. This suggests that an increase in labour supply with demand remaining unchanged results in:

(a) a reduction in the market wage level (w_a is lower than w), and
(b) an increase in the market level of employment (l_a is at a higher level than l).

The extent of the shifts will, as before, depend on the magnitude of the change in intentions and on the relative elasticities of supply and demand.

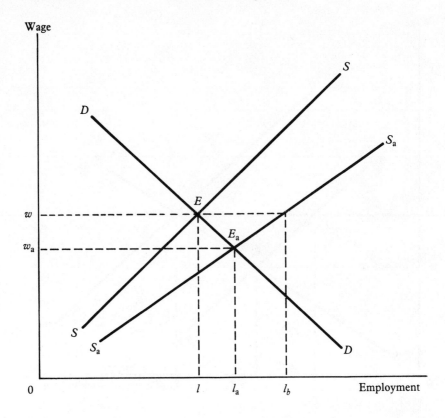

Figure 8.7 *Increase in labour supply and the competitive labour market equilibrium*

Decrease in Labour Supply and Market Equilibrium

Figure 8.8 shows a decrease in labour supply with demand held constant. At each wage level workers offer a smaller quantity of labour to produce a shift in the labour supply curve to the left, depicted by the new curve S_1S_1.

You should now be able to work through the consequence of the shift and see that the new equilibrium point E_1 indicates that this shift produces

(a) a rise in the equilibrium wage level (from w to w_1), and
(b) a fall in the equilibrium employment level (from l to l_1).

As before, the extent of the changes depends on the extent of the shift in worker intentions and on the relative wage elasticities of demand and supply.

Shifts in Both Demand and Supply

The above examples of labour market adjustments have all concerned changes either in demand with supply held constant or in supply with demand held constant. It is probably more realistic to examine situations where both the demand for and supply of labour are changing at the same time.

Clearly there are four possibilities: each may rise; each may fall; either may rise and the other fall. If you have followed the arguments in this chapter you should be able to work out the consequences of each possibility for yourself. However, the following examples outline the two most probable developments.

An Increase in Both Labour Supply and Demand at Each Price in a Given Range

The increase in the demand for labour causes the demand curve DD to move to the right, and this is shown by the new curves D_1D_1 and D_aD_a in Figures 8.9a and 8.9b, respectively. Similarly, the increase in the supply of labour is shown by the two supply curves S_1S_1 and S_aS_a, which are to the right and below the original labour supply curves SS.

When Figure 8.9a is considered a new equilibrium point E_1 may be identified, and when compared with the original equilibrium point E it will be seen that:

(a) the new equilibrium level of employment, l_1, is higher than the original level of employment l, and
(b) the new equilibrium wage, w_1, is higher than the original wage w.

However, when Figure 8.9b is considered and the new equilibrium point E_a compared with the original equilibrium point E it will be seen that:

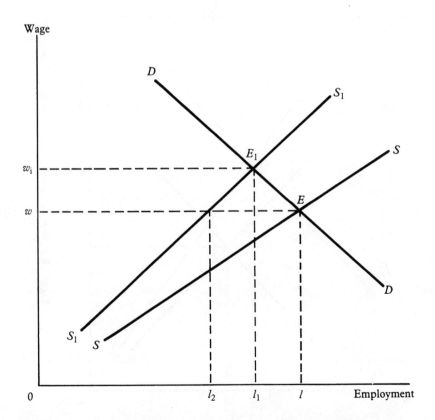

Figure 8.8 *Decrease in labour supply and the competitive labour market equilibrium*

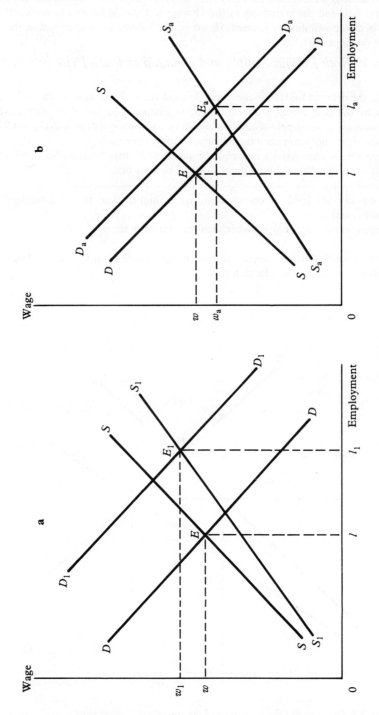

Figure 8.9 *Increase in both labour demand and supply and the competitive labour market equilibrium*

(a) the new equilibrium level of employment, l_a, is higher than the original level of employment l, and

(b) the new equilibrium wage, w_a, is lower than the original wage w.

When, therefore, there is an increase in both the demand for and the supply of labour, the equilibrium level of employment will rise. The extent of this rise, however, and the direction and extent of any change in the equilibrium wage will depend on the magnitude of the changes in demand and supply and on the relative wage elasticities of both labour demand and labour supply.

A Fall in Both Labour Supply and Demand at Each Price in a Given Range

The decrease in the demand for labour causes the original demand curve DD to move to the left. This is shown by the new curves D_1D_1 and D_aD_a in Figures 8.10a and 8.10b, respectively. Similarly, the decrease in labour supply is shown by the two new supply curves S_1S_1 and S_aS_a, which are to the left and above the original supply curves SS.

When Figure 8.10a is considered a new equilibrium point, E_1, may be identified, and when compared with the original equilibrium point E it will be seen that:

(a) the new equilibrium level of employment, l_1, is lower than the original level of employment l, and

(b) the new equilibrium wage, w_1, is higher than the original wage w.

However, when Figure 8.10b is considered and the new equilibrium point E_a compared with the original equilibrium point E it will be seen that:

(a) the new equilibrium level of employment, l_a, is lower than the original level of employment l, and

(b) the new equilibrium wage, w_a, is lower than the original wage w.

When, therefore, both labour demand and supply fall at a range of prices, there is likely to be a reduction in the equilibrium level of employment. How great the decrease in employment will be and whether the new equilibrium wage will be higher or lower than the original wage will depend both upon the magnitude of the decrease in the labour demand and labour supply and upon the relative elasticities of labour supply and demand.

This analytical approach suggests that a change in the conditions of labour supply or demand (or both) is likely to be followed initially by a period of instability before a new equilibrium position emerges.

The Period of Adjustment

For the purpose of analysis it has been assumed that this movement from the old equilibrium position to the new can be readily identified. The analysis, however, suggests nothing about the time period over which the adjustment takes place. In the real world of employment and labour markets the indications are that the adjustment period may be lengthy. There are two reasons for this.

(a) In the short term both the demand for and the supply of labour by individual firms is likely to be inelastic (see Chapter 4). Consequently, when changes in labour market conditions occur there may be a time lag before either labour demand or labour supply adjust to the

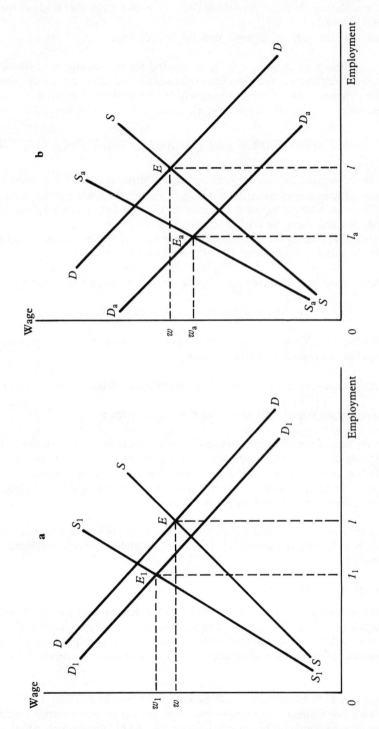

Figure 8.10 *Decrease in both labour demand and supply and the competitive labour market equilibrium*

new conditions. This delay may lead to either labour shortages or surpluses, as explained later in Chapter 11.

(b) Within the labour market there are institutions, for example employers' associations and trade unions, whose actions on behalf of their members may slow down the responsiveness of employers and/or employees to changes in the equilibrium wage. This delay will also induce either labour shortages or surpluses.

Questions for Discussion and Review

3 Rank the following individual labour markets in the order which you think approaches most closely the perfectly competitive conditions outlined in this chapter, i.e. the closest is ranked 1, the next closest 2, and so on: unskilled industrial labourers; crystal glass engravers; farm workers; helicopter pilots; infant school teachers; word-processor operators; office cleaners; commercial van drivers; stage actors and actresses. Give reasons and discuss your ranking.

4 Rank the same occupations in the order in which you think they are most likely to have suffered from unemployment in the period since 1976, i.e. the occupation with the most unemployment is ranked 1, etc. Discuss any similarities or differences between the two rankings. To what extent do you think any of this unemployment can be explained by the analysis outlined in this chapter?

5 Choose one of the models of changes in market equilibrium outlined in this chapter and use it to suggest possible effects on employment if institutional forces succeed in blocking any significant movement in the market wage level.

Equilibrium Conditions in Imperfect Markets

Relaxation of Competitive Conditions

The analysis of the previous section was based on some rather strict assumptions which meant, in effect, that the labour markets were considered to be perfectly competitive. In this section the consequences of relaxing some of these assumptions are examined, although at this stage we continue to assume that firms and workers are dominated by 'economic motives', i.e. that firms seek to maximise profits from the employment of labour and workers seek to maximise their wage returns.

The main effect of the relaxation of competitive market conditions is to recognise that firms are likely to be large and powerful enough to influence demand in their product markets and the demand for labour in labour markets. At the same time we also recognise that workers are able to form unions, which are also able to achieve power over the supply of workers.

Firms, of course, are sellers in product markets but buyers in labour markets in which the sellers are assumed to be workers or their trade unions.

The Firm with Market Power in the Product Market

The continued assumption of the firm's desire to maximise profits from its employment of labour means that its demand for labour is based on the revenue that can be earned from the additional product achieved by each additional unit of labour employed, i.e. the firm's demand for labour curve is its marginal revenue product of labour (MRPL) curve. In the competitive product market no distinction had to be made between the price of the product and the additional (marginal) revenue gained from each additional unit of product sold. If all units of product could be sold by the firm at the same price then this price (as shown earlier in Chapter 4) is the same as the marginal revenue.

However, if the firm is large enough to influence the price of the product through variations in its sales volume then this is no longer true. In this case the product demand takes on a shape similar to that of market demand, in that the greater the quantity offered for sale the lower must be the price to ensure that total market supply is cleared, i.e. sold to buyers in the market. The firm with market power thus has a product demand curve which is downward sloping. This, in turn, has an implication for marginal revenue. Assuming that at any given quantity level all units of the production are sold at the same price, i.e. there is no price discrimination practised for different buyers, then in order to sell more the firm has to reduce price, not only to the additional buyers it is trying to attract but also to all those who had previously been willing to buy at the higher price. The additional revenue gained from each successive unit increase in quantity sold is less than the product's unit price. For such a firm there is, therefore, a separate marginal revenue curve which lies below the price curve. In the absence of price discrimination the firm's price–demand curve is also, of course, its average revenue curve. If the demand curve is assumed to take a simple linear shape it can be shown that the marginal revenue curve will slope exactly twice as steeply as this, i.e. it will always bisect the horizontal distance between the average revenue and vertical (revenue) axis at each quantity level. This is illustrated in Figure 8.11.

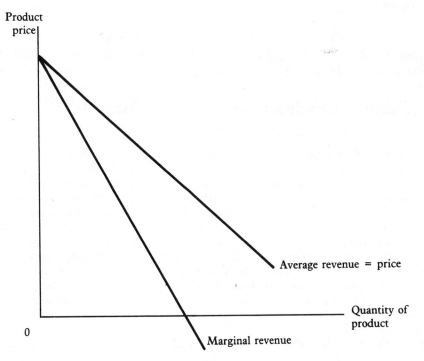

Figure 8.11 *Average revenue and marginal revenue curves in the product market. Average and marginal revenue in the product market where the firm's output decisions affect market price but where the firm does not practise price discrimination*

The effect of this on the firm's demand for labour can now be shown. Instead of having a single curve, the MRPL curve based on the assumption that the product's price is equal to its marginal revenue (MR), there are now two curves. One, derived from the price (average revenue, AR) × marginal physical product, is called the value of marginal product (VMPL) curve and the other, derived from the separate marginal revenue, is the MRPL curve. Using linear curves for simplicity, MRPL bears the same relationship to VMPL as MR does to AR; this is illustrated in Figure 8.12.

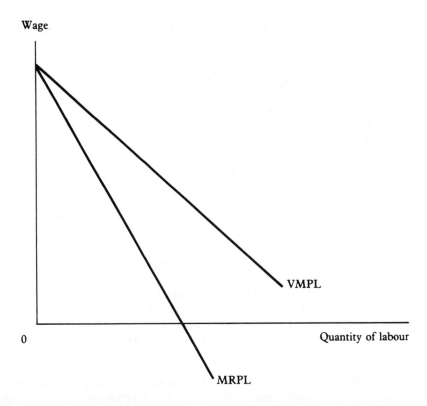

Figure 8.12 *The labour marginal product and labour marginal revenue product curves [Based on* **Figure 8.11***]*

At this stage the supply of labour curve (*SS*) is still assumed to arise from a perfectly competitive labour market and is thus horizontal. Given these conditions, illustrated in Figure 8.13, the firm will wish to employ *l* units of labour, the quantity level where the wage, which to the employer is the cost of each unit of labour, is equal to the MRPL.

Some economists compare this to the position that might be assumed to have held had the product market been perfectly competitive. In this case the employer might have been expected to pay a wage equal to VMPL because product price would then have equalled product marginal revenue. The difference between VMPL and MRPL, $a - b$ in Figure 8.13, is then described as representing a degree of 'monopolistic exploitation'. Alternatively, as suggested by Figure 8.13, workers employed by firms selling in a perfectly competitive product market might have expected to have been employed at the higher level l_p, where the labour supply curve intersects the value of marginal product curve.

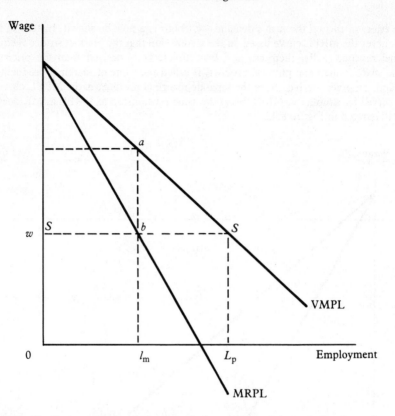

Figure 8.13 *The firm's equilibrium in an imperfectly competitive labour market. In product markets where firms have monopoly power and seek to maximise profits the demand for labour = MRPL. The employer wishes to employ $0 - l_m$ workers at a wage of w. In a competitive market employment might be expected to rise to $0L_p$. At employment level $0l_m$ there is monopolistic exploitation of a–b.*

If you have studied microeconomics you will recognise the similarity between this argument and that based on the 'monopoly model', where firms with some monopoly power are said to exploit the consumer by charging prices higher and setting output lower than would hold under perfect competition.

The Firm with Market Power in the Product Market and with Monopsonistic Power in the Labour Market

We now consider the position of the firm which employs a sufficient proportion of the available labour supply to affect the wage it has to pay. Under these conditions it can be expected that the supply of labour curve will cease to be horizontal, as previously assumed, and take the shape of the normal market supply curve, i.e. be upward sloping. As more workers are employed in a market with a fixed quantity the price or wage that has to be paid to induce additional workers to enter the market has to rise.

The employer with significant market power as a buyer of labour faces this upward sloping supply of labour curve. The term used to denote monopoly power as a buyer is 'monopsony', and power as a monopsonist affects the marginal cost of labour. This is because employers cannot, in practice, pay different wages to workers doing similar work. If, for example, the firm finds it has to pay £10 per hour to hire an additional worker with a particular skill when it is paying, say, £8 per hour to existing workers with similar skills, it will not only have to face considerable employee unrest but it will also find that some of the existing workers will leave. Assuming a limited supply of labour, £10 will have to be offered to them or their replacements to fill the vacancies. Firms, therefore, generally pay the market or going wage to all workers of the same level of skill. Consequently, the firm which employs more labour finds its additional (marginal) costs rise not only by the wages of the extra workers but also by the additional pay that has to be awarded to similar workers already employed to ensure that they do not leave. The firm thus faces a marginal cost of labour (MCL) curve which is to the left of the labour supply curve SS and, assuming simple linear cuves, also bisects the horizontal distance between the SS curve and the (vertical) wage axis. This is shown in Figure 8.14.

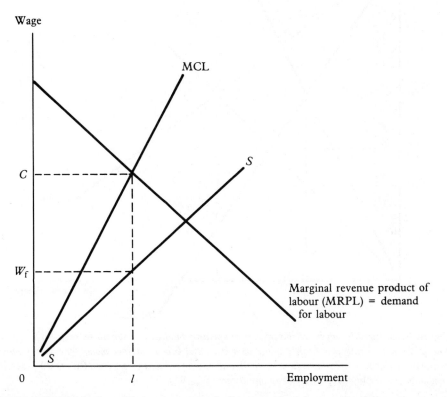

Figure 8.14 *The firm's equilibrium in an imperfectly competitive labour market facing a monopsonist labour supply*
The profit-maximising firm with monopoly power in product markets and monopsonistic power in the labour market needs to equate marginal cost of labour (MCL) with marginal revenue product of labour (MRPL) employing quantity 0l at wage 0W_f.

Given the normal profit-maximising conditions for the firm, i.e. that it seeks to equate its marginal cost with the marginal revenue achieved as a result of incurring the cost, the employer can be expected to employ that quantity of labour where the marginal cost of employing labour (MCL) is just equal to the marginal revenue product arising from that labour (MRPL). This occurs at labour quantity level l, where MCL = MRPL, in Figure 8.14. At this level of employment the wage paid is W_f and the marginal cost of labour is C.

Some further aspects of this position are illustrated in Figure 8.15.

Maintaining our assumptions of profit-maximising behaviour, the firm seeks to employ l_f workers at a wage of W_f, which is that quantity of labour where MCL = MRPL with the wage denoted by the SS curve.

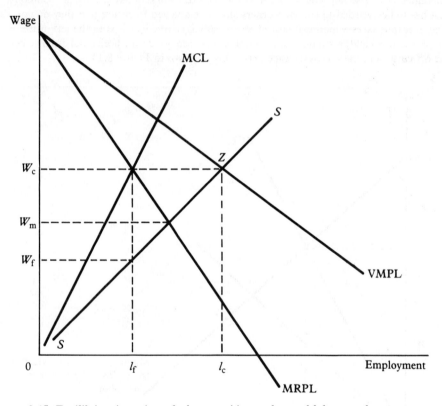

Figure 8.15 *Equilibrium in an imperfectly competitive product and labour market*
The profit-maximising firm with product monopoly and labour market monopsony power may be accused of reducing employment from $0l_c$ to $0l_f$ and paying reduced wages from $0W_c$ to $0W_f$ exercising monopoly power $(W_c–W_m)$ and monopsony power $(W_m–W_f)$.

It is suggested that such a firm is restricting employment and reducing wages in comparison with the position that would apply had both labour and product markets been perfectly competitive. It is argued that under perfectly competitive conditions labour employment and wage levels would be denoted by point Z, where SS = VMPL, i.e. at l_c units of labour and wage level W_c. It is also argued that, under this monopolistic–monopsonistic condition, workers are being subjected to exploitation of two kinds. These are monopolistic exploitation, represented by the wage difference $W_c - W_m$ (arising because MRPL is to the left of VMPL) and monopsonistic exploitation, represented by the wage difference, $W_m - W_f$ (arising because MCL is to the left of SS).

Bilateral Monopoly where Monopsonist Employer faces Monopoly Supplier of Labour

While there are millions of individuals in employment the idea of a labour supply monopoly may be difficult to imagine, but there are circumstances where it can, and does, occur.

The most obvious case will be where an individual offers on the labour market a very specific talent or training for which there are few, if any, substitutes. More commonly, monopoly power arises out of labour organisations. In Britain, and in other nations, it has been known for employees in certain professions not only to regulate entry but, at the same time, to operate an agreed set of charges for their services regardless of the level of demand for these.

It is sometimes suggested that trade unions exercise monopoly power over the supply of labour. There is little dispute that trade unions seek to raise the price of their members' labour above the going rate and sometimes achieve success in this. However, such a policy does not necessary make the trade union a monopoly supplier. The latter would, in theory, occur only if the trade union was able to purchase the labour services of its members and then resell these at a profit to an employer. Nevertheless, some employers have accepted, in practice, the principle of only employing union members hired through the union organisation to undertake work tasks either unilaterally defined by the unions or jointly defined by the union and the employer. It might be considered in such circumstances that the union could be approaching a position where it had a practical monopoly over labour supply. It could also be argued that although the union was not a monopolist and did not make 'profits' in the manner of a supplier in product markets, it behaved in much the same way when it exercised full rights of control over the wages, terms, and conditions under which members were employed. It might also be compared to a monopolist when it sought to maximise current members' interests at the expense of limiting supply and excluding other potential entrants to that part of the labour market which it controlled. Certain unions in the entertainment industry and the print unions before the mid-1980s might be considered to have operated monopolistic powers in their particular labour markets.

The theoretical model developed by economists to analyse the situation where a monopsonist faces a monopolist is that of bilateral monopoly, and this is illustrated in Figure 8.16.

In this diagram the demand for labour curve *DD* is the marginal revenue product (MRPL) curve and, looked at from the point of view of the monopoly supplier, is also the average revenue curve of the supplier—just as in product markets the consumers' demand curve is also the supplying monopolist's average revenue curve. Applying the normal rule for the relationship between linear average and marginal revenue curves stated earlier and illustrated in Figure 8.11, we can derive the monopolistic labour supplier's marginal revenue curve (MRS).

The monopsonistic employer has a marginal labour cost curve (MCL) to the left of the labour supply curve *SS*, as explained earlier. The profit-maximising employer seeks to employ labour at the level where MCL = MRPL (at X), i.e. at l_f units of labour, and this employer will seek to pay a wage of W_f (from the *SS* curve). This is the employer's equilibrium.

However, the monopolistic labour supplier's equilibrium is rather different. This occurs when the marginal revenue for supplying labour (MRS) equals the marginal cost of supplying labour, which we can assume to be set by the labour supply curve *SS*. The supplier, therefore, seeks to supply $0l_u$ units of labour and will press for a wage of W_u—the maximum that an employer is prepared to pay without reducing the quantity of labour demanded, i.e. the marginal revenue product at quantity l_u.

This leaves a gap between the two equilibrium levels of wages W_u and W_f, and the model itself does not tell us how the conflict is likely to be resolved. This gap can be regarded as a bargaining range within which the wage level can be negotiated. The more powerful or skilful

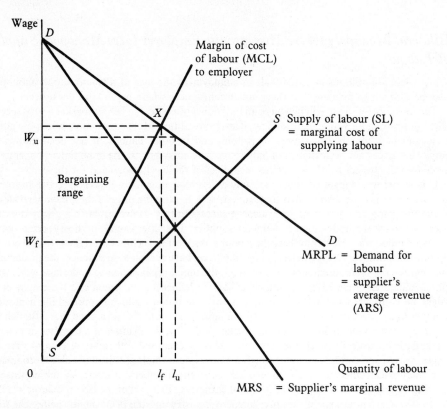

Figure 8.16 *The bilateral monopoly model of the labour market*
Bilateral monopoly with the trade union assumed to behave as a profit-maximising supplier of labour.
The monopoly-monopsony employer seeks to employ $0L_f$ labour (where $MCL = MRPL$) at wage $0W_f$
(from SS). The union seeks to achieve wage $0W_u$ and raise the employment level to $0L_u$. There is no
predictable equilibrium wage or employment level but a bargaining range (W_u–W_f and L_u–L_f).

the supplier (the trade union), the closer will be the negotiated wage to W_u. The more powerful
or skilful the buyer of labour (the employer), the closer will it be to W_f. Notice, however, that
under these conditions it is possible for a labour negotiator to secure increases in wages without
any reduction in numbers of workers employed. Indeed, the model suggests that a labour
supplier can negotiate an increase in both wage and employment level.

This model has been used to assist in explaining the remarkable success of some unions in
achieving pay levels above the going rate for very long periods without any significant loss of
employment for members. Nevertheless, it should also be pointed out that:

(a) Market structures can change very quickly and become more competitive, often as the
    result of new technology which changes employers' attitudes—as in the printing industry
    in the 1980s.
(b) High wages and secure employment for members may be obtained at the price of limiting
    the demand for the industry product with a consequent reduction in employment
    opportunities for young workers seeking, unsuccessfully, to enter the industry. A union
    operating in this way can become progressively smaller and less powerful until its monopoly
    powers suddenly cease to exist.

(c) Exercise of monopoly labour supplier power means that the employer is unable to achieve the desired labour–capital combination where the factor marginal product to price ratios are equal, so that intense pressure is built up to replace labour with capital. The longer this is resisted the stronger it becomes until a damaging labour conflict does eventually take place.

Questions for Discussion and Review

6 On the basis of the models introduced in this section, discuss the view that a powerful trade union can increase both the wages of its members and the number of members.

7 Taking into account the theoretical models introduced in this section and your own observation of labour market conditions, discuss the view that wages are likely to be higher in industries dominated by a few large firms than in trades or industries where there are large numbers of firms each having little power to dominate the product market. You may care to consider such industries as: chemical manufacturing; retailing; motor manufacturing; banking; insurance; legal services; estate agents. You should also consider local industries and firms.

8 Can some powerful trade unions be regarded as 'suppliers of labour'?

Limitations of Models Based on Profit Maximisation
The Challenge to Profit Maximisation

The assumption that the employer of labour seeks to maximise profits has been fundamental to all the theoretical labour demand, supply, and market models considered so far in this book. Nevertheless, we cannot ignore the fact that a powerful body of economic thought has challenged the traditional view that firms, particularly large firms operating in oligopolistic product markets, have as their only or even their principal objective the maximisation of profit. The main reason for the challenge has been the argument that large corporations having significant power in product markets are likely to be effectively controlled by their senior management who, for the most part, are not major shareholders in the companies they control. The shareholders, for their part, it is suggested, have no interest in the conduct and management of the company as long as it makes satisfactory profits. Consequently there is, effectively, a divorce between ownership (in the hands of shareholders) and control (in the hands of senior management).

A number of differing views have been put forward and some interesting models developed. It is not necessary to examine these, but, although they all suggest rather different objectives or sets of objectives, they do have the common feature that the pursuit of the shareholders' interest, assumed to be profit, can give way, in some degree, to the pursuit of managerial interests, among which growth in the size of the organisation tends to form an important part.

If they are correct in suggesting that managerially controlled firms do have a strong preference for growth then this suggests that managers also have a preference for employing labour beyond the value to the firm of its marginal product, and we can no longer regard the marginal revenue curve as the basis for the firm's demand for labour curve. Unfortunately, it is difficult to derive from these theories any single satisfactory substitute for the marginal revenue product curve, which remains an essential starting point for the analysis of employer behaviour in labour markets.

Further Problems of Marginal Productivity Models

Quite apart from the issue of the managerial theories of the firm, serious doubts have been expressed about the validity of labour market models based on the concept of the marginal productivity of labour. Some observers point out that it is very difficult to calculate the value of any additional product that can be attributed to any given change in labour employment. Productivity can often be varied by employers: for example, by changing the speed of an assembly track. Such changes may take place according to market requirements and the workers themselves may have little control over them. Where productivity is more dependent on worker skill and effort, this can differ between workers and for the same worker at different periods of time. Everyone who has lived in a motor manufacturing region knows what is meant by a 'Friday car'! The assumption of the marginal productivity models that labour is a homogeneous production factor is very far from reality.

Many economists have pointed out that a model based on a maximising objective makes an assumption of perfect knowledge, i.e. that a decision maker can calculate the precise consequences of the various choices of decision open to him or her at any given time, and that a decision is reached in full knowledge of all features of the economic environment in which it is made. This assumption is also far from the reality of labour markets, where communications are often poor and unreliable and where the search for information has a cost, as pointed out in Chapter 7.

The time scale envisaged in marginal productivity models is also open to question under modern conditions. The models imply that employers seek to equate marginal product with marginal cost over a fairly limited time period, perhaps a week or a month. As also pointed out in Chapter 7, there are many cases where employees are recruited in the expectation that they will contribute to the firm's success in several years' time. Some may even be retained in recognition of the contribution they have made in the past. The time horizons of both employers and workers are often rather longer than the span of a single pay packet.

If employer and worker attitudes and objectives can sometimes seem vague, there is often equal uncertainty about the objectives of labour organisations. Most observers accept that trade unions have an influence on pay and working conditions, but the precise nature and extent of this influence is often a matter of dispute. More advanced marginal productivity models do make some attempt to introduce different union objectives, such as maximising employment opportunities instead of maximising current wages, but these efforts do little justice to the complexity of unions, which are examined more fully in Chapter 16.

Industrial economists, under the influence of Simon (1957) and others such as Cyert and March (1963), have recognised that organisations may not seek to maximise anything but adopt 'satisficing' behaviour of the kind described in Cyert and March's 'A Behavioral Theory of the Firm'. This theory assumes that business decision makers are subject to multiple interest forces and are thus obliged to pursue multiple goals. In many respects 'Behavioral Theory' does appear to offer a suitable framework for the analysis of a number of important aspects of labour markets. Some writers, such as Walton and McKersie (1965), have applied the theory to particular aspects of organised labour behaviour, but we are not aware of any systematic attempt to analyse a labour market using the concepts and analytical framework of Behavioral Theory.

A less ambitious recognition of uncertainties in the labour market has resulted in the suggestion that the concepts of demand and supply curves in relation to labour should be replaced by fairly broad bands indicating that neither employers nor workers have completely

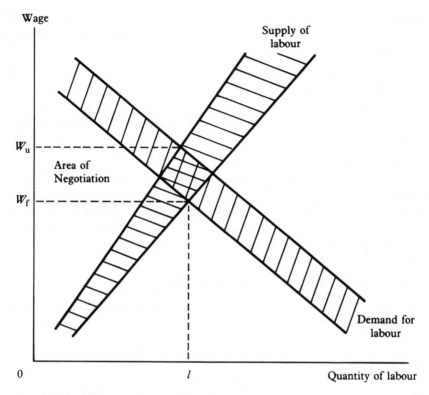

Figure 8.17 *The potential wage range for negotiation*
Notes: (a) The employer tries to agree a wage as close as possible to W_f
(b) The worker tries to agree a wage as close as possible to W_u.
(c) The actual wage agreed will depend on their relative strength and negotiating skills but
will lie between W_f and W_u.
If we assume flexibility in labour supply and demand the usual curves are replaced by broad bands to
give a bargaining area at the employment level (0l) determined by the market

formed intentions when they negotiate wages but are open to influence by individual circumstances. The result is illustrated in Figure 8.17.

The width of the bands, and hence the size of the negotiating area formed by their intersection, depends on the degree of uncertainty and extent of worker individuality. It is assumed that the employer will seek to negotiate a wage as close as possible to the lower limit of W_f and the worker, or his/her representative, seeks to negotiate as close as possible to W_u. The actual wage negotiated depends on their relative market power and negotiating skills.

This simple model recognises some of the complexities and uncertainties of actual labour markets. Further considerations and departures from the perfect economic market are examined in the next chapter.

Questions for Discussion and Review

9 Look at some pages of job advertisements in at least one local and one national newspaper. Estimate the proportion of advertisements that state or imply that the wage is 'negotiable', at least to some extent. How far does this support the view that labour supply and demand are 'bands' rather than definite 'curves'?

10 Discuss the special problems of estimating labour productivity faced by employers in the public sector of the economy. You may care to consider such areas as national and local government administration, teaching, the 'caring services' of social work etc., and the uniformed services such as police and fire fighting forces.

11 Discuss the view that managers have a vested interest in paying high wages and expanding the number of workers they control, e.g. because the larger the department managed the higher the manager's salary, and this salary can usually be expected to be higher by a given percentage than the best-paid member of the department. How may managerial attitudes on employment and pay in small firms differ from those in large firms?

Suggestions for Written Assignments

1 Explain and critically examine the view that the demand for labour is based on the marginal productivity of labour and that this is a major influence on the wage determined in labour markets.

2 Refer to the latest issue of the *New Earnings Survey*, which should be available in a good reference library. What evidence does this provide that membership of a trade union and employment in a large firm with significant market power in its product market are important influences likely to raise wages?

3 Use the theoretical models introduced in this chapter to analyse the possible consequences for employment of success by workers in simultaneously reducing hours of employment, raising pay, increasing the extent of paid holidays, and increasing employer contributions to pension provisions.

Suggestions for Further Reading

For a further discussion of the approach adopted in the early part of this chapter see Cartter (1959) Chapters 5 and 6.

Any good textbook of intermediate level microeconomics should give the main theoretical models based on marginal productivity under conditions of perfect and imperfect competition and bilateral monopoly. Your teacher will be able to recommend such a book. One example is 'Modern Microeconomics' by Koutsoyannis (1981), which also contains a useful outline of the main 'managerial theories' of large firms' behaviour which offer different analytical models from those based on an assumption of profit maximisation.

Further discussion of the managerial theories can be found in most textbooks on managerial or business economics and many on industrial economics. A general text covering this area is 'An Introduction to Business Economics' by Old and Shafto (1989).

Walton and McKersie (1965) applied Behavioral Theory to the specific issue of labour negotiations, and Pigou (1932) discussed the implications of the 'range of indeterminateness' created by the existence of wage bargaining.

9
Further Aspects of Labour Markets

Modifications to the Neo-classical Models
The Assumed Importance of the Wage–Employment Relationship

In the labour market models so far examined, the labour price (wage) has been seen as the main, though not the only, influence on the quantity of labour offered to and taken up by the market.

It has to be recognised that this does introduce elements of unreality. Other, non-wage factors do have key roles to play. This view is supported by many known examples where the wage has not been the decisive influence on the selection of a particular occupation. One reason why analytical models stress the price–quantity relationship is because the wage is easily quantifiable while other aspects of employment are not. Furthermore, by emphasising the wage it is possible to identify a consistent pattern of preference. All other things being equal, which they seldom are, we would all prefer a higher wage from our employment than a lower one!

Relaxation of Assumptions of Homogeneity

It is interesting that the economists who observed the early stages of Britain's modern economic development recognised the significance of non-wage influences and sought to incorporate these into their models of labour market operations. One important modification which has been made by these early writers and their later and more recent followers has been to relax the neo-classical, perfect-market assumption of homogeneity, i.e. that all workers were identical in skill and ability.

In his observations of the economy's operation in 'The Wealth of Nations', Adam Smith (1961), the 'father of modern economics', focused his attention (in Chapter 10) upon the labour market. In a fashion similar to that adopted in subsequent neo-classical models he acknowledged that in the long run there would emerge a stable, equilibrium position. The core of Adam Smith's approach is that while accepting differences in employment conditions and in workers he believed that there would be a tendency for the equalisation of the differing advantages and disadvantges for each type of employment. This was thought likely to occur within an area, which Smith termed a 'neighbourhood' but which might now be referred to as a 'local labour market'. He considered that if a particular type of work was seen as having advantages over other work then some, but not necessarily all, of the workers would seek the advantageous work and avoid perceived disadvantages. If this was to occur, employers offering the employment thought to be advantageous would be able to reduce the rewards offered and would be more selective in their recruitment of workers. Those employers offering work perceived as disadvantageous would experience shortages of labour and would need to respond by increasing the rewards they offered and by being less selective in their choice of worker.

Questions for Discussion and Review

1 List the features of jobs other than pay which you consider to be important in the choice of first job. Make at least four similar lists based on the views of other people you know. Identify the similarities and differences between these lists. Do you think there are any differences between the influences thought important by males compared with females?

2 If increased pay serves to make good some of the non-pay disadvantages of an occupation, what differences would you expect to find in the earnings of the following pairs of occupations? Dentist and doctor (general practitioner); farm worker and garage motor mechanic; office secretary and hospital nurse; police officer and long-distance lorry driver; ambulance driver and fireman. Try to check whether or not your expectations fit the facts. If they do not, then suggest possible reasons.

The Historical Development of Labour Market Models

The Contribution of Adam Smith

In this explanation of how a labour market operates there are two significant points. The first relates to occupational choice, the desire of the worker to seek what he believes to be the most advantageous employment. In Adam Smith's time (the mid-eighteenth century) the choice may have been to work in agriculture with a relatively low wage but with the advantages of a traditional occupation with well-established rights and procedures and some respect for the individual worker, or to work in one of the new manufacturing industries for a higher wage but with unaccustomed ways and restricting disciplines. Thus the labour market would distribute workers into differing sectors of the economy according to their individual preferences.

The second aspect relates to the consequences of these choices based on the relative advantages/disadvantages upon employment. No employer could afford, even in the short run, to lose all of his workers and consequently employers would engage in a continuous process of adjusting the employment reward package. Both the character of jobs being offered and individual workers' perceptions of the relevant advantages and disadvantages are likely to vary in practice. Neither work nor workers are homogeneous. Adam Smith was not suggesting that the labour market would, or could, ever lead to equality in monetary rewards, but rather that individual workers would seek always to act to try and maximise their own perceived advantage. In Adam Smith's approach to the labour market, therefore, it was perfectly acceptable for wages in different jobs to differ, even in the long run. This was because the features of the work undertaken, the physical characteristics of the workplace, the risks involved in the work, and the training required would all differ as well. These and other considerations would be taken into account by individuals in their evaluation of the relative packages of advantages and disadvantages attached to different jobs. These would tend to change in the light of employers' experiences of recruiting the workers they required.

In labour markets as perceived by Adam Smith, the employment choice was made on the basis of the net advantage, that is the advantages less the disadvantages, and not on the basis of the wage alone. Smith's model, however, as he himself recognised, made some important assumptions which were not always justified in practice. The model required that everyone was free to evaluate the net advantages of differing types of employment and then to make the appropriate choice. Such knowledge and free choice are not always present. Some major barriers that continue to limit the individual's choice of occupation were identified in Chapter 7. Other individuals may receive the wrong advice and be encouraged to enter inappropriate occupations. Finally, there remain those who, having begun one career, or even having worked in one location, find it extremely difficult to change either.

Despite these reservations, Adam Smith's explanation of the way labour markets operate still retains attractive features.

Modifications Introduced by John Stuart Mill

In the nineteenth century, later observers of labour markets accepted the hypothesis that individuals would seek to maximise their net advantages and in so doing these observers acknowledged the competitive nature of the market. Nevertheless, observation continued to show that labour markets were not necessarily competitive. Consequently, attention was concentrated upon the reasons for the lack of competition. This lack was seen as a cause of the disparity of monetary earnings between occupations. In the view of John Stuart Mill (1895) inequalities in occupational and industrial earnings were a natural consequence of competitive markets because such inequalities were thought to compensate for the 'circumstances of particular employments'. However, in the reality of nineteenth-century Britain the disparity of earnings did not accurately reflect the relative advantages and disadvantages of the differing types of employment. Mill noted that employment which he considered to be 'exhausting' and/ or 'repulsive', far from attracting the highest monetary rewards, was usually the lowest paid and undertaken by those with no choice at all in the matter. The unskilled, the aged, and those in poor health had to accept whatever employment was available. The less attractive the work the less likelihood was there that there would be any compensating monetary reward.

What was termed by Mill as the 'hardships associated with employment', far from being, as Adam Smith had suggested, directly proportional, seemed more likely to be inversely proportional to earnings.

John Stuart Mill did not suggest that Adam Smith was wrong, nor did he offer an alternative theory. Instead he acknowledged that the disparity in income levels did not necessarily reflect the relative advantages and disadvantages of employment in competitive labour markets. The non-competitive character of labour markets, he concluded, was a consequence of the heterogeneous nature of potential workers. Because of differing social backgrounds, and differing opportunities for education and training, workers were unable to compete freely with each other in the labour market. Mill argued that the supply side of the labour market consisted of numerous non-competing groups, and this distorted the way the market operated.

The Sociological Extension of Cairnes

By raising the question that social rank might influence an individual's position in the labour market, Mill was also beginning to raise wider sociological issues about labour market operations. This was also the approach of Cairnes (1974), who clearly recognised the existence within the labour market of non-competing groups.

Cairnes believed that the range of potential occupations available to individuals was determined by family background. Consequently, the levels of rewards offered in occupations outside the range available to a particular individual did not affect him because he had no opportunity to enter them.

Main Features of the Early Models

Common to these early studies of labour markets is the belief that if they are competitive then any disparity in pay ought to reflect the differences in other aspects of the work being undertaken. There is, however, an early recognition, by Adam Smith, that lack of knowledge of the available options, and constraints on the mobility of labour, may lead to a lack of competition and hence to a greater disparity in earnings than ought to exist. Subsequent writers, for example Mill and Cairnes, extend the explanations by acknowledging that lack of opportunities arising from family background and/or education can cause the evolution of non-competing groups in the labour market and consequently to the distortion of the pattern of rewards. Non-competing groups, made up of clusters of differing occupations and entry to which was restricted by social background and education, were thought to lead to the fragmentation of the competitive labour market.

Questions for Discussion and Review

3 Which of the approaches to labour market differences outlined above do you find the most relevant to your observations of modern labour markets? Give reasons for your choice.

4 A popular television series persuaded many young people that they would like to become veterinary surgeons. When these people started to investigate the possibility seriously most found that they could not hope to achieve this ambition. Suggest reasons for this.

Imperfections in Market Demand

The Contribution of Hicks

The studies so far mentioned in this chapter have all pointed to the apparent imperfections in the supply side. Writing of the 1930s, Hicks (1964) turned to the demand side. He observed that in the period between the recession of 1931 and the outbreak of the Second World War in 1939 there were two types of employment on offer within the labour market. In the first place many industries contained what Hicks referred to as 'regular' trades. The workers in these occupations and/or industries did not change their employer frequently. Consequently, the longer they stayed with an employer the more valuable they became to that employer. They gained new skills and increased their flexibility and productivity. In the terms of Chapter 7, employers were making a continuous investment in human capital through informal on-the-job training. Hicks suggested that the worker who was assured of regular employment would locate his home near to the place of work, and that this would significantly raise the cost of any subsequent change of job. Thus, in regular employment, the worker became more valuable to an employer and would benefit from higher wages. Any change in employment would cause the worker to lose these enhanced earnings and to incur the cost of moving to a new area. The employer would also benefit from stable employment through workers' increasing experience and higher productivity. These gains would lead to lower labour costs. In the 'regular' labour market both the employer and the worker were thought to enjoy direct benefits. Hicks also believed that there was a further benefit. Small variations in product demand were unlikely to cause the employer to dismiss workers or lead to their seeking different employment. Nor would variations in product demand necessarily lead to fluctuations in wages. The regular labour market was, therefore, characterised by stability in employment, growing experience and labour productivity, and relatively stable wage levels.

The alternative to the regular labour market was identified by Hicks as the 'casual' one. In the period until the Second World War many areas of employment, for example building and the motor car manufacturing industry, were reliant upon a casual labour force. In fact, Hicks took an example, a porter, from neither of these industries, but this illustrated the point he was stressing. There was, at that time, a regular demand for the work of porters whether in markets or other sectors of the economy, but the number demanded varied according to circumstances from day to day. One important example was a variation of the porter, a docker. The number of ships and the quantity and types of cargo to be handled varied daily so that employers were not able to guarantee constant work to a constant number of dockers and were unable to offer regular employment contracts. Dock work in Britain, until the introduction of a State-financed labour scheme, was traditionally unstable with highly unstable earnings, and sometimes no earnings.

Workers in this kind of unstable work could be expected to search continuously for different work and the cost to the individual of switching between employers would be regarded as small. Employers would also be unsure how long individual workers would remain in their employment and would not expect any to stay for prolonged periods. Consequently there would be little formal training provision to individuals, and workers leaving took with them little human capital investment.

In Hicks' opinion there were two clearly defined labour markets within the economy. One was for regular and the other for casual trades. Which of these markets a worker joined would depend mainly on the trade an individual followed. Occupational choice, therefore, which itself was seen by nineteenth-century economists as reflecting the individual's background and education, would determine the allocation to regular or casual employment.

Dual Labour Markets

The recognition that the demand side of the labour market might not be homogeneous, and that there could be significant differences in the characteristics of the employment packages offered to different groups of workers quite apart from differences in the nature of employment, is an aspect of labour market analysis which has become central to the work of those labour economists who seek an expansion of public policy initiatives. Although there are numerous threads to the various approaches adopted, Doeringer and Priore (1971) provided both a starting point and a possible link to the earlier work by Hicks (discussed in the previous section) and that of other labour economists. Though not the first to suggest the concept, they developed a 'dual labour market' theory relevant to the 1970s. In essence, they viewed the demand side of the labour market not as a unitary whole, as had the nineteenth-century writers, but rather as one which contained two distinct segments. Here the similarity with Hicks' earlier work is clear.

By the late 1960s, however, when Doeringer and Priore were developing their ideas, economic circumstances were rather different from those of a generation earlier, when Hicks' work first appeared. Changing economic circumstances, in particular the high levels of employment and corresponding low unemployment levels, had caused changes in the practices adopted by many employers within the labour market. For example, a high proportion of casual employment had been converted into regular employment. One probable reason for this was the difficulty experienced by employers in attracting casual workers. While Doeringer and Priore implicitly acknowledged that changes of this nature had taken place, they nevertheless concluded that there were essentially two labour markets, which they termed primary and secondary, and that workers were able to move from one to the other though there might be difficulties impeding such movement. Each of the two markets had distinct characteristics.

The Primary Market

This was composed, mainly but not exclusively, of jobs in larger firms and consisted of the 'better' jobs available. This implied that the jobs offered not only higher pay but also good working conditions and stable, long-term employment. Consequently, these jobs also offered longer-term prospects of training and promotion. Job holders could expect, and be expected, to receive further investment in human capital. In order to enter this market job holders would already have experienced education and/or training to a level above the average.

The Secondary Market

This comprised jobs with relatively low pay, poor working conditions, and carrying low social prestige. These jobs were generally perceived as being unattractive. Although jobs in the secondary sector were not casual in the sense earlier identified by Hicks, many had been casual in the past and an essential characteristic of casual employment had been carried over into the secondary market, namely instability of employment linked to a high rate of labour turnover. This instability did not necessarily arise because of decisions of employers to terminate employment but was more a consequence of the relatively low levels of skill required. Individual workers can enter and drop out of unskilled employment with little cost and no sacrifice of long-term prospects of rewards. In turn, the relatively high levels of labour turnover discouraged both the employer and the employee from engaging in the process of human capital formation.

In essence, therefore, the dual labour market was seen as consisting of 'good' jobs offering high rewards in return for high productivity arising from prior human capital investment, and 'not so good' jobs where the rewards, and labour productivity, were more limited and reflected an apparent failure to invest in human capital. The dual labour market theorists of the post-1945 era offered a radical alternative to neo-classical labour market models. This alternative approach sought not only to explain the day-to-day operation of labour markets but also to explain a series of public economic issues that had not been accounted for in previous theories. Dual market theory could also be used to justify increased State involvement in education and training as a deliberate attempt to provide the greater benefits of primary markets to a larger number of workers.

Dual Markets Today

There is some evidence that modern labour markets are still fragmented in the way suggested by proponents of the dual theory.

(a) Despite the prolonged post-1945 period of full employment and prosperity there remained people in regular employment who, nevertheless, continued to live in comparative poverty and whose earnings were supplemented by regular State benefit payments.

(b) The aggregate pattern of income distribution and earnings differentials appeared to have changed relatively little by the late 1980s.

(c) Unemployment has not been distributed randomly throughout the labour force but has been concentrated among specific groups of workers.

Indicators of this nature appear to lend support to the dual labour market hypothesis but they do not actually test the hypothesis. Cain (1975) set out a number of ways in which he believed it might be tested. Earlier work by Bosanquet and Doeringer (1973) noted that low-paid employment, of the type to be expected in a secondary market, tended to be concentrated in industries which were characterised by low skill requirements and low capital:labour ratios. In addition, the British evidence indicated that undesirable working conditions and lack of opportunity for advancement were usually to be found with employment offering low pay. While they were able to confirm that certain areas of employment had all these features in common, it was acknowledged that this was not necessarily proof of the existence of a dual labour market. However, after undertaking a series of further tests, Bosanquet and Doeringer were prepared to accept that there were similarities between British and US labour markets and, in spite of some differences, they accepted that there was a dual labour market in Britain.

Bosanquet and Doeringer based their analysis on data relating to recruitment, promotion, and training practices within firms. Such data were thought likely to lead to identification of the differing practices believed to be characteristic of the primary and secondary markets. Their research indicated that the initial distribution of employees based on the first job which represented the worker's occupational choice reflected both educational differences and discrimination. This implied that investment in human capital alone might not be sufficient to place an individual in the primary market if that person showed other characteristics, or signals, suggesting that the secondary market might be more appropriate. Once employment in either the primary or secondary labour market had been taken, the possibility of mobility between the markets was discouraged by firm-specific training. Those in the primary market received training and thus became more valued by their employers and received higher wages. Those in the secondary market did not receive training and thus did not gain the skills that would enable them to apply for jobs in the primary market. Mayhew and Rosewell (1979) expanded upon this work in relation to Britain using other data sources. Their conclusions were not dissimilar to those of Bosanquet and Doeringer in so far as they agreed that education, qualifications, and family background were important determinants of the kind of job that workers obtained in the labour market. On the other hand, they also recognised that chance might also play a part in obtaining employment.

Further support for the concept of the dual labour market might be thought to be given by recent experience of high unemployment in Britain. Unemployment, particularly long-term unemployment, appears to be heavily concentrated among workers in the secondary market. Some of the primary market workers who lost their jobs seem to have 'traded down' to take work in the secondary market where, because of their previous primary market experience, they become valued employees. One consequence of this movement has been that the long-term unemployed appear to be not the previously skilled workers from declining manufacturing industries but rather the young, women, and members of the ethnic minorities who had previously been employed in the secondary market.

Market Segmentation as a Modification of the Dual Market Theory

British analysis of the dual labour market hypothesis has been mainly directed at examining the characteristics of those in the two markets, identifying both their social background and educational qualifications. In contrast, Osterman (1975) sought to examine the dual labour market by reference to the characteristics of the employment offered. This led to the hypothesis that occupational rewards were primarily dependent upon the nature and demands of individual jobs.

He argued that the interesting question was how the market came to be segmented. He thus implicitly acknowledged the existence of segmentation within labour markets. Osterman's analysis led him to believe that the distinctions which existed between the segments, initially taken as primary and secondary, have to be explained in terms of different job and technical requirements. Accordingly it was these features of the offered employment that led to the different on-the-job training requirements which, in turn, led to segmentation of the labour force. Nevertheless, like other researchers, he recognised that the dual labour market hypothesis does lead to the identification of an extensive primary sector containing a considerable range of quite different types of employment. The differences between these appear more obvious than the common features. One possible solution to this problem is to introduce a further sub-division within the primary labour market only.

Osterman initially opted for a fairly crude division between non-manual and manual employment. However, he recognised that although there were obvious differences in the content and training requirements for employment in the non-manual and manual sectors, there is also a considerable overlap in earnings. Though he never fully abandoned the non-manual/manual division, he developed an alternative approach which was designed to sub-divide and classify primary-sector jobs on the basis of one aspect of job content. He considered that the extent of the worker's autonomy was central to the sub-division. In certain jobs, at the upper end of the primary market, workers enjoyed considerable autonomy in how and/or when they undertook their work. At the other end of the spectrum, the majority of the work in the primary sector was undertaken by workers with little or no autonomy.

This approach is not dissimilar to that of Reich *et al* (1973), who suggested that the primary labour market was sub-divided between subordinate jobs and independent jobs. The latter type of jobs required employees with 'creative, problem-solving, and self-initiating characteristics', while the former sought employees with 'characteristics of dependability, discipline, and responsiveness to rules and authority'. In their work Reich *et al.* also suggested other criteria which result in the segmentation of the labour market:

(a) *Segmentation by race.* Although they participate in the secondary market, and to a lesser extent in the primary market, ethnic minority workers are usually found in distinct segments of those markets. These workers tend to be concentrated in the secondary market but even within this some occupations may be closed to them or may have been closed in the past.

(b) *Segmentation by sex.* Within both the primary and secondary markets there has existed further segmentation. Certain jobs have generally been restricted to males while other jobs have generally been undertaken by women. This situation has led some observers to suggest that there are actually two primary and two secondary markets, i.e. separate markets for males and for females operating in parallel.

Evidence for both these forms of occupational segregation can be found in Hakim (1979). For studies based on women's work histories, see Martin and Roberts (1984); their work provides substantial evidence to support the idea that there are distinct male and female sectors of both primary and secondary markets.

Analysis of the segmentation of the primary market has led to the view that certain of the generally assumed characteristics of the primary market are not necessarily relevant to all jobs in that market. Certain jobs, especially those towards the top end of the primary market, have features in common with secondary jobs. In particular, it has been noted that senior managers and very many professionally qualified staff do not exhibit the same degree of employment stability that might be observed among other primary groups, such as school teachers or skilled engineers.

The employment stability patterns of senior management and professional staff resemble those previously associated with the secondary market. There is an apparent lack of loyalty to specific employers, leading to relatively high turnover rates. There appears, however, to be one essential difference. Those switching employment within the secondary labour market take almost identical jobs for usually the same range of pay. Those workers within the primary labour market who exhibit a high degree of job mobility take advantage of their accumulation of human capital to move to more senior, responsible, and more highly rewarded positions. They do not seek to advance their careers within one company or even necessarily within an industry, but instead appear to optimise the returns on their human capital investment.

Questions for Discussion and Review

5 In the period between 1960 and 1980, labour market trends were towards bringing occupations into primary markets or at least giving as many as possible features close to those associated with primary markets. In the post-1980 period, trends have tended to be in the reverse directions. Suggest at least two reasons for this change.

6 Between 1946 and 1988, the State has generally accepted the principle that lack of family income or wealth should not be a barrier to a suitably qualified person's ability to gain higher education. Discuss the consequences of this for recruitment to the following 'professions': medical practice; accountancy; the law; commissioned ranks of the Armed Forces; academic posts in higher education.

Further Aspects of Labour Market Segmentation
The General Pattern of Labour Market Segmentation

There appears to be widespread agreement that labour market segmentation has a long history and is thus probably an inevitable feature of modern industrial society.

The problem for the modern student of the economy is to devise a classification system and perhaps a model that will convey the essential nature of this segmentation and assist in predicting the likely impact on labour supply, demand, and rewards of changes in the economic, social, and demographic environment.

All the indications are that in modern industrial nations labour markets are segmented on the basis of occupation and industry.

(a) *Occupation.* Word-processor operators seldom, if ever, apply for work as watch repairers, or vice versa. The reasons for this occupational segmentation are complex and were examined in Chapter 7.
(b) *Industry.* There are some clear differences which may be identified when considering industrial fragmentation. These include:
  1 The type of product market. If an industry produces products which enjoy stable demand conditions, then firms in that industry may, if they wish, operate in the primary labour market. If, however, products face fluctuating demand, then suppliers will seek to recruit mainly in the secondary labour market.
  2 The structure of supply. If supply is controlled by a few (probably large) firms, then the labour market is likely to be primary, largely perhaps because workers become specialised to that industry and have few other possible employers. On the other hand, if there are a large number of relatively small, competing firms, the demand for labour by individual employers may well fluctuate even though industry demand for labour stays fairly constant. Consequently, firms will tend to try to ensure that they operate in secondary labour markets.

3 The nature of industrial technology. If capital equipment is expensive and at the frontiers of research (for example, a nuclear power station), then the firm needs skilled workers in the primary labour market. Where the level of technology is low, requiring skills that are widely available, then firms may be able to obtain their labour needs in the secondary market.

The type of industrial sector is thus of considerable significance in determining the characteristics of a labour market. McNabb (1987), however, largely discounted the importance of industrial features in determining differences in earnings. His research led him to place the main emphasis on the effects of labour market segmentation based on occupations. He believed that the earnings differences arose from differences in human capital investment.

A logical implication of McNabb's study would be that segmentation reflects different workers' backgrounds and their opportunities for taking advantage of educational opportunities. These, in turn, affect people's chances to gain the training and qualifications required for jobs in primary markets.

The logical conclusion of the dual labour market hypothesis is that individual employers may operate in both the primary and the secondary labour markets at the same time. The choice of market is dependent upon the type of labour required for different tasks, so that the various types of worker are sought in their appropriate markets. Higher education provides an example of this. Most of the academic staff, senior administrators, and the clerical and technical staff are normally drawn from primary labour markets. These employees have generally made varying amounts of human capital investment. They receive on-the-job training that can be expected to enhance their value to the employing institution as well as their own career prospects. Higher-education institutions, however, employ considerable numbers of other workers such as catering staff, cleaners, porters, and gardeners with relatively little human capital investment. These employees are in regular employment, as identified by Hicks, but their work, however valuable to the employing institution, requires little formal training. They can be easily replaced if they leave and very few can expect long-term career advancement or significant opportunities to raise their relatively modest wage levels. Higher-education establishments normally recruit these workers in the secondary labour market.

Questions for Discussion and Review

7 Discuss the extent of labour market segmentation in the following industries: oil; house building; agriculture; motor vehicle repairing; any other industry of which you have personal knowledge.

8 What effect do you think the increasing reliance of many employers on contract work has on the extent of labour market segmentation?

Local Labour Markets
The Geographical Basis of Market Segmentation

Whatever model or classification system adopted, there seems to be little doubt that modern labour markets are segmented both occupationally and industrially. There is, however, another aspect of segmentation of practical significance to both employers and workers. This is segmentation into local-area labour markets according to the time and cost of travelling between home and work. This is also likely to have a greater influence on secondary than on primary occupations. When pay is low, people cannot afford to travel long distances nor to obtain personal transport of the quality that makes long-distance commuting a practical possibility. It is also a feature of British working life that jobs at the lower end of the occupational and income hierarchy tend to involve longer and more rigid hours than those at the upper end. The longer the journey to work the greater the risk of being late and suffering a pay penalty—another feature of secondary as opposed to primary markets. A person with low earnings potential whose job requires daily attendance between, say, 8.30 a.m. and 5 p.m., unlike his highly paid senior manager, cannot realistically contemplate living in the West Midlands and working in London.

The extent of local labour markets, therefore, varies according to:

(a) *Transport costs in relation to income*. In general, the ratio of transport costs to income will probably be higher for employees in secondary and manual occupations than for primary and 'white collar' workers, who are also more likely to receive assistance with travel costs from employers.

(b) *Availability of transport*. This is more important than actual distance. Local markets are not circular with a fixed radius but tend to extend along important transport networks, such as main railway lines and motorways.

(c) *Working conditions*. Important considerations include flexibility of working time, enabling workers to avoid the most congested travel times, and, of course, the provision of company cars, a fringe benefit particularly widespread in Britain.

Although, as noted in Chapter 10, there are substantial barriers to geographical mobility for most workers, especially when they become responsible for homes and children, the general trend over the past half century has been for almost all local labour markets to extend in size. The days when most manual workers lived within easy walking or cycling distance to their place of work have gone. This is because incomes have risen, transport facilities have improved in most areas, and there has been a considerable increase in the ownership of private cars. The area within which work, or workers, are sought has generally become more extensive. Smart (1974) expressed the view that the emergence of a spatial aspect to labour markets reflected the modern industrial society within which residence and workplace became separated geographically.

Characteristics of Local Labour Markets

One major issue is that of definition, since the term 'local' implies a considerable degree of precision which may not actually exist in practice. When agencies of the British Government refer to 'local labour markets' they often mean quite different things. Population census tables, for example, are produced to show 'travel to work' areas. These are evidently thought to constitute local labour markets. On the other hand, the government agencies responsible for employment measures rely upon 'employment exchange areas'. Often these two approaches overlap to a certain extent, but it is unusual to find that the two areas coincide exactly. Employers and workers towards the centre of an employment exchange area frequently draw their workers or seek employment almost entirely from within a single travel-to-work area. However, those employers and workers on the fringes of one travel-to-work area may seek a part of their labour force or employment in other, adjacent travel-to-work areas. It is by no means unusual for workers to cross the boundaries that have been established for statistical purposes.

Cartter (1967) observed that it might be appropriate to think in terms of a series of concentric circles extending out from each major employment centre. Each succeeding circle would become fainter the further its location from the centre. This type of basic approach allows for the overlap which may often be observed. It does not, of course, permit the geographical boundaries of local labour markets to be defined precisely.

Goodman (1970) suggested that the boundaries of the labour market were largely set by the 'pecuniary and psychological costs' involved in the journey to work. He expressed the view that these costs resulted in the labour force being spatially sub-divided as well as being fragmented by occupation and industry. In this view, although what is meant by 'local labour market' is readily understood, the market boundaries cannot be measured or defined with any precision. Individual preferences are important because individuals differ in the distance they are willing to travel to work. One person may value his or her ability to go home for lunch. Others, who commute over long distances, may consider it quite normal to work a twelve-hour day, including travel time, and enjoy the 'social life' that develops on the inter-city train.

This kind of approach caused Madden (1981) to suggest that women would select their employment closer to home because their tendency to work short hours and to receive relatively low pay would reduce their net earnings after allowing for the costs of long-distance commuting.

An approach not dissimilar to the one by Cartter was adopted by Robinson (1968), who regarded the geographical area of a local labour market as 'containing those members of the labour force, or potential members of the labour force, that a firm can induce to enter its employ, and those other employers with whom the firm is in competition for labour'. What is interesting about this particular approach is that it recognises the possibility that similar, but individual, firms situated relatively close to each other may be, in effect, in differing local labour markets. Certainly there does appear to be some hearsay evidence that certain firms will not always be willing to offer employment to individuals who have worked for other firms in the same industry and locality.

Robinson's approach relates primarily to employers. Phelps Brown (1962), on the other hand, paid particular attention to how potential employees might react to local labour markets. He believed the answer to lie in the 'potentialities of individual access', a concept having two elements:

(a) *The costs of travel.* These include both direct payments for transport and the indirect costs which arise from the time and energy spent in travelling.

(b) *Access to information.* Information relating to employment opportunities and to which most individuals have ready access is usually available only within a restricted area. It is obtained mostly from friends and colleagues in the know and from the local press and employment agencies. Although these agencies are important sources of information within labour markets and are often parts of national networks, the detailed information which they provide of work available is usually limited to a local area.

The precise definition, therefore, of the local labour market presents some difficulties. For most purposes, however, precise definition is not really necessary. What is important is to recognise that spatial considerations will further fragment a labour market already segmented by occupation and industry.

Questions for Discussion and Review

9 Suggest changes in both personal and public transport that have widened local labour markets in the past two decades.

10 Discuss the effect of the following social changes on the size of local labour markets: a further rise in female economic activity rates and a further reduction in the difference between the average earnings of males and females; changes in the educational, including examination, system since 1987.

Suggestions for Written Assignments

1 Write a report on transport available to people travelling to work in your own area. Your report should show whether these transport facilities encourage or discourage an extension of local labour markets and which local occupations are most dependent on transport.

2 Towards the end of 1988 there were a number of press reports describing the growth of 'telecommuting', i.e. the practice of working from home with computers and transferring the product of that work to offices through fax and other electronic communications systems.

Write a report of not more than 1000 words in which you

(a) list the advantages and disadvantages of 'telecommuting' from the viewpoint of both employer and employee,

(b) identify the kinds of job and worker most likely to be affected by this development, and

(c) identify other consequences of the trend for the economy and community.

3 Identify and list three occupations which are available in your area for each of the following:

(a) 16-year-old school leavers with no examination passes.

(b) 16-year-old school leavers with 4 higher grade GCSE passes or BTEC equivalent.

(c) 18-year-old school leaver with 2 GCE advanced level passes or BTEC equivalent.

Classify your nine occupations as either primary or secondary according to the dual labour market concept outlined in this chapter. Give reasons for your decisions.

4 An 18-year-old student who expected to obtain satisfactory GCE advanced level passes was given the following conflicting advice from two different local employers.

'In this firm we rely almost entirely on the people we train ourselves and we like our managers to have experience of working at the lowest levels. We do not have any special regard for graduates and think that going to university or polytechnic is a waste of time that could be spent learning something useful.'

'My advice to you is to get a good degree. Each year our firm recruits several graduates in subjects with no special vocational relevance. We think that a graduate has qualities that, with further training, will produce a good manager.'

Write an essay of about 1000 words supporting the views of one of these employers.

5 Identify and discuss possible reasons for the main differences in the pay structure of manual and non-manual workers.

Suggestions for Further Reading

An overview of the approach by economists to the developing interpretation of the labour market concept was offered by Rottenberg (1956), who provided a concise summary of the differing contributions.

The concept of the dual labour market was given substance by the work of Doeringer and Priore (1971), but a more detailed and critical analysis is to be found in both Cain (1975) and Wachter (1974). Bosanquet and Doeringer (1973) sought to discover whether the concept was applicable to the British labour market.

For a comprehensive survey of the literature relating to dual and segmented labour markets see Cain (1976). Loveridge and Mok (1979) have provided a detailed survey of the numerous segmented labour market models.

Goodman (1970) has presented what is probably the best concise survey of the economic interpretation of the local labour market.

Subsequent work on local labour markets has tended to concentrate on the implications of their operation. MacKay et al. (1971) is a good example of this. A more recent, and not entirely convincing, study of unemployment and its resolution in local labour markets is to be found in Hasluck (1987).

Underlying the studies of the character of the labour market is the assumption that there will exist an employer–employee relationship. For a limited number of workers, however, mainly members of the 'professions', the relationship is that of practitioner and client. This special type of labour market for professional workers was examined by Whitfield (1982).

10
Mobility, Search, and Information

The Concept of Labour Mobility
Mobility and Market Equilibrium

One of the assumptions about labour markets made so far has been that labour was free to move from one job to another, i.e. was mobile, within a market. This assumption is essential to the neo-classical model of the labour market. Unless they are mobile, buyers and sellers of labour cannot respond to changes in the price of labour.

Without labour mobility wages, the price of labour, cannot provide a mechanism for attaining equilibrium between demand and supply in the market and wage differentials cease to be reliable signals of imbalances in labour demand and supply. Mobility allows workers to move to jobs where wages are high and away from those where pay is low to achieve a market equilibrium in which significant wage differences are smoothed away.

In neo-classical market theory, this movement is dictated by the shifting patterns of consumer demand. Labour is a production factor, the demand for which is derived from the demand for products. Labour mobility enables the labour factor market to respond to changes in the product markets. Some evidence that long-term changes in employment do reflect these shifts can be found by contrasting the decline in employment in, say, leather goods manufacturing with the rise in the travel and leisure industries.

Barriers to Mobility

It was pointed out in Chapter 7 that it is possible to identify different occupations by the combination of skills that each requires. The work of a secretary, for example, is different from that of a word-processor operator. These differences also apply to occupations of a similar nature but in different industries, and even firms. The work tasks for a secretary in the coal mining industry will differ to some extent from those of a secretary in banking. Consequently, the rewards offered to these different secretaries will not be the same.

It was also argued in Chapter 7 that the practical choices of occupation open to individuals tended to be restricted by a range of constraints, many of which would be outside his or her direct control. Similar constraints apply to mobility between occupations once work has been commenced. These restrictions also form barriers to the mobility of working people. This mobility is sometimes known as the 'propensity to move' of workers. The existence of this propensity is essential to any theory based on the achievement of market equilibrium between labour supply and demand, but its strength will clearly depend on the strength of the barriers which restrict mobility.

Besides affecting movement between occupations, industries, firms, and localities, barriers can also affect people's ability to progress in their chosen careers. The obstacles to movement affect both the supply and the demand sides of the labour market.

Barriers Restricting Supply

These can be summarised under two headings, as follows.

Lack of the Necessary Skills, Training, or Qualifications Required for Specific Jobs

It was shown in Chapter 7 that, for many reasons, individuals did not have equal opportunities to obtain the educational and vocational qualifications or the information and contacts needed to enter large numbers of occupations and some industries. For those unable to enter through the approved channels at the start of their careers, most of these jobs would remain closed throughout their working lives.

Socio-economic Barriers to Movement

Even if they possessed the required qualifications, older workers often face a daunting number of restrictions making mobility, especially geographical mobility, difficult and expensive. Those with families face barriers and costs of children's education, housing, spouse's career opportunities, and natural personal reluctance to tear up roots that develop over a period spent in a particular neighbourhood. Housing, in particular, has become a major barrier, with the lack of any significant rented housing market and the large regional differences in house prices.

Barriers Restricting Demand

Some employers in the same locality, or same industry, appear to operate 'no poaching' practices. Except in cases where firms are extending their operations and have to recruit specialists trained elsewhere, many employers are reluctant to recruit staff above certain grades from other firms in the same industry or the same local area. Employers acting in this way are able to restrict pressure for increased wages and ensure that they are able to retain the productivity benefits of past human capital investment

Question for Discussion and Review

1 Examine and discuss the implications of the entry requirements for pursuing the following occupations: veterinary surgeon; commercial airline pilot; skilled printer; barrister-at-law; electronics engineer.

Pressures for Labour Mobility

In terms of the economic analysis of markets, any movement must arise out of either demand or supply pressures. If the market is operating efficiently (in economic terms), the movement will take the market from one state of equilibrium to another. Applying this reasoning to labour markets suggests that mobility can arise from pressures on the supply side from workers or from the demand side from employers. At the same time the familiar economic distinction between the macroeconomy of the nation as a whole and the microeconomy of individual markets, industries, and firms raises the possibility that macroeconomic considerations may make it desirable for microeconomic labour markets to be more, or in some circumstances less, favourable to labour mobility.

Individual Workers and Job Changes

When the classical assumption that people will always seek to maximise their utility is applied to worker attitudes towards job changes, it is assumed that workers will move if the anticipated future benefits from the change are expected to be greater than the perceived (present and future) direct and opportunity costs of the change (see Figure 10.1). As with all forms of capital investment, the costs are easier to calculate than the future benefits, about which there is often considerable uncertainty.

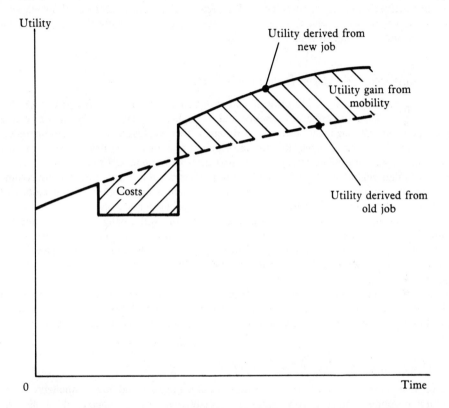

Figure 10.1 *Cost and utility benefit of individual worker labour mobility*

The major benefit likely to be expected from a job change is increased income or an improved chance of increasing income together with any anticipated improvement in working conditions and quality of work. The cost–benefit calculation has to take into account total costs, including those of searching and investigating possible job opportunities, any relocation costs involved, and possible increases in travel and housing costs. These last two are likely to be high in an area of rapid economic growth.

In view of the general uncertainties surrounding jobs and income levels, the time scale over which this kind of calculation can be made is usually fairly short. It becomes more complicated if a proposed move involves two income earners within the family. However, there is certainly evidence that people do make rough and ready calculations of costs and benefits before making moves, especially in occupations where there are rigid national pay scales. The reluctance of teachers from outside London and the South East to accept promotion posts in those areas are indications that pay differences are insufficient to compensate for increased costs, especially those of housing and travel.

Nevertheless, it has already been noted that the decision to move rarely involves monetary considerations alone. It also has social and psychological implications.

In addition to the social costs of moving from one area to another if this is needed, any job change involves moving from the social structure of one workplace to an entirely different social structure in another. This kind of change involves what are sometimes known as 'psychic costs'. Most people work in groups. Friendships are formed, status positions developed, and even non-work activities can be based on working relationships and conditions. Many workers appear to value the social relationships involved with work more highly than the monetary benefits that might be gained from a job change.

The Employers's Need for Labour Mobility

Some of the problems involved in creating and maintaining a workforce suitable to meet the needs of production in a period of economic and technological change will be examined in a later chapter. At this stage it is sufficient to recognise that employers must also compare the costs and benefits of job changes. Recruiting, training, and integrating new workers into the work team involve costs. There may also be past costs of training and the loss of increased productivity that might have been derived from training expenditure. In contrast, there is some uncertainty surrounding the benefits to be expected from a new worker. These costs and uncertainties may be reduced where employers follow a policy of relocating workers within, as opposed to recruiting from outside, the organisation, but this will usually involve assisting the employee with relocation costs and there is no guarantee that the worker will perform up to expectations after the move. All kinds of difficulties may unsettle the relocated employee. Every football manager knows the risks of recruiting a star player who fails to fit into a new team or to settle in a new area.

While not wishing to gain a reputation for inability to retain their workers, employers also need to be able to adapt the structure of their workforce to the pressures of changing demand and technology. The correct balance between these two objectives is not easy to achieve.

The Macroeconomic Need for Labour Mobility

An economic community must be able to adapt to changing demand and technology, i.e. to structural economic changes. New skills and occupations are developed: old skills and occupations are no longer needed. New industries rise up and old ones decline. Some regions become prosperous: others lose major employers. All this involves labour mobility. Economic growth and development can be delayed if firms in new or expanding industries cannot recruit the skilled labour they need. Governments pursuing economic growth thus tend to encourage labour mobility.

On the other hand, governments have to balance a number of different and often conflicting economic and social objectives. Labour mobility has a social cost for communities as well as for individuals. Stable communities form a social structure that not only provides a high degree of social and personal satisfaction for their members but also provides informally a range of welfare benefits, e.g. for the very young, the old, and the sick, that have to be provided by the State if that social structure collapses. It is also likely that unstable and rapidly changing communities generate increased rates of crime, social problems, and mental illness—all of which have an economic as well as a social and human cost.

Questions for Discussion and Review

2 Locate and interview three people who have changed jobs or moved areas during the previous three years. List the reasons they give for the changes and the problems they had to overcome. Discuss these in the light of your reading of this chapter.

3 Discuss the changes in housing and education that you think would remove some of the barriers to labour mobility.

The Extent of Labour Mobility

Perhaps surprisingly, in spite of the considerable barriers, there is substantial evidence in many countries, including Britain, that the degree of mobility, measured in terms either of new employment starts and/or employment quits, is extensive.

Estimates made on behalf of the British Government by Smith (1988) suggest that in any one year there are 7.5 million jobs taken with new employers by individuals exercising their right to be mobile in the labour market. There are four features concerning that figure which should be taken into account.

(a) The figure of 7.5 million new starts represents one third of the employed labour force in contemporary Britain. If this is a typical yearly figure then it clearly supports the hypothesis that labour mobility is a crucial element in the working of labour markets, however these may be defined.
(b) A total of 7.5 million new employment starts does not mean that 7.5 million individuals change their employment in any one year. An unknown number will change their employment two, three, or more times in any one year. This figure, therefore, is likely to overstate the number of individuals who are mobile in the labour market.
(c) Because of the substantial barriers to mobility already identified, the total of known job changers does not include many who could have moved but who, for various reasons, did not do so. Thus the figure of 7.5 million is likely to understate the actual degree of potential flexibility which may exist in the British labour market.
(d) This 7.5 million refers specifically to the number of jobs taken by individuals with new employers. It does not include people who change either their occupation and/or employment location without changing their employer. It therefore understates the actual degree of labour mobility which occurs within companies and consequently in the economy as a whole.

There is some further, if limited, evidence on trends in labour mobility. The British Department of Employment requires manufacturing employers to notify the number of employees leaving and new employees starting. Selected details are contained in Figure 10.2. These figures suggest that:

(a) The average monthly total of workers leaving their jobs in 1987 represented 1.6% of the labour force employed in manufacturing. Assuming that employers were able to replace these where they wished to do so, this implies an annual turnover of labour approaching 20%.
(b) For the twenty-year period ending 1987, the percentage levels of quits and starts do not usually coincide but the following pattern is found:

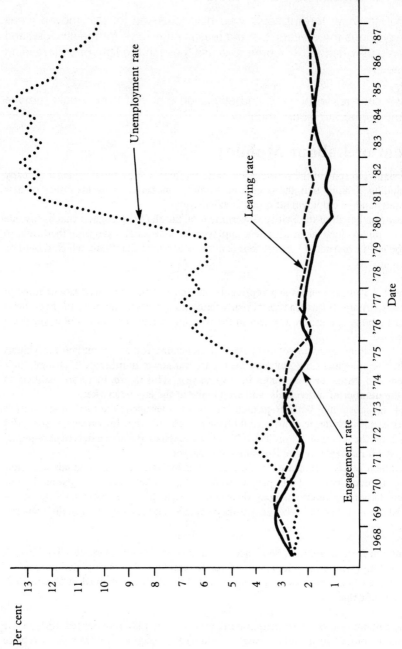

Figure 10.2 *Engagement rate, leaving rate and unemployment rate for manufacturing industry in Britain, 1968–1987, by percentage*
Source: Employment Gazette, various issues

1 Recruitment declines prior to a fall in quits, suggesting that manufacturing employers first respond to a decline in product demand by cutting back on recruitment and that employed workers also leave their jobs less readily, either because they recognise that getting a new job may be more difficult or, if they want to leave, they delay doing so voluntarily in the hope of obtaining redundancy payments.

2 Recruitment rises before quits start to increase, suggesting that employed workers delay leaving until they are certain that the general demand for labour in the market is improving or they feel that current prospects for increased earnings, promotion, etc. are improving.

(c) The general trend over the period, which has seen the re-emergence of large-scale unemployment, has been for a decline in the percentage of the manufacturing labour force leaving their jobs, from 40% in 1968 to 20% in 1987.

There is, of course, likely to be a difference in the predominant reason for job changes between periods of economic prosperity and growth and those of relative depression. When jobs are plentiful, most job changes are voluntary and initiated by workers. When the labour market is in recession and the economic future uncertain, many changes are employer-initiated and involve redundancies. At such times worker-initiated mobility declines as workers decide to stay in their current jobs.

Instead of pay differences declining during periods of recession and relatively low labour mobility, as might be expected, they appear to increase. There are several possible explanations for this. Voluntary job changes, perhaps, are encouraged more by the non-monetary features of work than by monetary considerations as long as the worker believes that another job can be found without undue expense or delay. Alternatively, employers take advantage of depressed labour markets to restore what they may regard as desirable wage differentials and only pay significant wage increases to workers for whom demand is still greater than supply. There were important shortages of skilled labour even during the worst years of high unemployment in the early 1980s.

Questions for Discussion and Review

4 Discuss the implications for labour mobility of an increasing trend for husbands and wives each to pursue careers.

5 Discuss the implications for labour mobility of the trend for skilled work to replace unskilled work, for non-manual work to replace manual work, and for the growth of 'telecommuting', where people work from home and make use of telecommunications systems.

Types of Labour Mobility

The general term 'labour mobility' embraces one or more of the following five types of movement.

(a) Entry, re-entry to, or exit from the labour force.
(b) Geographical.
(c) Occupational.
(d) Industrial.
(e) Inter-firm.

Although it is important to examine each of these, it must be recognised that any one job change can include more than one, and perhaps all, of the types.

For example, a person working as a banker in Scotland may be offered a position as a lecturer at a college in London. Such a change would show that the individual concerned was mobile geographically (moving from Scotland to London), occupationally (changing from banker to lecturer), industrially (moving from the financial sector to education), and between firms (moving from a bank to a college). Although all these together form a single job change, the individual has to consider each aspect and overcome the barriers relating to each. The banker may decide to decline the job offer for reasons connected with one or more of the mobility types, e.g. the family's desire to stay in Scotland or failure to find satisfactory housing in London, uncertainty as to whether the necessary teaching skills have been acquired, future pay prospects in education comparing unfavourably with those in banking, or anticipated difficulty fitting into the social structure of a college after some years in a bank.

Entry, Re-entry to, or Exit from the Labour Force

The basic form of labour mobility relates to entry to, or exit from, the labour force. Assuming an employed labour force of about 25 million, it might be anticipated that, say, approximately 600 000 men and women are approaching their respective standard retiring ages and about another 300 000 are likely to die. Assuming that an equivalent number of these vacancies from 'natural causes' is filled by a new entrant to the labour market, we can expect a basic level of aggregate labour turnover of a little under 1 in 25 (4%). In fact this base level is likely to be higher because of serious illnesses in families, the rising proportion of females in the working population, and possible trends towards retiring before the standard retiring age. Many women also wish to take a temporary break from full-time employment while their children are very young and not all want to return to their previous occupations. Some take advantage of continuing education facilities to make a career change.

The extent of entry/exit mobility is thus dependent on the following influences.

(a) *Social.* In particular these relate to attitudes of women to full-time employment and to the home, to community and employer provision for child-care facilities, and to changing attitudes to retirement from full-time work.

(b) *Socio-political.* These both respond to and influence social attitudes and changing patterns of life and employment. It is, however, political decisions that affect the minimum school leaving age, encouragement and financial provision for education, full- and part-time after the minimum school leaving age, the provision of pre-school care for children, the scale of personal taxes and welfare benefits which affect the monetary gains to the family from having both parents working as opposed to maintaining one at home during the early years of child development, and the ages at which pensions become payable and the scale of pension provision.

(c) *Economic.* Earlier it was suggested that the rising demand for female labour may have played a bigger part than is sometimes realised in bringing about the increased participation of women in the workforce. Demand for labour affects most aspects of entry/exit mobility including the amount of pre-work education and training considered to be necessary, suitable age for retirement, and the amount of time taken away from employment for reasons of family formation. If, for example, more large employers provide child-care facilities, more parents with young children are likely to remain in or re-enter full-time employment.

Inter-state Geographical Mobility of Labour

This occurs at two distinct levels: one is the international migration of labour (across national frontiers); the other concerns migration within a nation state as labour moves from one region to another.

In the long term, extensive shifts in population between nation states have had far-reaching effects on the character of host nation labour forces. This is proving as true for Britain in the 1980s as it was for the USA a century ago. The economic influences on international migration of labour are broadly similar to those affecting internal, regional labour mobility. The extent of political control, however, is much greater. Governments frequently seek to impose controls to maximise economic gains while minimising economic losses and the risks of social conflict. Historically this suggests encouraging the emigration of the unskilled, unemployed and underemployed, and those economically dependent on others, but discouraging and sometimes barring the emigration of the young and the highly skilled, especially those possessing scarce skills. Immigration controls usually have the reverse objectives—to encourage the young and the skilled to come while discouraging those likely to bring more costs than benefits. The extent to which countries can impose controls depends on their political attitudes and machinery, but few countries in the present age of cheap, fast, international transport can avoid having some controls on immigration. Relatively few of the industrial market economies take the political risks of attempting to control emigration. They appear to hope that the human capital gains and losses will be roughly balanced in relatively unrestricted international labour markets.

Geographical Mobility of Labour within Nations

This appears to receive less attention than international mobility, even though the numbers of workers involved are greater. In free market economies it is, of course, difficult to obtain reliable data on the numbers and characteristics of those whose job changes involve movement from one place to another. Statistics on population movements do not distinguish between the economically active and inactive.

For administrative purposes, Britain is divided into ten regions of varying size and population (see Table 10.1). In a normal year a million people, representing 12% of the recorded geographical migration within Britain, move between regions. Census data, however, indicate that the extent of movement within regions is much greater, 69% of migrants moving 10 km or less. Data based on the British 1981 Population Census indicate that migrants aged 16 years or more had a higher economic activity rate than the total population. This suggests that job mobility was a major cause of migration.

The one million figure represents the aggregate number of movements between regions, but a characteristic of geographical mobility within nation states is that it is a two-way process. In 1985, 54000 people moved out of the Scottish Region. At the same time there was a movement into the region of 46000. This cannot be explained on the grounds that individuals moved from Scotland to work elsewhere in Britain only to return to their homeland for their twilight years. Although 36000 15–44 year olds did move from Scotland, there was a return movement of 29000 in the same age group. Amongst those of 'pension age' there was a movement into Scotland of 3000, but this was balanced by an equivalent 3000 people in the same age group who moved out of the region. It must, of course, be recognised that migration is not a success for everyone, and any figure for geographical movement is likely to contain numbers of those who are reversing an earlier change.

Economic analysis of geographical internal mobility faces an apparent contradiction. People will be leaving one region expecting to improve their employment prospects and earnings. At the same time others with the same aspirations will be moving into the region. This is generally

Table 10.1   Inter-regional population movements, by age, in Britain during 1985 (in thousands)

Region		0–14	15–44	45–59/64[a]	59/64 and over[a]
				Age in years	
South East	In	35	164	16	13
	Out	43	146	28	27
South West	In	23	75	16	16
	Out	15	69	7	8
West Midlands	In	14	50	7	7
	Out	15	59	7	6
East Midlands	In	16	53	8	7
	Out	14	52	7	5
East Anglia	In	12	37	7	8
	Out	8	29	4	4
Yorkshire and Humberside	In	12	49	6	5
	Out	15	57	7	5
North	In	7	27	3	3
	Out	8	34	4	3
North West	In	15	56	7	6
	Out	16	66	8	7
Wales	In	9	31	6	5
	Out	7	31	3	4
Scotland	In	10	29	4	3
	Out	11	36	4	3

[a] *59 years for women, 64 years for men*
Sources: Office of Population censuses and surveys, and General Register Office for Scotland

explained on the grounds that the labour force is heterogeneous, i.e. it contains many different kinds of people and people with different skills and training. A case study of Scottish inward and outward labour migration might reveal the following.

(a) Those who are moving from the region may in the past have worked in, or have expected to work in, the old, slow-growing or declining sectors of the economy such as ship building or coal mining. They are moving to other parts of Britain where their skills are still marketable.

(b) Those who are moving into the region have the occupational skills required for the fast-growing new industrial sectors of the Scottish economy such as oil exploration or electronics. These migrants see their move to Scotland as enhancing their employment and earnings prospects.

Thus the gross geographical movements of labour are a reflection of the fragmentation of the labour market discussed earlier. A number of economists have been concerned with the fact that internal migration gives rise to large gross flows of people, but because the movement is in both directions the net, aggregate population shift is very small.

Sjaastad (1962), for example, examined this feature of flows between regions in the USA. He argued that:

(a) No conclusions could be drawn without examining at least the age and occupational structure of both the native and the migrant population.
(b) By itself the level of net migration did not indicate the impact of labour mobility on earnings and employment differences because of the heterogeneous nature of labour.
(c) The two-way nature of migration suggests that earnings differences have industrial and occupational, as well as geographical, origins.

An assumption that the underlying reason for workers to change their location is the economic desire to improve earnings and employment prospects suggests that knowledge of the costs and potential benefits of a move from one area to another should enable the economist to predict whether movement from one region to another is probable.

Comparison of monetary costs and benefits should not present too many problems, but the economist must recognise that many workers are more heavily influenced by the non-monetary considerations of the kind outlined earlier in this chapter. The longer the period a worker and family has been resident in an area, the greater will be the social and psychic costs of moving. Consequently young, single people are likely to have a greater propensity to migrate than older workers with families, particularly with families containing children at school.

Some costs, both monetary and non-monetary, can be reduced if the migrant moves to an area where others from the region have previously settled. There is a strong tendency for the existence of a strong migrant group from a particular region to attract other immigrants from that region.

Nevertheless, it is the younger people, especially those who have already had experience of living away from home during their education or training, who are most likely to migrate. These have relatively low monetary and non-monetary costs of mobility but can expect relatively high levels of benefit over their full working lives. This implies that a migrant population tends to contain an above-average number of the young, the more highly educated, and those with initiative and readily marketable skills. The implication, therefore, is that a community tends to gain from net immigration.

Molho (1984) concluded from his examination of inter-regional migration that the main motivating factor for geographical labour mobility was the 'pull' of increased earnings and job prospects, not 'push' factors such as unemployment.

Questions for Discussion and Review

6 Outline and discuss the social barriers to geographical mobility. Include in your discussion the view that improvements in transport and communications are reducing these barriers.

7 There are probably more British civilians working in countries outside Britain today than there were in the 1930s when Britain controlled a large empire. Discuss possible reasons for this.

Further Considerations of Labour Mobility
Occupational Mobility

Occupational mobility occurs when workers move from one occupation to another. The term 'occupation' is used in the sense defined earlier in this book, i.e. as employment requiring a unique set of skills. The interest here is not the social issue of changes in income distribution or socio-economic status but with evidence of occupational change and the factors that may influence it. Consequently 'inter-generational' occupational mobility—the movement by children to higher/lower occupations than those of their parents—is not examined.

The Need for Occupational Change in a Changing Economic Environment

Changing employment opportunities, especially over the last generation, have led to a decline in certain long-established occupations and to the rise of new ones. Many individuals, therefore, who wish to remain economically active may have to change their occupations at least once and sometimes twice or more during their working lives. This has further implications for both basic education and vocational training within the community.

Barriers to Occupational Mobility

If there is an economic case for increased occupational mobility, any natural or artificial barriers in addition to the geographical barriers arising when a change in occupation involves changing location must be of concern. It has always been difficult to move to jobs which require special education and training when this has not been acquired early in life. Some crafts remained exclusive over a long period precisely because they depended on successful completion of apprenticeships at the start of a worker's career. It is sometimes assumed that the decline of the apprenticeship system and the extension of adult education and training are helping to increase occupational mobility, but there are also market tendencies that may be working in the opposite direction. Labour market fragmentation, especially into primary and secondary markets, as explained in Chapter 9, may be restricting opportunities for occupational change. Those workers who are only able initially to obtain jobs in the secondary market may find it dificult to transfer to occupations within the primary market.

Because many of the data relating to changes in the occupational mix within the structure of the economy are only available in aggregate and generally only show changes over fairly long periods, it is difficult to separate actual occupational changes achieved by individuals from the inter-generation changes which occur when children enter different occupations and employment markets to those of their parents. It is not even certain what the effects of current trends actually are. For example, the long-standing tradition in British manufacturing, in contrast to, say, Germany and the USA, for supervisors, foremen, and the lower ranks of industrial managers to be promoted from the shop floor implied a channel for occupational mobility for some people to move from manual to non-manual work. The modern swing towards requiring managerial and many supervisory grades to have formal qualifications which may be difficult to obtain without a certain minimum level of general education may or may not raise standards of industrial management, but it may restrict opportunities for occupational mobility, with important social and economic implications.

Without this mobility, the long-term trend towards a decline in manual and unskilled occupations and the rise in non-manual work could condemn large numbers of manual workers and those in secondary markets to long periods of unemployment. Promises of improved job prospects in the long term for his children or wife provide little comfort to the redundant factory worker without hope of similar work in his home area.

Evidence on the Extent of Occupational Mobility

To try and measure the extent of occupational mobility excluding the inter-generation effect, 'cohort analysis' is frequently used. This identifies a specific age group, e.g. 20–29 or 45–54, and studies the career pattern of its members. Thus it is possible to examine members of a cohort who first entered employment between, say, 1960–64, identify their initial occupations, note subsequent changes in occupational status, and seek to distinguish the characteristics common to those who retain their initial occupations from the characteristics of those who change. Cohort analysis, therefore, tries to identify both the extent of occupational change and possible influences upon it.

Metcalf and Nickell (1982) based their analysis on data collected for the National Training Survey published by the Manpower Services Commission in 1978. This was based on interviews relating to the labour market experiences, for the period 1965–75, of 50 000 individuals. The information thus obtained was unlikely to contain inter-generation movements. When available occupations were grouped into six, broadly based categories it was estimated that 25% of the total number of respondents were in different occupational classes at the end of the decade compared with the beginning, though there were quite large variations between the classes. In three of the groupings, however—Professional and Managerial, Junior Non-manual, and Semi-skilled Manual—there was no change in the occupational groupings for three-quarters of those initially included. In the Intermediate Occupations, Skilled Manual, and Unskilled Manual groupings the degree of movement out of these categories was rather greater. Only 60% of the initial membership of Unskilled Manual workers were still in this group at the end of the period. Of those leaving, 90%, by 1975, were classified as being in either Junior Non-manual or Semi-skilled Manual.

Using a different, and smaller, cohort, Mayhew and Rosewell (1981) noted that those who moved to a lower occupation class also switched from one industry to another. Those, however, who were occupationally upwardly mobile tended to remain in the same industry.

Metcalf and Nickell sought to extend their analysis of the data to take into account the dual labour market (outlined in Chapter 9). They concluded that there was a high degree of stability in primary markets, where 90% of those surveyed remained in the same occupational group throughout the decade of the survey period, and that there was more mobility in secondary markets, with one in four workers moving from secondary to primary market occupations during the survey period.

Reasons for Occupational Mobility

Among studies investigating the reasons for this 'intra-generation' occupational mobility, those of Mayhew and Rosewell (1981) and Metcalf and Nickell (1982) suggested that human capital investment was the key element, though perhaps in different ways. Education—its length and the achievement of educational qualifications—was not found by Mayhew and Rosewell to be of great significance in determining occupational mobility, although they did recognise its significance in determining first occupations. On the other hand, educational influences were considered to be significant by Metcalf and Nickell, who expressed the view that occupational mobility was associated with qualifications. Both pairs of researchers acknowledged the significance of occupational, especially full-time, training, in influencing subsequent occupational mobility.

Factors of less significance identified by Metcalf and Nickell included age and marital status. Younger people tended to be more occupationally mobile, but contrary, perhaps, to expectations, single men were less so.

Greenhalgh and Stewart (1985) brought gender into the issue, finding that males tended to be more upwardly mobile than females. Over time, males and single females have benefited from the changing industrial structure by achieving higher occupational status, but as the aggregate occupational structure has shifted upwards, married women, often working part-time, have moved into lower-status jobs. The relative decline in occupational position by married women may also reflect the difficulty many experience in keeping their vocational skills up to date.

Inter-industry Mobility

Inter-industry mobility is defined here as the movement from one industrial sector to another (for example, from electrical engineering to the construction industry). As with occupational mobility, the long-run observed movements between industrial sectors are, to some extent, between generations, with children entering different industries to those which employed their parents.

A study by Lindley (1976), for the period 1959–68, provided evidence of inter-generation mobility. In certain, mostly expanding, industrial sectors there were fewer workers retiring than there were young entrants. In other, declining industries with falling job opportunities, the workers retiring outnumbered those entering. Over a period as short as ten years, the relative employment levels of industries can change significantly, mainly as a result of the different flows into and out of employment.

Inter-generation industrial mobility helps to induce long-term adjustments to the structure of labour forces to bring them into line with the industrial structure of the economy. Nevertheless, some short-term movement is also likely from currently employed workers, away from declining or stagnating industrial sectors into those with better growth or stability prospects.

One study, de Wolff (1965), noted that labour mobility tended to be set in motion by 'lay-offs and new hires'. Declining industries do not reduce wage rates, preferring, or finding it easier, to reduce the number of workers employed by not recruiting. At the same time, expanding industries tend to increase the number of workers hired. The economic motives for such movement appear straightforward. On the other hand, the expanding sectors offer improved prospects of employment and earnings. Increased pay is usually necessary to induce workers to accept the risks and costs of transfer from other industries. There is evidence supporting the view that expanding industries tend to pay above average wages.

It must also be recognised that only a relatively small proportion of jobs in the new or expanding industries are likely to be industry-specific. Many are in occupations that are found in most or all sectors of the economy. These include specialists in purchasing, marketing, finance, and office administration as well as many kinds of office staff such as secretaries and word-processor operators. It is these workers who may have to be encouraged to become industrially mobile by higher pay.

Modern industry, over a long period, has also tended to require specialised and managerial employees to have a higher level of general education and professional or vocational training than in the past, when more stress was placed on serving an apprenticeship within the industry. More recently trained workers are thus likely to be occupation- rather than industry-orientated and more prepared and able than their precedessors to pursue their chosen occupations by transfer between industries.

Inter-firm Mobility

Much movement takes place between firms in the same local labour market area. This can, but need not, involve a degree of geographical, occupational, and industrial mobility. While recognising the importance of redundancies and forced movement, particularly in recent years, the emphasis in this section is on voluntary, unforced movement initiated by workers themselves.

Parsons (1972) found evidence to suggest that workers who were mainly responsible for funding and arranging their own training, i.e. increasing their personal stock of human capital, were more likely to move to different firms.

The precise extent of local inter-firm mobility is difficult to determine, though some estimates put it as high as 80% of all labour mobility in Britain. Nevertheless, the net flows between firms appears to be relatively small and closely associated with firms' needs to expand or contract their labour forces.

In general, therefore, individual firms are able to recruit workers to make good losses from voluntary quits. Consequently, the motives for local inter-firm movement must be mainly personal to the workers themselves. These motives can be many and varied. They may include 'pull' factors based on beliefs that movement will increase the monetary and non-monetary benefits of working. These are, for example, increased pay, improved working conditions, greater job security, more work experience—an element in the accumulation of personal human capital—more congenial fellow workers, and more suitable or flexible hours of work. They may also include 'push' factors to reduce the costs of working, e.g. a wish to reduce the time and cost of travelling or to escape from an environment that has become irksome. Some movement, especially among unskilled, routine workers with little or no prospect of occupational mobility, may simply be to overcome boredom, seeking some stimulation in change for its own sake.

A detailed mobility study by Harris (1968) concluded that the major reason for moving between firms was the desire to enhance either earnings, prospects, or both.

Nevertheless, there must be some doubt as to the importance of improved pay as a motive for local labour mobility because if this were a major influence we would expect to find more evidence of continuing upward spirals of local wages—and firms combining together to check such a tendency. Consequently other motives, such as those listed above, must be present.

Research findings are, to some extent, conflicting. Survey material reported by Harris (1968) provided evidence that two-thirds of those engaging in localised inter-firm mobility knew which employment they were to enter before beginning the process. Smith (1966), however, suggested that those engaged in this form of mobility actually had little information concerning the job opportunities being provided by their new employer. In a detailed case study relating to the establishment of a new plant, Jones (1969), who studied successful, and unsuccessful, manual worker applicants, concluded that those seeking voluntary job changes were three times more likely to be motivated by a 'desire to obtain greater security' than by financial motives. In a study of members of the British Institute of Management, Nicholson and West (1987) reported that the possible financial rewards arising from mobility were given a low priority compared with the desire to work in an environment which provided learning opportunities and a personal challenge.

Economists have been interested not only in why localised inter-firm mobility occurs but also in the characteristics of those most likely to be involved. Firms need this knowledge because such localised movement of people between roughly similar jobs does not significantly alter the structure of local employment but it does add to business costs through additional training, loss of past human capital investment, and lost production. Most firms would like to reduce this kind of labour mobility. Jones (1969) sought to test two hypotheses, that voluntary job changes were most frequently made by (a) young and (b) short-service workers. Of the total successful and unsuccessful applicants for employment, Jones found that 44% were aged under 30 years and only 17% were aged 40 or over. This support for the first hypothesis has been strengthened by other research, including a study by Richardson et al. (1977) examining aspects of the London labour market. By focusing upon 'leavers' rather than 'joiners' Richardson et al. found that workers under 30 years of age retained their employment for shorter periods than did older workers.

However, Jones concluded that the second hypothesis concerning length of service could not be supported by his evidence. This conclusion was supported by Richardson and his colleagues' London study.

Nevertheless, the London study did indicate that in certain government departments and for some white collar employees, persistent job changing appeared to affect their long-term employment prospects adversely, and that after a period of job instability individuals tended to become less mobile. This apparent job instability may be motivated by the perfectly rational economic desire to gain experience and test the market before deciding to settle down.

Questions for Discussion and Review

8 Discuss the effect on each of the classes of labour mobility of an increase in the proportion of workers who have received higher education and professional training.

9 Discuss the consequences for each of the classes of labour mobility of the many mergers that took place among large firms in Britain in the 1980s.

Labour Mobility and Search Activity

The Need for Search Activity

Any kind of job movement implies that both workers and employers become involved in search activity. This also, of course, applies to new entrants to the labour market seeking their first job and to employers recruiting new entrants.

Workers and would-be workers have to search in order to acquire information concerning:

(a) *The jobs available.* Labour market communications are far from perfect, and some effort and costs usually have to be incurred to find out the demand conditions for any particular kind of work.
(b) *The type of work offered.* No two jobs are really alike, even if their descriptions are similar. Differences increase when there is movement to different occupations, industries, and regions.
(c) *The rewards available.* The wage offered and other aspects of the reward package vary between employers.

Employers also have to incur search costs when they recruit labour because no two workers are exactly alike. There are always differences in human capital as well as in attitudes and ability to fit into the existing work team. It might be expected that, in a period of high unemployment, these costs fall. This is not always the case, however, as employers are then likely to be faced with choosing between large numbers of people, many of whom appear very capable of doing the job offered.

The Search Process

Increased search experience enables both sides to learn and to adjust their objectives and expectations, both monetary and non-monetary, in order to reach conclusions more quickly and with less cost.

Employers, of course, especially large firms, have more opportunities to gain experience because they employ specialist personnel departments which are constantly involved in recruitment and able to monitor and adapt their search techniques.

The search process, whether by employers or potential employees may be either extensive or intensive.

(a) *Extensive.* This is the case when individuals obtain information concerning large numbers of jobs or when firms seek to attract a large number of applicants. This appears to give considerable choice, although the amount of information that can be absorbed is limited.
(b) *Intensive.* This is where more detailed information is sought, but only in relation to a limited number of jobs or applicants.

In practice, the two approaches are often partially combined. For example, the final-year undergraduate will initially conduct an extensive initial search, but then concentrate on a few firms and apply to these after a more detailed investigation. Similarly, the employer seeking graduate recruits may encourage a large number of applications and possibly conduct many first interviews. Serious consideration, however, may be given to only a few individuals from a few favoured educational establishments. The extensive initial search is clearly used chiefly to monitor the effectiveness of a predetermined selection procedure.

Although graduate recruitment is a special case, similar processes are found elsewhere in labour markets, and the choice of extensive or intensive methods tends to be associated with particular types of market. People seeking entry to or transferring within primary markets are usually willing to enter into extensive and intensive, and sometimes costly, search activity because the potential future benefits of success can be considerable, and errors expensive. Employers are also likely to be well aware of the monetary and non-monetary penalties of choosing unsuitable primary market workers. Search in secondary markets, where job changes are more common and expected, is likely to be less extensive because errors for both workers and employers are more easily and inexpensively corrected.

Changing jobs has earlier been seen as an investment made in anticipation of increasing the net benefits of employment. The direct and opportunity costs of job search are part of that investment, and the longer the period of search the less the time available for enjoying any gains in benefit.

Search Models

Two different theoretical models have been evolved by economists to explain how search activity might be optimised. Too long a period of search raises costs beyond any likely expectation of benefit; too short a period may result in failure to identify more beneficial jobs or applicants.

The models outlined below take the viewpoint of a job applicant.

Stigler's Model

The first was developed by Stigler (1962), who sought to apply the marginal principle to job search. He believed that individuals would continue the search process until the marginal cost of further search would equal the marginal benefits to be achieved (see Figure 10.3).

Before point X, where the marginal cost of search equals the marginal benefits (for example, at points $Y1$ and $Y2$), the marginal benefits exceed the marginal costs, thus indicating further search is worthwhile. However, at points $Z1$ and $Z2$ marginal costs exceed the marginal benefits, and search at these points results in loss of benefits.

The assumption made in this model is that applicants determine their optimal period for search. Any job offers received are stored and the search is continued for the optimum period, point T in Figure 10.3. At this point all offers received are compared and a decision is taken to accept the one that appears most favourable.

This may be possible for those entering a labour market from full-time education but, as Salop (1973) has shown, it is not the normal practice for the majority of work vacancies. Employers usually allow only a short time for acceptance or rejection of a job offer, and although partial storage can be achieved by later rejection after acceptance, this can be dangerous in local or specialised markets. Generally, therefore, individual applicants have to accept or reject each offer when it comes along.

McCall's Model

The inappropriateness of Stigler's model to most labour markets has led to different approaches. One, developed by McCall (1970), assumed that the potential worker had:

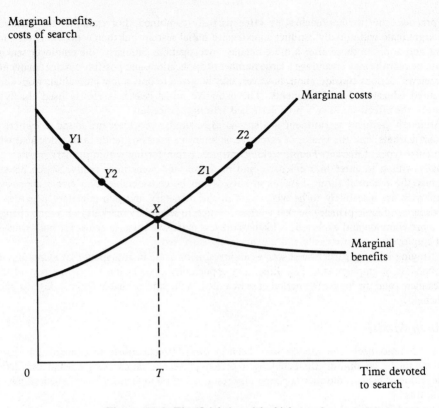

Figure 10.3 *The 'Stigler' model of job search*

(a) some information concerning employment opportunities and approached firms in a preferred order; thus, the longer the period of search the less attractive potential employers are likely to appear, and

(b) a reservation wage level below which he or she was unwilling to accept employment, even if this should be from a preferred employer.

McCall believed that the individual engaged in a labour market search would begin with the most favoured possibilities and while rejecting any offer below the reservation wage level, W_i in Figure 10.4, would accept the first offer above that level. Because firms in this model are approached in favoured sequence, the first to offer employment above the reservation wage will be preferred to the second to do so. A need for the storage of offers does not arise. In this approach an inter-relationship exists between the reservation wage level and the time devoted to search. It is anticipated that it will take longer to find an employer prepared to offer above a high reservation wage than below it. This is shown in Figure 10.4 where the frequency of potential job offers, by wage level, is shown by the curve $f(W)$ with the reservation wage signified by W_i. The higher the value of W_i, the greater the proportion of jobs which will not be considered.

There remains the question of the establishment of the reservation wage in the McCall model. This will vary for individuals depending upon circumstances. For example, those in employment can be expected to set a reservation wage above their current wage. On the other hand, the unemployed are likely to adjust their expectations downwards the longer the period of unemployment and as pressure to find work increases. Salop (1973) suggests that this tendency indicates that the worker is responding to information gained during the search process, namely that his/her initial reservation wage is too high to allow return to the employed labour force.

While acknowledging the validity of the McCall approach, another observer, Pissarides (1982b), noted that manual employees who had lost their jobs during a downturn in the economy would often be re-hired subsequently by their former employer. He considered that anticipation of possible re-hire might modify a worker's search strategy. Pissarides' study indicated that workers in the group studied would only search if they considered the chance of re-employment to be small. Both workers and employers recognised that re-hire would give both firm and worker the opportunity to benefit from the past acquisition of firm-specific skills.

Questions for Discussion and Review

10 Re-state the two search models outlined in this chapter from the viewpoint of the employer.

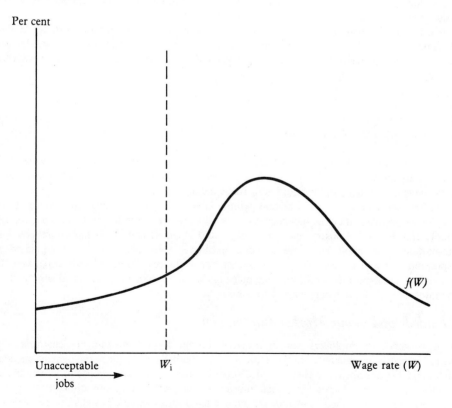

Figure 10.4 *The 'McCall' model of job search*
Notes: f(W) represents frequency distribution of wage offers
W_i represents the 'reservation' wage level

11 Large firms have many advantages over small firms in recruiting workers, although career opportunities in small firms are often very attractive. Explain why large firms may have these advantages and discuss this statement.

Job Search and Information

The Importance of Information to Labour Markets

As noted earlier, employers and employees can only come together within the labour market if information is available about potential job opportunities. The methods whereby information is communicated and the sources of information used by participants have a bearing on the search process. They are also likely to influence the operation of the labour market. Should labour market information be either limited or difficult to obtain, then it may be regarded as a scarce economic good and to acquire it will involve costs. These can be monetary or involve the sacrifice of time. Inadequate and/or inappropriate information will act as a labour market imperfection, making it difficult for the market to achieve equilibrium between demand and supply.

Economists have only recently shown interest in the information mechanism of labour markets. Earlier observers believed that failure to achieve equilibrium resulted from the natural heterogeneity of labour or to the lack of necessary information. These explanations do not satisfy economists in an age of information technology!

A number of researchers have recognised the importance of information. Stigler (1962), examining the significance of information to workers, recognised that complete knowledge was unlikely to be forthcoming but considered that individuals did need to obtain information relating to:

(a) wage rates,
(b) stability of employment, and
(c) other determinants of job choice.

Because people had different requirements, expectations, and attitudes to work they were likely to have very individual determinants in other respects, so that full awareness of these could only really be gained when employment had actually commenced.

Stigler also noted that information within labour markets became obsolete in time. Employers adjusted their labour requirements and reward offers to meet changing market supply and demand. Consequently, not only would potential employees have unreliable and out-of-date information but some existing employees were likely to be disappointed in expectations that had been based on different circumstances. Stigler clearly recognised the importance of labour market information on issues far wider than wage rates, and also saw how the information could change with changing market conditions.

Channels of Labour Market Information

Both workers and employers gain information through formal and informal channels. The formal information channels are those provided by public, or private, employment agencies including, for example, the career advice services provided in education and in newspaper articles and advertisements. Informal information networks are more difficult to specify precisely, but are assumed to include on the one hand information other than career articles, reports, and advertisements gleaned from the mass communication media or information provided by friends and associates. For their part, employers gain information about the labour market from the number and nature of enquiries from job seekers. The diverse character of the informal communication channels may help to explain the rather mixed information that generally circulates within labour markets.

Rees (1966) studied the Chicago labour market, where he found that 80% of blue-collar and 50% of white-collar workers obtained employment through informal information networks. On this evidence he argued strongly that both employers and employees favoured informal mechanisms in preference to more formal channels.

Reid (1972) did not challenge the formal/informal division but suggested that the informal methods, on occasions, might be highly structured. If this is correct it could explain how, in practice, some groups of workers, such as ethnic minorities or females, might be discriminated against in certain firms or industries, despite the apparent lack of evidence that such discrimination is practised. Rees believed that informal channels, especially those based on the introduction of applicants by existing employees, represented a screening device operated by a satisfied workforce at little or no cost to the employer. Existing employees were unlikely to introduce workers liable to disrupt existing employment patterns. From the applicants' viewpoint, Rees believed that the informal information network offered the opportunity to gain rather more detailed information from existing employees than a personnel department could offer. New entrants would also have the advantage of having friends in the firm. This would reduce the psychic costs of employment change.

Although informal networks appear attractive to both the buyers and sellers of labour, employers may not always be willing or able to take advantage of them. Rees found companies which had ceased to use this method because of the development of cliques in the labour force. These tended to reduce labour productivity.

Stigler pointed out that if the offered employment package was not sufficiently attractive employers had to spend more in the formal information network. This appeared to imply that there was some kind of trade off between the employment package, perhaps extending beyond the wage level, and spending on information within the labour market.

Rees found that where employers had to resort to the more formal networks, the value of the differing available methods varied. Employers in Chicago were generally more satisfied with both the service they received, and the employees gained, from private than from public employment agencies, a result which may reflect the initiative of individual applicants as much as the level of service provided. One interesting aspect from the use of private agencies was the variation in fees over time and between occupations. These applied to manual and non-manual worker recruitment and indicated the extent to which search costs could vary.

In their comparative study of two local labour markets in Britain, MacKay et al. (1971) also found informal information networks to be of considerable significance in job changes and in finding work following redundancy.

Because of the significance of informal networks in allocating labour, Reid (1972) sought to examine their effectiveness, especially in aiding workers made redundant. He concluded that these informal networks were important for both the voluntary and the involuntary mobile workers.

A note of caution, however, should be sounded when assessing the results of Stigler, Rees, Reid, and MacKay. These and other studies on the same theme were undertaken in periods of relatively low unemployment, when labour demand was greater than supply and employers sought to find potential workers of the desired calibre. Existing employees and specialist employment agencies are probably the most efficient channels under these conditions.

In periods of high unemployment with labour supply in most markets exceeding demand, employers can choose from many more applicants through all available channels. The high screening costs of formal methods may cause many to prefer informal channels. The informal channels may represent an additional fragmentation of the labour market favouring those in employment at the expense of the unemployed. A study by McCormick (1988) for the period

1971–83, when unemployment rates rose fivefold, revealed that the share of new jobs secured by those in employment remained unchanged. People in work tend to have access to informal channels denied to many of the unemployed who become increasingly reliant on public employment agencies. These may well not be the favoured recruitment channels for most employers.

Questions for Discussion and Review

12 A number of towns have formed clubs for the unemployed where services are provided to assist in job search and where local unemployed can meet. In the light of this chapter discuss the value of such clubs to people seeking to return to the active labour force.

13 List and discuss the information you would want to have available in looking for your next (or first) job.

Suggestions for Written Assignments

1 Outline the main changes in the regulations regarding movement of workers between member states of the European Community resulting from the 1992 relaxations. Describe the main remaining barriers to the creation of a single European Community labour market.

2 In the 1950s the insurance offices in Britain were selling pension schemes to employers on the grounds that they helped firms to retain scarce labour. In the 1980s the British Government introduced transferable pensions, claiming that these would help to produce the increased degree of labour mobility required in a period of economic and technological change.

 Discuss the influence of pension provisions on labour mobility and describe and comment on other 'social barriers to mobility' that government has the power to influence.

3 Discuss the effect on labour mobility of:
 (a) the growth of contract labour firms,
 (b) the growth of part-time work, and
 (c) the growing proportion of women in the labour force.

4 Describe the main services available to assist school leavers in searching for a job if they decide not to continue full-time education. What information do you consider is needed by such a school leaver and how far is it provided by the services you have described?

5 What public and private sector services are provided in your locality to assist unemployed adults to find employment? How effective do you consider these services to be in providing the information needed by the job seeker?

Suggestions for Further Reading

In spite of its date, the work edited by E. Wright Bakke (1954) contains several essays which are relevant to the various aspects of labour mobility discussed in this chapter. Molle and van Mourik (1988) examined aspects of geographical labour mobility, both within nations and within Europe, in the context of the policies and objectives of the European Community. Rolge (1981) and Molho (1984), however, concentrated their studies specifically on inter-regional mobility in Britain.

The character of occupational mobility and the economic influences on it are the subject of studies by Mayhew and Rosewell (1981) and Metcalf and Nickell (1982). Each of these has provided an insight into this type of labour mobility.

The economic considerations initiating inter-firm labour mobility have been examined theoretically and empirically by Parsons (1977).

Two studies undertaken by the Organisation for Economic Co-operation and Development (OECD), the first produced by de Wolff (1965) and the second by the OECD itself (1986), drew upon a comprehensive range of data relating to labour mobility.

The character of labour market information, especially that relating to job search, was the subject of an essay–literature review by Pissarides (1985).

11
Labour Market Disequilibrium

Elements in Labour Market Disequilibrium

British official statistics refer to the 'workforce'. This approximates to what economists call the total supply of labour. Both terms include those in employment and those described as unemployed. Total labour supply is therefore made up of those in work and those wishing to work but without paid occupations.

Similarly, the demand for labour includes not only those who are actually employed but also the unfilled vacancies which employers offer on the labour market. Economics is concerned with the allocation and use of scarce resources. Consequently, economists are interested in the reasons why a proportion of the supply of labour remains unused and why a proportion of labour demand remains unmet. To the economist the existence of either indicates that the labour market is not bringing demand and supply into equilibrium. For the individual, failure to find a job when vacancies exist can suggest that discrimination is being practised. If this is the case, then the economist must recognise that the market is imperfect and seek to find out which people or groups are the victims of discrimination and the reasons why it exists.

Unemployment
Definition and Measurement of Unemployment

It is not possible to measure anything until there is a clear understanding of what is being measured. As a consequence of its political, social, and personal importance, a great deal of attention is paid to the extent of unemployment. Few people are able to agree about its precise extent simply because there is no general agreement on how unemployment should be defined.

The Lloyds Bank Economic Bulletin for September 1987 (from which Figure 11.1 has been taken) discussed the problem and showed that there were very wide variations in the extent of unemployment in Britain depending on the definitions employed. A very wide definition of an unemployed person might be one who is seeking and is available for work but cannot find a job. Even this is not satisfactory because it begs the question of the suitability of work available to the talents, training, and skills of the person seeking work. An extreme, if unlikely, example would be a brain surgeon whose best job offer is for work as a builder's labourer. Is such a person unemployed?

Clearly it is not possible to say that everyone without a job is unemployed or even everyone who has left full-time education but not yet retired with a pension. There remain many difficult questions. How should we define young mothers wishing to work but unable to find jobs suited

Table 1   Criteria for being unemployed

	Claiming benefit	Sought work last week	Sought work last 4 weeks	Wants a job	Available for work	Worked in last week	Worked in last 4 weeks	Number 000's
1	Yes	Yes	—	—	Yes	No	—	2002
2	No	Yes	—	—	—	No	—	826
3	Yes	—	Yes	—	Yes	—	No	101
4	No	—	Yes	—	Yes	—	No	47
5	Yes	—	No	—	Yes	—	No	859
6	Yes	—	No	—	Yes	—	Yes	206

Note: A dash indicates that the criterion at the head of the column does not form part of the definition summarized by the row.

Alternative definitions of unemployment

		000's	%*
Labour Force Survey estimate	1 + 2 =	2828	10.6
Alternative (ILO/OECD) estimate	1 + 2 + 3 + 4 =	2976	11.2
UK national definition: claimants	1 + 3 + 5 + 6 =	3168	11.7
Widest definition	1 + 2 + 3 + 4 + 5 + 6 =	4041	14.3

* *Per cent of employed labour force plus unemployed.*
Source: 1986 Labour Force Survey

Figure 11.1 *Problems of defining unemployment*
Reproduced with permission from Lloyds Bank Economic Bulletin, No. 105, September 1987

to their talents and available time? How should we regard those who have been persuaded to accept 'voluntary early retirement' but who would really prefer to be employed?

It is obviously impracticable to try and measure all those who want to work but who cannot find work they consider suitable. Some countries, including the USA, attempt to measure unemployment from surveys, though not with such a wide definition as this, but surveys conducted by government agencies are often suspected of being manipulated by administrations anxious to minimise the problem. Statisticians prefer to have something rather more concrete than 'desires' to measure.

British figures for unemployment are based on the numbers of people claiming benefit who are seeking and available for but who have not found work. The precise method of compiling the figures and the unemployment rate, however, was altered many times between October 1979 and July 1986 with a consequent estimated reduction in the rate of over 1.4%. Details are shown in Figure 11.2, reproduced from the Lloyds Bank Bulletin referred to above.

Basing a measure on those claiming benefit must always lead to some distortion. The total will include a number who are not genuinely seeking work either because they are already earning an income in the 'black', unofficial (cash-payments only) economy or who have left the labour force 'for family formation' or to retire but who are entitled to receive unemployment benefit for a period. At the same time the total does not include some who do genuinely want to

Table 2   Changes in the unemployment statistics

Date	Change	Effect
10/79	Fortnightly payments of benefits	+ 20,000
11/81	Men over 60 offered higher supplementary benefit to leave working population	− 37,000
10/82	Registration at job centres made voluntary Computer count of benefit claimants substituted for clerical count of registrants	− 190,000
3/83	Men 60 and over given national insurance credits or higher supplementary benefit without claiming unemployment benefit	− 162,000
7/85	Correction of Northern Ireland discrepancies	− 5,000
3/86	Two-week delay in compilation of figures to reduce over-recording	− 50,000
		424,000
Total effect of changes to seasonally adjusted figure without school leavers in 4/87		458,000
7/86	Inclusion of self-employed and HM forces in denominator of unemployed percentage	− 1.4%

Sources: Employment Gazette, October 1986, p. 422. Unemployment Bulletin, no. 20, summer 1986, pp. 14–15, and statistical supplement, May 1986, p. 6

Figure 11.2 *The changing basis in the measurement of the unemployed*
Reproduced with permission from Lloyds Bank Economic Bulletin, No. 105, September 1987

work but who are not entitled to receive unemployment benefits. Apart from the reluctant early retirers, this group consists largely of women wanting to return to the workforce after a period of absence due to family reasons. Some of these may wish to work part-time or to offer hours that local employers are unwilling to accept. Many would wish to return to employment if there were adequate local facilities for looking after pre-school children or for covering the gap between school and normal working day closing hours. Some others may have work skills that have become outdated during a period of absence and lack re-training opportunities.

All these possibilities are relevant to the use of scarce human resources and, therefore, are of interest to economists. Similarly, while the concept of a job vacancy is a familiar one, investigation by Rosewell and Robinson (1980) suggests that published figures for vacancies seriously understate the true total.

The Pattern of Unemployment

In the twenty-year period following the Second World War, the levels of unemployment experienced in many nations were significantly lower than those between 1919–39. Nevertheless, during the post-1945 era there were often significant differences in the levels and trends of unemployment between industrial nations. For example, in Britain between 1948 and 1966 there was a relatively slight trend for unemployment to rise. In contrast, in the Federal Republic of Germany over the same period unemployment was declining. In more recent times, after 1966 for Britain but later in the case of other nations, unemployment levels have been significantly higher than those in the two decades following 1945. It is hard to identify any figure to attach to any 'natural' rate of unemployment in industrial nations. The level of unemployment at any given time appears to reflect the particular circumstances of a nation at that time, though these circumstances are likely to be influenced to an increasing extent by international factors.

When considering the higher levels of unemployment in the 1980s, a number of factors have to be taken into account:

(a) Even when unemployment levels are perceived to be high, the great majority of the labour force remains in employment. This is not to say that concern ought not to be expressed by economists, and everyone else in the community, when one in ten of the workforce is unemployed. It is, however, just as important to recognise that the other nine remain in work.

(b) The unemployed, much like the employed labour force, do not form a homogeneous group. The unemployed, for example, vary by sex, age, health records, previous human capital investment, and previous employment history.

(c) For the majority who become unemployed, the experience is relatively short, although a hard core of long-term unemployed is present in most nations.

Recognising this last point, economists have made a distinction between the numbers of people unemployed on a particular date—the stock of unemployed—and the number of people who suffer unemployment during a particular period—the flow of unemployment. The two are not likely to be the same. If, for example, the stock of unemployed as at 1st September is compared with the stock at 1st December of the same year, the total number may be the same but only a proportion will be the same people. Many of those unemployed in September will have found jobs by December while others will have lost their jobs between September and December; some will have lost and gained jobs during the period. Figure 11.3 shows stocks and flows in a typical labour market, while Table 11.1 provides a quantitative analysis of unemployment flows in the UK for selected years.

Table 11.1   Flows into and out of unemployment for the United Kingdom for selected years (in millions)

	1980	*1985*	*1986*	*1987*
Excluding school leavers				
Inflow into unemployment	3.85	4.40	4.60	4.31
Outflow from unemployment	3.21	4.43	4.99	4.85
Change in 'stock' level[a]	+ 0.64	− 0.03	− 0.39	− 0.54
School leavers' unemployment	+ 0.04	+ 0.06	+ 0.06	+ 0.03
Changes in unemployment stock	+ 0.68	+ 0.03	− 0.33	− 0.51

[a] + *indicates an increase in stock,* − *indicates a decrease in stock*
Source: Employment Gazette, various issues

The inward flow of unemployment is made up the following groups.

(a) People who were in employment but who voluntarily become unemployed.

(b) People who were in employment but who become unemployed for involuntary reasons, such as termination by the employer or failed self-employment.

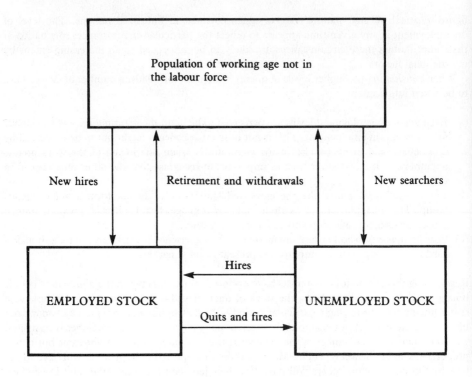

Figure 11.3 *Labour market stocks and flows*
Note: Arrow signifies labour market flow

(c) Those who have not previously been employed but who are seeking employment for the first time. Most of these will be people leaving full-time education or government-sponsored programmes such as work experience schemes, but there will also be a number of women who chose to occupy themselves in family formation rather than enter the labour market after completing full-time education.

(d) Those previously employed but seeking re-entry to the labour force after a period of absence; for example, women who wish to return after being occupied full time with a family and some older people disillusioned with early retirement.

It should be noted that some of these groups, e.g. women returning to the workforce after a period of absence, may not appear in British official unemployment statistics because they are not entitled to unemployment benefit. The sizes of all the groups are likely to be influenced by the prevailing state of the economy. The more vacancies there are, the easier it is to obtain work and the greater will be the temptation for those out of the workforce voluntarily to return and for others not to leave.

Variations in the Extent of Unemployment

The size of the unemployment flow is unlikely to be constant throughout the year or from year to year. Seasonal variations have long been recognised and are allowed for by long-established statistical smoothing techniques. British Press and other reports usually give the actual figure of the unemployment stock at given dates and with this they usually quote the 'seasonally adjusted' figure. Variations in successive stock figures are usually considered to be fairly reliable indicators of trends in the flow. This is reduced by:

(a) People who gain new employment or who enter government-sponsored schemes that remove them from the official unemployment statistics.
(b) Those who decide to give up the search for work and leave the labour force and the official total of unemployed as they cease to be eligible for receipt of unemployment benefits. Most of these are likely to be the early retired, but some will be those who have embarked on a period when they are fully occupied with families, usually caring for the very young or the old and/or infirm.
(c) Any who are discovered to be illegally claiming benefit or who decide to stop illegally claiming benefits because they fear discovery. No one, of course, knows the precise scale of illegal claiming.

Changes in the Structure of the Unemployment Flow

Changes can also occur in the relative sizes of the groups unemployed, i.e. in the structure of unemployment. Official British figures classify the numbers unemployed by age, sex, industry, region, and by duration of unemployment. These classifications do not, of course, match the groups identified in this chapter, but changes in the totals do give some indication of probable trends. They also encourage the development of policies aimed at assisting those groups which seem most at risk from current economic conditions and thus help policy makers move away from the over-simplified ideas current in the 1950s and 1960s, when it was assumed that any rise in unemployment justified injections of government spending into the economy in order to increase the total demand for labour. It was later realised that these could increase labour shortages without having more than a slight effect on the flow of unemployment.

Unemployment and Underemployment

Unemployment is essentially a feature of labour markets in industrial nations. In agrarian economies the potentially unemployed, those who do not have sufficient gainful work to keep them fully occupied, are absorbed into the occupied labour force which consequently experiences considerable underemployment. In developing countries a large group of people, often young people, apparently live off a single small shop or farm. These people share the proceeds of the small enterprise under traditional family obligations, but as the country becomes urbanised and industrialised many of these underemployed drift to the exploding towns to seek work and higher living standards. Those who fail in this quest become 'unemployed' in the sense outlined in this chapter.

A number of the planned economies have, in the past, also proclaimed that they do not have an unemployment problem. More recently they have been obliged to admit to a problem of underemployment so large that it has prevented them from achieving an acceptable level of economic growth.

Some unemployment, therefore, seems to be a feature of an industrial economy. If this is to be kept to a socially acceptable minimum, detailed analysis of the various possible causes and types is desirable.

Questions for Discussion and Review

1 Discuss the view that underemployment is a more serious economic problem than unemployment.

2 'Although the true extent of unemployment in Britain can never be measured exactly, the official figures nevertheless indicate trends with reasonable accuracy.' How far do you think this statement is true?

Causes and Types of Unemployment

The Classical Economic View of Unemployment

Classical economists, believing in the power of unregulated markets to achieve equilibrium between the forces of demand and supply, explained the existence of unemployment in terms of market disequilibrium. A simple model is shown in Figure 11.4. In this diagram the aggregate labour supply curve SS intersects the aggregate labour demand curve DD at the equilibrium point X. At this point the intentions of all buyers and suppliers of labour are satisfied at an equilibrium wage W_e and quantity of labour L_e. If, because of imperfections in the market mechanism, the market wage is actually at a higher level, W_i, then demand falls to L_d and

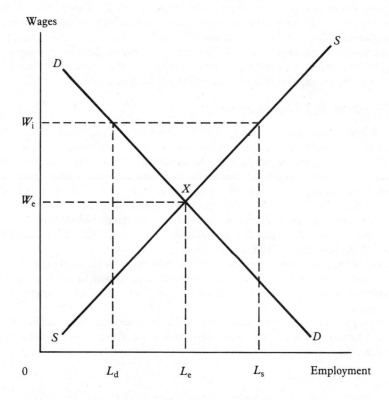

Figure 11.4 *The classical economic view of unemployment*

supply is encouraged to rise to L_s. The difference $(L_s - L_d)$ represents the quantity of unemployment.

This rather simple explanation of the market mechanism ignores the multiple and fragmented nature of labour markets and gives no explanation of how labour demand and supply are derived, why they change, or why the wage has moved to a level of disequilibrium. Nevertheless, the model and later refinements of it have exerted a powerful influence on policies designed to reduce aggregate unemployment.

The main deduction drawn from the model and its successors is that the chief cause of unemployment is too high a wage level. Attempts to reduce wages have met resistance from organised labour (trade unions). Consequently, it has been assumed that trade unions have been the main reason for pushing the wage level above market equilibrium. The natural policy measure to follow from this reasoning is to reduce the power of trade unions in order to secure reductions in the wage level and so achieve market equilibrium and the elimination of significant unemployment.

It was this kind of argument that led to the reduction in miners' wages and the 'General Strike' of 1926. The social divisions this produced together with the long-term persistence of high levels of unemployment up to the second year of the World War of 1939–45, despite fluctuations in real wage levels, encouraged some fresh thinking on the whole problem of unemployment and, in particular, to the dominance of the arguments of Keynes. These, in their turn, were to have an enormous influence on the industrial market economies until about the mid-1970s.

The Keynesian Challenge on Unemployment

Writing and teaching against the background of social divisions resulting from the General Strike, the economic depression of the early 1930s, the rise of national socialism in Italy and Germany, and approaching war, Keynes challenged the classical economic ideas of his day. He did not dispute the basic truth of the economic model outlined in Figure 11.4 but pointed out that the process whereby equilibrium would be achieved would take a long time and involve a degree of social suffering and strife that was not only ethically unacceptable but politically dangerous. For all practical purposes, therefore, Keynes argued that the national labour market could be in long-term equilibrium at a level of employment that could leave large numbers of people seeking work but unable to find jobs. There could thus be a long-term and persistent gap—a deflationary gap—between the equilibrium and the full employment levels of national production and income.

In making this link between equilibrium in the labour and product markets, Keynesians make an important assumption that the supply of labour is able to respond in aggregate to changes in the demand for labour induced by changes in aggregate product demand. In basic Keynesian models, therefore, any increase in aggregate demand in the economy is likely to lead to a fall in unemployment as long as there is a significant level of unemployed resources. Only when full employment is reached will further increases in demand lead to inflationary wage and price increases. This contrasts with the extreme classical model, where the supply of labour is regarded as independent of the demand so that increases in demand lead to wage and price increases rather than to reductions in unemployment. This difference is illustrated in Figures 11.5a and 11.5b.

One of the major consequences of this disagreement between Keynesians and classical economists and the modern revival of classical theory, often referred to as neo-classical economics, is that Keynesians believe deficiencies in aggregate product demand to be a major cause of unemployment. Since, for reasons explained in any good macroeconomics textbook, Keynesians do not believe that unregulated markets by themselves are capable of making good

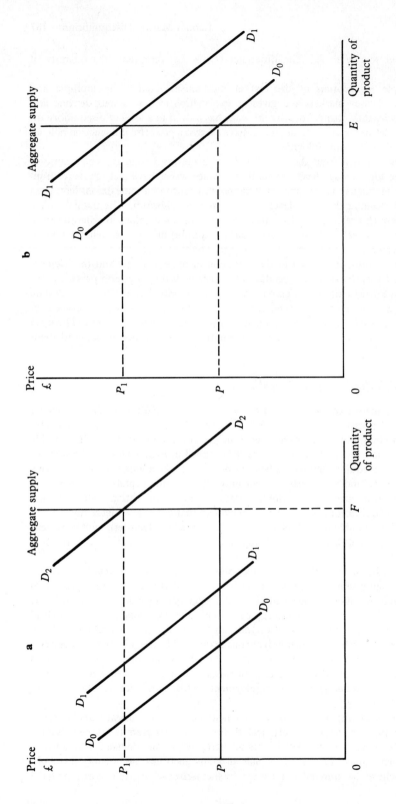

Figure 11.5 *The Keynesian view of unemployment*

Figure 11.5a *represents the extreme Keynesian view that aggregate supply responds immediately to an increase in aggregate demand (D_0 to D_1) and so increases employment at all levels of national product below the full employment level ($0F$). Further increases in demand (D_2) will raise price ($0P$ to $0P_1$). The extreme classical view of* **Figure 11.5b** *regards aggregate supply as fixed and independent of demand, so that demand rises produce immediate price rises with no change in employment.*

these deficiencies in aggregate demand, the only satisfactory solution is for the government to act as the stimulus to inject the necessary extra demand into the economy when the private sector forces of household consumption and business investment are insufficient on their own. Keynesians, therefore, believe that governments both can and should so manage demand that they maintain reasonably full employment in labour markets.

Because of the close association between the idea of demand deficiency as a major cause of unemployment and Keynesian analysis of the national economy, this is sometimes termed Keynesian unemployment. Neo-classical economists do not accept the assumptions underlying this analysis.

Further Causes of Unemployment

Although the dispute over demand deficiency is still very much alive, it is normal to identify a number of other, less controversial, types of unemployment.

Unemployables

Within every society there is a small proportion of the population who for medical and/or mental reasons are not able to pursue employment of any character, not even employment within special sheltered conditions. By the 1980s, however, many nations had made provisions for maintenance that avoided the need for such people to keep reporting that they were available for employment but unable to find work.

Seasonal Unemployment

It has long been recognised that certain groups of workers, such as those in construction and tourism, were able to gain regular employment, often with the same employer, at specific times in the year while being unemployed at other times. Some sectors of manufacturing are also subject to strong seasonal variations in product demand but, to avoid the costs of redundancy and re-hiring, they have sought to reorganise their production and marketing strategies.

Frictional Unemployment

This arises out of the normal wear and tear of working life. At any given time some workers will lose patience with employers or colleagues and leave their jobs. Some will be dismissed for personal reasons and some will just be bored and feel like changing. Most frictionally unemployed workers can expect re-employment in a few weeks, but in a period of high unemployment the average time is likely to be extended to increase the total number of short-term unemployed. This kind of unemployment cannot be eliminated but it can be partially reduced by improved communications and by strengthening agencies whose function it is to match jobs and job seekers.

Structural Unemployment

This originates from three main causes:

(a) *Shifts in product demand which cannot always be accommodated by the same employers.* In the 1950s and 1960s manufacturers of ladies' stockings were mostly able to switch to making tights, but men's tailors were less capable of moving from formal suits to blue jeans.

(b) *Changes in production method.* These enabled firms to make a greater quantity of product while employing far fewer workers. Computerised accounting systems displaced large numbers of office workers and automated production lines have eliminated the jobs of a great many factory machinists.

(c) *Changes in product following new technology developments.* There are many examples where electronic products have replaced older mechanical devices. These include electronic calculators (replacing adding machines and slide rules), electronic watches and weighing machines, and many more. All these changes have had major employment consequences for the older industrial nations, since many of the new products are made in the newly industrialised nations.

The effect of such structural changes is not only to reduce the number of workers needed by an industry at any given level of output but to de-skill many workers who had previously held privileged, respected, and well-paid positions in their firms. Relatively few are able to re-train and acquire new skills to regain or retain their old status. Most have either to come to terms with the fact that they are now unskilled or accept early retirement from the active workforce. Economists can argue that structural change, in the long run, tends to create rather more employment opportunities than it destroys. It opens up new and often more interesting occupations and offers new scope for business enterprise and human ingenuity. These gains, however, are made at a high price in terms of personal losses and tragedies for the people whose jobs have been destroyed and who find it difficult or impossible to find satisfactory employment in the new technological environment.

Regional Unemployment

Another consequence of structural change is that the new activities are frequently in different geographic areas to the old. The first industrial revolution shifted the main centres of economic activity (other than London) from the south of England to the North, the Midlands, central Scotland, and South Wales. The second industrial (electronic) revolution has tended to move activity back again to the southern half of Britain. Table 11.2 gives an indication of the large differences in regional unemployment in Britain in 1988. The pressures for locational mobility were explained in Chapter 10, which also noted the powerful social, psychological, and economic barriers to such mobility. If there are genuine economic benefits from increased labour mobility, society has to face the human challenges this presents.

Table 11.2   Percentage unemployment level for Britain by region

	1978	1982	1987
South East	3.6	7.7	7.5
South West	5.5	9.1	8.8
West Midlands	4.9	13.6	11.9
East Midlands	4.4	9.9	9.6
East Anglia	4.3	8.5	7.5
Yorkshire and Humberside	5.3	12.2	12.2
North	8.1	15.5	14.8
North East	6.5	13.6	13.4
Wales	6.9	3.8	13.0
Scotland	7.1	13.0	14.0

Source: Employment Gazette, various issues

Statistical Methods of Classifying Unemployment

It may seem cruel to try and classify those facing the intensely personal tragedy of unemployment. Their urgent problem is to try to return to the active workforce. Yet governments need to know causes, and the relative importance of different causes, if they are to have any hope of finding appropriate policy measures to solve the problem.

Work by Dow and Dicks-Mireaux (1958) indicated that an inverse relationship normally existed between recorded unemployment and vacancies notified to the public employment services. This relationship has provided a basis for subsequent methods of categorising unemployment. The U–V (Unemployment–Vacancy) methods assumed that the supply and demand for labour were in equilibrium when the numbers unemployed equalled the number of available vacancies. From that assumption, differing statistical models were developed for classifying unemployment. Leaving aside the unemployables and seasonally unemployed, three major forms of unemployment remained and each could be related to vacancies in the following fashion.

(a) If, in a local labour market, the number of vacancies equalled or exceeded the number of unemployed, then those without jobs should be able to gain employment after a time when information on vacancies became available to them. The majority of these unemployed people would be regarded as frictionally unemployed.
(b) If, in certain local labour markets, the number of unemployed exceeded the number of vacancies at a time when other local labour markets were in U–V equilibrium, then it was assumed that there was disequilibrium in the distribution pattern of labour demand and supply and that this was evidence of structural unemployment in parts of the economy.
(c) If the total number of unemployed exceeded total vacancies in the national economy, and if the imbalance was widely spread throughout the economy, it was considered that aggregate supply was greater than aggregate demand and that there was demand deficiency (Keynesian) unemployment.

For a time, statistical approaches of the kind used by Gleave and Palmer (1980) appeared to offer results useful for guiding the policy decisions of governments. Later it became clear that they failed to provide adequate information when there were levels of unemployment much higher than available vacancies.

A simple assumption, that unemployment equal to the total of vacancies was frictional and the excess due to demand deficiency, failed to take account of known structural change in a period when, for example, coal mining, steel making, and much heavy manufacturing was suffering severe decline in many parts of Western Europe.

The Revival of Classical Views of Unemployment

By the mid-1970s it was becoming evident that Keynesian demand management policies were failing to cope with increasingly severe inflation. At the same time, there was a growth of 'stagflation'—when inflation and unemployment rise together—a tendency difficult to explain from Keynesian models of the economy. Keynesian economics in general and Keynesian explanations of unemployment in particular came under severe attack, and there was a reversion to two nineteenth-century economic models which economists trained in the 1960s had assumed to have been destroyed by Keynes' arguments. On the one hand there was a revival and modernisation of classical ideas based on market equilibrium and the ability of unregulated labour markets to achieve a full-employment equilibrium; on the other there was renewed interest in Marxist explanations based on the view that large-scale unemployment was inevitable for the preservation of a capitalist economy. Because the classical revival became the foundation for much government policy in the 1980s this is examined first and in some detail.

The first problem faced by a neo-classical economist in the early 1980s was that, with an officially recorded figure of unemployed which at one stage was well over three million, labour markets were evidently not in a state of full-employment equilibrium. This problem was largely overcome by developing models based on voluntary and natural unemployment and on market failure caused by institutional forces.

The idea of natural unemployment was not new. It had been associated with the so-called Phillips (1958) 'relationship' between rates of wage–price rises and of unemployment, and was explained as the rate that remained when there was no demand deficiency in the national labour market, i.e. when total labour demand and supply in the economy as a whole were in equilibrium. According to Keynesian analysis, therefore, the natural rate of unemployment was the sum of frictional and structural unemployment. As explained in Chapter 16, Keynesians also recognised that this natural rate would rise in a period of high price inflation as workers sought to increase their incomes in anticipation of future price rises.

The neo-classical economists saw the evident disequilibrium in labour markets, including the persistence of high levels of job vacancies and rising wages in spite of high unemployment, as evidence of market failure. This failure was explained partly by the power of institutions and partly by worker attitudes fostered by the institutions and by the prevailing economic and social climate.

A simple model explaining this position is shown in Figure 11.6. This shows a normal

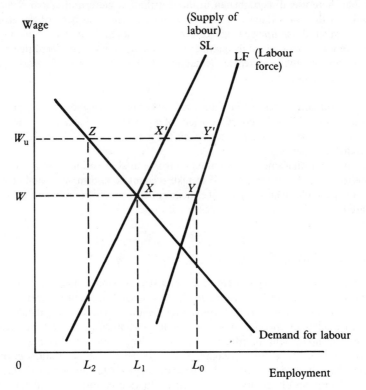

Figure 11.6 *The natural rate of unemployment*
The labour force curve (LF) represents the total of those in employment and registered as seeking work. The supply of labour (SL) curve represents those actually prepared to accept work at available wages. At wage W the difference $(Y - X)$ is the natural rate of unemployment $(L_0 - L_1)$ which is largely voluntary. This can be increased to $Y^1 - Z$ if workers support unions in increasing wages from $0W$ to $0W_u$. The gap between LF and SL is made possible by current market imperfections and social policies.

demand curve for labour but two supply curves. The one to the right (LF) represents the labour force, made up of all those in employment and those registered as seeking but unable to find work. In British labour statistics this is the workforce. The curve to the left is a different supply of labour curve (SL) made up of all those in work and prepared to accept work at prevailing wages. At wage W, where labour demand is in equilibrium with the actual supply of labour, the difference XY is the natural level of unemployment ($L_0 - L_1$).

This relatively high natural rate is also seen as voluntary because it arises from the ability of workers to risk frictional unemployment in the knowledge that their families, and to some extent themselves, will be protected by the safety net of State welfare and unemployment benefits, and also because structural unemployment is high owing to slow adaptation to the realities of structural, especially technological, change. Former skilled workers, encouraged by unions, anti-change social attitudes, and earnings-related unemployment pay, continue to look for work at their old level of earnings as skilled people and are slow to recognise that if their skills have been overtaken by technology they must re-train or accept unskilled status and earnings.

Unemployment, seen as 'voluntary' in this sense, is further increased if trade unions are powerful enough to push wages up higher, say to W_u. This further reduces the employment level, to L_2. The gap between the two curves at wage W_u, ($Y' - Z$), is also considered by classical economists as voluntary because workers are prepared to support unions in spite of the employment consequences of their actions.

The policy implications of this model for a government wishing to reduce unemployment and restore labour markets capable of achieving a full employment equilibrium are to reduce the power of trade unions, to reduce the level of unemployment and State welfare benefits, and to create more welcoming attitudes to technological change.

Another market imperfection is identified as large market monopolies, especially State monopolies (the nationalised industries), thought to be weak in their resistance to trade union wage claims because of the absence of commercial pressures to make profits. The policy of privatisation is thus also regarded as assisting the general return of more economically efficient labour markets. Notice that in this classical model of the labour market, demand deficiency unemployment, so important to Keynesian analysis, is considered to be non-existent or insignificant. Unemployment is almost entirely associated with market failure, and policies are designed to restore effective economic markets.

The Marxist View of Unemployment

This revival of another nineteenth-century view of the labour market is sociological in essence but also makes use of some basic economic concepts. The Marxist model sees the competitive, capitalist, market economy as encouraging technological change which requires additional capital. The constant addition of more and more capital leads to diminishing profit returns and to over-supply. This makes it harder for firms to survive and increases the pressure for survival through more advanced technology and capital investment.

It is argued that this competitive process leads to large-scale unemployment because some firms fail in the competitive race and others survive by replacing people with machines. The process also requires firms to accumulate capital while reducing the profitability of capital investment. Survival thus depends on squeezing profits from business activity through exploiting labour—paying subsistence wages and robbing workers of the fruits of their labour. Employers are able to do this because of the large numbers of unemployed who have to compete with each other to obtain jobs.

It is central to the Marxist model that the economic system in which capitalists are dominant can only survive as long as there is a large reserve force of labour, chiefly made up of unemployed. If unemployment falls, workers challenge the dominance of capital and are able to secure higher wages. Owners of capital still need profits and competition between wages and profits forces up prices and puts the whole financial structure of capitalism under strain. The capitalist class, faced with this danger, ensure a return to government policies designed to weaken labour through unemployment and restore the dominance of capital.

The capitalist system is thus incapable of achieving a full employment equilibrium at a socially acceptable living standard for workers. Revolutionary change is the only possible cure.

Keynesian policies of government demand management designed to avoid the two problems of unemployment and inflation had been seen as a convincing answer to the Marxist predictions of inevitable revolution. They also undermined the class conflict argument by showing that employers needed the high levels of consumer demand induced by high wages. In Keynesian economics, employers have nothing to gain by exploiting labour and paying low wages. It is, therefore, not surprising that the apparent collapse of Keynesian demand management economics and the return of classical economics, together with high unemployment and changes in labour laws, should revive interest in the Marxist model.

Questions for Discussion and Review

3 Discuss possible reasons for the lack of success in Britain in securing full employment without experiencing other economic problems, especially price inflation.

4 Discuss the case for suggesting that technological changes bring unemployment in the short term but greatly expanding employment in the long term. If this suggestion is believed to be true, does it mean that there is no need for a government to have a policy on unemployment?

Labour Shortages
The Neo-classical Model of Labour Shortages

A shortage of workers in certain occupations in spite of unemployment in other parts of the economy is commonly found in modern market economies. The term 'labour shortage' is used by economists to describe a number of different situations, but a shortage of labour can initially be explained through a neo-classical labour market model, illustrated in Figure 11.7. Here there is a single labour supply curve SS, and this is in equilibrium with labour demand (DD) at X. When the labour market is in equilibrium, the market wage is W_e and the quantity of labour supplied and demanded is L_e. Should the market wage be below the equilibrium level, at W_i, then the quantity of labour supplied would be L_s, which is less than the equilibrium quantity. At wage W_i the quantity of labour demanded rises above the equilibrium, to L_d, and the difference between demand and supply, ($L_d - L_s$), represents the shortage of labour in the market.

This model, explaining labour shortage in terms of excess demand over supply at the current wage level, is the most common static definition of a labour shortage. Recognising, however, that an economy is dynamic, i.e. changing, rather than static, this model is sometimes modified to the view that shortages are caused by the failure of labour supply to increase as rapidly as demand at wage levels that have prevailed in the recent and immediate past.

The analysis of consequences and remedies for labour shortages must distinguish between localised shortages, which in some cases could apply only to one company or to workers with specific skills, and a general shortage of labour in the economy as a whole.

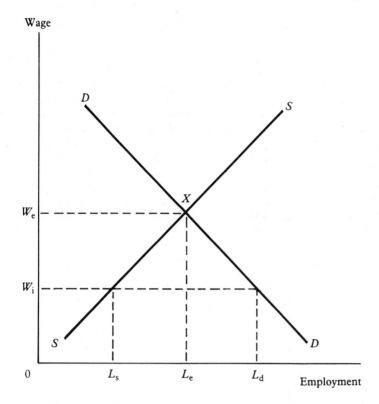

Figure 11.7 *The classical economic view of a labour shortage.*

Labour Shortages at National Level

A national shortage is, nevertheless, often associated with specific occupations, e.g. doctors or professional engineers. This arises because either demand is increasing more rapidly than supply or supply is declining more rapidly than demand. Each of these situations reflects a failure to make adequate investment in human capital in a previous period. Any national labour shortage of a skilled occupation occurs because an insufficient number of people have received the appropriate training and/or are prepared to work at the current pay rate.

If the shortage occurs in an occupation where demand is increasing more rapidly than supply, this lack of investment could reflect past failure to anticipate its future evolution or expansion. In the late 1970s, for example, few would seriously have forecast the growth in microcomputer ownership or the need for the associated software writers. Current wage levels for these writers have encouraged an increase in the numbers training and, in time, no doubt, this occupational labour shortage will disappear.

Economists associate this process with the concepts of economic rent and quasi-rent.

Economic Rent

This can be defined as the element in the earnings of a production factor that result from the operation of the factor market and which does not influence the decision of the factor's owner as to whether to enter or leave that market. In simple terms it can be defined as any excess of market or actual price over the factor's transfer earnings, where the transfer earnings are the next best earnings that could be obtained by the factor in another market. This concept is illustrated in Figure 11.8.

In this simple market model the market equilibrium price, where the demand for and supply of labour are equal, is W. The supply curve represents a range of workers, each of whom would be willing to enter this market at a particular wage. It is assumed that workers will only enter a given labour market when the wage offered is equal to or more than the next best available wage from a different market. Thus the worker L is prepared to enter the market at wage W_t. If the market wage dropped below W_t, worker L would leave because he or she could obtain W_t elsewhere. This is L's transfer earnings. However, because of the supply and demand conditions in this market, worker L actually receives the market wage W. However, the worker would be prepared to stay in the market at any wage down to W_t. The difference $(W - W_t)$ is therefore economic rent for L. There is economic rent in the earnings of most people who have stayed in the same job for some years and who have not invested in additional training. In Figure 11.8 only the worker(s) whose next best transfer earnings are equal to the market wage of W do not receive any economic rent.

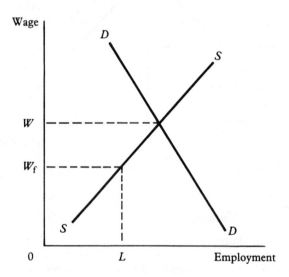

Figure 11.8 *Transfer earnings and economic rent*
Note: $0W_t$ = *L's transfer earnings*
W_tW = *L's economic rent*

Quasi-rent

This idea can be extended to the situation where there is a significant rise in labour demand which people have not anticipated and prepared for, as illustrated in Figure 11.9. Here there is a rise in the demand for labour from DD to D_1D_1. Because this rise in demand had not been foreseen and it takes time to gain the qualifications or skills needed by workers in this occupation, supply, in the short term, is completely inelastic. The supply curve is initially represented in Figure 11.9 by SS_a so that, following the demand rise, wages rise from W to W_0. All workers fortunate enough to be in that occupation enjoy economic rent of at least $W_0 - W$ and in many cases more. However, as others observe the incomes and Porsches enjoyed by these workers some, with the necessary ability or basic education, will acquire the additional

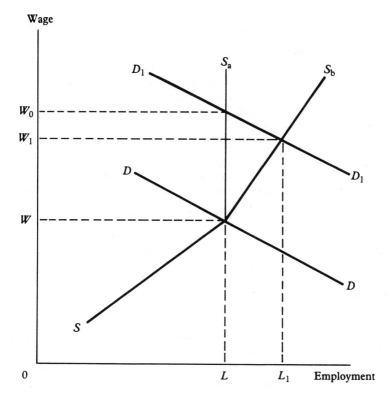

Figure 11.9 *Labour earnings and quasi-rent*
Note: SS$_a$ represents initial labour supply curve
SS$_b$ represents subsequent labour supply curve

skills or qualifications required. The supply curve, in the medium term, becomes less inelastic and moves, say, to SS_b with a consequent fall in the market wage to W_1. This process is likely to continue until wages in this market come into line with wages in other occupations requiring similar skills, qualifications, and investment in human capital. In this case the initially high economic rent falls as market supply adjusts to the new conditions of demand and is generally known as quasi-rent.

A shortage arising because labour supply is declining more rapidly than demand also reflects failure to invest in the relevant occupational training in a previous period, during which the market wage did not offer a sufficient return to stimulate sufficient human capital investment in training.

Remedies for National Labour Shortages

When there is a national labour shortage in an occupation there are short- and long-term solutions. An immediate remedy might be found in the encouragement of those with the relevant occupational skills to migrate. A longer-term solution can be found through an increase in human capital investment. Both require an increase in the relevant occupational market wage as implied in the model of Figure 11.7 so that this kind of labour shortage is sometimes referred to as a 'salary rise shortage'.

Salary-associated Labour Shortages

Controlled Price Shortages

Wilkinson and Mace (1973) have identified a special form of a national occupational labour shortage, termed a controlled price shortage. This arises when a national group of individual employers, e.g. local government agencies, apply an agreed level of wages below the general market level. These employers are likely to suffer a shortage while other employers recruiting staff with the same occupational skills do not.

Salary Rise Shortages

A labour shortage in an occupation occurring either within a specific local labour market or with a specific employer in a local labour market is likely to be a salary rise shortage. Resolution of this problem is unlikely to require an increase in the market wage level. Labour shortages in these circumstances will be overcome by the employer(s):

(a) offering increased wages which will also have to be offered to all employees in the shortage occupation; the marginal cost of recruiting new workers is thus higher than the wages they are paid,
(b) engaging in a more extensive search activity, possibly in other local labour markets, or
(c) lowering their previously applied hiring standards and simultaneously offering on-the-job training to develop the required skills.

Failure by an employer to take any action may well result in inability to attract suitable labour of the required standard even though the wider labour market has surplus supply.

Further Aspects of Labour Shortages

An occupational labour shortage is usually signalled by changes in relative wages as employers wishing to employ those with special occupational skills increase the level of wages they offer. However, other forms of signalling do exist, e.g. a lowering in the hiring standards generally applied to the occupation and/or an increase in the vacancy–unemployment ratio for the occupation. Individual firms may also react to a labour shortage by persuading those in the affected occupation to work overtime or increase the amount of overtime worked.

This section has considered labour shortages as evidence of labour demand exceeding supply at the market wage level. Thomas (1973), however, questioned whether this was the appropriate approach for many employers. He regarded labour demand as representing employers' desired employment levels as distinct from their short-term requirements, which were often subject to 'indivisibilities' in the form of fixed labour–plant ratios, as explained in Chapter 4. The firm's labour needs could also be governed by the requirements of planned output and targets.

The implication of the Thomas approach is that individual employers do not necessarily react immediately when demand exceeds supply for particular occupations. They are confident in their ability to retain their own labour. If, however, they start to lose their workers or if they are unable to recruit sufficient new employees, then they act to remedy the situation.

Questions for Discussion and Review

5 In the Autumn of 1988, when the official number of unemployed people in Britain totalled over 2 million, there were many reports in both national and local newspapers that firms in the South East and Midlands areas of England were being prevented from expanding by a shortage of skilled workers. Discuss possible reasons for such shortages in a period of high unemployment. Are there labour shortages of this kind in your area?

6 How far and by what means does the British (or your own national) Government seek to encourage training for young people? How successful do you think these efforts are in raising the level of labour skills?

Discrimination

Unlike unemployment and labour shortages, discrimination, although it results in a kind of disequilibrium, results less from defects in the labour market mechanism and communications systems than from conscious or unconscious prejudice on the part of employers directed against particular groups of workers.

Initial prejudice is generally biological in origin and concerned with gender, colour, or ethnic origin; it has economic consequences for both discriminators and those discriminated against.

Problems of Identifying Discrimination

It is not sufficient to show that there are differences in the average earnings of two groups of workers to prove that discrimination is being practised. It is, for example, widely recognised that the average earnings of females are below those of males. This difference, however, could arise from a number of reasons.

(a) Males might, on average, work longer hours than do females.
(b) Males might achieve higher levels of productivity than females.
(c) Males might, on average, achieve a greater degree of continuity of employment within industries, occupations, and firms.
(d) The two sexes might, in general, pursue different occupations, and occupational differences might originate in different sets of preferences for the physical characteristics of the work involved.
(e) Differing occupational preferences might owe more to educational and family influence than employer preference.

It could, of course, be observed that some of the above differences, if they exist, result from a wider degree of discrimination prevalent in society as a whole, for example, a tendency to condition females to acceptance of home-making roles so that careers are subordinated to the demands of the home and family, or to acceptance of positions subordinate to males in the business office, or towards literary and descriptive subjects in higher and further education as opposed to the male-dominated scientific and analytical subjects which, on average, tend to lead to the better-paid occuptions. Of course, it may not be entirely possible to separate employer prejudice from wider social discrimination. After all, business managers and employers are products of the same social conditioning as their employees.

Economists try to distinguish between what are called pure and statistical forms of discrimination. The former is said to arise when one set of labour market participants exhibits a prejudice against others. The latter arises primarily because of insufficient information within the labour market to permit the making of decisions free from distortion by conventional stereotyping.

Discrimination and Earnings

Labour market discrimination often results in earnings differences. These can arise from the kinds of jobs offered (pre-market discrimination) or checks to career development (post-market discrimination).

At one time railway companies in the USA would not admit black workers to the high-paying occupation of engineer but recruited them freely to the low-paying occupation of conductor. This was pre-entry discrimination. In the modern British education system the majority of teachers are female but the majority of school heads and holders of senior posts are male. This suggests post-entry discrimination.

Wages and earnings differences do provide an apparent indicator which is readily · measurable. Accordingly, wage difference is the main reference point for the major economic analysis undertaken by Becker (1957). He assumed that discrimination reflected the 'tastes' of employers and workers. Although Becker's work was based on observations of blacks in the USA, the principles established are applicable to other forms of discrimination. Becker's model assumes that employers have a dislike, or 'distaste', for certain participants within the labour market. Should they wish to discriminate against that group they are prepared to incur higher wage costs, and hence lower profit levels. A discriminating employer incurs the financial cost of discrimination when discriminated labour may be hired at a wage W_m but for the purposes of making the employment decision he/she regards the wage as being $W_m(1 + d)$. Here d represents the employer's discrimination coefficient, and is the price paid by the employer for the satisfaction of not employing the disliked groups. If equal marginal product is assumed to be available from employing either discriminated or 'normal' workers, then introducing the discrimination coefficient suggests a number of possible predictions:

where W_n = the wage paid to the 'normal' group of workers
W_m = the normal wage paid to the disliked group
$W_m(1 + d)$ = the wage the discriminating employer is prepared to pay to avoid employing the disliked group
d = the employer's discrimination coefficient

(a) When $W_n < W_m(1 + d)$, 'normal' labour is employed, the employer acting as though disliked labour has a greater monetary cost.
(b) When $W_n = W_m(1 + d)$, the employer is indifferent as to which labour group is employed, regarding both as having the same monetary cost.
(c) When $W_n > W_m(1 + d)$, disliked labour is employed, the monetary cost being more powerful than the employer's prejudice.

Becker's conceptual framework also suggests the further prediction that the greater the supply of discriminated participants in the labour market, the lower their wage will be in relation to the normal market wage. This is illustrated in Figure 11.10.

Should identical wages be offered to both 'normal' and discriminated workers, then $W_m/W_n = 1$.

When the wage offered to discriminated workers is below the wage offered to 'normal' workers, $W_m/W_n < 1$.

Unlike previous diagrams, the demand curve for discriminated workers in Figure 11.10 is based on their wage *relative* to that paid to normal workers.

When employers pay both groups an identical wage ($W_m/W_n = 1$), the demand for discriminated workers, relative to normal workers, is represented by a–b on the curve DD.

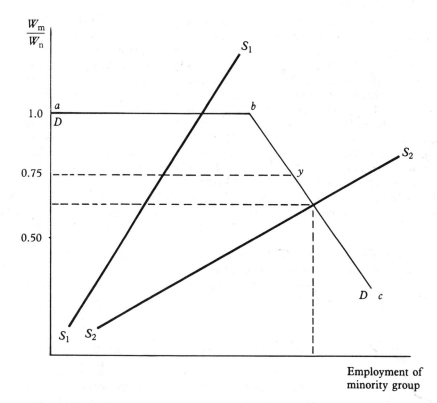

Figure 11.10 *Wage and employment differentials caused by employer prejudice*

Employers in this situation are indifferent to the type of worker employed. Employers discriminating against disliked workers offer employment only when the relative wage is below unity ($W_m/W_n < 1$). This causes the labour demand curve for these workers to be downward sloping (b–c on the curve DD). As the difference in the relative wage level increases, the possibility of employment by employers exercising discrimination becomes greater.

When the quantity of discriminated labour supplied is limited to curve S_1S_1, all such workers can obtain employment on equal terms with other workers in non-discriminating firms (section a–b on the demand curve DD). However, should the quantity of discriminated labour supplied be indicated by the curve S_2S_2, then the value of the relative wage for discriminated workers falls below unity to encourage the discriminating employers (section b–c on the demand curve DD) to offer employment. The relative wage differential between the different workforce groups is influenced not only by the strength of employer discrimination but also by the quantity of discriminated labour seeking work.

These predictions suggest that when $W_n > W_m(1 + d)$ or $W_n = W_m(1 + d)$, prejudiced employers, discriminating against a disliked group, face higher wage costs than are necessary. This, in turn, leads to potentially lower profits unless the higher cost of providing goods and services can be passed on to consumers. The US and British evidence sugests that it was the larger firms, operating in less competitive markets, which 'traditionally' employed white males. They appeared to exercise some discrimination against black people and/or women. These groups tended to be employed in relatively smaller firms operating in more competitive product markets.

If these assumptions are correct, then large employers could discriminate at little cost to themselves. They could pass on the costs of discrimination to their customers.

The framework of discrimination analysis so far examined assumes that it is employers and managers who are the originators of discrimination. It must be recognised, however, that some groups of workers also have a 'distaste' for other labour groups, and may be the prime movers in causing discrimination, sometimes in spite of public protests to the contrary from their trade union leaders. Interpreting this behaviour in the framework of the Becker model suggests that 'normal' employees, asked to work with people from the disliked group and offered the normal wage W_n, would value this as $W_n(1 - d)$. For such employees the value of d is their discrimination coefficient and represents the value of the lost satisfaction which the workers anticipate experiencing if required to work with a member or members of the disliked group. To compensate the prejudiced workers would necessitate paying a wage above the normal, i.e. with a value greater than W_n. This would be the normal wage plus the discrimination coefficient, $W_n + d$. Consequently, an employer who did not wish to discriminate against any section of the workforce would have to pay the higher wage ($W_n + d$) to all employees to retain the prejudiced workers.

If the Becker model implications are correct, an employer unwilling to accept these higher wage costs would lose prejudiced workers and would have to replace these by recruits from the discriminated group. Unless social attitudes changed the non-discriminating employer could eventually find that only disliked-group members were being employed in the working areas affected.

Economic Implications of Labour Market Discrimination

This analysis suggests that the economic consequences of discrimination include higher labour costs paid by employers, higher product prices because employers tend to be less willing to resist these increased costs where they believe they can be passed on to product buyers, and the creation of a further set of wage differentials. There is the further opportunity cost of the lost benefits where workers are employed below the levels of their personal skills and abilities. Many observers comment on the scarcity of people with the abilities needed to manage large enterprises at the most senior levels. Other observers point to the relatively small number of women in the most senior posts in large companies and in the public sector. If we accept that abilities of all kinds are likely to be fairly evenly distributed between both sexes, the implications are clear. Women capable of running large organisations are not obtaining opportunities to do so because of labour market discrimination or wider, social discrimination that prevents them from obtaining the necessary education, training, or qualifications. Similar observations could be directed towards other areas of skill shortage and other groups suffering discrimination.

It is not clear whether there are any economic causes for discrimination. Lianos (1976) investigated its origins and concluded that it arose from a set of preconceived social attitudes. There is, of course, ample evidence that the socialisation agencies of family, school, and neighbourhood groups tend to reinforce traditional attitudes towards female roles in what many regard as essentially a patriarchal society. There is equally strong reinforcement, in some sections of society, for hostility towards some immigrants. The causes of these attitudes are far too complex for analysis using simple economic or even sociological models, but economists concerned at the economic costs of discrimination and wishing to indicate possible remedies cannot ignore causes. These, in common with many other contemporary social attitudes, may have origins in much earlier economic conditions. To give a very simple example of this, the dominance of Jewish families in some sections of banking and finance may have its ultimate origins in the hostility to trading in money shown by the mediaeval Christian Church. A greater awareness of the roots of discrimination may help to show its irrelevance to, and the costs of its survival in, modern economies.

Discrimination and Fragmented Labour Markets

Discrimination is difficult to measure and analyse in economic terms, partly because of the fragmented nature of labour markets. Each segmented market demands its own set of qualities from entrants. It becomes easy, therefore, for those who control entry to these markets to require entrants to have certain qualities which are only acquired by people from a favoured group. All outsiders, not just members of the discriminated groups, are thus excluded.

Examining labour markets of a century ago, Cairnes (1974) showed the importance of non-competing groups. These were identified not only by gender but also by family background and education. Pre-entry discrimination on the grounds of social and educational background was, and probably still is, widely practised. Discrimination is also reinforced when individuals appear to confirm the attitudes on which discrimination itself is based or rationalised. When a female management trainee gives up her job because her husband is promoted and moved to a different area or because she wishes to form a family, she may unwittingly reinforce the belief of a senior manager that women are not suitable for preparation for or promotion to higher management. Male domination of senior management can thus continue without any sense of social guilt or economic loss.

For this kind of reason, education and vocational training for the discriminated groups may concentrate on preparation for secondary markets rather than on the more highly rewarded primary markets. Some school 'business studies' courses appear mainly to prepare girls for work as keyboard operators on computers and word processors with little or no scope for entering business management. Other groups of boys may be studying mathematics, physics, economics, and the more analytical subjects, with little immediate vocational content, but more likely to lead to well-paid, primary occupations. This deep-rooted social difference is likely to encourage a continuation of the 'statistical discrimination' measured purely by differences in average earnings of males and females.

Discrimination may also be reinforced by demand-side features of fragmented markets which, like the workers, are far from homogeneous. This, of course, is not just a modern feature. Different jobs have always demanded different qualities, but older occupations usually had easily recognisable physical requirements, such as the physical strength of a blacksmith or the delicate manual dexterity of a cotton spinner. Different qualities are still required in modern, technologically advanced economies, but these are often linked to personality and are less immediately visible. If employers find that people with a particular social and geographical background are more likely to have the personal characteristics they require, and consequently offer a higher level of productivity, then they will tend to recruit from these groups and others will be excluded.

An increasing number of primary occupations now have a pre-entry requirement of educational qualification gained from a prolonged period of formal education. Inability or unwillingness to undergo this education may condemn individuals and groups to the relatively low-paid occupations, often in secondary markets. On the other hand, fee-paying schools, whose survival depends on their ability to convince parents that a substantial financial investment will bring an appropriate, future income return are more alive to the changing demands of the better-paid sections of the labour market and more ready to adapt their courses and teaching methods accordingly. By the 1980s such schools were producing pupils with the educational qualifications and personal qualities likely to lead to successful managerial careers in the major multinational companies. Their success tends to reinforce the belief that social discrimination exists in modern labour markets.

Clearly, labour market discrimination goes much deeper than the personal prejudices of contemporary employers and worker groups.

The persistence of statistical wage discrimination in spite of legislation aimed at eliminating it suggests that such laws have only limited effect. Nevertheless, statutes such as the Equal Pay Acts, 1970 and 1983, Sex Discrimination Act 1975, and Race Relations Act 1976 do help to change social attitudes and market behaviour, as well as indicating changes in attitude among social and political leaders and the opinion formers within the economy.

Questions for Discussion and Review

7 Which courses in your own school or college could be identified as being mainly followed by females? Discuss the pressures and influences leading to this situation.

8 What is meant by 'positive discrimination'? Discuss the case for introducing a measure of such discrimination in favour of one group of people you believe to be discriminated against in contemporary labour markets.

Suggestions for Written Assignments

1 Summarise the current law in Britain relating to the employment of either women or ethnic minorities. Why have such laws been considered necessary and desirable? How do you explain continued evidence of apparent discrimination in spite of these laws?

2 Even in periods of high unemployment firms operating in Britain have complained of shortages of skilled workers, young workers and of all workers in certain regions.
   (a) Explain possible reasons for these shortages.
   (b) Describe any measures being taken to overcome these problems.
   (c) Discuss the likely success of these measures.

3 Write a report, supported by data available to you, on the current state of unemployment in Britain or your own country. In your report you should pay attention to the following:
   (a) The proportion of long-term unemployed (out of work for one year or more).
   (b) The industries most affected by unemployment.
   (c) The age groups most affected by unemployment.
   (d) Your assessment of the reliability of the available data.
   (e) Your brief explanation of the findings under a–c above.

4 With the help of appropriate macroeconomics textbooks, define and explain the concept of 'demand deficiency' unemployment and the reasons why neo-classical economists largely rejected this concept. What evidence is there, in current unemployment in Britain or your own country, for the existence of demand deficiency as a cause of unemployment?

Suggestions for Further Reading

The increase in unemployment levels from about 1977 to 1987 has led to a parallel increase in the output of commentators and economists on the topic. A visit to any reference library will provide the opportunity to choose from a wide range of texts which examine and/or analyse unemployment from the viewpoint of the economist, the social scientist, and the politician. A useful starting point is the relatively modest-sized, but comprehensive, book by Hawkins (1987).

The eight essays which cover various economic questions concerning unemployment in the book edited by Creedy (1981) provide a sound basis for extending your understanding, as does the work of Greenhalgh et al. (1983).

The rise in unemployment levels has not been unique to Britain, and Hughes and Perlman (1984) provide a comparative analysis of the experiences of Britain and the USA. A significant feature of contemporary unemployment has been the impact it has had on females, and this is examined, within the European context, by Paukert (1984).

Questions relating to labour shortages, both in the general economic sense and in specific occupations, are discussed by Thomas and Deaton (1977). This book offers not only a set of theoretical explanations but also uses these to analyse three different occupations. A rather less analytical but, in practical terms, comprehensive examination of labour shortages is to be found in Hunter (1978).

The available academic literature on the nature and consequences of labour market discrimination is extensive. A comprehensive survey of that literature has been provided by Sloane (1985).

Discrimination, on the basis of sex, was the subject of articles by Chiplin and Sloane (1974) and by O'Donnell (1984). The view that discrimination on social grounds was largely the consequence of segmented labour markets has been discussed by Flanagan (1973).

12
The Firm in the Labour Market

The Firm's Demand for Labour

The basic principles of market behaviour discussed in previous chapters provide an analytical framework within which the strategies and behaviour of individual employers can also be analysed.

Influences on the Firm's Demand for Labour

It is fundamental to neo-classical economics to regard the demand for any production factor as derived from the demand for the product. At the individual firm level this means that the basic influence on the demand for labour is the demand for the product of the firm. The firm seeks to produce its product at the level which enables it to meet demand at its desired price—or the price determined by the product market as a whole. If demand changes, the firm must adjust its planned output, or the product price, or both, and this will have implications for the desired level of employment. In the long run, the firm cannot under- or over-produce without inducing market difficulties that will have repercussions in future periods.

However, it is not always possible to establish a direct, functional relationship between product demand and the demand for labour without making assumptions concerning the production method. If the production method remains unchanged then such a functional relationship will exist, but a significant output change frequently leads to the firm making a change in the production method (for example, purchasing more advanced machines). It is conceivable then that, under certain circumstances, an increase in output could lead to a reduction in the demand for labour. It could certainly lead to a demand for a different kind of labour. Another possibility is that the firm could make more intensive use of machines—for example, by introducing another shift. Only when there is a fixed capital:labour ratio dictated by the nature of the equipment used and when there is no choice of equipment or possibility of varying the intensity of use of equipment can we be sure of predicting the effect of a rise in demand on the firm's labour requirements. The effect of a fall in demand is even less predictable, especially in the short run. If the firm believes that the reduction will be reversed in the future or be replaced by alternative products, it may decide to retain its existing labour, to avoid redundancy and re-hiring costs, to maintain the goodwill of its workers, or to prevent valued employees moving to competitors.

Achieving a Desired Employment Level

These production uncertainties do not apply to the individual firm at a given time because the production decisions which determined the output level, the kind of equipment to be used, and the labour required to use it will have been taken previously. Indeed, until they are taken the firm cannot determine its future labour needs with any certainty. Assuming they have been made, the firm is then able to determine its needs for various kinds of labour. If its current labour force does not match these needs in size and structure, then the firm has a demand for labour. Such a situation is illustrated in Figure 12.1.

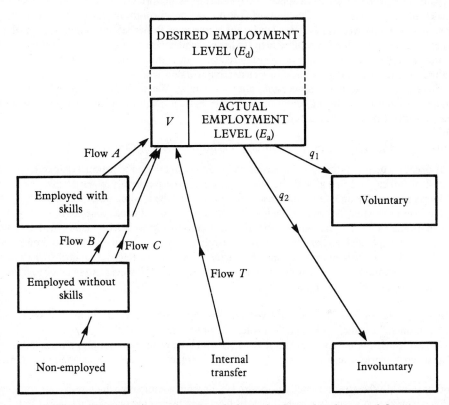

Figure 12.1 *Employment stock and alternative inward and outward flows*

Here the labour force requirement is shown as the desired employment level E_d. The firm's existing labour force and its skill structure is shown as its actual employment, E_a. Because actual employment is below the desired level ($E_a < E_d$) there are vacancies (V) for additional workers with certain required skills. Thus:

$$V = E_d - E_a$$

In this situation the firm will endeavour to recruit a suitable labour force to fill the existing vacancies while retaining the existing labour force.

The existing labour force can be regarded as a stock of labour, but any movement of workers into or out of this stock is a flow. The size of the firm's labour force stock is subject to the following flows:

(a) An inward flow of new employees to the firm arising from the various sources indicated in Figure 12.1. These are flows of:
   A, people with the required skilled currently employed by other firms,

      B, people currently employed elsewhere without the required skills but thought capable of achieving them with training, and

      C, people not currently in employment and perhaps not yet in the labour market.

(b) A flow outward from the firm consisting of existing employees.

In trying to fill its vacancies and achieve its desired employment stock, the firm can be expected to make the best possible use of the inward flow but restrict the outward flow. The importance of retaining existing workers is indicated by the findings of Roper (1988). These suggest that 80% of all labour recruited is a replacement for people who have left their existing employment.

If the employed labour stock is of the required size but is not of the required skill structure then the firm has the further option of transferring workers who are surplus to requirements elsewhere to fill the vacancies, if necessary after re-training. Where this is not possible, the firm then becomes subject to the influences of the labour market(s) within which it is operating, and these may affect its own labour policies.

Short-term Remedies for Temporary Labour Shortages

Firms operate under conditions of uncertainty, especially in relation to product demand. Given the cost of 'hiring and firing' and the legal protection now frequently given to job security, employers are usually unwilling to increase the size of the labour force until they are sure that any increase in product demand is likely to be sustained. One possible short-term strategy to meet an increased need for labour of uncertain duration is to ask the workers concerned to work overtime. As explained earlier, this normally involves payment of premium overtime rates though, in Britain, this extra cost may be partly mitigated by relative savings in national insurance contributions as compared with hiring new workers. However, a policy of overtime working can have other effects, including:

(a) An increase in the number of workers leaving (often termed 'quits') if overtime requirements conflict with their work–leisure preferences.

(b) A need to require overtime for some workers who are not in short supply, a need that can arise when work groups are made up of teams of people with differing occupational skills.

Another possible short-term remedy is to hire labour from a company which rents out suitably qualified workers on a contract basis. 'Temps' have long been a feature of office work, but the extension of this practice to a much wider range of occupational skills is a development that, in Britain, belongs mainly to the 1980s. This fairly new feature of labour markets may be seen as an important way in which employers seek to resolve the dilemma of increasingly competitive and uncertain product markets combined with labour markets where social attitudes, supported by legislation, have tended to strengthen security of employment. For workers this trend means that many people who might formerly have expected ready and stable employment in primary markets now have to resort to secondary markets, at least for a time pending the securing of a more stable job. On the other hand, some workers may prefer the greater flexibility of agency or contract work and be prepared to pay a price in lost security to gain this flexibility.

Questions for Discussion and Review

1 In 1988 British Airways was successfully privatised as an efficient and profitable company. Ten years earlier it had been suffering large losses and there had been reports of low labour morale. Observers attributed the transformation to *flexibility* in both capital, e.g. by leasing instead of buying aircraft, and labour, e.g. by having reserve, trained cabin crews who could be called on as required. Explain the need for flexibility in the case of a major airline and show how it can contribute towards achieving increased efficiency and profits. Suggest possible problems that a policy of flexibility might bring to the company's suppliers, shareholders and employees.

2 Discuss the circumstances under which a worker may prefer part-time to full-time work.

Worker Recruitment
Aspects of Selection

When an employer decides to recruit from outside the firm it usually has to select the individuals required from a greater number of applicants. The information the employer really needs to make a fully rational choice can only be gained after a period of employment. Selection, therefore, normally has to be made in the light of incomplete and uncertain information. Observers, such as Spence (1973), have regarded this decision as an investment made under conditions of uncertainty. Naturally, managers in charge of recruitment seek to reduce this uncertainty as much as possible; especially uncertainty surrounding a worker's potential productivity.

Spence regarded various applicant characteristics such as age, sex, and educational attainment as signals relating to potential productivity. Each signal would be taken as an indication of high or low productivity potential and employment decisions would be made in the light of their total effect. If this is a correct analysis, and assuming that workers as a group learn from experience gained from labour markets, then people can increase their potential benefits from employment by investing in those signals, such as education, which they can influence.

Employers have a choice as to which of the inward flows of new workers they wish to attract. Each supplies a different kind of labour, and subject to current labour market conditions it can be assumed that employers will prefer the flow which appears to offer the greatest productivity benefit in relation to recruitment cost. It is therefore helpful to examine the characteristics of each of the three potential inward flows identified in Figure 12.1.

Question for Discussion and Review

3 Discuss the view that the interests of employer and employee must always be different because the employer is always looking for the greatest potential productivity at the lowest possible cost while the worker is always looking for the greatest possible payment for the least possible sacrifice of time and effort.

Recruitment of Trained Workers from Other Firms
Advantages of Recruiting Trained Workers

This is Flow *A* in Figure 12.1. Each recruit from this source is also a quit from another employer and is an example of inter-firm mobility already discussed. The process may also involve geographical and/or industrial mobility.

The main advantage of this type of recruit to the employer is the low cost of training, which can often be reduced to a brief period of induction to the new firm. Careful selection on the basis of predetermined signals can reduce the chance of recruiting workers that other employers are happy to lose because of their unsatisfactory personal qualities. In a US study, Lazear (1986) concluded that employer 'raids' were selective and that the best workers were the ones most likely to receive outside offers. Employers who decide to encourage recruits from this flow can employ a number of different strategies.

Recruitment Strategies for Trained Workers

Pay Inducements

An obvious attraction is payment of higher wages than those of other firms which employ workers with the desired qualifications. On the other hand, there is evidence to suggest that wage is not the only consideration affecting inter-firm mobility. Workers, it was suggested in Chapter 10, also value job security and look for long-term employment prospects.

Other problems can also arise from a high-wage inducement strategy. The high wage must also be given to workers of the same category, already employed. Not to do so involves a high risk that they will become dissatisfied and quit, thus creating further vacancies. Thus high wages involve either an increase in the marginal cost of employing new workers or raises the rate of labour turnover. A further result may be to reduce the productivity of existing workers. This can result if these workers have a particular target income which can be reached with less work following a wage rise. (If you are unsure of the wage–leisure preference analysis which is often used to support this conclusion, you should re-read Chapter 6.) It must be borne in mind that workers can vary their work input by changing their attitudes to overtime work or by absenteeism, even where pay is not directly related to quantity of production.

Improvements in Fringe Benefits

Most firms are now subject to statutory obligations to provide certain benefits such as sick, holiday, and retirement payments. Legislation normally provides for minimum standards, although these can be exceeded by firms if they perceive benefits in so doing. Tendencies in recent years have moved away from older, collective benefits such as canteens and sports and social facilities in favour of individual 'insurance' type benefits such as the sickness and retirement schemes already mentioned. It is debatable how far these influence workers to change employers, but they are likely to encourage some workers to stay with their present employer as benefit levels tend to rise with length of service.

Increase in Search Activity

Instead of increasing payments and benefits to workers, a firm may decide to spend more in trying to find suitable employees and/or to obtain better value from its search expenditure. Firms may seek improvements by:

(a) changing and/or extending the information networks used, e.g. by moving from or supplementing existing informal networks with more formal approaches such as advertising in local or trade press or by trying a number of different methods, and/or
(b) extending the search activity to other labour markets, such as other geographical areas, or by looking for people with suitable skills or background in other industries or occupations.

In a study of recruitment methods in Britain, Roper (1988) found that the choice of search activity significantly affected the time needed to fill vacancies. Some produced speedier results than others. Further reductions in the time needed to fill vacancies could also be achieved by using more than one form of search. Increasing or changing the current search methods could, therefore, be an effective way to increase the supply of new workers requiring the minimum of additional training.

Reducing Hiring Standards

Firms frequently specify a number of conditions to be met by applicants for skilled vacancies. For example, a degree may be requested in addition to a professional qualification, or a skilled manual worker may be required to have completed an 'approved' apprenticeship which may be a code for training by one of the leading firms in the industry. Advertisements frequently specify a minimum number of years' experience and are sometimes combined with age expectations that severely limit the number of potential applicants. Research by Reder (1969) suggested that there was a close association between hiring standards and time taken to fill vacancies; hence a change in hiring standards might enable a firm to increase the inward flow of trained workers. There is a danger that reducing hiring standards may reduce the level of productivity of the labour force, but this may not always apply since some of the pre-entry conditions may have been designed more to reduce selection costs than to produce high-quality candidates, while others may have been due chiefly to the social and educational prejudices of personnel officers and have little foundation in genuine candidate quality.

There is research evidence that employers tend to favour modification of search and hiring strategies rather than raise wage levels when faced with a supply shortage. Manwaring (1984) found a preference for varying recruitment methods, whereas Mace and Wilkinson (1977) found a preference for modifying hiring standards. This is not really surprising. If firms believe that the shortage is likely to be short-term they can revert to earlier practices, but any increase in wages will be permanent and could lead to a damaging 'wage war' with other employers in the locality or industry. Such attitudes in the labour market might be seen to be similar to attitudes to demand falls in product markets, where firms are more likely to respond initially by changing marketing methods than by reducing price.

Head Hunting

An interesting development which took place in the 1970s and 1980s has been the growth of what has become known as 'head hunting'. This describes the process where a firm seeks to recruit a senior manager by asking a specialist agency, usually closely linked with or having its origins in management consultancy, to locate and approach a suitable applicant and persuade that person to move to the hiring firm. The person located by the head hunter is often in a position similar to the vacancy and in most cases is likely to be employed by one of the hiring firm's competitors. Specialist head hunters will make it their business to know the successful managers in a range of occupations and be ready to fit names to vacancies as they arise. The hiring firm prefers to use a specialist agency to avoid the charge of direct poaching from competitors and to keep recruitment discreet. They may not want competitors to see an open advertisement which discloses a weakness in a key area of management.

Questions for Discussion and Review

4 Discuss the view that an employer who has paid for an employee's training and then finds that this employee is being recruited by a business competitor should be able to recover the training cost from either the employee or the competitor.

5 How can it be argued that an increase in wages is likely to reduce the value of work performed by a group of workers? Support your answer with leisure–income preference analysis.

Recruitment of Employed People without the Skills Required

Implications of Adopting this Approach

Workers in this group were identified as belonging to Flow B at the beginning of this chapter. Unlike those discussed in the previous section, these people are prepared to be occupationally mobile as well as possibly being mobile in the other senses identified in Chapter 10.

An employer's decision to recruit workers in this group represents a change in:

(a) search methods, in that the firm may be moving from informal to formal methods in order to widen the area of search and increase the number of applicants, and

(b) hiring standards, since by definition this group cannot have pre-recruitment experience of exercising the skills required nor, of course, the skill qualifications expected from the previous group.

Training and its Costs

Before recruits from this group can become productive to the standards required, training is necessary. It is assumed that recruits will have the necessary prerequisites of general education and, of course, some work experience. Training, as already indicated, is a form of investment in which a present cost is incurred in anticipation of future benefits. Except in the relatively few cases where financial assistance is available from outside (usually from government-sponsored training agencies), this cost may be borne by the employer, the employee, or a mixture of both. Since the firm is actively recruiting workers with a training need, it may be assumed that it will bear all or the greater part of the cost, though it may ask for a contribution from the recruit as evidence of determination to acquire the new skill within a reasonable period. The training cost contains a number of elements, not all of which are immediately obvious.

(a) *Production loss.* If an untrained person replaces a trained employee, there is likely to be an immediate loss of production. This loss will be made good after the successful completion of training, but lost production is unlikely to be recoverable. It can, however, be minimised by making productive use of any spare capacity available in the form of underemployed existing workers. If there is no spare capacity among existing skilled workers, these may be asked to work longer hours—at a cost to the employer. It is generally thought that on-the-job training will reduce the potential loss in production because the new employee should start to make a growing contribution to production as his or her training and experience develops. However, off-the-job training might reduce the total training time and for some skill or professional qualification may be a requirement of the training authority.

(b) *Diversion of existing resources.* Training of any kind is likely to require some input of managerial, supervisory, or other skilled workers' time with an opportunity cost of lost production from these employees.

(c) *Trainees' wages.* Because the trainee is gaining additional human capital investment which will improve his or her future marketability and income-earning potential, it would be logical to require him or her to work without pay and even to pay for the training. This, however, would be unrealistic. If workers are to be induced to leave their current jobs they will have to be paid a wage that seems reasonable or attractive to them. Employers are more likely to pay reduced wages during the period of training, perhaps increasing the pay on successful completion of definite stages of training. Employers will usually wish to hold out the prospect of significant pay rises on successful completion of training to induce workers to keep the training period as short as possible. Both employer and employee are likely to be aware that the employee may leave soon after completing training, in which case the employer's investment has not brought a profitable return. This is an investment risk which the employer will seek to reduce by good worker management. It cannot, however, be eliminated, and employers have frequently sought to offer only firm-specific training to recruits from other firms to try and limit their marketability. Consequently, where governments of industrial nations have sought to increase occupational mobility they have tended to recognise that this can only be achieved if a substantial part of the training cost is borne by the taxpayers and not by individual employers.

Observation of business practice suggests that the content of the training offered is likely to influence the apportionment of training costs between employers and employees.

Where the training is mainly firm-specific so that the trainee gains relatively little increase in his or her value to other firms, the training wage is likely to be relatively high. On the other hand, the post-training wage will be at a level which enables the employer to gain a return on the investment.

Where the training is mainly not firm-specific, so that the trainee is increasing his or her personal human capital of value to other firms and so increasing personal marketability, then the employer is likely to pay a training wage relatively lower than the previous case and trainees are also likely to be asked to share some of the training costs. On the other hand, the post-training wage is at a higher level, both as an inducement for the employee to stay with the employer and to permit the employee to gain a return on personal investment.

Question for Discussion and Review

6 Discuss the considerations likely to influence an employer who is unable to recruit a person with a required skill and who may be wondering whether to either train an existing employee and replace him/her from the outside market or recruit from another firm a person with the capability of being trained to the skill standard required.

Recruitment of People not Currently Employed

General Features of this Flow

This represents the group identified as Flow *C* at the beginning of the chapter. By definition, recruitment of workers in this group cannot involve inter-firm mobility but may involve geographical, industrial, or occupational mobility. This flow can arise from three possible sources: new entrants to the workforce, those returning to the workforce after a period of voluntary absence, and those who are involuntarily unemployed. These all represent distinct groups with different characteristics and, therefore, requiring different recruitment strategies.

New Entrants to the Labour Market

Most of this group enter the labour market after recently completing their full-time education, and individuals are distinguished chiefly by their age and the educational level achieved. In spite of the growing tendency for the final years of full-time education to contain an element of work experience, relatively few can be expected to be of productive value to an employer, who must thus undertake substantial general and firm-specific training. Consequently, employing these recruits in anything but totally routine and unskilled work represents a long-term commitment by a firm towards developing a future labour force.

As discussed in Chapter 7 in relation to apprentice training, firms may seek to pass some of the training costs to the trainee, although there has been a growing tendency in the industrial nations for government agencies to contribute to training costs, which are thus paid by the community as a whole through taxation.

As an immediate means of filling an employment vacancy this is not the most appropriate source for most firms. Recruiting school and college leavers involves a high cost and a high risk of receiving an unprofitable investment return.

On the other hand, a newcomer to the workforce offers the employer the chance to mould that person's attitudes to work to fit the requirements of the firm and to ensure that further training is industry- and often firm-specific, thus reducing the chance of losing the employee after training.

When there is no shortage of recruits from the other flows, employers may limit recruitment to those whose educational attainments or efforts to acquire 'work experience' suggest that they possess above-average productivity potential.

However, when, as in 1988, unemployment and the numbers of young people in the population start to fall, this flow begins to look more attractive. In that year employers were being warned that the number of school leavers could be expected to fall by about 25%. Firms wishing to attract recruits from this dwindling pool would need to adopt one or more of the following strategies:

(a) Market its employment opportunities actively in the schools and colleges likely to offer recruits of the standard required.
(b) Reduce the height of the educational hurdle over which recruits were required to jump before being considered for employment.
(c) Offer professional training or financial inducements for training in an effort to divert some school or college leavers from possible higher or more advanced education.
(d) Increase the starting pay of its younger trainees.

During 1988 there were several press reports of firms adopting one or more of these measures. The main banks, for example, were reported to be increasing the pay of young recruits, and other financial and engineering sector firms were also reported to be active in recruiting school leavers.

People Returning to the Labour Market after Voluntary Absence

In addition to females returning after a period of looking after a family, this group may include some of those who took early retirement in the depressed years of the 1980s or who wished to leave the pressures of full-time careers as they got older. Many members of this group may seek part-time employment, at least initially. Few are geographically mobile, but many show a considerable amount of flexibility in the work they are able and prepared to do and in hours of work.

In sectors other than office clerical work, the growth of this segment of the labour market is a recent but significant development. Formal channels of recruitment are not as developed as in other parts of the market so that both employers and workers are heavily dependent on informal search and recruitment, with many firms poorly prepared for making the most productive use of this source of labour.

Returnees to the workforce often require training, and some seek occupational changes. On the other hand, they can also contribute considerable general experience both of work and life and can help to stabilise the social structure of the work place.

This is another source of labour which becomes more important as other flows decline. To tap this source an employer may need to:

(a) Make working conditions more attractive to women, for example, by making arrangements for child care or by adapting or being flexible over working hours.
(b) Ensure that part-time workers are still able to qualify for promotion within the firm, perhaps creating senior part-time posts where this is feasible.
(c) Take a more flexible attitude to recruitment standards, being prepared to set aptitude or other tests for recruits who did not have the same educational opportunities as their younger colleagues.
(d) Assist with home removal or travel costs and arrangements where this is likely to extend the geographical area of recruitment.

Recruiting the Involuntary Unemployed

Like most labour groups, this is very far from being homogeneous. The general term 'unemployed' covers a wide range of people from the highly skilled and qualified who are frictionally unemployed for a short period to the almost totally unqualified who have been unemployed for long periods and may never have experienced any prolonged period of stable work.

The frictionally unemployed present no special problems and firms may prefer to recruit someone who has already left previous employment than risk any accusation of 'staff poaching' from fellow local employers. Their main concern is likely to be to ensure that such an employee does not have characteristics that could upset the social structure of the current labour force.

When people have been unemployed for some weeks or months there is a danger that they lose the habit and discipline of work. Employers are likely to look with more favour on those who have kept themselves occupied in a constructive way, e.g. by taking advantage of any re-training or further education that may be available, by doing voluntary or part-time work or work at a lower skill level.

The problem with the really long-term unemployed is that they are for the most part the people for whom there are the least vacancies. This is illustrated in Table 12.1. This group is composed chiefly of the young with no educational qualifications or vocational skills and the old with similar lack of education and skill or with skills that have been rendered unmarketable by technological development (and sometimes with attitudes that are difficult to reconcile with modern conditions).

Because of these problems and the expense of overcoming them, employers tend to recruit from this source only when other sources fail—unless they are offered financial assistance or inducements from a government wishing to help the long-term unemployed for social, ethical, or political reasons.

Questions for Discussion and Review

7 In 1988 press reports indicated that some firms in South East England were '. . . increasing the recruitment of part-time women staff; reducing recruitment standards; introducing their own tests to replace educational qualifications; recruiting in all parts of the country; and encouraging women to return after raising a family. . .'
Discuss the reasons for these actions and additional measures that you think these firms would need to take in order to attract the desired new recruits.

8 Examine the job vacancies section of your local newspaper over several weeks. Which of the flows identified in this chapter appear to be of main importance on

Table 12.1 Percentage rates of unemployment [by (a) selected occupations and (b) qualifications] for those aged 16 years and over for 1986

Selected occupations	Male	Female	Total
Managerial and professional	3.2	3.9	3.5
Clerical and related	5.8	5.0	5.2
Craft and similar	7.8	9.2	7.9
General labourers	21.3	17.8	21.0
All occupations	11.1	9.9	10.6

Qualifications	Male	Female	Total
No qualifications	17.3	11.2	14.5
GCE 'O' level or equivalent (16-year-old school leaving examination)	10.5	9.8	10.1
GCE 'A' level or equivalent (18-year-old school leaving examination)	8.6	9.7	9.4
Post-schooling higher qualifications	4.0	5.6	4.6
All or no qualifications	11.1	9.9	10.6

Source: Department of Employment data

the evidence of your findings? How far do you think your locality is typical of the national pattern of recruitment?

The Outward Flow of Workers from Firms

The Cost of Labour Turnover

The outward flow of workers is made up of people leaving the firm as a result of their own or the employers' decisions. Unless the firm is reducing the size of its workforce under the impact of declining demand or changing production technology, most worker quits give rise to a vacancy and exercise of hiring procedure. There is thus a cost to the employer, usually increased by some reduction in the output of labour until the new employee is fully trained and assimilated. Employers prefer to keep these direct costs of labour turnover as low as possible. They are also aware that a high rate of labour turnover, without good reason, is considered to be evidence of poor labour management and, in extreme cases, can lead to the refusal of some employment agencies to send job applicants to them.

Involuntary Quits

Some workers leave voluntarily for their own reasons. Some leave involuntarily because of employer decisions. Workers in this latter group, represented by q_2 in Figure 12.1, may lose their jobs for one or more of the following reasons.

(a) Inability to continue in current employment because of poor health or advancing age. In some cases workers are able to transfer to a different occupation within the firm or elsewhere. Others may have to leave the labour force. Individuals reaching the normal retirement age usually have to leave the firm and most leave the workforce, though shortage of workers may lead to their re-entry as part-time workers.

(b) Dissatisfaction of the employer with the productivity or conduct of the individual employee. In many countries, including Britain, employers expose themselves to the risk of incurring financial penalties if they are deemed to have 'unfairly' dismissed an employee whose job is covered by employment protection legislation or if they break the terms of an employment contract. What is 'unfair' is defined by legislation and codes of practice which often have the force of law. Some employers try to avoid compulsory dismissal by making it clear to the worker that he or she has little prospect of advancement within the firm in the hope that this will lead to early 'voluntary' departure. However, this kind of conduct can lead to charges of 'constructive dismissal' and financial penalties.

(c) The need or decision by the firm to reduce its employment levels. The employer then initiates a system to bring about 'voluntary' or involuntary redundancies and/or early retirement schemes, or indicates that, as far as possible, job leavers will not be replaced. This situation, of course, has implications for remaining employees not being made redundant and may encourage those who have marketable skills to look for a change in employment. The line between voluntary and involuntary departure is sometimes very thin.

Employer Attitudes to Redundancy

When workers are dismissed or retire, assuming that there is no pressure to reduce the size of the labour force, they will normally be replaced, though not necessarily by a worker with similar skills. Employers may take advantage of changes in personnel to change the skill structure of their workforce. However, redundancies will accompany a general reduction in the number of workers employed though it may be necessary to recruit some people with new skills.

Research by economists suggests that most employers try to avoid having to implement large-scale redundancies.

This was the view of Oi (1962) when he suggested that in a modern industrial economy labour had become a quasi-fixed factor. This was partly because of the cost of eventual replacement when the economic problems giving rise to the redundancies had been overcome, and partly because long-serving workers were valuable to the firm because of their experience and the amount of in-firm training they had received. Labour economists believed that firms tended to choose labour 'hoarding', i.e. toleration of a period of underemployment, as a preferred and less costly alternative to dismissal and re-hiring at different stages of the demand cycle.

Parsons (1972) sought to develop this view further by concentrating on the implications of human capital investment in firm-specific training. When a firm was responsible for investment in this kind of training Parsons believed that, in normal periods, a worker's marginal revenue product value would exceed the wage paid. The value of the difference represented the firm's anticipated return on the investment it had financed. Consequently, in a recession, when product demand declined, firms would prefer temporarily to forgo the return on their human capital investment. This was less damaging than the capital loss incurred on a substantial amount of redundancy.

Although not necessarily denying this widespread belief in firms' reluctance to resort to large numbers of redundancies, Jones and Martin (1986) were able to compare the experience of the 1970s with the outcome of the post-1979 recession. They observed that in the latter period there was often pressure upon employers to reduce manpower levels and in many, but not all, instances this was achieved by 'forced separations' (redundancies). Their study highlighted two contrasting situations. Industries, and one may assume, firms in different industries, which normally experienced a high level of voluntary quits found it less necessary to resort to dismissal by redundancy. They also drew attention to a tendency for firms using workers with specific skills to be more willing to make them redundant when there was a rising rate of unemployment for this kind of labour. Employers were less likely to hoard labour which they anticipated could easily be replaced when necessary.

At any given time there are likely to be some influences operating against redundancies and others against labour hoarding. For example, Britain has had redundancy payments legislation since 1964 which increases the cost of laying off workers. Operating in the opposite direction there have been massive mergers and take-overs in British commerce and industry since the mid-1960s. This has led to the formation of some very large groups and a reduction in feelings of personal loyalty between employers and workers. Increased international competition, more competitive world markets, and the emergence, at the head of growing business groups, of old-style profit-seeking entrepreneurs, including some from countries with a much tougher tradition of labour management, probably reduced resistance to redundancies in sectors of industry which had to adapt rapidly to changed conditions. Most business economists agree that the companies which emerged from the depressed years of the early 1980s did so looking much 'leaner and fitter', an achievement usually made possible by some quite large-scale redundancies.

Voluntary Quits

Workers' voluntary decisions to leave their present employment form a further and substantial part of the outward flow of labour from firms. Except for early retirers and those opting for a period of work in the home, it can be assumed that most voluntary leavers will join other firms. It appears that the volume of voluntary quits tends to rise in periods of economic expansion and decline during depressions. Workers take a rational view of their chances of finding new employment quickly and with little cost.

The main reasons for voluntary quits identified in the earlier discussion of labour mobility were that young and recently employed workers were more likely to leave than the older, longer-serving employees and that a desire for job security and sound future prospects were more important than short-time income rises.

Another influence was observed by Parsons (1972), who found that where a worker bore the greater part of the cost of acquiring firm-specific human capital investment that worker, after training, was likely to receive a wage higher than he or she could expect with another firm. This increased income could be regarded as a return on the cost of the human capital investment and also as a discouragement from leaving the firm where the skills were acquired.

The generally agreed view that recently appointed employees are more likely to leave their employers voluntarily may reflect the way firms and workers engage in search and the rather poor channels of communication in labour markets. Departure from a job after only a short time represents a loss on the investment in search for both employer and employee and necessitates fresh search expenditure for both. Some research has been directed towards finding possible ways to reduce these costs.

Salop and Salop (1976) believed that the main problem was that firms lacked adequate information about job applicants. They suggested that employers should abandon their reliance on over-generalised and unreliable indicators, such as age, sex, and past work experience, and instead pass the major cost of the investment in job change to the worker. Workers could be permitted to choose their employer but would be required to bear the main cost of firm-specific training, receiving a wage equal to their marginal revenue product. Workers would be more careful in selection and much less likely to leave because they would be faced with the major part of mobility costs. This suggestion appears sound in economic logic but rather impractical. It overlooks the fact that firms are in competition for workers of high quality who, after all, represent the most valuable of all scarce resources. The costly search to locate, attract, and employ the best workers went on vigorously throughout the years of very high unemployment in the early and mid-1980s.

Monitoring Voluntary Quits

Firms, of course, do recognise and seek to reduce the high cost of voluntary quits. It is also helpful to measure the scale of any problem, so that an acceptable way of monitoring voluntary quits is desirable. Most firms are familiar with and use a simple measure of labour turnover. This divides the number of employees leaving during a specified period by the average number of workers employed in that period. The result is usually multiplied by 100 to form an easily recognisable percentage.

This is a simple and easy to use measure, but it is weak in two respects.

(a) It does not distinguish between voluntary and involuntary quits. The latter can usually be predicted and prepared for. The firm's greater need is some reliable measure for individually unpredictable voluntary quits. The measure can be modified quite simply to meet this objection by replacing 'the number of leavers' by 'the number of voluntary leavers' in the numerator of the division. The measure then becomes one of voluntary labour turnover, and this is more useful for making comparisons between firms and between different periods.

(b) Harris (1964) pointed out a second weakness of the simple labour turnover measure when used for inter-firm comparisons. The measure would not distinguish between some very different situations. Harris took the example of two firms, A and B, each with a labour force of 100. Over a twelve month period firm A lost and replaced half of its labour force once. In the second firm 10 of the original employees were replaced. However these replacements left and had to be replaced. If this took place five times then firm B also suffered 50 quits, but unlike firm A only 10% of the jobs were affected. Thus the economic consequences for the two firms of identical labour turnover rates would be quite different. Some observers, Bowley (1969), for example, have suggested that a more relevant measure would be to study employment stability rather than employment mobility.

A labour stability measure could be found by dividing the number of employees with one year or more of service by the number of employees employed in the previous year, again multiplied by 100. This measure would identify the clear difference between firms A and B in the Harris example. Whereas both firms would experience a labour turnover of 50%, the level of labour stability in firm B will be 90% compared with the 50% figure in firm A.

A careful analysis of labour stability might be expected to enable a firm to redirect its search activities and/or modify its current hiring standards. There are various measures available for examining the relative level of quits within a firm. Each measure has its strengths and weaknesses. The actual choice of technique to be used will be determined by the circumstances in which a firm finds itself. The main object is to obtain reliable and relevant facts to help the firm solve any particular problem which it happens to be facing.

Questions for Discussion and Review

9 The following table relates to two firms, A and B, in the same industry.

	Firm A	Firm B
Number of workers employed at start of period and average employed in the previous period	400	500
(including those with service of 1 year or more)	(350)	(400)
Number of workers employed at end of period	420	500
(including those with service of 1 year or more)	(380)	(385)
Number of workers leaving during period	46	50
(including voluntary leavers)	(30)	(40)

Calculate suitable measures of labour turnover and stability for these firms. Which firm do you consider to have the more stable workforce? What further information do you think might increase your knowledge and, perhaps, cause you to change your mind?

10 An organisation, under pressure to reduce its workforce in a period of high unemployment, pursued a policy based on 'voluntary redundancies only' and a 'freeze' on new recruitment. At the same time it introduced generous financial provisions to encourage early retirement. Some years later unemployment fell and serious shortages of skilled labour of all kinds developed. Discuss the problems likely to be faced by the organisation in the changed labour market and how you think its situation would compare with a similar organisation which had pursued a policy of compulsory redundancies with selective compulsory retirement and hiring based on perceived organisational need. Discuss the social and economic implications of the two contrasting policies for the workers involved, including those not made redundant under either policy, and the community as a whole.

Internal Labour Markets

The Importance of Internal Labour Markets

The high degree of success enjoyed by British firms in retaining their employees was confirmed by a study of job duration made by Main (1982).

Using British Government employment data Main calculated that, in 1968, the average completed job tenure of all full-time male holders was 20 years, with 60% of his sample spending a minimum of 10 years with a single employer. Although Main was studying a single specific period he believed that the years he chose were representative and that his results could be taken as a 'rough approximation' for any period. Main's findings imply that the majority of male workers only very rarely come into contact with the competitive labour market. On average, contact is made with this market about once every decade.

This apparent isolation of a high proportion of the labour force from the labour market has led to the recognition that internal labour markets exist within firms, a possibility recognised by Main.

Internal labour markets allow workers to change their jobs without changing their employers, for they simply transfer from one job to another within the same firm. This market is very relevant to the options open to firms when filling job vacancies because it permits transfers within the firm. This option was represented by Flow T in Figure 12.1.

The possible transfer of a worker to a more senior job benefits the firm through a significant reduction in search costs. Moreover, worker awareness of the possibility that career progress can be made by transfer within the internal market is likely to reduce the scale of voluntary quits from workers seeking better jobs. Workers are relieved of the costs and uncertainties of periodic job search in the open labour markets and, at the same time, they have financial incentives to undertake informal firm-specific and on-the-job training.

Implications of Internal Labour Markets

When a vacancy is filled by transfer within the firm, assuming that the person transferred is promoted to a more senior position, then this person's move creates another vacancy—the post from which promotion has been made. Mace and Wilkinson (1977) found that firms tended to rely on internal promotions and tried to restrict recruitment from outside the firm to jobs near the bottom of the occupational hierarchy. Some firms even try to keep to this process when they change their skill structure and require people with skills not formerly employed. Their first choice is often to try and find employees with suitable educational backgrounds and aptitudes willing to be re-trained, and only recruit from the external labour market when insufficient employees can be found or if the time scale of change does not permit the necessary training.

A policy of internal promotion implies that the firm maintains adequate records of existing employees and maintains a regular internal report system to ensure that it knows the capabilities, strengths, and weaknesses of existing employees. This further implies that managers who are not specialist personnel officers nevertheless do have some skills in human resource management and are willing and able to prepare their subordinates for promotion opportunities. It is not certain that all firms do fully appreciate the implications and costs of efficiently operating an internal labour market.

Doeringer and Piore (1971) recognised that an efficient internal promotion and career development system is an essential part of the concept of primary jobs. They attempted to define an internal labour market as one located within an organisation and which was not governed by conditions in the external labour markets but by a set of administrative, formal, and informal rules developed over a period by the firm and employees in their joint interests. They can be explained in economic terms as a consequence of employers and employees wishing to maximise the returns to be gained from their respective costs of job search and training. The longer an employment relationship lasts, the greater the benefit from the initial investment made by the two sets of participants.

Preference for internal promotion has certain further implications for recruitment. It has already been pointed out that recruitment will be concentrated on jobs, or 'ports of entry', at the lower end of the various occupational ladddders in the firm. Recruitment will be from the external labour market in competition with other firms, but the employer, operating an internal promotion policy, seeks not only the ability to do the immediate job on offer but also the characteristics, educational background, and personal qualities thought to be required for more senior posts. The screening process employed will be directed towards this objective. The firm is aware that it is proposing to make a substantial capital investment in training and that appointments that do not lead to successful careers within the firm must be judged investment losses.

The larger firms have some advantages over small firms in this process. The small firm cannot afford to make many mistakes, nor can it afford to repeat the investment too often. It may have to live with partial failures, i.e. recruits who do not live up to initial hopes and promise but who are reasonably competent. A large firm can afford to recognise that not all appointments will be successful. It may, for example, recruit ten new employees each year and judge the operation to be a successful investment if, say, two of these reach senior levels within a target period. The value to the firm of these two may justify the expenditure on the other eight, some of whom will have decided to pursue careers with other firms while others are deemed to have not lived up to expectations and are asked to leave or told that they are unlikely to receive promotion. The employer will justify this policy by arguing that experience shows that out of each ten recruits, two will be successful in the terms defined by the recruitment and promotion strategy. What the selectors do not know for sure at the time of selection is which two, so that all ten start their careers on equal terms and then, in effect, select themselves for further training and promotion.

Applicants will also be aware of the employer's attitudes and strategy when making their applications. They all believe that they have the qualities for long-term success, and firms with known internal promotion preferences are likely to receive more applicants than those known to recruit senior staff from the external market. Such firms are therefore likely to be able to raise their hiring standards.

Manwaring (1984) suggested that there existed in certain firms and industries 'extended internal labour markets'. In these cases initial recruitment was made through existing employees who became part of the market communication system.

By restricting entry to a limited number of ports of entry, a firm places a greater emphasis than normal on a life-time investment in training. However, in an internal labour market the worker will derive long-term benefits from enhanced promotion prospects and wages and, consequently, may be prepared to share in the investment cost. This is more probable if the employee knows that the firm operates an efficient training and formal promotion system where workers are able to know what the requirements are for promotion and how they can meet those requirements. Personnel officers still report that a surprisingly large number of firms are prepared to go to considerable trouble and expense to maintain and care for their physical assets but appear to have little awareness of the importance of developing and getting the most from their human capital investment.

It may be objected that this emphasis on internal labour markets does not fit the apparent growth, in the 1970s and 1980s, of the relatively new practice, in organised form, of head hunting as described earlier. The two tendencies can, however, be reconciled. In a competitive period of rapid technical change, firms are forced to look for people with new attitudes and relevant experience of new methods. Firms which have traditionally relied on internal promotions to fill senior posts may be aware of their lack of skill in recruiting from external markets at this level and prefer to rely on the expertise of specialist agencies. Furthermore, the practice may be more widespread in market sectors where there has long been a fairly high rate of labour mobility, even at senior level. Under competitive conditions, firms are aware of the increased importance of senior posts and seek specialised help in filling these. Recruiting a senior manager, head hunted from another employer in the same industry, may be thought to strengthen the recruiting organisation while weakening the competitor, the manager's former employer.

Internal Labour Markets and Wages

At the lower port of entry levels, firms usually offer the market wage rate, though some of the large multinational employers may offer a premium slightly above the recognised normal rate. Once workers begin to progress through the hierarchy of jobs, other considerations arise. There is a case for the wages offered in an internal labour market to be similar to levels in the external market. If the firm were to offer a wage below the external market level it would risk suffering voluntary quits and loss of its human capital investment as workers began to realise they could earn more with other employers. It could also be argued that a rational employer would not pay an internally promoted worker more than the wage at which a worker with a similar skills could be recruited from the external market. To do so would suggest that the employer was sacrificing any return on its training costs as well as paying more than the market price for a factor input.

The reality appears to be that for certain jobs, for example machine operatives or clerical staff, the training received in the firm is likely to have a ready, market, transfer value to the worker. In these cases the offered wage will be broadly in line with the market wage. It should be recognised that this is more a 'wage range' than an absolute amount, i.e. $£X \pm £y$ per week (or other customary period) to allow for a certain amount of individual flexibility.

Other workers whose training, however extensive, is firm-specific, adding little to the employee's market transfer value, are likely to find it more difficult to compare their pay with an external market rate. These workers fear that if they quit they will lose from their investment in training and may also risk a fall in income if their next best alternative employment is at a lower skill and pay level than their present occupation.

Firms relying heavily on internal labour markets have to fix their wage levels high enough to encourage workers to undertake training. This implies that they will bear a high proportion of the training cost. They must then maintain a wage level which will discourage trained employees from quitting. This implies sharing the benefits of training with the people receiving it.

Mace and Wilkinson (1977), in their study of professional engineers, found little evidence that the most costly skills to acquire necessarily commanded the highest wages available.

The firm has a difficult task in structuring its wages policy. It cannot upset the internal structure with its in-built pattern of differentials, rewards, and inducements for the encouragement of workers to develop the skills required by the employer and for them to stay with the firm during the period when it is gaining the benefit of past human investment costs. If the firm has to pay special wages and/or give additional fringe benefit inducements to recruit some categories of skilled workers from the external market, this can upset the internal structure and force some major revisions. These, of course, add to the marginal costs of recruiting from outside sources. On the other hand, if the employer encourages and helps to finance employees to acquire scarce skills which make their holders attractive in outside markets, it also has to pay the going rate in pay and fringe benefits after training in order to retain them.

A further requirement of the internal wages structure may be to permit flexibility in the use of labour, particularly in a period of rapid economic and technological change. Job evaluation exercises, examined in Chapter 14, have been traditionally concerned with recognising the skill and other requirements for particular jobs rather than particular people. At the same time we have to recognise that when employees have developed firm-specific skills, their value can lie as much in the knowledge of the ways of the firm and how colleagues react under given circumstances as in the exercise of a specific general skill. It is difficult to build this into job evaluation, but it clearly cannot be ignored.

Some of the problems arising out of separating the internal and external labour markets were examined by George and Shorey (1985). Their research suggested that employers had to recognise that:

(a) Employers attach importance to the acquisition of skills that are specific to the firm.
(b) The expectation that employees will progress in the occupational hierarchy and will need to acquire additional skills as they continue in employment is an important influence on selection, screening, and recruitment.

(c) Firms prefer to recruit at the lowest end of hierarchies and to fill the more senior jobs by internal promotion.
(d) Employers like to control the training process.
(e) Employers have to reconcile the internal pay structure with conditions in external markets.

Observations suggest that the structure of an individual firm's internal labour market tends to develop by trial and error. If the firm is judged to be successful on its performance record and also achieves a stable workforce, then senior managers believe that their human resource management policy is also successful. Most of them probably came through the internal market very successfully! They are then likely to formalise the structure and convince themselves that· they are practising manpower planning. Stability and complacency can be rudely shattered if the firm has to meet unexpected market conditions, as in the early 1980s, or is taken over by another firm with different policies, perceptions, and objectives.

Manpower Planning

The term 'manpower' is also used to refer to female employment. If the firm is to have the labour resources it needs to carry out the activities necessary to the achievement of its objectives, it must manage its human capital resources carefully. This, however, is more difficult than the management of physical resources. Before purchasing a machine, a manager can find out precisely its capabilities, its needs for maintenance and upkeep, and its projected life. Costs and benefits can, therefore, be calculated with reasonable accuracy—if its product is sold according to plan.

People are not as predictable nor always as reliable. Machines cannot walk out of the door and join a competitor. People can and do. People cannot be put on one side and replaced easily and without cost. People grow old and less productive (as, of course, do machines, but machines do not have to be provided with pensions), and the way an employer treats its long-service and loyal employees will be observed and have an influence on the attitudes of others.

Consequently, employers need to be able to forecast their probable human resource needs in advance, preferably some years in advance, and to plan their current recruitment and training strategies accordingly. Manpower planning seeks to achieve this. Success depends on:

(a) Formation of clear company objectives and the forecasting of likely success in achieving these.
(b) Awareness of developments in production methods and their implications for personnel requirements.
(c) Predictions of future quits for all the reasons outlined in this chapter.
(d) The application of skilled personnel management techniques to search, screening, selection, and training of workers.
(e) Co-operation with specialist agencies in government, education, and other specialist manpower services.

All investment contains an element of uncertainty, and investment in human capital is no exception. Some flexibility is essential, particularly in the modern period of rapid economic and technological change. Employers, therefore, now show a preference for workers able to cross the traditional skill demarcations and for those with educational backgrounds that encourage adaptability and capacity for re-training, perhaps several times during their working lives.

The manpower manager has to discard many myths and prejudices relating to groups suffering discrimination and be both imaginative and realistic in assessing employment needs and devising ways of meeting them. It seems strange, perhaps, that the management of human resources does not always seem to attract quite the same share of the best ability as the management of the firm's financial and physical capital.

Questions for Discussion and Review

11 Discuss the case for and against the policy of promoting from within the firm from the point of view of
(a) the firm's employees, and
(b) the future stability and success of the firm.

12 It has been argued by some observers that the pension arrangements developed since the 1950s have been a powerful force for discouraging workers aged over 35 from voluntary movement between firms. To what extent do you think that labour mobility will be increased by measures to encourage individual workers to arrange their own pensions which are not tied to specific employment organisations?

Suggestions for Written Assignments

1 Explain why firms often need to have flexibility in the number and types of workers they employ. How far and in what ways might it be possible to reconcile this flexibility with the worker's need for job security and income stability?

2 Interview a personnel officer from a company employing 200 or more workers. Write a report of approximately 1500 words, excluding data appendices, outlining the most difficult problems faced by the firm in the recruitment, training, retaining, and dismissal of its workers and the steps taken by the firm to overcome these problems.

3 'One of the major causes of low morale in education is the almost total lack of manpower planning arising out of the inability of organisational managers to control their own staffing levels or the kinds of staff they employ.'
Discuss this statement in relation to one school or college known to you. What is likely to be the effect on educational manpower policies of the transfer of greater financial reponsibility to individual organisations under the terms of the Education Act 1988?

4 'The scale to which head hunting is engaged in is a good indication of the extent of competition in a business sector.'
Explain and discuss this statement. If possible, give examples from one industrial or occupational sector known to you.

5 Why is a high rate of labour turnover often assumed to be an indication of inefficient management? Explain and discuss the difficulties associated with measuring labour turnover and suggest occasions when an increase in this rate might show that managers are becoming more efficient.

Suggestions for Further Reading

This chapter has sought to extend the ideas and concepts developed in previous parts of the book and to apply them to a single employer. If you are uncertain of the meaning and significance of the general concepts incorporated in this integrated approach, you should refer to the appropriate earlier sections.

Different approaches to the identification and filling of job vacancies may be found in Thomas and Deaton (1977), chapter 2 and appendix A.

Work by Courtney and Hedges (1977) and Hedges (1982), based on samples of engagements made by employers, provided interesting data relating to the differing recruitment methods adopted and the relative success levels of these various methods.

Pettman (1975) drew on both international and wider social science data to examine labour turnover, and complemented the work mentioned in the preceding paragraph. Parsons (1977) offered both a theoretical and empirical survey of the economist's approach to labour market turnover.

Doeringer and Piore (1971) still provide the best single description of the concept of the internal labour market, and reference to their work is essential for anyone making a further study of this subject. Nowak and Crockett (1983) have provided a case study, based on three firms, of internal labour markets in operation.

A non-economist's explanation of the concept and practical implications of the efficient planning of manpower is to be found in Bramham (1988). He described various manpower techniques in current use.

13
Wage Determination and Differentials

Wages in Theory and Practice
The Limitations of Wage Theories

As explained in Chapter 4, the basic idea underlying the theory of wage determination is that employers continue to hire workers to the point where the value of the last worker's contribution to output, the marginal revenue product, would be equal to the cost of employing that worker. This, for simplicity, is often assumed to be the same as the wage paid to that worker. On the labour supply side, the wage at which each worker is prepared to enter employment is determined by that individual's set of wage–leisure preferences. The neo-classical model of wage determination in labour markets depends on the two forces of employer demand and worker supply interacting to arrive at equilibrium levels of employment and wages. In its simplest form the basic market model appears as illustrated in Figure 13.1.

Models of competitive markets assume that the market equilibrium wage established by demand and supply will set the wage rates paid by employers operating in that market.

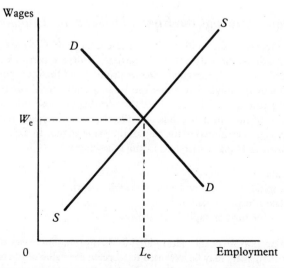

Figure 13.1 *Employment and wage equilibrium in the neo-classical competitive labour market*

However, observation suggests that the wages actually paid by firms are subject to influences that go beyond the basic market models. These influences can affect both supply and demand in ways that are not always taken into account in the neo-classical market models.

In particular, as recognised in Chapter 8, the conditions for a perfectly competitive labour market are rarely found in practice. Most labour markets are highly imperfect. Communications, for example, are often poor, leading to inadequate information and poor decisions. There can be powerful barriers to the entry of workers to some markets. These take various forms, including the need to make a financial investment in human capital that is beyond the means of many workers capable of performing adequately in those markets. These imperfections can distort the flow of supply, causing under-supply in some markets and over-supply in others where the barriers are lower or less effective. Such distortions in supply have major consequences for wage determination.

Other important market imperfections (in the pure economic sense) may arise from government intervention (as outlined in Chapter 15), the organised, collective actions of workers, i.e. trade unions (see Chapter 16), to influence supply, or associations, formal or informal, of employers designed to limit competition in the demand for labour. Consequently, when the actual pattern of wages paid by firms is examined it can seem significantly more complex than the relatively straightforward theoretical models outlined earlier in this book. Theory can sometimes seem rather remote from the daily reality of wages seen from the viewpoint of the practical employer and manager. Instead of the ordered and predictable interaction portrayed in most labour market models, both firms and workers may be perceived as operating, with inadequate knowledge, under conditions of uncertainty and reacting in response to pressures from labour organisations, governments, and other external agencies.

Fortunately, perhaps, the objective of economic analysis is not to explain or predict specific wage or employment levels for any given firm, occupation, or industry at a particular time but to identify, explain, and sometimes to predict, in more general terms, trends in the pattern of relative wages paid to workers in different occupations, industries, and firms. The economist should be able to use the theoretical models and concepts of economics to explain why one group of workers is likely to be paid more than another group but is less likely to be able to use these to suggest why the wage of worker X should be £y per week in a specific firm and industry.

Marginal Productivity and the Firm's Demand for Labour

Value added statements, of the kind used for Table 13.1 and which are produced by many commercial organisations, provide a useful starting point for considering the relationship between the value of a worker's marginal revenue product and the wage paid to that worker. A value added statement is designed to show the value a commercial organisation adds to the input of productive resources. These include the services of those undertaking sub-contract work before the sale of the finished goods or services. A commercial organisation's ability to reward labour and capital is limited to the sum of the value added. In Table 13.1 the sum of the value added is shown as being distributed in the following ways:

(a) Payments to labour.
(b) Payments to capital (that is, dividends to shareholders).
(c) Payments of taxes to public authorities.
(d) Money retained for further capital investment.

The retention of a proportion of the value added for investment increases the total worth of the company and, consequently, may be expected to increase the value of the ordinary shares at no direct cost to the shareholders. Any profits retained for further investment could also have been

Table 13.1   Source and disposal of value added (in £m.)

	1985	1986	1987
Turnover	5598.5	5291.3	5705.5
comprising: initial purchases	3107.3	2843.8	2966.7
value added	2482.2	2447.5	2738.8
Disposal of value added			
To government (taxes, duties, levies, and rates)	912.8	930.6	1011.6
To employees	1052.1	1026.7	1017.4
To owners of capital	189.8	191.6	226.1
Retained for investment	327.5	298.6	483.7

Source: Grand Metropolitan PLC Accounts, various years

paid to shareholders in the form of dividends in the current period had the directors so decided. The amount of retention, therefore, is effectively an indirect payment to the owners of capital. A value added statement thus indicates the total revenue product paid to capital and makes possible the calculation of the marginal revenue product applicable to one unit of capital. The unit might be seen as a unit of money, say £1, or as a single ordinary share.

In the same way the value added statement shows the amount of total revenue product paid to labour, and so makes it possible to calculate the marginal revenue product applicable to one unit of labour, i.e. one worker. The marginal revenue product of labour identified in this way is, of course, an average—the arithmetic mean—covering all kinds of workers, and like many averages arrived at in this way may not actually apply to any one specific worker.

The value added statement also shows taxes of various kinds payable to central and local government. These reduce revenues which would otherwise be available for distribution as wages, share dividends, or retentions for investment. Taxes, therefore, reduce the returns to capital and labour available for distribution from the value of the marginal revenue product of both capital and labour.

If all taxation effects are ignored, then the total value added by an organisation is divided between labour and capital. In perfect markets an assumption could be made that the apportionment between capital and labour is made on the basis of their relative contribution to production. If capital owners are paid less than the value of their marginal product, investment declines and the long-term future of the firm is threatened. If workers are paid less than the value of their marginal product, labour becomes difficult to recruit, and without labour the firm ceases production. Nevertheless, even if the full value of the marginal product paid to labour does equal the value of product attributable to all the workers employed, this does not mean that every worker receives a wage equal to his or her personal contribution to production.

The Wage and Marginal Productivity

If it could be assumed that a firm, operating in a perfectly competitive labour market,

(a) employed a workforce that was completely homogeneous,
(b) made a total payment to labour equal to the revenue value of the total product attributable to labour, and
(c) paid each worker a wage equal to the total payment to labour divided by the number of workers,

then all would receive an identical wage equal to each worker's marginal revenue product.

In reality, the labour force will be heterogeneous: individuals will contribute different skills and will have differing levels of productivity. Individual members of this heterogeneous labour force will also receive differing levels of wages. In these conditions it remains possible that the differing wages may equal the differing values of the marginal product contributed by the individual workers.

Frank (1984), however, did not believe that this possibility matched the reality of actual wage payment patterns. He suggested that wage levels were influenced by other factors such as education, training, and work experience and could not therefore be explained simply in terms of differing individual marginal productivities.

As a partial explanation for this failure of employers to match marginal productivities and wages he suggested that it was too expensive to measure individual contributions to production so that wages were based on other, simpler and less expensive criteria. Frank studied in detail a number of different types of workers, even including university professors, and concluded that the most productive employees appeared to be paid less than their marginal revenue products while the least productive employees received a wage above their marginal products. That this result did not lead to conflict between workers within organisations was due, Frank believed, to social rather than to economic considerations. Individual workers appeared to be concerned primarily with their relative position within a wages hierarchy rather than with the actual level of wages received.

Other contributions to the discussion of marginal product and its relevance to the individual worker's wage have focused on the longer-term relationship thought to develop between the firm and the individual and, by implication if not always specified, on the consequences of individual workers acquiring firm-specific skills. Oswald (1981) suggested that as workers gradually acquired skill and experience from their continuing employment relationship their marginal product contribution to the firm increased more than the increase in pay they received. Oswald's model implies that the younger members of a firm's labour force are likely to receive a wage above the value of their marginal product. This may be intended to encourage them to remain with the employer and to acquire relevant, firm-specific skills. In contrast, the more senior, and hence experienced and valued, employees receive a wage below the value of their marginal product. Ideally the firm would prefer to employ only the more 'senior' workers, who are paid less than their marginal product, but is also obliged to employ the unprofitable junior workers to ensure an experienced labour force in the future. In effect, Oswald developed his approach on the basis that a firm returned to labour the value of marginal product attributable to labour. In the process, however, it redistributed the marginal product between individual workers in the firm's longer-term interests.

While acknowledging that employers may not offer all workers a wage equal to their marginal product, another commentator, Pissarides (1985), suggested that both the employer and worker recognised the value of an extended employment relationship, and when circumstances permitted this to occur neither the employer nor the worker might be concerned at any particular time to ensure equality of wage and marginal product. They were both more likely to be concerned with long-term benefits. Consequently, a firm might offer a new employee a wage below the anticipated marginal revenue product. If the employee stayed with the employer the wage was likely to rise faster than the increase in marginal product. This would encourage the worker to stay with the firm rather than go to a new job where again the wage would be less than the value of the marginal product.

Pissarides also suggested that employers might adopt this approach because they were withholding a proportion of the worker's initial real value as a kind of deposit held against the worker's future actions and behaviour. The firm could then partially repay this as it satisfied itself of the worker's long-term contribution. Repaying the deposit allows the firm to raise the worker's wage more rapidly than might seem to be justified by the increase in marginal revenue product. The firm, however, retained part of the deposit to be returned to the worker as a retirement pension.

These models assume, therefore, that, in the absence of exploitation made possible by monopolistic or monopsonistic power or by the existence of large-scale unemployment, firms operating in competitive labour markets are likely to return to labour the aggregate value of its marginal revenue product. On the other hand, at any given time all the individual workers may not receive wages equal to the value of their individual contributions to the firm's production. Employers are likely to use wage payment systems to ensure that some redistribution of marginal product takes place because of the heterogeneous nature of labour and because workers become more valuable to their employers as their skills and experience within the firm increase.

Questions for Discussion and Review

1 Some firms are prepared to recruit trainees who are graduates in subject areas of no immediate business relevance at salaries very similar to those received by employees having several years' work experience. Discuss the arguments for and against this practice.

2 If it is easier for an employer to measure the marginal productivity of a manual than of a non-manual worker, would this suggest that the arguments presented in this chapter are more or less relevant to manual than to non-manual employees?

Individual, Inter-firm, and Regional Pay Differentials

Pay Differentials of Individuals within the Firm

Observation suggests that employees in the same firm may be carrying out identical work tasks but receive different wages which do not necessarily reflect differences in the workers' marginal productivities. Explanations for these differences can be based on the employers' desire to:

(a) operate relatively simple and administratively inexpensive wage payment systems based, as Frank (1984) suggested, on easily identifiable and measurable criteria (these could include, for example, length of service and/or qualification levels), and
(b) retain the existing labour force which, in time, is assumed to become more productive as workers accumulate firm-specific human capital made up of both on-the-job training and work experience.

Wage hierarchies, which often owe very little to marginal revenue product hierarchies, are known to exist within firms in industrial market economies. In their comparative study of Britain and Japan, Collier and Knight (1985 and 1986) attributed this to the willingness of employers to offer 'seniority pay' based upon length of service. Seniority pay was seen as an incentive to individual workers not to seek alternative employment. Employers were thought to gain from this practice through a reduction in labour turnover with a resulting reduction in the cost of firm-specific training and through the opportunity to recover the previous 'sunk' costs of earlier selection and training.

The Collier–Knight analysis implies a link between the ages and wages of workers. Although this link does exist, as shown, for instance, by the work of Creedy and Hart (1979), this can arise for other reasons. A pay scale based purely on seniority, measured by length of service, could result in a young worker of several years' service earning more than a much older worker with only, say, one year's service.

Pay Differentials between Firms

Workers can pursue identical occupations in the same industry but work for different firms. Bank cashiers do very similar work in each High Street bank. An engineering lathe turner can often choose from very many employers within the same local labour market. Thus workers are often able to choose between different employers in the same industry, and one factor influencing their choice may be the difference in wages offered for similar skills.

Any consideration of inter-firm pay differentials must recognise the difference between the money wage and the total reward package offered by an employer. Part of this total package can be quantified, and includes the money wage, payments in kind (such as company car, help with expenses such as telephone rentals, lunches, or travel to work costs), and fringe benefits such as sports facilities that enable some workers to pursue private interests at very low cost. In addition, however, the total package includes unquantifiable aspects of employment such as physical working conditions and opportunities for gaining experience useful for further career progression. Thus, an outside observer may note that firm A pays a higher monetary wage than firm B and perceive this as an inter-firm differential. However, workers in the industry may consider that firm B is offering a total reward package likely to provide a higher degree of satisfaction. Firms frequently offer a higher monetary wage to compensate for other, unattractive aspects of the total reward package. This difference between the monetary wage alone and the reward package seen as a whole may account for some elements in inter-firm pay differentials.

Nevertheless, even when allowance is made for any equalising elements within total reward packages, empirical studies such as those in Robinson (1970) indicate that inter-firm differentials do remain. One reason may be that certain firms offer higher rewards as a means of recruiting labour. The higher wage payments may be seen as a substitute for the increased search costs that would otherwise be incurred.

Information that a firm is offering higher wages to reduce search activity is likely to spread through a labour market through informal communication channels. Some workers currently employed at other firms may apply to join the high-wage employer, who may then be able to be more selective in recruitment and try to employ only those workers with above-average marginal productivity potential. If they succeed, inter-firm wage differentials may reflect differences in the marginal productivity of individual workers. High-wage firms may be able to employ the more productive workers with the low-wage firms able to recruit only the less productive. This, in turn, may enable the high-wage firms to be more profitable and better able to pay higher wages and so retain their dominance in the labour market.

Research Findings on Inter-firm Differentials

Research, largely conducted in the USA, has indicated that a significant influence on inter-firm differentials is the size of the working establishment or plant, as measured by number of workers employed. Several studies suggest that there is a statistical relationship between size of working establishment and of differentials in the reward package. Firms which mainly operate in large establishments tend to offer packages that are superior to those offered by firms which have small production units. Lester (1967) found differentials of the order of 20–25% in large areas of US manufacturing. He considered this to be paradoxical, questioning why firms who might be assumed to have the greatest power in the labour market offered superior reward packages. Masters (1969), whose research was undertaken over a similar period to that of

Lester, reached broadly similar conclusions and expressed the belief that his results provided further evidence that plant size was a significant influence upon inter-plant differentials. While identifying the existence of the statistical relationship between plant size and differentials in reward packages, neither of the above researchers offered explanations for this. Miller (1977), however, suggested that in many US industries the larger firms achieved higher than average levels of labour productivity. Consequently, the higher reward packages offered by such firms might be assumed to reflect the greater value of their labour's marginal product. The relationship between pay differential, firm, and establishment size seems clear, but this does not rule out other influences and explanations.

(a) In many industries large firms which are likely to include at least some large plants are often able to exert a greater degree of product market power than do small firms. Consequently, the larger firms with large plants may exercise their product market power to enable them to pay higher wages and pass these on to buyers through higher prices.

(b) Mayhew (1976b) suggested that large plants might benefit from economies of scale, and that employers then shared these benefits with the workforce in the form of higher than average wages.

(c) Labour organisations may find larger workforces not only easier to organize but also to have professional managers who are willing to negotiate with them.

(d) Given the choice, workers may prefer to work in smaller work units where there may be a greater variety of work tasks and more extensive personal relationships than are usually found in a large work establishment. Thus the statistically significant higher reward packages associated with large plants which are usually associated with large firms may be offered as compensation for the loss of utility arising from what Blanchflower (1986) terms 'a more structured work setting' with 'more formal rules' associated with employment in such establishments.

Inter-regional Differentials

There is general recognition of the existence of a pattern of regional wage rates around the national average. This is shown for Britain in Figure 13.2.

These regional variations, however, conceal pay differentials that exist between different occupations and industries. Neither of these are evenly spread throughout the regions so that an attempt to measure pay differences due entirely to regional causes must be based on figures that have been corrected for the uneven distribution of industries and occupations. Fuchs (1967) showed how this could be achieved. Regional figures corrected in this way show a much reduced regional differential, but nevertheless there is still a pattern of regional differences in the earnings of workers in some occupations and industries.

It is difficult to determine the precise reasons for the long-standing and relatively stable pattern of regional pay differentials. Many economists, such as Cowling and Metcalf (1967) and Thirwell (1970), have been more concerned with mechanisms whereby wage increases which may have originated in one industry or part of the country have spread throughout the regions. They have appeared to accept the existence of a pattern of regional differences without too much concern about how or why these have developed and remain.

The absence of any clear theoretical model to explain the pattern has led some economists, such as Blackaby and Manning (1987), to suggest that regional differentials might have institutional (trade union) causes. At the same time these and other observers have recognised the importance of 'key regional characteristics'. Brown (1972) has suggested that regional differences arise in part because a 'region has some constant source of advantage, for example location'.

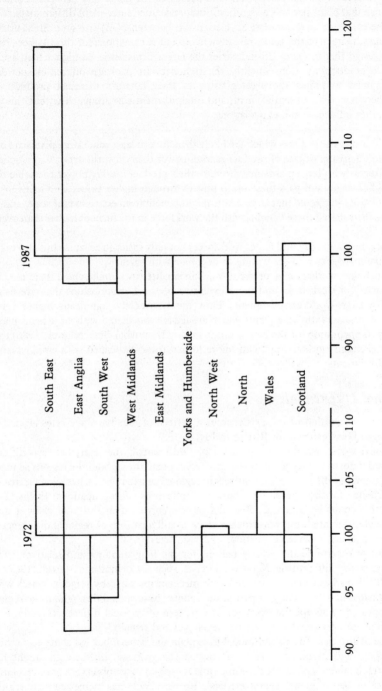

Figure 13.2 *Regional earnings pattern for male employees, 1972 and 1987*
Note: Average gross weekly earnings of adult full-time male employees by region expressed as a percentage of average of all regions
Source: Personnel Management (London), October 1988

Explanations of this type seem a little less than convincing, but other economists, for example Johnson (1966), who used US data, remain convinced that, with modifications, the neo-classical competitive model does provide an adequate explanation on the basis of supply and demand differences in regional labour markets.

Though difficult to explain through economic analysis, inter-regional differentials have persisted in modern industrial economies over a long period. From their study for the period 1914–68, Hart and MacKay (1975) concluded that the inter-regional hierarchy was stable although the size of the differentials tended to diminish over time.

A more cautious approach is adopted by Mayhew (1976a), who pointed out that inter-regional wage variation is less than

(a) inter-regional productivity variation,
(b) inter-industry wage variation, and
(c) intra-regional wage variation.

Mayhew accepted that pure regional differences existed and were statistically significant, but he believed that they normally explained only a small proportion of the earnings variation for specific occupational groups within an industry. Different industries appeared to present different patterns of regional differences. A region with relatively high pay in one industry might not have a similar position in other industrial sectors.

It appears that we have to accept that regional earnings differentials are not explicable through simple, clear-cut analytical models.

Questions for Discussion and Review

3 One consistent feature of regional pay differentials has been the relatively high earnings of workers in London and South East England. Discuss reasons for this and for factors that might substantially reduce the pure regional differential when other differences are taken into account. How might the supremacy of London earnings be affected if the total reward package is considered in place of just pay?

4 Discuss the possible consequence for employment and earnings in public sector activities such as teaching, postal work, and the police force of the relative lack of inter-organisational and inter-regional pay differentials in comparison with conditions in most parts of private industry and commerce.

Occupational Pay Differentials
The Adam Smith Framework

Any newspaper provides clear evidence that certain occupations offer higher monetary rewards than do others. This fact of life may well help to explain your own study of economics. Economists are interested in the underlying reasons for differences in the earnings of people in different occupations and in the way these have changed over time. They have sought explanations for these tendencies through neo-classical models of labour markets within which supply and demand interact to produce equilibrium price (wage) levels and they have looked for other factors which may have modified or partially replaced normal markets. Adam Smith (1961) considered this matter to be of such significance that, in his examination of the British economy in the eighteenth century, he set out five propositions which he considered relevant to the explanation of occupational pay differences:

(a) Agreeableness of the employment.
(b) Cost of learning the business.
(c) Constancy of employment.
(d) Trust to be reposed.
(e) Probability of success.

In spite of the enormous changes that have taken place in the structure of production and employment in the two hundred years since Adam Smith formulated these propositions, remarkably they still provide a useful starting point and framework for an examination of occupational pay differentials.

Attractiveness of Employment

In the first of Adam Smith's features it is being suggested that if a job has attractions which have a utility to a worker then the worker is prepared to pay a price for this in the form of reduced pay. On the other hand, a disagreeable job reduces utility and this has to be made good by increased pay. Although the attractions of present-day work may be rather different from those of the eighteenth century, when the main considerations may well have been the actual physical working conditions, the concept is wide enough to embrace aspects of work which are relevant today. Its underlying truth may, therefore, be tested against contemporary evidence.

For example, Bosworth and Dawkins (1980) suggested that not only were there different levels of disutility between occupations because some were more or less risky or dirty than others but that there would also be different degrees of disutility depending upon other features of the employment, such as the hours the worker is required to work. For instance, bakers are required to work at night and postmen begin work when most people are still asleep. These and similar workers may expect to receive extra pay for the disutility of their 'unsocial' working hours. This received some formal recognition during the period of incomes policies, 1966–79.

Bosworth and Dawkins recognised that the payment of a premium to certain occupations for working unsocial hours represented an additional cost to the employer which might indicate the employer's belief that an economic advantage was being gained.

Similarly, Marin and Psacharopoulos (1982) suggested that one obvious non-pecuniary disadvantage for some occupations was that they exposed individual workers to an above-average risk of death or serious injury. They acknowledged that apparently risky occupations—they specified mining and window-cleaning—were not necessarily among the highest paid, but that fact alone did not mean that their pay did not contain an element of risk compensation.

In a review article of research undertaken in the USA, Smith (1979) concluded that there was evidence, when other considerations were held constant, of the existence of compensating occupational wage differentials which did reflect the degree of risk of fatal injury occurring in certain occupations.

In modern employment a wide range of factors may affect the 'agreeableness' of an occupation. In addition to the hours of work there is the extent of what is often termed 'job satisfaction'. Academic observers, who may be projecting their own attitudes, usually assume that work gives more satisfaction if it enables the operator to have greater control over pace, to exercise individual discretion, or to be involved in several stages leading to final completion of a product. They assume that 'machine minding', where work is limited to relatively few activities all governed by the pace of the machine, offers very little satisfaction and is performed only for pay. Many would agree with this judgement, but there are also workers who do not want any kind of work responsibility and are happy to operate in a controlled situation, often taking considerable pride in a repetitive movement involving a fairly high degree of manual dexterity and precision. Nevertheless, it is generally expected that relatively high rates of pay are needed to compensate for lack of job satisfaction when work is highly controlled and monotonous.

Examining payment levels in the engineering industry, Mayhew (1975) found that skilled workers did not always receive more pay than semi-skilled machine operators. The traditional rewards for skill and training in some industries were less than the compensation thought necessary to persuade people to do the monotonous work.

Rewards for Human Capital Investment

Human capital investment is the modern term for Adam Smith's 'cost of learning the business'. This issue was examined in Chapter 7 and has been investigated by a number of researchers, including Psacharopoulos and Layard (1979). Research findings still support Adam Smith's view that workers expect compensation in the form of higher pay for personal expenditure in education and training, or, perhaps more correctly, they and their parents are only prepared to incur education and training costs if they believe that these will lead to increased future incomes.

Further Issues Raised by Adam Smith

Although research designed to test the validity of the remaining considerations proposed by Adam Smith has been very limited, there is no evidence to suggest that they have become irrelevant. On the contrary, examination of the assumptions and techniques underlying job evaluation structures as outlined in Chapter 14 indicate that these are largely based on an expansion of all of the five propositions made by Adam Smith, whose ideas remain a solid foundation for the analysis of occupational pay differentials in a modern economy.

Stability of Occupational Pay Differentials

One reason for the continued acceptability of Adam Smith's observations is the remarkable stability of occupational pay hierarchies over long periods. This stability was revealed by evidence supplied in the work of Phelps Brown and Hopkins (1955, 1956, and 1961). These three studies examined the relative pay differentials between certain groups of skilled building workers and unskilled workers over a period of seven centuries. Their findings indicated that in spite of occasions when occupational differentials might contract due to 'shocks', such as severe price inflation, elsewhere in the economy, there appeared to be a long-term trend, at least until 1914, for the old occupational differential pattern to reappear.

In contrast, however, evidence assembled by Hart and MacKay (1975) and Routh (1980) suggests that from about 1914 the scale of relative occupational differentials has significantly changed. The changes have affected the differences not only between skilled and unskilled workers but also between those in manual and non-manual employment. Nevertheless, it must be recognised that although the changes appear to have affected the relative differences in pay between the various occupations—the spread around the average is less today than in the nineteenth century—the occupational pay hierarchy remains constant. Allowing for occupations that have appeared and those that have disappeared, Figure 13.3 shows that most of those at the top and bottom in 1913 were still in much the same position in 1978.

When considering modern tendencies there is some uncertainty as to whether the changes in occupational differentials are permanent, representing a fundamental shift in labour market conditions, or whether they are temporary, so that a return to the nineteenth-century pattern can be expected.

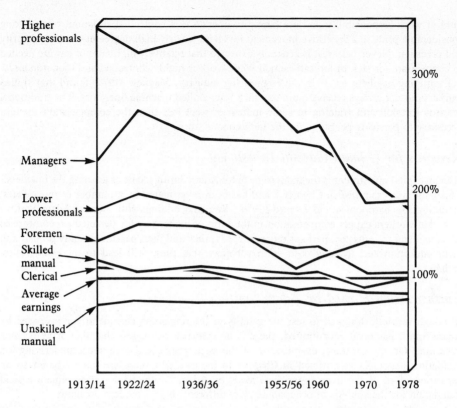

Figure 13.3 *Earnings of occupational groups expressed as a percentage of average earnings, various years*
Source: 'An A to Z of Income and Wealth', HMSO, London, 1980

Routh put forward the hypothesis that significant changes had occurred in labour demand and supply to produce fundamentally changed market conditions. There have been major changes in the provision of secondary, further, and higher education so that a much increased proportion of young people are gaining qualifications leading to employment in the non-manual sectors of labour markets. Proportionally fewer school leavers are seeking manual work.

At the same time technological developments have brought about shifts in labour demand. New processes tend to require fewer workers for any given level of production but can be heavily dependent on relatively few people possessing special skills.

Routh's approach, therefore, suggests that educational and technological developments have produced shifts in supply and demand large enough to reduce the range of occupational pay differentials in favour of manual and at the expense of non-manual workers. To be valid, this hypothesis requires an expansion in the supply of workers qualified for non-manual work greater than the growth of demand for these workers and a contraction in the supply of people seeking manual work greater than the reduction in demand for this kind of labour. Changes in differentials within these two broad worker groups would also be explained by similar movements in supply and demand if Routh's approach is correct.

For different reasons Reder (1955) reaches a largely similar conclusion. He considered that a major contributory factor to changing occupational differentials in the twentieth century had been the different pattern of aggregate employment compared with previous periods. Reder showed that in periods of full, or relatively full, employment there was a tendency for the earlier scale of wage differentials to contract. This could be accounted for by competition between employers for scarce labour and increased willingness to train workers for the new skills required.

Reder cited the experience of major industrial nations during the two World Wars. During both periods large numbers of men served in the armed forces and formerly male-dominated skilled and managerial occupations were 'diluted' by introducing female and unskilled workers. In both periods relative pay differentials became smaller. A similar contraction in pay differentials also appeared to take place in periods of low unemployment. When, however, unemployment rose again there was no tendency to re-establish the old scale of differentials. Employers, in a buyer's market for labour, did not need to bid up the wages of skilled workers. Although it might have been in their economic interests to force down the wages of unskilled labour, employers were prevented from doing so by prevailing social pressures, including the social attitudes of their own managers. This suggests a 'ratchet' effect on differentials. They tended to close in periods of low unemployment but failed to spring back to their old levels when unemployment levels rose. There was little change in response to 'normal' fluctuations in the levels of economic activity. On the other hand a later study by Walsh (1977), using Canadian data, suggested that there could be some widening and narrowing of differentials as they responded to short-term economic fluctuations.

The twentieth-century narrowing of occupational differentials may only be temporary. The period during which differentials have contracted has also been one of prolonged price inflation, during which there has been considerable social and political pressure to raise the wages or maintain the real purchasing power of the 'low paid' and restrain pay increases for the 'well off'.

Hawkesworth (1978), for example, examined the movement of engineering skill differentials in Britain between 1951 and 1976 and concluded that notions of 'equity' and 'fairness' in periods of high price inflation offered a sounder explanation for the trends he was able to identify than did conventional economic forces. In a more limited study for the period 1972–75, Brown (1976) observed that during this period of government anti-inflationary prices and incomes policies there was a rapid compression of occupational wage differentials. When, therefore, twentieth-century style inflation eventually comes to an end there could be a restoration of older scales of occupational earnings differentials.

Turner (1964) advanced an institutional explanation for the twentieth-century tendency. He saw the cause as the special pattern of multi-unionism existing in Britain. This, he felt, led to competition to raise wages for the largest groups, formed of unskilled workers. In this competition the numerically smaller groups of skilled workers had less power. Turner's case is weakened, however, by the fact that the British experience of narrowing occupational differentials reflects a world-wide tendency.

In practice all the influences identified in this section are likely to have had some effect on the changing occupational pay structure, but it remains to be seen whether or not the changes are permanent.

Questions for Discussion and Review

5 How far do you think the pattern of occupations dominating employment in London and South East England contributes to the relatively high levels of pay in these regions?

6 There is some evidence to suggest that occupations containing a relatively high proportion of female workers tend to be at the lower levels of the occupational earnings hierarchy. Name three occupations which you think support this suggestion, and discuss possible reasons.

Inter-industry Pay Differentials

Related Factors Influencing Industry Pay Levels

Before examining the differences in pay attributable to differing industries it is necessary to recognise that a number of associated features can also have an influence. These include:

(a) *Shift work and overtime.* If an industry relies heavily on shift working and/or overtime then the pay averages for that industry are likely to be affected by the hours worked.
(b) *Firm and establishment size.* This effect has already been noted and could influence the pay levels in industries whose firms or work establishments are predominantly larger or smaller than the average.
(c) *Regional location.* Again this will affect some industries, particularly those which are heavily concentrated in high- or low-pay regions.

Nevertheless even when, as in the work of Hood and Rees (1974), allowance has been made for these influences, there are still pay differences that remain linked to different industries and which have been stable over fairly long periods.

Differing Occupational Structures in Industrial Labour Forces

No two industrial labour forces contain the same mix of occupations. The proportions of skilled, managerial, non-manual, and unskilled manual workers employed are all likely to differ because of differing requirements of technology and organisation. Clearly those industries which contain a relatively high proportion of the more highly paid occupational groups are going to have above-average levels of average pay.

Differing Proportions of Male and Female Workers

In spite of equal pay legislation women, as explained in earlier chapters, continue to face problems securing genuine equality in labour markets. Consequently, any study of contemporary employment is likely to reveal that there is a close association between high levels of pay and male domination of a labour market, whereas industries which contain a high proportion of women tend to be among the lower paid.

One explanation may lie in the occupational structures. An industry may be low paid because it contains a high proportion of female workers. Alternatively, of course, it may contain a high proportion of women precisely because pay is low. Employers are more ready to employ women because pay levels do not attract high-quality male workers.

Economic Explanations for Industry Differentials

Most of the above explanations are statistical or social in basis and owe little to economic analysis, nor do they provide complete explanations for inter-industry differentials. A number of economic features can be associated with differences in pay levels.

The Labour–Capital Ratio

A worker's wage level has been assumed to reflect the worker's own level of productivity. This, however, depends not only on individual attitudes to work and personal skills but also on the equipment and tools with which the worker is supplied. The quality and quantity of these reflect the physical capital investment made by the employer. Thus the firm's investment of capital also influences a worker's productivity and, if we accept the assumption that pay is linked to marginal product, it has an effect on the likely wage level. Industries having a high proportion of capital investment are likely to have the more highly paid workers.

This association between capital-intensive industry and relatively high pay does appear to exist, but before assuming that high capital investment always leads to high pay some warnings need to be stated.

(a) One of the arguments of Chapters 4 and 5 was that an increase in wages without an equivalent increase in marginal productivity could lead to employers replacing labour with capital. It could be, therefore, that a high ratio of capital investment was the result, rather than the cause, of high wages.
(b) A high investment in capital means that the firm's fixed costs are high and that the potential losses from any interruption in production can be very great. Under these conditions employers may pay relatively high wages either because they pay a premium for workers expected to be reliable and of high quality or because they are vulnerable to organised threats of labour disruption and the cost of a wage rise is small compared with the losses from a stoppage of production. In either case employers are more willing and able to pay high wages where wage payments are a relatively small proportion of total costs.

Nevertheless, differences in capital–labour ratios do provide an explanation of the tendency for industries based on new technology to pay higher wages than those still dependent on old technology. New technology usually implies a high level of physical capital investment per worker and a high marginal product of labour.

The New, Growing Industries

It is often observed that it is new or growing industries which top industry wage hierarchy tables. One possible explanation is that they are usually highly capital intensive, with the consequences outlined above. Another explanation may be related to the fact that they tend to employ a high proportion of workers with occupational skills in demand in numerous industries. Young and growing firms, which have not had time to develop their own internal labour markets, have to persuade workers with the skills they need to become industrially mobile, and this usually involves having to offer attractive reward packages. It is not usually possible to pay new recruits wages higher than existing employees of equal skill levels, so these tend to gain from the need to entice workers away from other employers.

The Product Market and Market Structure

As explained in Chapter 4, wages are linked to marginal revenue product and the revenue element depends on the firm's ability to sell the product and on the structure of the market in which the product is sold. In general it was earlier suggested that the less price elastic the product the less wage elastic was the firm's demand for labour likely to be, as wage costs could more easily be passed to buyers in product prices. The greater the market power of the employer, the less price elastic the product can be expected to be. Consequently, a product monopolist is more likely to pay high wages than the firm supplying products to a highly competitive market. Moreover, at least in the short term, economic analysis indicates that the monopolist may be able to pay increased wages without reducing employment levels, in contrast to the competitive supplier who may have to reduce the numbers employed after a wage increase.

Introductory economics textbooks usually accuse monopolists of making 'supernormal' profits. In fact these are only found infrequently in reports of the Monopolies and Mergers Commission. It is possible that employers, aware of public disapproval and possible government action following evidence of such profits, prefer instead to share their monopoly profits with employees in the form of increased wages. High wages can also be expected to lead to even higher reward packages to senior managers, whereas profits have to be distributed to shareholders.

The Size of Establishments

Until recent developments in micro-technology, industries with a high level of physical capital investment would normally consist of firms operating production units of above-average size. Such units would also be expected in markets dominated by a few large firms. Observers usually found, therefore, that industries where production was concentrated in a relatively few large establishments tended to have wage levels near the top of the industry differential league. Conversely, industries containing large numbers of small production units tended to be at the lower level of the industry wage hierarchy. It is questionable, therefore, whether the observed association between establishment size and wage level is accounted for by the factors already explained or whether there are additional influences that should be taken into account.

The association between establishment size and wage levels was discussed above in relation to inter-firm differentials, and the factors identified there also apply to industry differentials.

Trade Unions

As also noted earlier, high wage levels have also been associated with high levels of trade union power. Unions need not be powerful throughout the industry. If they are able to raise the wages of certain key occupations who have a particular ability to cause heavy costs through a work stoppage, this increase may then spread through other occupations through the operation of firms' payment structures. This process has been suggested by Dunlop (1964).

The extent of possible trade union influence, the conditions favouring its growth, and the ways it may be exercised are examined in Chapter 16. It may be noted at this stage, however, that unions are most likely to be able to raise wages when they can influence the supply and demand forces within labour markets. The methods they can use to do this are also examined later.

If firms desire or are under pressure to maximise profits, the short-term success of a trade union in pushing wages above the level that is in the best interests of the firm is likely, in the long term, to lead to the replacement of labour by capital, the removal of the production unit to a region or country where labour costs are lower, or the failure of the firm as consumer demand for the product declines. The long-term result, however, may be delayed for a considerable time, as in the rather special case of newspaper production, perhaps until the structure of the industry becomes more competitive and subject to changed managerial control.

Some Research Findings on Inter-industry Differentials

Any consideration of inter-industry wage differentials should, therefore, take into account a range of possible influences and possible interaction with other forms of differential as outlined in this chapter. A group of studies, each of which concentrates on one particular aspect, is likely to produce apparently conflicting results, as in the following examples.

(a) Blanchflower (1986) expressed the view that high wages in an industry represented compensating differentials for conditions of work and unsocial hours required in large plants.
(b) Garbarino (1950) argued that the variables of productivity, concentration, and unionism explained the majority of the differential patterns, but that employment change was also significant.
(c) Kamerschen (1967) believed that industry differentials were dependent upon differences in

productivity, industrial concentration, unionism, and growth rate, with a strong presumption that productivity was the key.

(d) Phelps Brown and Browne (1962) considered there to be an association between the rise of earnings across industries and the level of establishment employment concentration.

(e) Ross and Goldner (1950) identified three influences—unionisation, employment change, and oligopolistic market structure—but then acknowledged it was usual to find all three operating together and that they were unable to separate them.

(f) Tylecote (1975), while finding the degree of industrial concentration to be significant, also expressed the opinion that an industry's labour costs in relation to its sales were important.

(g) Weiss (1966) attributed the differentials primarily to industrial concentration within which trade unions, or the threat of trade unions, produced high wages, although, as a rider, he expressed the opinion that such industries also attracted the more productive workers.

Although failing to agree on the causes of industrial differentials, there is greater consensus among economists concerning trends.

In their separate studies of trends in the post-1945 British economy, both Crossley (1966) and Phelps Brown and Browne (1962) found only modest changes in the relative positions of industries in the wage hierarchy during the limited periods studied. Similar stability was found for a 14-year period in the USA by Ross and Goldner (1950).

It might be argued that a decade or so was too short a period for inter-industry wage differential patterns to change, but Cullen (1956), in his analysis of the US economy, found a high degree of stability over the fifty-year period 1899–1949. A British study by Tarling and Wilkinson (1982), which was generally critical of the concept of long-run inter-industry differential stability, nevertheless acknowledged that the structure of money earnings did remain stable over long periods. However, in a companion paper to that of Tarling and Wilkinson, Lawson (1982) expressed the view that inter-industry earnings differentials were in the process of changing. He attributed the previously identified stability to the fact that in the post-war period of price inflation, most wage increases represented compensation for price rises. Because of this they tended to be of a similar size. When this common element was allowed for, Lawson believed that change could be detected.

Questions for Discussion and Review

7 Choose three of the following industries and find out their approximate position in the industrial wage hierarchy: the retail trade; agriculture; hotels and catering; the chemical industry; coal mining; oil refining; electricity generation. Discuss possible reasons for the relative positions of the industries you have chosen.

8 Identify the dominant industry in your own area and discuss its position in the national wages hierarchy in the light of the arguments presented in this chapter.

Suggestions for Written Assignments

1 Suggest reasons for the apparently greater degree of stability between industrial wage differentials and occupational pay differentials over the past half century. How far is it possible to reconcile this difference?

2 Identify the most important occupations and industries in your area. What similarity is there between the relative levels of these in their respective pay hierarchies and your area's place in the pattern of regional pay differentials? Suggest reasons for any differences you observe in the various differentials.

3 Write a report outlining the main differences between the pay of non-manual and of manual workers and suggesting reasons for trends in the pay differential between these two groups of workers.

4 'The firms and occupations which offer the highest pay are the ones that are the most difficult to enter.' Discuss, using suitable examples, the accuracy of this statement. Suggest reasons why it is true for at least some firms and occupations.

Suggestions for Further Reading

Analysis of the theoretical concepts related to the determination of the reward for labour and a consideration of the influences upon the differing types of wage differentials were examined in Phelps Brown (1977) and Wood (1978). A number of the wider socio-economic issues associated with the subject of this chapter were discussed in Donaldson and Philby (1984).

14
Wages and the Firm

Pay and Conflicting Objectives
The Employer's Desire to Link Pay and Production

The examination of the individual's supply of labour in Chapter 6 identified a simple relationship in which the wage received for working was a reward for leisure sacrificed. The individual's relative preference for income and leisure determined the number of hours per week that person was prepared to work.

For this choice to be effective there must be employers wishing to employ labour. Employers, however, are interested not just in the work done by the worker but in the production achieved from that work. The product of a period of work depends not only on the length of the period but also on the effort made by the worker. Sitting at a typewriter does not, in itself, type letters.

Consequently, any payment system operated by an employer is likely to be designed not only to persuade workers with the required skills to give up their leisure or present occupations to work in the firm but also to encourage them to devote their energies to achieving the production objectives of the employer.

This suggests a possible conflict of interest between employer and employee. Classical economics assumes that participants in the economy seek to maximise their own utilities. This could mean that workers aim to achieve the highest possible income combined with the lowest possible sacrifice of both leisure time and freedom at work. Employers, on the other hand, seek to obtain the highest possible quantity and quality of product from their workers at the lowest possible cost.

Many students of labour relations would argue that this is a very great over-simplification of the employer–employee relationship, that people have motives for working that are not directly related to pay, and that a full understanding of these can enable employers to achieve high levels of labour productivity without paying inflated wages and yet still allow workers to achieve most of their own individual work objectives. Discussion of these arguments is beyond the scope of this book, and this chapter is concerned only with payment systems and the part they may play in helping to overcome any conflicts that there may be between the objectives of workers and their employers.

It might be argued that the observed failure of normal employment contracts to make specific reference to work effort was an important element in the development in the early 1960s of 'productivity agreements', some of which attempted to be more specific in relating pay to effort. Most of these, however, were chiefly concerned with modifying collective agreements or long-established custom and practice which reduced labour productivity and which had been designed to maximise employment prospects and increase pay without any corresponding increase in the sacrifices made by workers.

Whatever the system of labour management and whatever assumptions might be made about the workers' motives for working, there is ample evidence to suggest that many employers believe that work effort can be influenced by wage payment methods. Pencavel (1977) has pointed to the importance placed by employers on different wage payment methods despite their lack of knowledge about the degree of effort likely to be made by potential employees and how this was likely to be affected by differing methods of payment.

It is common to classify the different payment systems into two main groups:

(a) *Time payments*. Under a time payment system workers are rewarded according to the length of time spent at the place or places of work. Such systems clearly require a supervision and management structure to ensure that workers are actually working during the time for which they are paid.

(b) *Payment by results*. Under this system workers are rewarded by predetermined work performance measures. This, in turn, involves costs and systems for assessing performance and making payments. Whether these schemes require more or less work supervision and inspection is a matter of some uncertainty.

The Worker's Desire for Pay Stability

Employees might recognise the employer's need to link pay with production but they are also conscious of the following:

The Need For Income Stability

The work of Azariadis (1975) on implicit contracts recognised that workers were typically 'risk averse' and preferred earnings stability to fluctuating incomes even though the latter could, over a period, provide higher rewards. Modern social trends, especially dependence on home mortgages and consumer credit, rely heavily on the worker's ability to maintain income stability. A sudden reduction in income results in a damaging reduction in living standards, loss of social position, and often family disruption. Pay fluctuations were less damaging in older market economies when land and house rents also fluctuated and workers owned few personal assets and rarely became involved in long-credit schemes.

The Dependence of Labour Productivity on Factors Beyond the Worker's Control

More important than a worker's personal effort may well be the equipment provided by and the managerial standards achieved by the employer. A typist may be working very hard and accurately but productivity might be much improved with the provision of a good word processor, adequate training, and well-planned work. Efficient office managers can often reduce the actual physical effort and work load of office workers while increasing productivity.

Diversity of Workers

The typical modern firm employs many different kinds of workers, and a pay system that might encourage greater effort from one group might produce unproductive activity or even hostility in another. The firm, therefore, can be expected to operate a number of different payment systems at any given time.

In most industrial or commercial enterprises the employees are engaged in a complex range of interlocking but different activities. Regardless of the type of organisation examined, similar patterns of activity may be identified. For example, in a manufacturing organisation there are on the shop floor two distinct groups of manual, often described as blue collar, employees. One group, that may or may not be classified as skilled or semi-skilled, operates machinery and equipment leading directly to the production of goods. A second, more diverse group of skilled and unskilled workers supports those employees while not actually participating directly in the production process themselves. The term 'production' is here being employed in the more limited sense common in industry, of actually making goods, and not in the wider economic sense of any work that contributes to the satisfaction of a private or public 'want'.

How and what is being produced will be determined by managerial, administrative, and technical workers. These are often known as white-collar workers and today, perhaps more for historical reasons than for significant differences in the conditions of their employment contracts, they are also known as 'staff'. Managers, at varying levels, depending on the size of the organisation, are responsible for initiating, regulating, and supervising activities. Technical staff provide the specialist skills needed to turn managerial decisions into reality. Administrative workers help to co-ordinate all the different activities within the organisation and in relation to the outside world. Workers who provide the skills and services to support production are also known as 'indirect production' workers.

Nearly all types of organisation have a broadly similar employment structure. The terminology developed to describe manufacturing is also often applied to services, where the employees engaged in actually providing the service directly to the public are described as production workers.

Overcoming Diversity and Conflict

The employer's problem is to devise a pay structure whose cost bears some relationship to the contribution of labour to the success of the enterprise, which enables workers to know what they are earning and what they can do to increase their earnings, and which provides incentives for workers to improve the quality of their work and its contribution to the objectives of the enterprise but which does not encourage activities that are detrimental to those objectives.

At the same time, the employer has to recognise that the firm is operating in a labour market in which the best workers are able to choose between competing employers. Nevertheless, pay should not be so high that it leads to the employment of workers who are over-qualified for the work they are expected to do and who then become frustrated. High pay can never fully compensate for the neglect of these non-monetary rewards from work which can be included in the general term 'job satisfaction'.

Questions for Discussion and Review

1 Make a list of the categories of workers in the educational establishment where you are now or where you most recently studied. Classify your categories as either production or indirect workers. Discuss any problems you had in making your classification. Which workers if any, could have part of their pay related to the results of their work?

2 Suggest ways in which a wage payment system might encourage a worker to appear to do more work without increasing the saleable output of the employer.

3 Discuss and comment critically on the methods you might choose to measure the productivity of the following workers: word-processor operator; tax accountant; delivery van driver; office manager; school teacher; policeman.

Time Rate Payments

The Use of Time Rate Systems

The principle of time rate payment, the system under which most employees in Britain are paid, is that the employee's reward is not directly related to success or otherwise in the tasks undertaken but to time spent on the employer's business. This method may imply that the work does not permit individual performance to be measured in the short run, e.g. managerial decision making, or that the quality of the work undertaken is of greater significance than the quantity of output, e.g. in the maintenance of machinery. Provided that the manager is available over a specified time period to take the relevant decisions, or the millwright is available when required, then these people will be paid the agreed amount. In making the payment it is not immediately relevant whether the manager is taking the correct decisions or that the millwright successfully repairs the machine.

Indirect manual employees are usually paid a time rate, but this method is also used when employees directly engaged in manufacturing processes undertake tasks which are machine controlled and/or where the activities of groups of employees are closely linked and there is an emphasis on the quality of output.

Time rate payment systems are also normally used for non-manual employees, such as secretaries, whose work tasks and work loads vary over the day or longer period.

In the short run, payment depends on time spent working and not the quality of work. Should, however, the effort made in the time period be considered unsatisfactory or of very high quality, it has to be assumed that the employer would take this into consideration in other ways. For example, the employer's view of a worker's suitability for promotion to better-paid work would depend very largely on current performance in the present job.

Salaries and Status

A distinction, discussed by Khan (1956), is often made between 'salaried' and 'day work'. This arises from the implied status given to different groups of employees, their differing opportunities for advancement, and the time periods involved. For salaried employees it is the practice to specify the level of pay over a twelve-month period, e.g. £20 000 per annum, although payment is made monthly. For day work the period specified will be shorter, for example £300 for a 39-hour week, or, say, £7 an hour. The actual level of reward for the specified time period is often the subject of negotiation between trade unions and employers or their representatives. This has been the established practice over a prolonged period for day work employees in many industries, and has increasingly become the practice for salaried workers, especially where the employer is in the public sector.

Salary payments continue to retain an element of implied superior social status. This has often been associated with a greater degree of security and with a number of privileges such as longer holidays, a shorter working day, and sickness and pension scheme benefits. These privileges, however, have been eroded by legislation and by moves to harmonise conditions. Some manual worker trade unions have made strenuous efforts to obtain 'staff privileges' for their members, and personnel managers have often been sympathetic to this objective.

Salaried staff still tend to have opportunities to progress to higher positions and pay levels that are denied to day workers. Salary structures often contain a series of grades, scales, or classes. A typical structure might have, say, 5 grades: Grade 1, £6000–8500; Grade 2, £9000–12 000; and so on, with perhaps opportunities to rise to a higher system of 'managerial grades' or to individual contracts with individually negotiated salaries. New employees begin at one of the lower scales, which one depending on previous experience or educational level, but anticipating movement through the grades by stages. There may be formal, and publicly known, incremental scales through which the employee can progress for a period more or less automatically with little or no appraisal of individual effort or merit. It is assumed that the worker is accumulating human capital in the form of skills and experience. This type of approach is found in the public sector and often for lower grades of salaried employment in the private sector. A modified approach to this is found more commonly in the private sector. The modified system continues to place the employees in grades, but the boundaries of these may not be known; progress through a grade owes much to assessment by immediate superiors who can determine the speed of progress. This particular method, designed to appraise individual performance, is often based on differing forms of merit rating.

Time Pay and Incentives

All the different forms of time payment systems tend to share similar limitations. Because payment is not linked directly to the effort put into the work, there may appear to be no immediate incentive for an employee to work hard. Time payment schemes, therefore, are unlikely to stimulate employees to improve efficiency or productivity. A pay scale may be easy to understand, but if it is inflexible and externally negotiated by people remote from the individual worker it offers little opportunity for workers to increase their income levels within the specified work periods. In some cases there may be opportunities to increase income by overtime working, rewarded by higher (premium) pay rates. In other cases, particularly for more senior grades, workers may be expected to work overtime as a normal part of the job.

Questions for Discussion and Review

4 List what you consider to be the advantages and disadvantages of a time rate payment system from the point of view of the individual employee.

5 Under what circumstances could the amount of time occupied on the employer's business be an unreliable guide to the worker's contribution to the success of the firm?

Payment by Results

The Case for Payment by Results

When an employer feels it necessary to use pay to encourage greater effort, some form of incentive scheme is likely to be used. The general term 'payment by results' is used to refer to any scheme which involves financial incentives for increased or improved work. It covers, therefore, a very wide range of schemes. These can measure individual or group effort, units of work produced or time spent on specified work, or indeed any other kind of measurement that employers can devise.

In the purest form of payment by results, an employee is rewarded only for personal output during a specified period. Failure to achieve output, however caused, results in a loss of earnings. While individual payment by results schemes are considered to be appropriate for direct production workers, they also frequently apply to those selling goods or services who receive a commission calculated on the level of sales.

Schemes for Payment by Results

The simple, basic, payment by results principle of 'no output, no reward' has been developed in two main ways:

Piecework

Under this, the employee is rewarded with an agreed sum for each unit of output sold or produced. The item unit is given an agreed monetary value and the reward is simply the number of units produced or sold multiplied by the monetary value. Figure 14.1 provides an illustration.

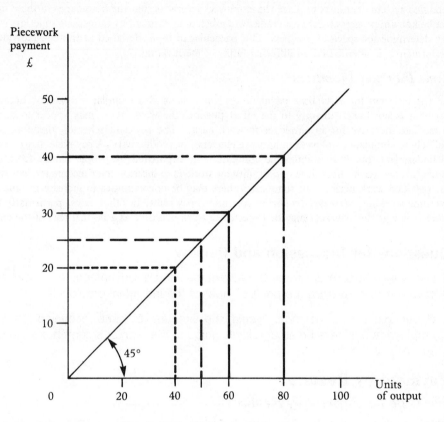

Figure 14.1 *Piecework payment diagram*
Note: Each piece valued at 50p

Time Allowance

This is often adopted for the more complicated manufacturing tasks. It uses what is known as the standard minute. The objective is essentially the same as that of piecework. The employee's reward is based upon a time value for output achieved. The length of each production process is specified in terms of standard minutes, calculated by a recognised work study procedure. At the end of the period the work achieved is measured by adding the number of standard minutes allotted to each item produced. In an eight-hour shift an employee may contribute more or less than 480 standard minutes of work. The employee's pay for the shift is found by multiplying the agreed monetary value for the standard minute by the number of such minutes worked. This is illustrated in Figure 14.2.

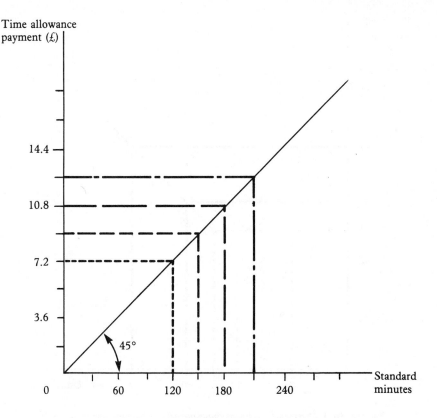

Figure 14.2 *Time allowance payment diagram*
Note: Each standard minute valued at 6p

Payment by results schemes are intended to encourage those employees who are able to control both the method and speed of their work to operate more effectively. The direct link between pay and output enables the worker to increase pay by increasing output. It also benefits the employer by spreading fixed production costs over a larger number of units.

Stability of Earnings

Methods of payment by results also have limitations. A disadvantage for employees is that earnings are no longer stable; they can fluctuate from week to week for reasons beyond the employee's own control (e.g. work tasks may change; machines can break down, interrupting the flow of material). When tasks are changed, workers are often paid for a specified period an agreed rate based on the average of either the employee's own earnings over the previous period, or those of fellow employees already skilled in the task.

There are many ways to protect workers from loss of earnings caused by circumstances beyond their control. Individual schemes are chosen or modified to suit particular circumstances. There are often standard, collective arrangements for such general eventualities as machine breakdown. For schemes covering work on the employer's premises it is common practice to incorporate a 'fall back' element. This is illustrated in Figure 14.3.

When, for reasons beyond his or her control, an employee is unable to achieve the output

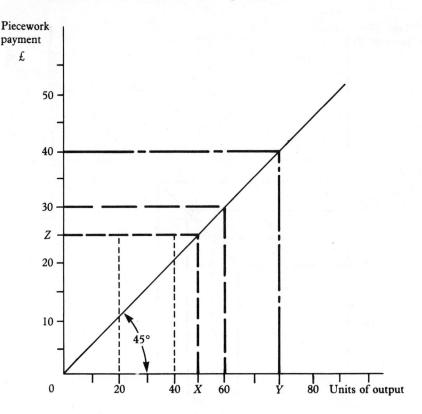

Figure 14.3 *Piecework payment diagram with minimum fall-back payment*
Note: Each piece valued at 50p

level X shown in Figure 14.3, a guaranteed wage of £Z will be paid. Beyond output X, expressed in items produced or standard minutes of work, the financial incentives to increase efficiency and production become effective. Thus, an output level of Y will be rewarded with a higher wage.

In the example of Figure 14.3 the permitted earnings increase is directly proportional to the increased level of output. This clearly is the simplest approach, but it is not the only one. Some others are indicated in Figure 14.4. These approaches are used by manufacturing industry, and each has its own advocates.

An obvious prerequisite for payment by results schemes is to establish standards. These inform the employee of the monetary value of the item being produced or the time in standard minutes it should take to produce. Correct standards are essential both for the employee, whose earnings are dependent upon them, and for the employer, for whom they are a production cost.

With some exceptions, it is usual for these standards to be established at company level. Although there are still some organisations where 'rate fixers' determine the relevant monetary or time values by methods more dependent upon their own experience than any scientific procedure, this is becoming much less common. Greater reliance is now placed upon specialist work study techniques. Nevertheless, the determination of piecework prices or standard minutes is not, and probably never will be, an exact science. Errors are made and disputes arise on the shop floor. These problems have to be solved by negotiation and this is costly in management time. A further criticism of payment by results is that, in the short run, management is unable to control the level of output and/or the wage bill.

In spite of these widely recognised difficulties, some important benefits are often claimed. The main advantage is that financial incentives are believed to encourage worker efficiency and output levels. Supporters of such schemes argue that incentives provide sufficient self-motivation to reduce the amount of supervision necessary. To provide a net advantage, of course, any gains from these benefits must be greater than the costs of establishing and maintaining standards for each job and the management time required to deal with disagreements.

A further complication arises when direct production workers are able to increase their earnings while indirect workers, who are more dependent on materials, maintenance, and other factors outside their control, have fewer opportunities to do so and become resentful.

Discussions of payment by results systems frequently assume that it is the individual worker's effort that is being measured and rewarded. This is often true, but in many cases modern technology also makes it possible to measure the work of a clearly defined team of workers to permit a group scheme. This is sometimes thought to be preferable because it

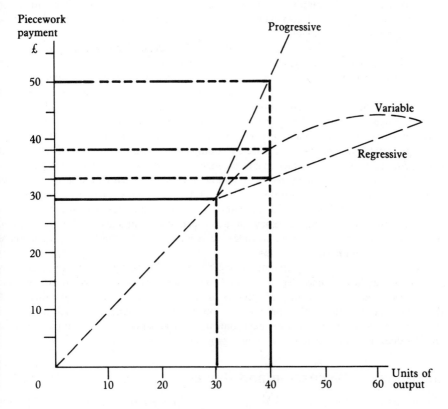

Figure 14.4 *Piecework payment diagram with alternative rewards*
Note: (a) Output 40 units payment – progressive payment £50
*   – variable payment £37.50*
*   – regressive payment £32.50*
*   (b) Minimum fall-back of £29 for up to 30 units*

introduces an element of group discipline and competition between teams. Fellow workers can be tougher than supervisors in dealing with a colleague thought to be threatening the team's earnings. On the other hand, teams which become used to achieving a high rate of performance on a particular set of tasks can be very hostile to any kind of change. A payment scheme that increases the costs and problems of management or impedes change is self-defeating.

Limitations of Payment by Results

All wage systems have their strengths and weaknesses. Payment by results schemes are not practical in all situations. To have the best chance of success the following conditions should be met.

(a) Output should be capable of being controlled and influenced by those whose pay depends on its size.
(b) Output should be subject to accurate measurement.
(c) Volume of output should be more important than quality.

It is clear, therefore, that payments by results schemes are most appropriate for tasks that are fairly simply, short, and repetitive, and where the speed of work is not controlled entirely by the machine. Where quality of workmanship is important, e.g. for machine maintenance, these schemes are not generally suitable.

It must also be recognised that there is no indisputable evidence that payment by results does lead to higher output. When payment by results schemes are introduced production levels do tend to increase, but it is usual for other changes to be made at the same time. For example, modifications may be made in working methods, in work flow, or in organisational structure. It may be that it is these, rather than just the financial incentives, that produce the higher output levels. Sociologists also recognise what they term the 'Hawthorne effect' (so called because of the association with some famous experiments carried out by George Elton Mayo at the Hawthorne works of the General Electric Company in Chicago in the 1920s). This acknowledges that any change which makes the members of the work team feel that people are taking an interest in them is likely to raise morale among the workers involved. For a time after the change, therefore, work improves, only to return to previous levels after the workers themselves have returned to their old anonymity. If, subsequently, the old working practices are restored, there is the same tendency towards a period of temporary work improvement. This is a reminder that management attitudes are as important an influence on production as working practices and payment systems.

There is also evidence that workers dislike uncertainty and fluctuations in weekly or monthly pay. After a time they become adept at learning how to achieve a desired level of earnings and then they use their mastery of the task process to take additional leisure or make their work easier. They may fear that if they produce too much then management will look for further increases in production when pay rates next come up for negotiation. It is evident that payment by results does not automatically raise labour productivity.

Questions for Discussion and Review

6 Attempts are made from time to time to introduce payment by results schemes for office workers such as typists and word-processor operators. Discuss the problems likely to arise with these attempts.

7 It is often said that people do not work just for pay. What other rewards do you believe are sought from work?

Time and Results Schemes

Measured Day Work

Because of the uncertainties and limitations of payments by results schemes, attempts have been made to evolve ways to remove the fluctuations from workers' pay while preserving the financial incentive to achieve higher levels of output. One approach which has been adopted in numerous British firms over the past quarter century is known as measured day work.

This is based on a particular approach to employee rewards, but there are very many variations. The fundamental principle of measured day work schemes is to provide a fixed payment which is additional to the worker's basic (daywork) rate in return for some specified extra effort on the employee's part.

The additional payment can vary according to the type of work undertaken or effort involved. It is made on a regular, usually weekly, basis for as long as a specified level of output is maintained. The target level of output for each employee, or defined group of employees, is determined by work measurement techniques. In practice, targets are likely to be similar to those thought to be achievable by average employees working under a payment by results scheme.

Under measured day work, however, detailed working practices are determined by managers, not production employees. Should a worker not achieve the required standard due to his or her own fault, e.g. through carelessness, then the additional sum would not be paid. Should, however, the failure to reach the standard be attributable to factors for which the management is responsible, then the extra payment is made.

Supporters of measured day work believe that this approach combines the encouragement of higher output with preserving managerial control over working methods, output levels, and wage costs. For the employee, such a scheme does offer the opportunity of achieving increased wages while avoiding the fluctuations associated with payment by results. On the other hand, there is a reduction in the elements of personal motivation and incentive which have always been seen as an essential part of payment by results. The employee also loses control over individual output. It must, however, be recognised that in many modern integrated and highly mechanised or automated manufacturing processes there is now very little scope left for workers to vary individual output or working tasks.

Participating in the Success of the Firm

Payment systems based on 'pieces' of output achieved have a long history. They were basic to the 'outwork' manufacturing methods employed before the industrial revolution brought work into mills and factories. The modern emphasis, however, on the 'energy effort' that is a feature of payment by results and measured day work schemes originates from the ideas of the Scientific School of Management. This stressed financial incentives linked to individual effort in performing specific tasks designated by management.

Other schools of management thought, in particular the Human Relations School, have placed less emphasis on the individual contributions of employees and paid more attention to the collective contribution of the workforce. This rather different approach has contributed to the growth of factory and company-wide payment schemes which seek to motivate an entire workforce. The objective of these schemes is to influence general attitudes and especially to promote a spirit of worker–management co-operation. The intention is to foster feelings of common interest between workers, managers, and shareholders in the financial success of the organisation.

The simplest example of this type of approach is where a bonus payment based on output levels and/or sales for a particular period is paid to all employees. The actual amount of payment is often a percentage of the individual's normal earnings. Payments can be made monthly, quarterly, or annually. For such a scheme to work there must be an agreed level of output or sales to provide a base line from which to measure changes and to determine future bonus payments.

Another approach, again often based on previous sales levels, is the payment scheme known as the Scanlon Plan. This seeks to establish a factory-wide bonus scheme which would supplement the normal wages paid. It is designed to include all employees at every level. The size of the bonus paid is determined by a ratio which relates the average labour costs to total sales values over a previous period. The plan assumes that the ratio of labour cost to sales value declines as the production achieved per worker rises provided that the increased output is actually sold.

Under Scanlon Plan schemes a proportion of the 'savings' in labour costs from increased output per worker would automatically be made available for bonus payments.

The concept of supplementary bonus payments based on collective teamwork was developed in a slightly different fashion in the Rucker Plan. This particular variation used value added (roughly the financial difference between revenue received from sales and payments made to other firms for goods and services purchased) in preference to sales value. In other respects the underlying approach is much the same. A proportion of the higher net revenue resulting from the increased average output per worker is shared among all the employees.

These schemes, and others like them, have been designed to overcome some of the limitations of both payment by results and measured day work. Emphasis is placed on the inclusion of all employees and not just those whose work could be measured.

From a 'human relations' viewpoint the Scanlon and Rucker Plans are valuable in that they could make individual employees aware of their contribution to the whole organisation. However, it is often considered that their effects on pay are relatively small. Indeed, these plans suffer from the limitations of all such bonus schemes, namely that there is a very weak link between increased effort from any one individual and that worker's subsequent bonus payment. This bonus also usually represents only a small percentage of the total wage payment. It is even possible for an individual and/or group to increase effort and then to find that the subsequent factory bonus declines. When bonus payments are based on output, sales, value added, or some other measure of company achievement they can be unpredictable and, of course, depend on events such as changes in taxation or raw material prices which are outside the control of the workforce. They may also depend on certain crucial strategic managerial decisions such as whether to enter or leave a particular market or purchase a certain kind of machine. The great majority of workers have no influence on these decisions. When regular bonuses are achieved they come, after a time, to be regarded as part of the normal wage, and any reduction in the bonus tends to have a disruptive effect.

Some organisations have sought to relate bonus payments to the level of the employer's profits in the previous accounting period. In these cases the bonus may take the form either of money or of shares in the company. While the criteria adopted to determine the size of the bonus clearly differ, there are many similarities to the production- or sales-related schemes. Profit-related bonus payments are designed to encourage employees to take a wider interest in the fortunes of their employers, but provide few incentives to individual employees to increase their own efforts. Estimates suggest that by 1987, when the Government announced its intention of providing tax incentives to encourage profit-related earnings, about 5% of employees in Britain were covered by profit-related bonus schemes.

Government Encouragement of Profit-related Schemes

The idea of profit-related pay received government support in the Budget of 1987. The Government, however, was more interested in making wages more flexible than in encouraging workers to put more effort into their work. The Government sought to restore efficient, unregulated markets and these required prices and wages to move down as well as up. Since most people were aware that profits could fall as well as rise, linking pay to profit appeared a promising way to encourage the change in attitudes that a restoration of unregulated markets seemed to require.

The Budget proposals of 1987 contained generous tax incentives to encourage the spread of 'profit-related pay' (PRP). The Finance Act of that year provided that no income tax should be charged on half an employee's profit-related pay up to the stage where it made up one-fifth of the worker's total income, including PRP, or £3000, whichever was the less. This substantial tax relief is administered through the normal Pay As You Earn system, and employers have to register schemes with the Inland Revenue and supply a periodic report from an independent accountant.

This kind of scheme is only likely to appeal on any scale to higher-rate taxpayers and is unlikely to make wages in general much more flexible.

Questions for Discussion and Review

8 Discuss the case for profit-related pay from the point of view of (a) employers, (b) employees, and (c) the community.

9 Suggest activities where measured day work schemes are likely to be appropriate. Why might measured day work be preferable to piecework schemes in these cases?

Additional Aspects of Wage Payment Schemes

Overtime and Premium Rates

The major approaches to employee financial rewards have now been identified. These indicate that where the concern is with time effort only then the practice is to use time rate payments, and where the concern is with energy effort only then the practice is to adopt some form of payment by results. The intermediate stage of measured day work incorporates elements of both the time and energy efforts, the former being reflected in the basic pay level, the latter in the supplement paid. Other approaches have made use of bonuses or profit sharing and these generally apply to the workforce as a whole.

There are two further supplements which are often paid to individual employees under schemes catering for an organisation's entire labour force. Where employees work hours in excess of those in their contracts they are normally rewarded with additional premium rate payments for the overtime worked. These premium rates are higher than those applying to work in the normal contracted time and they may vary according to the time actually worked. For example, a higher premium usually applies for a Sunday than a Wednesday. They may also vary according to the total additional hours worked, e.g. a higher payment is made for the second ten hours in a month than the first ten hours.

A simple theoretical justification for the payment of premium rates for overtime working can be made using the concept of wage–leisure preference and the analytical technique of indifference curves introduced in Chapter 6.

When the possible consequences of an increase in wage rate were examined in Chapter 6 it was found that economic analysis could not predict the effect on hours worked without knowing the workers' wage–leisure preferences at the relevant income level. Consequently, a simple increase in pay for all hours worked could lead to a desire for more leisure rather than to a greater willingness to work, as required by the employer.

Suppose, however, that the employer offers the higher (premium) rate only for hours worked above the original number. This is illustrated in Figure 14.5, where the income–leisure possibility line $L_0 Y_0$ branches at point L, Y to indicate the increased maximum income possibility of Y_2. This new line enables the worker to reach a higher level of satisfaction I_1, but this time the amount of leisure is reduced. In this case the new leisure choice of L_1 is below the old level of L. In order to earn the higher income of Y_1 the worker has to give up some leisure and work the additional hours required by the employer.

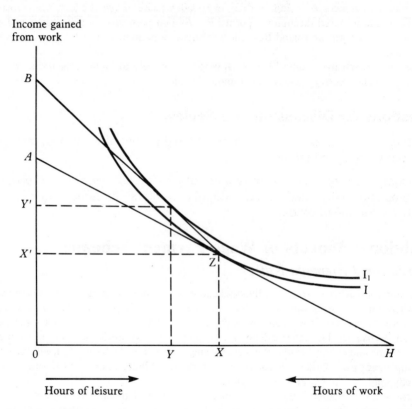

Figure 14.5 *An increase in working hours achieved by paying premium rates for overtime working*

It is also common practice, especially for manual workers, for normal rates to be supplemented should work be required on a shift basis which may involve either regular early or late working or work through the night. Any overtime or shift-work premiums are paid additionally to the normal pay entitlement, and both are based on either a percentage of normal earnings or a pre-determined flat rate. This practice of compensating workers by paying different pay rates for different working time periods is explored by Bosworth and Dawkins (1980).

Questions for Discussion and Review

10 'Income tax must be reduced in order to encourage people to work more.' Discuss this statement in the light of your study of this chapter.

11 'People who work anti-social hours should always receive higher pay.' Should they?

Job Evaluation

The Objectives of Job Evaluation

Where employees are paid under payment by result schemes, a differential pattern of earnings will emerge based on the differing levels of energy effort the employees contribute. Employees who contribute a high degree of energy effort will expect to receive a higher reward than those contributing less. The differences in earnings levels ought to reflect differences in the contributions to production achieved. However, where employees are rewarded under time rate payment schemes, the pattern of differentials cannot be developed on the basis of energy effort since there is no mechanism for its measurement. Nevertheless, it has long been recognised that there are differences in the value to the firm of workers subject to time rate payments and that these differences should be measured and reflected in the wages actually paid.

Techniques of Job Evaluation

The practice of job evaluation has been evolved as a contribution towards solving this problem. The technique of job evaluation involves assessing the relative value of different jobs within an organisation and linking appropriate rewards to these. It assesses and relates pay to the job and not to the individuals who actually perform the job tasks. Job evaluation is not used directly to determine the actual level of reward for employees; rather it is a method to assist in determining an organisational pay structure based on the relative value of the jobs which are undertaken within the organisation. For this reason the practice has become increasingly significant in resolving questions relating to equal pay for male and female workers.

Several basic forms of job evaluation have been developed and there are a number of modified forms to suit the needs of different organisations. Because job evaluation is based on human judgements it is always likely to remain an inexact technique and one liable to be swayed by personal considerations. Although they recognise its inexact nature, advocates suggest that the differing approaches do provide systematic ways of comparing the total demands of one job with another. It is held, therefore, to provide a basis for developing a logical and acceptable wage structure. However, because of the differences in the content and character of differing jobs within an organisation, two or even more job evaluation schemes may be operating at the same time. One, for example, may apply to manual employees and another to white-collar, clerical grades.

As organisations grow in size and complexity and develop internal labour markets of the kind outlined in Chapter 12, so does the task of trying to keep the rewards for different jobs in their appropriate relationship to each other in an acceptable wage structure.

Ranking

In small firms, or large ones with only a limited number of differing types of job, it remains possible for an individual to know the content of each job in considerable detail. In these instances it is then possible to use a simple form of job evaluation known as 'ranking'. A manager, or a small committee, will meet and place the jobs in an agreed rank order of value to the organisation. When the rank order is established, the payment levels to the differing jobs can be examined to confirm that the order in the pay structure corresponds to the rank values. The ranking approach does not analyse the different jobs, it only indicates a rank order of job difficulty and a possible wage structure. It gives no guide as to size of differentials between different jobs, only the order of pay between the highest and lowest.

A simple example of a ranking job evaluation for engineering manual workers is shown in Figure 14.6.

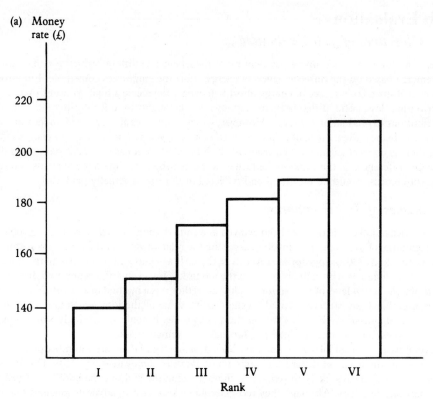

Figure 14.6 *Ranking job evaluation for engineering manual workers*

Jobs in company	*Rank order (i.e. relative value of job to company)*
Machine operator	*IV*
Press operator	*III*
Bench assembly	*II*
Inspector	*V*
Storekeeper	*I*
Toolfitter	*VI*

Job Grading/Classification

The ranking approach is thus dependent upon the subjective evaluation of particular managers. The same is partly true for job grading or classification. Under this approach an initial decision is taken as to how many grades or classes there should actually be within the organisation. For example, it may be decided that non-managerial and non-technical white-collar jobs should each be placed in one of six grades. Once the decision has been taken on the number of grades/classes then a careful definition, based upon clearly specified criteria such as education or training requirements, can be made of the type of job expected in each grade/class. When this stage has been carried out, the job description of each of the jobs may be evaluated and can be compared with the agreed criteria definitions to determine the appropriate grade/class for each job. This approach again says nothing of the relative size of the differentials between each grade/class. Establishing the pay differentials is a matter for managerial decision making, often after discussion or negotiation with worker representatives.

An example of a classification/grading structure for non-manual staff is shown in Table 14.1.

Table 14.1   Classification/grading job evaluation for non-manual staff

		Criteria		
Grades	Salary scales	Educational requirement	In-company training	Sample of jobs evaluated
A	3650–5000	—	5 days max.	Radiographics; postroom staff
B	4400–6600	3 'O' levels; 3 CSEs	15 days max.	File clerk
C	5500–7700	5 'O' levels	30 days max.	Receptionist; copy typist
D	6750–8500	'A'-level study	50 days max.	Secretary; word-processor operator
E	8000–10 000	2 'A' levels; ONC/D	50 days +	Personal assistant; buying process clerk

In the more complex approaches to job evaluation it is necessary to examine in detail the actual content of job tasks. When, for example, manual jobs are considered, it is usual to examine each job in terms of four 'core factors'. These are skill, effort (physical requirements), responsibility, and working conditions. Each of these factors will be further sub-divided. For example, the skill factor might be considered in terms of the education standards required, length of training, years of experience, degrees of dexterity, initiative, etc. Should, however, non-manual clerical jobs be the subject of this form of job evaluation, the core factors might be accountability, knowledge, mental skills, and social skills.

Factor Comparison Evaluation

One of the two 'scientific' approaches to job evaluation is the 'factor comparison method'. For manual employees this will incorporate the four core factors identified above. When the factor comparison method is first used a dozen or so key jobs will be selected and ranked under each of the factors being used. These might be factors such as length of training and working conditions. When the rankings of the factor components of each job have been agreed, the existing wage rate for each of these key jobs will be sub-divided between the factors used. Each factor is, therefore, allocated that proportion of the existing wage rate which is considered to reflect its relative importance within the job.

An example of this approach helps to clarify the operation of the system. Table 14.2 shows a

Table 14.2   Factor comparison job evaluation for engineering manual workers; comparison ranking by factors

Key jobs	Skill requirements		Physical requirements		Responsibility		Working conditions		Current wages
	R^a	MU^b	R	MU	R	MU	R	MU	£
Machine operator	4	50	3	50	2	30	4	30	160
Press operator	3	45	1	40	1	15	6	50	150
Bench assembly	2	30	5	60	4	40	2	15	145
Inspector	6	65	2	45	6	55	3	25	180
Storekeeper	1	20	6	75	3	35	1	10	140
Toolfitter	5	60	4	55	5	45	5	40	200

[a] R = core factor ranking
[b] MU = wage allocation

possible factor comparison structure for engineering manual workers. Each of the first four columns indicates the core factor ranking (R) and the wage allocation (MU) for each of the selected key jobs (machine operator, press operator, etc.).

Notice that the machine operator is ranked fourth for skill, third for physical requirements, second for responsibility, and fourth for working conditions. The existing wage of £160 is apportioned on the basis of £50 to skill, £50 to physical requirements, £30 to responsibility, and £30 to working conditions. In this ranking system 1 is at the bottom and 6 is at the top.

In making the payment allocation it is important to ensure that this does not modify the initial factor rankings. The allocation of a proportion of the wage to each factor shows why each job receives its current level of pay and ensures that jobs carrying higher levels of responsibility, skill, etc., receive the higher pay. When the factor/reward framework for the key jobs has been established it is then possible to fit all similar jobs into the grid. The key jobs provide reference points for fitting all the others into their appropriate places.

When the factor rankings have been established the monetary rewards to be related to each factor can be decided, and these provide the rate of pay for each job. Table 14.3 shows how these stages are carried out. Here, payment rates have been established and the key jobs fitted into their appropriate places in the grid. One additional job, that of millwright, has been added. Any number of additional jobs considered to be similar can also be included. Notice that the millwright's pay will be:

    £50 (skill)
  + £65 (physical requirement)
  + £50 (responsibility)
  + £45 (working conditions)
  Total £210

Like ranking, this approach does not analyse individual jobs, but unlike ranking, it does permit the formation of a systematic payment system. The factor comparison approach is widely used in the USA and in US-owned companies in Britain. British-owned companies, however, tend to favour another 'scientific approach', that based on 'points rating'.

Table 14.3   Factor comparison grid: key jobs plus millwright

£	Skill requirements	Physical requirements	Responsibility	Working conditions
90				
85				
80				
75		storekeeper		
70				
65	inspector	MILLWRIGHT		
60	toolfitter	bench op.		
55		toolfitter	inspector	
50	machine op. MILLWRIGHT	machine op.	MILLWRIGHT	press op.
45	press op.	inspector	toolfitter	MILLWRIGHT
40		press op.	bench ass.	toolfitter
35			storekeeper	
30	bench ass.		machine op.	machine op.
25				inspector
20	storekeeper			
15			press op.	bench op.
10				storekeeper

Points Rating Evaluation Systems

In the points rating approach about eight to ten factors common to all the jobs under evaluation are identified. These are then ranked in order of their assumed importance bearing in mind the class of jobs being considered. Numerical points are then allotted to each factor influence so that the points weighting reflects their importance.

For example, suppose three of the factors are educational level, practical experience, and responsibility. If it is decided that responsibility and practical experience are of equal importance but that each is a little more important than educational level, then out of a total of 200 points to be allocated over, say, eight factors, educational level may be awarded 20 and practical experience and responsibility 25 each.

Each of the chosen factor influences must then be carefully defined and graded into 'degrees'.

For example, it may be decided to identify five degrees of educational level, with degree 1 representing the least qualified and degree 5 the highest likely to be considered in this class of job. The highest degree is then allotted the maximum points score with progressively fewer points allotted to the lower degrees.

A possible classification might adopt the following pattern:

Factor–Education–20 Points

Degree	Minimum for Job	Points
1	No qualification	3
2	3 GCSEs	6
3	5 GCSEs (high grades)	10
4	Studied 'A' level	14
5	2 'A' levels, ONC/D	20

When this definition and points allocation process has been completed for all the factor influences, a comprehensive grid will have been formed. It is then possible to evaluate each of the jobs under consideration according to the criteria that have been established. Each job will have a score of points with a theoretical maximum for any one job of 200 points—or whatever the total chosen. To obtain the maximum the job would, of course, have to be allocated to the highest degree in each factor influence—a virtual impossibility.

The next stage will involve setting grades according to points ranges. For example, on the basis of a total of 200 points there might be, say, five grades:

Grade	Points Range
1	40–59
2	60–89
3	90–119
4	120–149
5	150–200

A score of 40 will be the theoretical minimum for the job placed in the lowest degree in each factor influence.

Each job is placed in a grade according to its own points score.

The degree of precision achieved by this evaluation method is deceptive and the reality is often less scientific and objective than is claimed. The choice of factors and their relative weighting can reflect the personal prejudices of the managers involved, and these choices and the points allocations for specific jobs can be the result of a certain amount of horse trading between the different managers and worker representatives who make up the job evaluation committees. It is a basic principle of all job evaluation systems that it is the job that is being evaluated, not the person. In practice, members of evaluating committees are usually well aware of the implications of their grading decisions for individuals in factories or offices. This awareness cannot fail to influence their judgements.

Choice of Scheme

All job evaluation schemes try to establish and maintain a rational payment structure related to existing jobs and based upon known definable criteria. The payment structure is designed to allow for pay differentials between different jobs which are dependent upon the perceived value of each job to other jobs within the organisation.

How this is achieved for any given organisation must depend largely on the size of the organisation, the structure of its working activities and the workforce, and to some extent the history of the firm and the nature of its past and present labour relations.

There have been cases where job evaluation exercises have been associated with managerial attempts to reduce total labour costs by eliminating and downgrading jobs. Not surprisingly, in these cases, later exercises are treated with considerable suspicion and hostility.

There is no 'best' system for all organisations, and any one of the systems outlined in this chapter is likely to have to be modified in some way to suit the circumstances of a particular firm. On the other hand, the more the managers concerned know about the principles and techniques of evaluation, the more likely are they to develop a system suitable for their special case. It is also important to realise that job grading and payment structures quickly get out of date in the modern, rapidly changing business environment. Job evaluation is not a once and for all exercise but a process that is likely to need repeating at fairly frequent intervals.

Questions for Discussion and Review

12 Choose a set of eight factors which you think should influence the pay structure of a commercial office (or any other workplace with which you are familiar). Allocate points to these factors to reflect your view of their relative importance.

13 'Workers are sometimes hostile to job evaluation exercises because they recognise that it is the person who is being paid and the person that matters— not the job.' Discuss this statement.

Suggestions for Written Assignments

1 Employers and workers have different perspectives on wage payments. Explain the main differences in these perspectives. Is conflict between employers and employees inevitable over pay or are there ways of reconciling the differences? Explain your conclusions.

2 'Many professional workers have the incentive in their early years of work that success is likely to lead to becoming a partner in their firm. If they achieve a partnership they have the incentive that growth and rising profits increase both income and social prestige. Managers in industry do not have the same incentives to identify with the objectives of the firm.' Discuss this statement and suggest ways in which industrial firms may be able to stimulate and reward effort from their managers. If possible, seek an interview with an industrial personnel manager, discuss the statement with this manager, and include his or her comments in your discussion.

3 'One of the advantages of payment by results schemes is that they reduce the costs of supervision.'
   'Payment by results schemes are often expensive to administer; they are a frequent cause of labour disputes and costs are reduced if they are abandoned.'
   Discuss these conflicting views of payment by results schemes. Include, if possible, your report on any investigation you are able to make of actual schemes operating in local firms.

4 Explain and discuss the problems of introducing incentive schemes into public sector services such as teaching, local government administration, and the police and fire services.

Suggestions for Further Reading

This chapter has examined the way in which firms operate payment systems, a theme developed in greater detail in a number of specialised books of which the following are a selection.

Beacham (1979) discussed the practical issues relating to the differing payment schemes while Marriot (1968) provides the 'classic' explanations for the various types of payment by results.

Bowley (1975) is a handbook containing 32 chapters designed to cover most aspects of pay and payment systems and Lupton (1972) contains previously published articles and/or extracts from other books covering the matters discussed in this chapter.

The Institute of Personnel Management, London, has published several books for those who have to propose and implement the management of pay. These include Smith (1983) and Thomason (1985).

Three articles bearing upon this chapter demonstrate the economist's approach to the analysis of wages in the firm: Pencavel (1977) examined the strategies open to employers and workers; McCormick (1977) covered a similar subject and incorporated industry case studies; Addison (1976) focused on the remuneration of manual workers.

A number of quasi-governmental reports have been published in relation to the approaches available for rewarding workers. The National Board of Prices and Incomes produced Report No. 65, 'Payment by Results Systems' and Report No. 83, 'Job Evaluation'. There were two further reports from the Office of Manpower Economics entitled 'Incremental Payment Systems' and 'Measured Daywork'; both were published in 1973.

15
Wages and Society

Government Interest in Wages
Reasons for Government Interest

All economic issues have a social dimension. While there may be excellent reasons for believing that economic markets provide an efficient mechanism for the distribution of resources, there can always be occasions when the results are not acceptable to the social conscience of the community, and in these cases some modification or replacement of the market system may be necessary for social or ethical reasons.

The modern, highly specialised market economy works on the assumption that households provide labour to the producers of community needs. In return the producers pay wages which households use to provide for their needs, including the need to maintain the non-wage-earning members of the family and to contribute to a pension fund to secure continued income for the worker whose wage-earning days are over. If this system were not modified to some degree any household unable to provide a worker or workers capable of earning wages would not be able to survive.

Areas of Government Interest

Governments, therefore, may become involved in the provision of incomes in a number of ways:

(a) To provide basic incomes from community funds (taxes) to those households and individuals which, for socially acceptable reasons (such as physical or mental handicap or the need to look after the very young, the old, or handicapped people), are unable to seek wage-earning work. It may also have a duty to support those old people who did not have past opportunities to provide adequately for retirement from work and a further duty to assist those unable to obtain wage-paying work because of apparent failings in the operation of the economic system.

(b) To use its law-making and law-enforcement powers to ensure that wages paid to those people who do secure wage-paying work at least meet the minimum standards set by current social beliefs.

(c) While most economists would accept that a government has the above obligations, some go further and argue that it has an obligation to intervene in labour markets to secure greater equity between wage earners.

There is a tendency to think that any attempt by government to intervene in matters of wage and income regulation and distribution only commenced in modern times following the breakdown of the *laissez-faire* market economics of the nineteenth century. It would be more accurate to see non-interventionist *laissez-faire* attitudes as a relatively modern departure from a long history of attempted government regulation and intervention. There were, for example, laws to fix wages for certain occupations as far back as the sixteenth century, and the highly regulatory activities of the medieval craft guilds were apparently fully supported by the political authorities of their day.

Although social welfare structures can have important implications on wage–leisure preferences, this chapter is more concerned with attempts to establish a socially based minimum wage and the attempt to influence wage and income distribution.

Questions for Discussion and Review

1 If it is accepted that the government has a duty to ensure that every household has a socially acceptable basic income, does this mean that the government also has a duty to ensure that all those able to engage in wage-earning work in fact do so?

2 If a government accepted a duty to provide work for all those able to work, what would be the implications for existing labour markets?

Low Pay

The Measurement of Low Pay

Social and economic concern is usually focused on the low paid not only because of normal human concern at the personal suffering and indignities associated with poverty but also because the social and economic deprivations frequently associated with low pay are often held to aggravate problems such as crime, mental and physical disease, and marital breakdown, all of which create social and economic costs for the community.

The term 'low pay', however, is relative. People feel poor if their incomes are lower than others that they can observe and compare with their own. The monetary sum which represents low pay in contemporary Britain would not only have represented enviable wealth fifty years earlier but would still be regarded as such in many developing nations today.

Because society's conception of what is 'low pay' is constantly changing it is necessary to have a recognised, standard, non-monetary measure that can be used for comparison and analysis. A common practice in Britain and in other nations is to assume that those in the lowest decile of the pay structure represent the low paid. A variation of this definition was used by the Royal Commission on the Distribution of Income and Wealth of the late 1970s. The Commission defined a person '. . . as low paid if he or she works full-time (this means 30 hours a week or more) and earns no more than those in the bottom tenth of male manual workers . . .'.

If you are not familiar with the term 'decile', imagine a group of 100 workers whose weekly earnings range from £40 to £400. If these are arranged in order from the lowest (£40) to the highest (£400) they can be divided into ten groups each of ten workers. Suppose that the ten lowest paid workers contained two whose weekly earnings were £40, three earning £40.50, and five earning £50 per week (all the other 90 workers had weekly earnings higher than £50). We could then say that the lowest decile group received weekly wages of not more than £50 and not less than £40.

Another very useful measure for wage comparison purposes is the median. This is the value of the central item in a series. For simplicity the example is modified slightly. Suppose the total group of workers numbers 101 and the weekly wages they receive are again ranked in monetary order. The worker whose weekly earnings are placed 51st in the ranking order is the median worker. Assuming that no other worker receives exactly the same wage, this worker's earnings represent the median amount. Notice that the 51st worker in a total of 101 has exactly the same number (50) earning less as the number of workers whose weekly earnings are higher. If the value of the median wage is, say, £100, then this indicates that the majority of the group are paid at rates nearer the lower limit of £40 than the upper limit of £400. A median value of, say, £300 would carry the opposite implication. Notice that these measures have been explained in terms of actual earnings rather than wage rates. People paid at low basic rates can, in practice, have many opportunities to earn additional amounts through bonus payments, commission, overtime at premium rates, and other methods. In other cases workers receiving an apparently high rate have no opportunities to increase their basic pay.

Any statistical measure can give a distorted impression of the characteristics of the total group if it is used on its own without further support. The use of the lowest decile as a measure of low pay is no exception. It is always possible, for example, that there are special reasons why a particular sub-group is paid less than other, superficially similar, workers. Used with care, however, the recognised statistical measures can be very useful. Labour economists frequently relate the value of the lowest decile to the value of the median to give an indication of the spread of wages of particular groups. They, and fellow social scientists, have been especially interested to observe that, in Britain, this percentage has remained remarkably stable over the century or so for which reliable figures have been available.

In spite of major changes in the structure of employment, business cycles of boom and depression, and a period of massive inflation during which the average money value of wages has increased two-hundredfold, in Britain, the value of the lowest decile has stayed within a relatively small band of 67–71% of the median wage (see Figure 15.1).

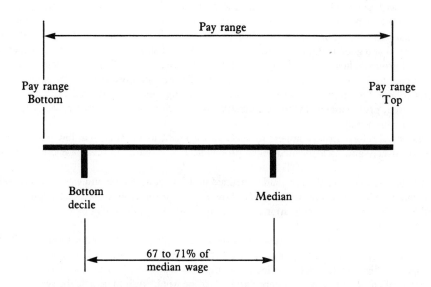

Figure 15.1 *The relationship of the 'bottom decile' to the median*

The Low Pay Problem

Given the way 'low pay' has been defined it must clearly continue to exist as long as there are differences in wages. Whether it necessarily constitutes a major social and economic problem raises rather more complex issues.

Low pay becomes a social problem if there are groups of workers unable to afford to maintain that standard of living which current social attitudes regard as an acceptable minimum, or if the range of pay between the lowest and highest deciles is such that it causes social bitterness and political disturbance with possible threat of civil conflict.

It becomes an economic problem if it interferes with the community's capacity to make adequate use of the scarce resources at its disposal, i.e. if it leads to the waste or under-use of scarce productive resources so that the living standards of the whole community are lower than they could be. This could result from income support measures for the following reasons:

(a) The payment of income support benefits may reduce the willingness of the low paid to work longer hours, seek more productive employment, or make the non-financial sacrifices involved in increasing personal human capital investment. It is often pointed out that some of the highest marginal rates of tax are paid by those who succeed in obtaining better-paid work and who then lose entitlements to welfare benefits and become liable to pay personal taxes.

(b) Income support and other welfare payments represent a substantial subsidy paid by profitable and successful firms and their workers to keep in being less productive and efficient firms which cannot afford to pay adequate wages to their employees.

The total effect may be to reduce incentives to improve productivity and to make domestic business less efficient and competitive in world markets.

Assumptions regarding links between low pay and social deprivation have to be modified by recognition that social attitudes change and that feelings of deprivation depend on what is being compared with what. The British industrial worker might be thought wealthy by a villager in a drought-stricken region of Africa but has been pitied by the German employer reported as saying that he would be ashamed if his worst-paid employee could not afford to take his family out to a meal at a good restaurant at least once a week. Nor should it be forgotten that there are organised groups whose survival depends on their ability to arouse feelings of deprivation and envy among the lower paid in order that they can gain their support in action designed to seek continued increases in pay and more comfortable working conditions. Even charity has become an organised, professionally managed industry whose success depends on its capacity to arouse the social conscience.

Some social reform groups appear to make an automatic assumption that low pay is a direct cause of poverty and its associated social problems. It is essential to recognise the following:

(a) A high proportion of the low paid as defined in this chapter are second wage earners within a family. They may have deliberately chosen work on the grounds of hours, convenience, flexibility, or other considerations. Far from being 'poor', they may be part of affluent or 'comfortably off' households.

(b) Low pay may be the result rather than the cause of poverty, poor education, bad health, social misfortune or inadequacy, or a host of other reasons linked with individual failure to cope with the hazards and complexities of modern urban life. In some cases, of course, this is part of an inherited cycle of deprivation. No one would wish to belittle the severity of this kind of social problem, but it does not help to cure it if too much emphasis is placed on low pay as a causal factor and too much hope placed on the establishment of minimum earnings as a sure cure for long-standing social evils.

Characteristics of Low-paid Groups

A recognised definition and measure of low pay makes it possible to identify groups of workers which meet the definition and to analyse their characteristics. Studies of the pre-1939 era indicated that the low paid were predominantly concentrated in the manufacturing sector, but by the 1960s they had become concentrated in the service sector and in public sector employment. This change may be partly explained by the relative contraction of manufacturing employment and changes in manufacturing technology with its increased reliance on the more highly skilled and highly paid workers. Consequently, workers with limited skills and relatively low productivity have moved to the expanding service sectors of the economy. Pockets of relatively low pay continue in certain sectors of manufacturing. These are usually characterised by the employment of an above-average percentage of females.

Contemporary evidence based on British Government earnings surveys appears to indicate that workers are more likely to be low paid in occupations requiring little skill and low basic education (see Table 15.1).

Table 15.1   Full-time adult male occupations where in 1987 one-third or more received an average wage of under two-thirds the national average wage of £199

	Per cent
General farm workers	65
Salesmen/shop assistants	58
Gardeners/groundsmen	54
Other cleaners	54
Barmen	53
Hospital porters	51
Butchers/meat cutters	50
Chefs/cooks	46
Caretakers	43
Craftsmen's mates/building labourers	42
Goods porters	40
Stockmen	39
Records and library clerks	37
Roadsweepers	36
Storekeepers	35

Source: 'New Earnings Survey—Occupational Tables', 1987, HMSO, London

Marquand (1967) began the work of identifying the low paid in contemporary Britain, and a detailed study of the low paid in Britain, undertaken by the National Board of Prices and Incomes (1971) provided detailed data of the characteristics of adult males who were classified, at that time, as receiving low pay. The Board identified these common characteristics as:

(a) Modest educational attainment.
(b) Above the average age of male workers.

(c) Below average in general health, as measured by absenteeism from employment.

(d) Containing a higher than average proportion of the disabled.

These characteristics collectively imply that the individual workers concerned had relatively low potential levels of productivity. Consequently, they tended to be employed in relatively undemanding jobs for which the rewards were relatively low.

Since this particular study, the rapid growth of female employment has changed the character of the labour force to a great extent. Any study of the low paid in contemporary Britain would reveal that women constitute a significant proportion of the low paid. Women receiving low pay, regardless of their health, education, and prior training, tend to be concentrated in a limited range of undemanding occupations within the secondary labour market.

Questions for Discussion and Review

3 Discuss the view that State provision of income support benefits
   (a) discourages the unemployed from seeking work, and
   (b) enables employers to pay low wages without accepting responsibility for the social consequences,
and consequently tends to increase the extent of low pay in the economy.

4 Before 1939 it was common for employers to pay married men higher wages than those paid to single men doing similar work on the grounds that they needed more money to provide for their families. Discuss the view that pay should be related to income need rather than to the work performed.

Minimum Wages
The Arguments for a Minimum Wage

The assumption that low pay leads to poverty and contributes to social deprivation leads to the social pressure to establish a legal minimum wage. To some extent this is supported by the economic arguments that forcing employers to pay 'adequate wages' would relieve the State from having to pay substantial welfare and income support benefits funded from taxes paid by profitable firms and productive workers. Those employers unable to pay the legal minimum would be forced out of business to release resources for use more productively and profitably by more efficient firms.

The function of economic analysis is to examine the probable consequences for employment and unemployment (and, therefore, for the use of scarce resources) of a national minimum wage, whether this is established by statute or whether it appears in practice as a result of a particular State welfare benefit payment system. For the purposes of this analysis it is assumed that a person will not knowingly work for a net wage that is less than the amount obtainable from welfare benefits if these also permit the retention of unrestricted leisure.

Minimum Wage and Firms Operating in Competitive Labour Markets

The model of the competitive labour market, the basis for Figure 15.2, was discussed in Chapter 8. This market assumed that all workers were homogeneous, that there were no impediments to the effective interaction of labour supply (*SS*) with labour demand (*DD*), and

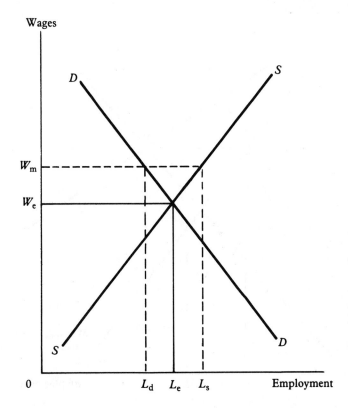

Figure 15.2 *Theoretical impact of an enforced minimum wage upon a competitive firm*

that these would react to wage movements to produce an equilibrium wage and quantity of labour employed in the market (initially at W_e and L_e in Figure 15.2).

If a legally enforced minimum wage is introduced above the equilibrium at, say, W_m, then the demand for labour falls to L_d while the higher wage encourages an increase in supply to L_s. The market is no longer in equilibrium and there is a surplus supply $(L_s - L_d)$ of workers seeking employment in that market. This surplus contains some $(L_e - L_d)$ who were formerly employed in the market, and these can genuinely be regarded as people rendered unemployed as a result of the wage increase. It is not so clear whether the number $(L_s - L_e)$ who were formerly not in the labour market but encouraged to enter by the introduction of a minimum wage can be regarded as being unemployed because of the higher wage.

Workers who retain their employment benefit from the higher wage, but there will be an economic welfare loss arising from the employment reduction if the unemployed are unable to find work in other markets. Individuals will have lost their employment even though the value of their marginal product was above their reservation wage.

The Monopsony Model

Where the labour market is not competitive (for example, where an employer is the sole source of employment for a particular group of workers, i.e. is a monopsonist), Stigler (1946) suggests that the introduction of a minimum wage will not necessarily lead to employment loss. Before the introduction of a minimum wage, the wage paid to labour is below labour's marginal cost, as

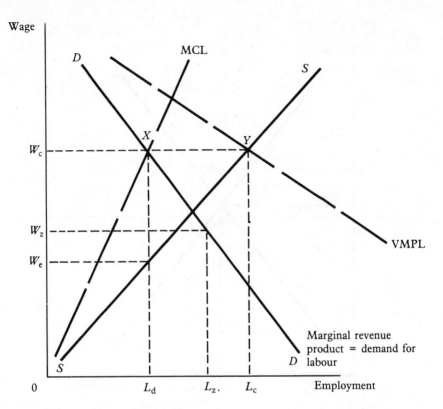

Figure 15.3 *Theoretical impact of an enforced minimum wage upon a monopsonist*

illustrated in Figure 15.3. In the case of the monopsonistic and profit-maximising firm, labour will be employed until the marginal cost of labour (MCL), is just equal to the employer's marginal revenue product. As explained in Chapter 8, the marginal revenue product curve is the basis for the employer's demand for labour curve under imperfect labour market conditions. This equality occurs at point X in Figure 15.3, where the quantity of labour demanded by the employer is L_d. At this quantity level the wage (from supply of labour curve SS) is W_e. Given that the firm is the sole employer of a particular type of worker, it is reasonable to suppose that it has monopoly power in the product market. The firm's marginal revenue product curve (derived marginal revenue × marginal physical product of labour) is thus below its value of marginal product (average revenue × marginal physical product), as explained in Chapter 8. Under competitive market conditions it might be expected that the wage and employment would be at the higher levels of W_c and L_c where labour supply (SS) equals the firm's value of marginal product (at Y). If we also assume that, under imperfect market conditions, labour is organised in trade unions we would expect the unions to press for wages and employment levels above those desired by the employer (W_e and L_e).

Under these circumstances we cannot predict the precise consequences of the introduction of a legally enforced minimum wage. Unless labour organisations and negotiating ability are very weak, the probability is that the national minimum wage will be below the levels already negotiated and will only affect a few very low paid workers. If the employer has been very powerful and been able to keep wages and employment at or near the profit-maximising levels, then the national minimum will increase labour's bargaining power and in all probability raise both the wage and quantity of labour employed. A minimum wage of W_z, for example, might be expected to increase the demand for labour to L_z (from the demand curve DD), but at this level the marginal cost of labour is very substantially higher than the marginal revenue product so that employers can be expected to resist expanding employment as much as this.

Economic analysis alone does not enable us to predict the precise effect of establishing a minimum wage on employment where product and labour markets are very imperfect, but it is reasonable to suppose that, at least in the short run, there is unlikely to be a reduction in the employment level and there could be an increase, particularly if the bargaining power of labour is strengthened. If the minimum wage does raise the pay of a small group of low-paid workers in a large firm we might also expect that pressure to restore former pay differentials will lead to upward movement in the pay of those earning above the minimum. In the long run, however, employers forced to pay wages above marginal cost can be expected to look for ways to reduce labour employment, probably by substituting capital for labour as opportunities for this arise.

The Two-sector Model

In those nations where a legal minimum wage has been introduced it has seldom been applied to all sectors of the economy. Specific industries have usually been included in the law but other industries and sectors have been excluded.

In Britain no attempt has been made by government to introduce national minimum wage legislation. Nevertheless, for much of the twentieth century there has been a quasi-legal minimum wage mechanism. This initially operated through Trades Boards and subsequently through Wages Councils. These provided a mechanism whereby voluntarily agreed minimum rates of pay in certain industries could be legally enforced. In the industries where Wages Councils operated it was felt that, even in periods of full employment, existing bargaining machinery had not gained the strength to negotiate satisfactory pay and working conditions without legal support. This view was encouraged by Armstrong (1966). These industries included the long-standing 'sweated labour' occupations such as hotels and catering, the retail trade, and farm workers. Even in these sectors the Councils were officially encouraged to stimulate the development of 'normal' collective bargaining machinery in the hope that this could take over wage and employment conditions bargaining and enable the Councils to be abolished. Indeed, they have ceased to exist in some industries, for example, lace finishing and road haulage.

It is, therefore, necessary to consider the possible consequences where a proportion of the labour force is subjected to a statutory minimum wage while other parts of the labour force are not.

Figure 15.4a represents a competitive industry A which is subject to minimum wage legislation. Before the introduction of a minimum wage the labour demand DD interacts with labour supply SS resulting in an equilibrium level of employment L_e at an equilibrium wage W_e. Following the introduction of a minimum wage, wages are assumed to rise to W_m and labour demand declines to L_m, although L_s workers now wish to work in the industry. In this competitive model $(L_e - L_m)$ workers become unemployed.

Industry B, represented by Figure 15.4b, is also a competitive one. This industry, however, is not subject to minimum wage control. Initially labour supply (S_xS_x) and labour demand (D_xD_x) are in equilibrium, with an employment level of L_x workers at a wage W_x. After the introduction of a legal minimum wage in industry A some workers in that industry lose their employment and then seek to enter industry B, whose labour supply curve rises to S_yS_y. As a result of this increase more workers are employed in industry B but the equilibrium wage falls to W_y.

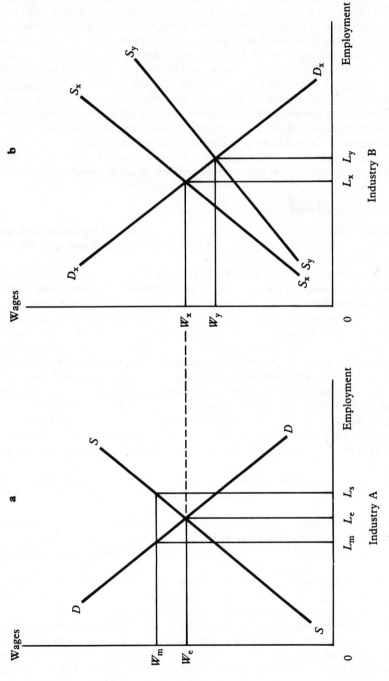

Figure 15.4 *Theoretical impact of an enforced minimum wage upon a two-sector competitive industry model*

In this two-sector model there is a spill-over effect. A proportion of workers in the industry covered by minimum wage legislation lose their jobs and seek work in industries not so regulated. Those workers remaining in the industry with a legal minimum wage rate enjoy an increase in their wages. On the other hand, workers in industries not so covered risk unemployment and/or a fall in wages.

Studies into the Consequences of Minimum Wage Policies

The neo-classical labour market models, as Peterson (1962) shows, may be used to predict the effects of a legal minimum wage introduced to solve the problem of low pay. Theoretical findings can also be checked against the observed consequences of actual legislation in various countries. Campbell and Campbell (1969) measured changes in employment and unemployment levels in certain US states when minimum wage levels were raised. These researchers futher undertook a comparative study of employment, unemployment, and labour force activity rates between states with and without minimum wage legislation. Brown et al. (1982), in their review article on the effect of minimum wage legislation on US employment and unemployment, surveyed the numerous research studies and drew the following conclusions:

(a) Minimum wage legislation produced an adverse effect upon the employment of teenagers. On the basis of both time series and cross-section studies, an increase in the minimum wage level of 10% reduced the level of teenage employment by amounts ranging from 1% to 3%. (The long-term consequence of this employment loss for teenagers may be greater than these figures suggest. Teenagers obviously seek work for wages, but they also do so to gain opportunities for on-the-job training and generalised work experience as a prelude to life-time employment.)

(b) Minimum wage legislation had a negative effect upon the potential employment opportunities of young adults aged 20–24 years. This, however, was not as great as that suffered by teenage groups.

(c) The consequences of minimum wage legislation for adult workers were less clear. There was some evidence of a negative effect leading to higher unemployment and/or lower activity rates upon certain groups of adult workers. This is in line with the predictions of the theory discussed above. At the same time there was evidence of a positive employment effect arising from employer preferences for employing adults when the wage differential between young workers and adults was reduced. Furthermore, given that adult workers are not a homogeneous group, minimum wage legislation sometimes favoured certain groups, male workers gaining at the expense of female workers, for instance.

The general view that emerges from research findings, supported by France's experience in the 1980s, is that minimum wage legislation leads to a net decline in labour employment, higher unemployment and, where potential workers become discouraged, lower activity rates, and also, Hashimoto (1982) believed, to a reduction in job training. Nevertheless, these are aggregate effects. The impact on specific labour market groups can and does vary. There is evidence that the net employment decline understates the real employment reduction as firms substitute part-time female labour for full-time workers covered by minimum wage regulations. Thus the fall in hours worked is greater than the decline in the actual number of people at work.

One result of minimum wage legislation which has not been studied in detail is its effect upon the prices of goods and services produced by firms affected by the changed wage rates. Standard economic theory interprets this as a simple change in production costs (the analysis being similar to that used for changes in expenditure taxes). The full effects of this would depend on the price elasticities of product demand and supply at the relevant price ranges. It is normally assumed that the more price inelastic the demand, the less the effect on product demand and employment and the greater the effect on price. The more price elastic the product supply, the greater will be the effect on production and employment and on price. If you think about this carefully you will see that this is what should be expected. If people continue to buy a product in spite of a price increase they will pay more. The easier it is for producers to change their production methods, the more quickly and effectively they will respond to a change in production costs to maintain their profits. The greater the effect on the quantity of product supplied to the market, the more likely it is that the numbers employed in production will also be affected. These arguments are illustrated in Figure 15.5, which shows the changes in product quantity and price under several combinations of demand and supply price elasticity.

However, there is no guarantee that a change in labour cost alone will change the demand for labour. The neo-classical models examined in Chapter 4 indicated that firms' preferences between employing labour and capital depended on their respective marginal productivities as well as on their relative prices. The full, long-term effect of any change in wage costs, including the effect of minimum wage legislation, must depend also on what is happening to labour productivity and to capital costs and productivity. Realistically, of course, it is likely that a government introducing minimum wage legislation is also likely to pursue other policies favouring labour and the objectives of labour organisations and these may well result in reductions in the marginal productivity of labour and increases in the non-wage costs of employing labour, e.g. more provision for holidays, sick pay, pensions, training, safety, etc. A combination of reduced labour productivity and increased labour costs is most likely to produce a reduction in labour employment and rising unemployment.

Questions for Discussion and Review

5 Some political groups have argued in favour of a national minimum income level to apply to all households whether anyone was at work in that household or not. Discuss the probable effects of such a policy on the levels of unemployment.

6 'The people most likely to be affected by a national minimum wage law are the ones most likely to suffer from high unemployment rates, so that such a law would increase the proportion of these people unable to obtain work and so increase the extent of poverty and social deprivation.'
Discuss this statement in the light of the analytical models introduced in this chapter.

Government and Income Distribution

Dissatisfaction with the apparent employment and income results of free markets led to the belief that governments should intervene in the national distribution of income to encourage greater equality of incomes. This belief was encouraged in the 1930s by Lord Keynes, who held out the hope that governments could and should manage the economy in ways that would improve social welfare and especially reduce unemployment.

It was thought that governments could most effectively influence the distribution of net incomes through direct taxation, but some economists, such as Fogarty (1961) and Wootton (1962), also argued that governments should additionally seek to influence the pattern of incomes so that the rewards of work accord more closely with society's view of the worth of that work to the community.

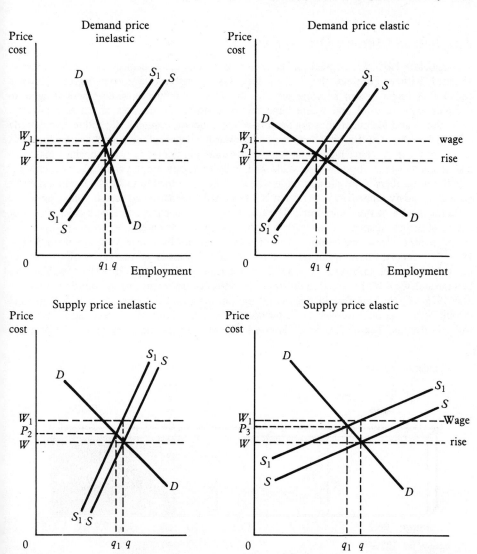

Figure 15.5 *The consequences of a wage rise upon employment in different product markets*
Note: In each case employers try to recover the cost of the wage rise ($W_1 - W$) and supply curves fall from SS to S_1S_1. The effects on market equilibrium price and quantity depend on product price elasticities of demand and supply. The effect on production ($0_q - 0_{q1}$) and hence on factor employment are greatest when demand and supply are price elastic.

Taxation and Income Distribution

Those, before 1979, who argued for the use of taxes as an instrument of social reform always assumed, without question, that social justice was equated with a greater degree of income equality. A social system allowing some to live in great influence while others struggle to maintain bare survival and where large numbers suffer the diseases of extreme poverty, deprivation, and malnutrition is not acceptable to a modern, economically and technologically advanced society. On the other hand, pressure towards a degree of incomes equality which fails to reward those who have made a substantial investment in human capital and which makes no distinction between those whose skills and abilities create employment and incomes for significant numbers of people and those who are only concerned to make the minimum effort needed to satisfy immediate supervision can be equally offensive and just as damaging to the economic health of the community. The question of whether there is such a thing as a 'just degree of income dispersion' is clearly a highly complex and contentious issue.

The issue of income and wealth distribution was examined by a Royal Commission in the late 1970s. Its reports draw attention to some of the difficulties of measuring the extent of inequality. Figures 15.6–15.8 are taken from the Commission's 1980 Report—'An A to Z of Income and Wealth'. Figure 15.6 illustrates the effect of tax on income distribution in the tax year 1976–77, showing that in this period the top income decile received over 26% of total income before tax but just over 23% after tax, whereas the bottom decile received 2.5% before and 3% after tax. Tax made little difference to the share of income going to the middle decile

Population divided into tenths

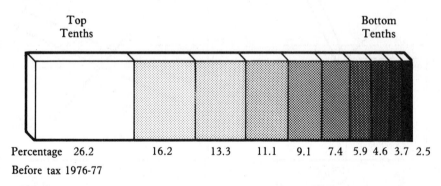

Top   Bottom
Tenths   Tenths

Percentage   26.2   16.2   13.3   11.1   9.1   7.4 5.9 4.6 3.7 2.5
Before tax 1976-77

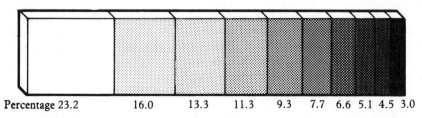

Percentage 23.2   16.0   13.3   11.3   9.3   7.7 6.6 5.1 4.5 3.0
After tax 1976-77

Figure 15.6 *The spread of income before and after tax, in 1976–77*
Source: 'An A to Z of Income and Wealth', HMSO, London, 1980

groups. These years were towards the end of a long period of governments which accepted as desirable policies that were directed towards a greater degree of incomes equality. Attitudes changed after 1979 and income and tax changes in the 1980s have tended to widen the dispersion between the higher and lower income groups.

On the other hand, simple figures such as these are subject to much criticism. The effect of taxation on the highest income groups is probably much exaggerated. High personal tax rates lead to large-scale tax avoidance, including the removal of capital and income to areas of lower taxes, payment in kind (company cars etc.) rather than in money, payment of business 'expenses' on a scale that makes a significant contribution to family income, and a host of other devices.

Figure 15.7 illustrates another effect of high taxes imposed as part of social reform policies. This chart shows the increases in tax suffered by different income groups between 1959 and 1977. Because of the difficulty of increasing already high tax rates, the greatest burden of tax rises has been borne by the middle and lower income groups, the largest increase being suffered by the third lowest decile (hardly the best-off section of the population) which suffered a massive 600% increase in its tax burden, expressed as a proportion of income. Very heavy increases in tax were experienced by the middle income groups, whereas the highest decile suffered the relatively modest rise of 34%.

During the period when income distribution was remaining remarkably stable, there were significant shifts in the relative position of occupational groups. The occupational income

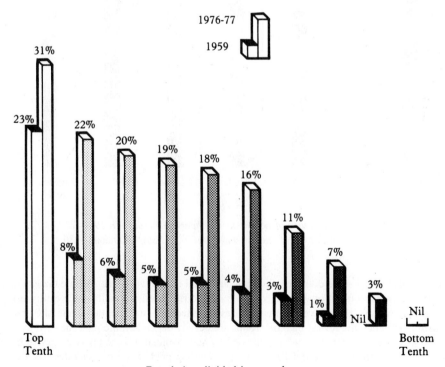

Figure 15.7 *Percentage of income paid in tax by different tenths of the population*
Source: 'An A to Z of Income and Wealth' HMSO, London, 1980

changes were illustrated in Figure 13.3 (Chapter 13), which clearly shows the narrowing dispersion between 1913 and 1978. The apparent paradox is explained by the differing importance of earnings from work as a proportion of total income. This is shown in Figure 15.8. For the top 1% of income receivers, employment earnings account for only 52% of total income. Self-employment is next in importance and over a fifth of income came from investments. In contrast, the middle income groups were almost wholly reliant on earnings for their incomes. At the lower end of the income scale, transfer payments such as pensions and social security payments became major sources of income.

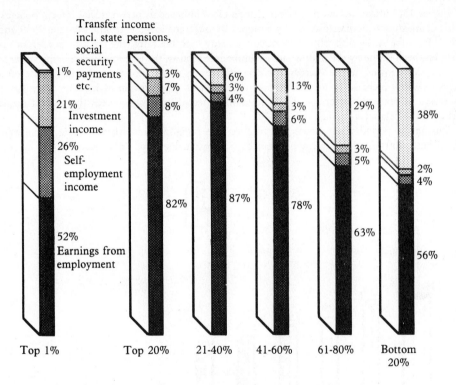

Figure 15.8 *Source of income to specific income groups in 1976–77*
Source: 'An A to Z of Income and Wealth', HMSO, London, 1980

These figures cast some doubt on the popular, social reform view that income tax is a major tool for the redistribution of income from the rich to the poor. In reality the wealthy usually manage to insulate themselves from the harsher effects of income tax while the transfer payments on which the lowest income groups are heavily dependent are paid for by those with modest incomes. The extent to which the wealthy have avoided income tax is suggested by the experience in both the USA and Britain where total tax paid at the higher rates has actually increased when these rates have been reduced.

Whatever the social and economic consequences of seeking of equalise incomes, income tax seems a very inefficient policy instrument for that objective. It might even be a powerful weapon for the extension rather than the relief of poverty.

Incomes Policies and Income Redistribution

The idea of an impartial body to determine wage increases had some appeal to social reformers in its early days. Some saw this as a possible step towards achieving a wage system which came closer to their ideals of social and economic worth. When the concept of a pay review body was taken up by a Conservative Government as a means of taking pay determination out of the party-political battleground, many aspirations were raised. In the early 1960s the British Government set up a National Incomes Commission, but this immediately met with hostility from the then politically powerful trade unions, who objected to any encroachment on their traditional freedom to engage in collective bargaining.

In 1964 a Labour Government was returned to power and immediately sought the co-operation of the unions in setting up a National Board for Prices and Incomes in the hope that this might become a means for achieving and sharing the benefits of increased economic growth. In fact, this hope was soon dashed by economic crisis, and a Prices and Incomes Act was passed in 1966 which froze all pay increases for a period of six months and then used the new Board as an instrument for controlling pay increases in line with government policy, which was solely concerned with short-run economic problems.

British incomes policies, therefore, never became a vehicle for income redistribution as desired by people like Lady Wootton. It did, however, contribute to changes in the pattern of pay differentials more or less by accident. The Labour Government believed that an incomes policy could only operate with the goodwill of the trade unions. Given the structure and politics of the trade union movement this, in practice, meant the support of the leadership of the large general unions such as the Transport and General Workers' Union (TGWU). As the price of their support, these leaders ensured that the mass of their members, a high proportion of whom were low-paid unskilled and semi-skilled manual workers, secured substantial pay rises while the main pressure to resist wage increases was kept on the skilled, better-paid industrial workers. At one stage, for example, Jack Jones, then leader of the TGWU, secured a flat rate national increase of £6 per week and this was hailed as a great exercise in pay restraint. For large numbers of his union members it actually represented a very significant percentage pay increase! Although in subsequent years most pay increases under the national incomes policy were expressed in percentage terms, and so might have been expected to have preserved the pattern of pay differentials, in practice the realities of negotiation and the power of large unions to cause industrial disruption and embarrassment to the Government ensured that it was these that were able to secure pay rises with or without dubious promises of future increases in labour productivity. For much of the period between 1962 and 1979, years of intermittent reliance on incomes policies, pay changes depended more on political power and influence than on the interaction of economic forces within labour markets.

Consequently, wage patterns were considerably distorted. The self-employed and the higher managerial staffs were able to evade incomes controls (and higher rates of income tax) through negotiating 'fringe benefits', payments in kind, and other devices. The unionised lower income groups were able to improve their relative position so that the main sufferers were non-unionised low income groups, the better-paid skilled manual workers (who were also suffering from changing technology), and the lower ranks of managers and industrial supervisors. Basic economic forces brought the inevitable: a shortage of skilled workers. Managers and supervisors could be recruited quickly once effective labour markets were restored, but time is needed to produce people with the higher level engineering, electronic, and other key industrial skills. Even at the height of unemployment in the 1980s employers were complaining of shortages of skilled workers, and this shortage became more serious as the economy recovered from recession.

Another group of workers with little power to withstand the distorting effects of government income regulation was the public sector, whose special problems are examined in the next section. Growing militancy among public sector workers helped to wreck both incomes policy as an instrument of government and the political power of the Labour Government. Although a Standing Commission on Pay Comparability survived until 1980, it had no place in the Conservative Government's plans for a return to unregulated markets, and incomes policies, as understood in the 1970s, really died during the 'winter of discontent' of 1978–79.

Questions for Discussion and Review

7 Prepare a list of 15 different occupations. Ask about 10 different people at different times and places to rank these occupations according to how they think they ought to be paid, with the highest as number 1, the lowest as number 15. In the light of the results of this exercise, discuss the problems of regulating pay according to ideas of social fairness.

8 Discuss the economic and social case for continued efforts to redistribute incomes in a market economy such as Britain's. What problems arise when income tax is used as an instrument for achieving income redistribution?

Pay and the Public Sector

Employment in the British Public Sector

Public sector employment in Britain has three sections: those, such as civil servants and members of the Armed Forces, employed directly by central government; those, such as most school teachers and workers in the environmental services who are employed by local authorities; and those who work for public corporations such as the Post Office and British Coal, in the nationalised industries. All countries have a public sector, but almost all differ in the kinds and scale of activities which are included in it.

Between 1979 and 1987, the numbers employed by central government have fallen slightly, those working for public corporations have dropped by nearly 52% following privatisation, but employment by local authorities actually increased slightly. Between 1940 and the mid-1970s, the general world trend had been towards expansion of the role of the State in economic and social affairs. More recently, the movement in Britain has reflected a more general world retreat from this position though with only a limited impact on employment by the late 1980s (see Figure 15.9).

The long period of expansion of State ownership and control into almost all sectors of activity and employment has had an important impact on the development of modern labour markets. Even after some years of active privatisation, the British Government still effectively owns and controls many large and complex enterprises employing many different groups of workers. Modern schools, colleges, and hospitals, for example, are much larger and more complex institutions than were their counterparts of the 1930s. Consequently, the influence of government on labour markets can be expected to be much greater than in the past.

Features of Public Sector Employment

The actual work activity of most employees in the public sector is no different from that of a worker in a similar occupation in the private sector. Driving a passenger coach along the M25 or operating a word processor require the same skills whether the coach or computer belong to

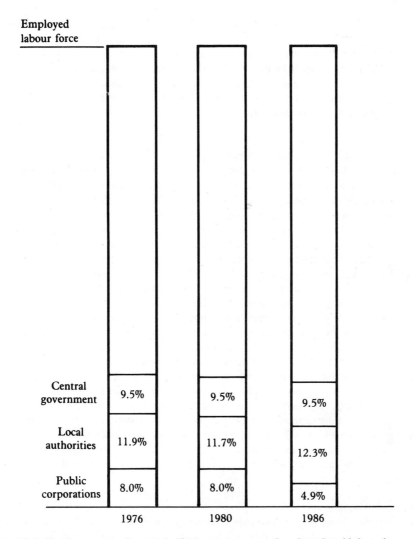

Figure 15.9 *Public sector employment in Britin as percentage of total employed labour force, various years*

State or privately owned organisations. However, there are many important aspects of employment in the public sector which do have a material affect on pay, working conditions, and job prospects.

Lack of Clear Organisational and Managerial Objectives

With the exception of those activities such as the Armed Services, which constitutionally operate under the authority of the Monarch, public sector organisations operate by authority of Parliament under terms and conditions established by the legislature through which they are constitutionally responsible to the community as a whole. Although Parliament may have given very specific powers to these organisations, their objectives have often been set in such general terms that they have little real meaning and are, therefore, subject to different interpretation by successive governments and, often, conflicting intepretations by chairmen of corporations and government ministers. Eventually, in 1978, the nationalised industries were given a definite financial obligation in terms of a target rate of return on the capital invested in the organisation, an objective rather different from the ideals of their original socialist founders!

Similar problems apply to public utilities and services. To 'preserve law and order', 'protect against fire', or 'provide a satisfactory education' are all so general and vague that they offer little help to management in making decisions on how and in which direction to allocate scarce resources.

Difficulties in Measuring Efficiency

If an organisation does not have clear objectives it has no clear way to measure efficiency at organisational or individual level. Because human beings must have some objective to work for, this gap is filled either by individual managers who set their own objectives in the belief that they are the true interpreters of best interests of the community or, where there is no firm local management, by each individual pursuing his or her own self interest. Thus one police chief may undertake a crusade against pornography, another against alcohol, each sincere in his dedication to the public interest. For practical purposes managers have to set some measurable criteria for individual promotions, but these are likely to differ in different parts of the same service or even in different sections of the same establishment. These 'efficiency measures' may also distort day to day activities. If police are judged by the proportion of reported crimes they succeed in solving they will avoid reporting crimes they know they are unlikely to solve, or persuade individuals likely to be convicted of one crime to 'admit to' large numbers of other similar crimes. If teachers are judged by examination successes then examinations will multiply and ways will be found to ensure that most entrants will gain passes and high grades.

When it is impossible to give an agreed definition of efficiency it is equally impossible to accuse any organisation or individual of inefficiency. This gives managers and large numbers of non-routine workers a very high degree of employment security regardless of their competence at work. A profit-seeking insurance company cannot afford to continue employing an insurance salesman who is unable to sell insurance, but teachers who cannot teach may stay in the classroom for many years. Many escape via the committee room to become managers of more competent teachers. Similar problems are reported from other areas of the public sector, including hospitals!

Political Influence

In practice, public sector organisations are effectively controlled by central or local government politicians and administrators who influence the share of taxation received by the organisation. Nationalised bodies are in a particularly difficult position because, constitutionally, they enjoy independence in day-to-day management. Apart from the practical difficulties in deciding precisely what is day-to-day management, this prevents Parliament from questioning ministers on matters held to relate to such management even though the political pressures involved are widely recognised. Central and local politicians have notoriously short-term political objectives and the common underlying aim of obtaining support from voters. In practice this means that public sector managers have to trim their decisions to the prevailing political wind which can veer rapidly as politicians come and go or change their minds to fit what they perceive as their current political interests.

Consequently, the flow of funds to particular parts of the public sector depends on political interpretations of public opinion and on the political skills of managers and their supporting politicians. Until recently, standards of efficiency based on the profitable use of scarce resources, considered normal in the profit-seeking private sector, have had little meaning in the public sector.

Administrative Rigidity

If objectives have been uncertain and volatile, public sector operations are often rigidly administered. For example, employees are subject to grading systems and pay structures which have the force of Parliamentary Statutes. Managers have very little freedom to adapt these to local conditions or discretion to reward individual merit or penalise individual failings. Rigidity arises out of organisational origins in Parliamentary Statute and its ultimate purpose is to protect public funds and to ensure that workers are treated fairly. It usually has the reverse effects. Strict budgets applied with little regard to local variations virtually guarantee that resources are wasted. Far from having incentives to reduce costs, managers gain from being large spenders. Failure to spend the whole of a budget one year can lead to reductions in next year's allocation, while evidence of financial shortage helps to support a case for a future budget increase. It is rarely possible to transfer money between budgets legally. Thus a manager can be powerless to prevent the loss of an employee who is offered a higher salary in the private sector but have ample funds to purchase equipment having no really useful purpose.

Consequences for Public Sector Labour Markets

The neo-classical models presented earlier in this book have no direct relevance to public sector employment, which, however, does not operate in complete isolation. The market forces operating in the private sector at home or in other countries must eventually influence conditions in publicly owned and controlled undertakings. In spite of years of public sympathy, British nurses only began to secure significant improvements in pay and working conditions when hospitals found they had to hire staff from private agencies and when there was a sizeable private hospital sector to offer alternative employment.

Public sector labour markets, therefore, are still markets and can be examined against the normal framework of demand and supply.

Demand for Labour in the Public Sector

Because organisations do not generally have to make profits nor, in most cases, have to determine their level or even direction of activity in accordance with their customers' willingness to pay for services, public sector demand for labour is not based on any recognisable marginal revenue product. The demand for labour in the short term is not always directly determined by the demand for the product of labour. Indeed, in some cases the nature and quantity of product is determined by the existence within organisations of particular groups of workers for whom there is an obligation to find employment. Nevertheless, demand for the product does ultimately influence the demand for labour though there may be significant time lags and waste of resources between the two sets of changes. The rapid fall in the British birth rate between 1972 and 1977 resulted in cut-backs in teacher training and large-scale early retirements among teachers in the 1980s. However, the slow pace and rigidity of the response failed to prevent major education labour market distortions when the birth rate and economy recovered in the 1980s. Dealing with excess demand by early retirement and by not replacing voluntary leavers led to shortages in those subjects where teachers had alternative employment opportunities and the loss of large numbers of experienced workers.

For similar reasons it is often difficult to measure the productivity of public sector workers. Crime reduction depends on many factors, not all of which are related to the number of police employed. Quality of education may have more to do with teacher quality than quantity, assuming it is possible to agree on how to measure the quality of a teacher. Consequently, labour demand in the public sector has often been determined by political negotiation in which labour organisations have played an important part. The demand for teachers, for example, has been influenced by reductions in class sizes, by the introduction of an increased number of different subjects (again reducing average class sizes), and by negotiating management structures and activities (e.g. pastoral care) which take teachers out of the classroom and often into committee rooms. Because there is no agreed measure of educational efficiency, it is impossible to say whether changes in demand are associated in any way with changes in productivity. Similar problems are experienced in the health and other 'caring' services.

Supply Conditions in Public Sector Labour Markets

People enter public sector employment for a number of reasons. These include chance and convenience. Office workers, for example, may take a particular job simply because it is convenient to home or transport route or offers working hours that suit family circumstances. In a period of high unemployment they may enter the public sector if they cannot obtain employment elsewhere when seeking the first job. Some workers choose an occupation for which the public sector offers the only or the main source of employment or where public sector organisations offer training and qualifications that are valuable in the private sector. These incude members of the Armed Forces, particularly those seeking valuable trade skills, scientific research workers, many medical and social workers, and, of course, teachers and lecturers.

A further reason for seeking work in the public sector may be that such employment may appear to be more congenial and less demanding than similar work in a profit-seeking firm in the private sector.

Potential employees within a market economy are assumed to desire to maximize their utility, as reflected in their wage–leisure choices. If a worker is able to choose between a wage of £X and £$(X + x)$ for the same number of hours of work, it is assumed that the higher wage will be chosen. When a worker is offered either a time rate wage of £X or the opportunity under payment by results to earn £$(X + x)$, the latter will be chosen when the worker believes the relevant marginal physical product level may be achieved without difficulty or risk. A worker anticipating achievement of only a relatively low marginal physical product is more likely to choose the time rate.

Few tasks within the public sector are rewarded under payment by results. The consequence of the public sector's dependence on time payment systems is that:

(a) Workers with a potentially high marginal physical product tend to seek employment where high earnings are probable. This usually means employment in the private sector where payment by results exists.
(b) Workers with a low potential marginal physical product tend to seek employment rewarded by time rates of pay. This often means entering the public sector.

Thus, the public sector offers rather undemanding work to those with low marginal product for relatively low wages. That such a strategy may lead to relatively high wage and production costs may not be noticed or seem important to managers whose training and experience centre chiefly on meeting externally imposed budgets and who do not know how to measure or even define the actual product of the activity they claim to be managing.

Public Sector Pay

Labour market equilibrium as understood in the private sector does not exist in most parts of the public sector. Political forces and organisational structures are major influences on product supply and labour demand. Consequently, these same influences are likely to operate on pay and conditions of employment in the public sector where they are generally determined by negotiation beween representatives of government and trade unions. They are thus the result of a political struggle and their outcome is largely determined by political power and influence. This usually means the ability of one side to inflict expense and loss of public approval on the other. Where the labour side does not have formal representational machinery, as in the case of the Armed Forces and the so called 'top people' (judges, very senior employees, etc.), pay may be determined by a Review Board set up under authority of Parliament.

Whatever the actual method of pay negotiation, the negotiators must be guided by some kind of principle. It is chiefly the lack of a principle generally acceptable to government, unions, union members, and the public as a whole (who have to pay public sector wages through taxation) that causes so much confusion and conflict in the public sector. As already suggested, politicians tend to be subject to short-term considerations and they tend to see public sector pay in terms of their strategy towards achieving wider political goals. For example, a government seeking to reduce the powers and privileges of trade unions and anticipating public violence may seek the co-operation of the police by making generous pay awards to them.

Occasionally governments have tried to avoid the inevitable unpopularity associated with major pay settlements—it cannot please both the workers involved and the taxpayers—by referring the problem to 'independent' review bodies. This procedure has proved unpopular with a government seeking to keep taxes as low as possible because such bodies tend to give expensive awards, e.g. the Houghton (1975) and Clegg (1980) awards to teachers. Moreover, these bodies do not generally have the power to consider structural changes which the government may wish to enforce as part of a pay settlement.

In the absence of market forces as understood in the private sector, attempts have been made to develop conceptual guidelines to influence public sector pay determination. Bowley (1980) suggests that the most important of these include 'comparability' and 'indexation'.

Comparability

Periodic attempts have been made in Britain, as in other countries, to relate public sector pay levels to those in other sectors of the economy by comparing pay for specified groups of public sector employees with 'equivalent' groups in the private sector.

In practice this is not as simple as it might seem. For many activities, and consequently for many occupations, the public sector has a near monopoly on service provision and hence employment. There is, therefore, only a limited range of activities for which direct comparison is possible. Other pay levels have to be determined by administrative mechanisms such as job evaluation. Moreover, private sector firms, subject to competition and profit objectives, demand high levels of performance. Workers unable to meet these are likely to lose their jobs. Private sector employment, therefore, is not strictly comparable with the relatively secure and often undemanding work available in the public sector to people with comparable skills and qualifications.

Indexation

An alternative suggestion has been that of indexation. When this has been adopted the existing wage structure within the public sector, and its relationship with external wage levels, have been assumed to be 'correct' and in subsequent periods public sector wages are adjusted according to changes in either a retail price index or a more general wage index. Consequently, occupational pay levels within the public sector wage structure retain their relationship, but change according to wider economic influences.

Neither approach has proved practical in the long term. When short-term problems relating to public sector pay have arisen, the solution has been to switch from whichever approach was being used to the alternative.

The economist can point to the failure of each to take account of:

(a) *Changes in labour supply and demand.* Indeed the existence of the internal labour market into which public sector employment is integrated is designed to limit the consequences of such changes.

(b) *Ability to pay the wage levels determined*. The internal labour market mechanism establishes the wage levels to be paid without necessarily taking into account the income flow required to pay them.

(c) *Productivity levels*. The difficulties in defining and measuring productivity in the public sector have already been identified. There is often a belief that because many public sector activities are personal services considered to be intrinsically desirable, e.g. health care and education, it is automatically assumed that an increase in individual productivity must produce a decline in the quality of the service provided and should not be encouraged.

It has to be admitted that economic analysis alone is unable to offer a solution to the problem of public sector pay, though it can sometimes show that proposed solutions are unlikely to achieve their declared objectives. It is not perhaps surprising that governments, including the British, recognising that they cannot solve the problem, try instead to reduce its size by a policy of transferring as many activities as possible to the private sector. It is possible, however, that pay determination in the privatised sectors remains a problem because it is the nature of the activities as much as the fact of State ownership and control that create difficulties in to reconciling the various economic, social, and political interests involved.

Questions for Discussion and Review

9 In the mid-1980s it was reported that large numbers of senior staff in the Civil Service and Inland Revenue were moving to jobs in the private sector. Discuss the reasons for and the consequences of this tendency.

10 Discuss possible ways to measure and raise productivity levels of the following categories of workers: teachers; railway train drivers; officers in local authority environmental and planning services; hospital surgeons.

11 Suggest reasons why the British Government, in 1988, made the governing bodies of schools responsible for their own financial budgets.

Suggestions for Written Assignments

1 Find out the approximate current social welfare benefits payable to the following: a married man with two young children unemployed, previous job unskilled manual; a divorced woman with one young child, previous job word-processor operator; a married man, children now independent and with wife working as a schoolteacher, previous job office manager. Find out the ratio of each of these benefits to the current average wage. To what extent, if any, do you think these benefits provide a minimum wage below which the people concerned are discouraged from finding new employment?

2 Discuss the proposition that all governments have to have an incomes policy if only for their own employees.

3 'If "low pay" were defined in terms of average earnings for workers throughout the world, no one in Britain would be classed as low paid.' If this statement is correct, does it mean that Britain has no low pay problem? Justify your answer.

4 Discuss the view that privatisation is the only effective solution for solving the public sector pay problem.

Suggestions for Further Reading

When considering the questions discussed in this chapter, it has to be appreciated that they all have socio-political as well as economic perspectives. Economists may use their analytical techniques to give advice on these questions, but the solutions this might suggest are not always the ones that society considers the most desirable.

On the issues of relatively low pay and poverty, Layard *et all.* (1978*b*) undertook a study for the Royal Commission on the Distribution of Income and Wealth. Questions relating to low pay, its consequences, and possible remedies are examined in Field (1973 and 1984). Low pay in a wider context was considered by Atkinson (1983).

Government incomes policies have been the subject of numerous books and Mitchell (1972), who was both a professional economist and a member of the Prices and Incomes Board, provided an analysis of the issues involved. Clegg (1971), on the other hand, expressed doubts about the actual operation of major attempts to develop incomes policies. An examination of numerous aspects and implications of incomes policies operating in a market economy was provided by Charter *et al.* (1981). This last work did not refer to the public sector, but the more general issues involved in public sector pay were considered by Elliot and Fallick (1981).

16
Wages and Trade Unions

Outline of Trade Union Organisation
General Significance of Trade Union Activity

Any analysis of labour markets has to take into account institutions with aims to influence market operations. Labour organisations, i.e. trade unions, are important in the determination of public sector pay and they are also thought to be significant in wage bargaining at company level and at the aggregate level of wages in the economy as a whole. Acknowledgement must also be made of organisations on the other side of the bargaining table, i.e. associations of employers.

Unions and the Firm

It is commonly believed that unions are able to negotiate for their members wages that are higher than would be obtained without union representation. In the short term, when major changes in production method cannot be made, the higher wages raise production costs and result in reductions of profits paid to the owners of capital invested in the enterprise and/or increases in product prices paid by customers. Long-term effects are less certain, as the neo-classical analysis suggests that firms seek to restore equality between the marginal productivity–factor price ratios of labour and capital by changes in production methods involving increased use of capital and increases in the marginal productivity of labour.

Unions at the Aggregate Level in the Economy

If unions succeed in raising the aggregate level of wages faster than the rate of growth achieved by the economy then, in the absence of foreign trade and assuming that other factor and input prices, factor ratios, and levels of marginal product stay the same, there must either be an increase in the share of national income paid to labour at the expense of capital or an increase in consumer prices. The foreign trade effects depend on whether any rate of decline of monetary purchasing power, i.e. the rate of price inflation, was greater than in competing countries. If domestic inflation rates were higher than those in the trading partners, consumers would buy foreign goods and this would reduce the rise in inflation; however, there would be a balance of payments crisis as imports rose and exports fell.

Again the longer-term effects are more difficult to predict because they would depend on the measures taken by government to try and halt the balance of payments deficit and the price and wage inflation, and the reactions of trade unions when they found that the purchasing power of past wage rises was being eroded by product price increases.

It is perhaps misleading to treat company and aggregate effects as separate issues. The aggregate economy is the sum of its individual parts, and action at firm level must be reflected at the economy level. Similarly, the decisions of company managers are influenced by actions taken by governments and by their perception of trade union policies as reflected in statements by union leaders and decisions of central union organisations. Consequently, the long-term changes that would be predicted from market analysis at the 'pure' theoretical level may be distorted, delayed, or even avoided altogether by a prolonged series of short-term reactions to the actions of unions and government.

The General Structure and Importance of Trade Unionism in Britain

Although most industrial countries have trade unions, these differ so much in such fundamental issues as strength, objectives, freedom from government control, and independence from political movements that a discussion of general features is impossible in one chapter. We therefore confine ourselves to the contemporary British trade union movement, although the market models used are applicable to any industrial nation such as Britain, Australia, and the USA where unions operate as largely independent labour organisations within the framework of a market economy.

Trade unions are organisations formed by groups of workers with the objective of improving their pay and working conditions in all their aspects. Millward and Stevens (1988) estimated that 58% of all employees were members of trade unions in Britain in 1984. Individual workers appear to believe that trade unions do secure improvements in both pay and working conditions.

Ross (1948) and Flanders (1970) showed that trade unions often have wider social and political objectives than the economic ones directly related to the employment contract, but for the purpose of this chapter these wider objectives are assumed to be secondary. The majority of rank and file union members join because they believe that doing so ensures that they gain the best possible returns from their employment. Unlike their more politically minded leaders, few have any clear wish to change the structure of the society in which they live, perhaps having a rather cynical view of the benefits that such changes would bring to the ordinary working person.

Table 16.1 Trade unions: numbers and membership in Great Britain for various years

	1975	1980	1985	1986
Number of trade unions	470	438	373	335
Per cent having 100 000 or more members	5	5.7	6.5	7.2
Total trade union membership (in thousands)	12 026	12 947	16 821	10 539
Per cent of members in unions having 100 000 or more members	77.9	79.3	81.2	80.8

Source: 'Annual Abstract of Statistics', HMSO, London, 1988 and *Employment Gazette*, 1988, Vol. 96, pp. 275–8.

Measured by number of members, the sizes of trade unions vary greatly. In Britain there are unions with a dozen members at one extreme to those with a million or more members at the other. However, in 1986 56% of the membership belonged to the 9 largest unions, each having 250 000 or more members. Unions, like the business firms employing their members, have been and continue to be subject to a merger movement.

British trade unions are as varied in their organisation as they are in size, the variations reflecting their different histories and traditions. Of particular importance is the distinction between those that trace their origins to the local craft societies of skilled workers in a single trade of the first half of the nineteenth century and earlier, and those which began as large groups of unskilled workers operating across industries, many commencing in the closing years of the nineteenth century or later. Those that have developed from skilled, craft beginnings, mainly through amalgamation of previously independent (often fiercely independent) bodies, tend to have much looser central and national organisations and place great weight on reflecting the aspirations and objectives of their members. Those with beginnings as general groups of unskilled workers who tended to migrate between firms and industries had to have strong central and national organisational structures and to place greater emphasis on leadership-inspired and -dominated policies and activities and also on gaining and exercising political power. The contrast underlies modern conflicts between unions such as the Electrical, Electronic, Telecommunciation and Plumbing Union (EETPU), with its strong craft origins [and believed, in 1988, to be considering merger with another old craft union, the Amalgamated Engineering Union (AEU)], and the Transport and General Workers' Union, which started among the dock and gas workers (often the same people) in the late 1880s.

This distinction could be accused of being an over-simplification of a very complex historical pattern. One problem with studying trade unions is that whatever is said is likely to be both true and false. Such is their diversity. For detailed information on internal organisation you should refer to more specialised work such as, for example, Bain and Price (1983) and Hyman (1983).

What makes the structure of British trade unionism so different from the pattern of other industrial nations is the diversity of unions to be found representing similar groups, and sometimes the same group of workers within both firms and industries. The withdrawal, in 1988, of the EETPU from the Trades Union Congress (TUC) and its Bridlington Agreement, which was supposed to prevent competition beween unions for the same members and the consequent open canvassing for members by unions fearing a severe membership decline, seems likely to increase this diversity.

By contrast, an employer in the USA is required to bargain only with a trade union which successfully organises a minimum of 50% of employees. Thus US law eliminates possible multi-unionism. In the Federal Republic of Germany, employers collectively are required to bargain with one trade union only for an industry and individual employers are not required, indeed are legally forbidden in many cases, to bargain with any trade union. In Britain, employers often have to negotiate simultaneously with numerous trade unions, each having differing objectives.

On the other hand, the difficulties this causes employers are often exaggerated because unions, even at establishment level, often have organisational structures to enable them to unite and bargain collectively with employers on major negotiating issues. After all, different groups of workers do have different problems and interests even if they all work for the same firm or in the same industry and groups. Workers, such as electricians or maintenance engineers, who are present in small numbers in many different firms, may feel that they prefer to be represented by their own union rather than be submerged in some all-embracing industry-wide grouping which is likely to ignore the wishes of its minorities when these do not fit in with the interests of the majority.

Questions for Discussion and Review

1 A further type of trade union is the one often referred to as the 'white-collar union'. Name three such unions and discuss the differences which you think

are likely to exist between these and former craft unions such as the Amalgamated Engineering Union.

2 Find out, outline, and discuss the part played by the TUC in the British trade union movement.

3 Discuss possible reasons for the fall in membership of the British trade unions in the 1980s.

Bargaining by Trade Unions

Trade unions in Britain normally seek to pursue their objectives by bargaining with employers and/or their representatives. This process, however, takes place at different levels in the industrial structure.

Bargaining at the Industry Level

Negotiations take place between individual unions or groups of unions and representatives of all, or the major, employers within an industry. The essential characteristic of bargaining at this level is that it usually results in multi-employer agreements. All employers who are party to the bargain, and often others who are not, agree to apply the terms of the settlement. This, incidentally, is similar to the practice followed in the Federal Republic of Germany. Unlike Germany, however, where the agreements have the force of law, British agreements rarely have this legal status.

There are also important differences between practices in the public and private sectors of the economy.

Public Sector Practice

National settlements usually establish the terms and conditions which actually do apply in practice to all relevant employees, whether or not they are in a trade union. The terms of the agreement are often given the force of law by subsequent action by a government minister under the authority of Parliament. This gives public sector pay and working conditions the rigidity mentioned in Chapter 15.

Private Sector Practice

National agreements usually establish a basic minimum which may actually apply in some cases but, more often, is the foundation on which local or company agreements or custom and practice are based. Consequently, a percentage increase in the nationally agreed wage is likely to lead to similar percentage rises in the rates actually paid by firms, and an extension of holiday or reduction in weekly working hours will also result in adjustments to local and company arrangements.

Bargaining at the Company Level

Companies, of course, are of diverse sizes, but a relatively small company by national standards may be an important employer in a local area or within a particular industry so that unions may give it particular attention. Negotiations at company level are usually handled by full-time union officers who deal with senior management or senior personnel or labour relations management, depending on the size of the company. Company agreements affect practices throughout the company, whether it operates from a single establishment or from many establishments. Most union negotiations in the USA are at company level.

Since the 1960s there has been a trend in British multi-establishment companies for managers and union officials to try and standardise agreement terms throughout the company and sometimes throughout a complete company group. National standardisation has been relatively easy in single-industry companies such as the major motor manufacturers (though even in these it has produced anomalies where individual plants have offered wages and conditions that are significantly different from those of other firms in a locality) but more difficult, and less common, in company groups covering a diverse range of industries and activities.

In some industries and companies, national company agreements are subject to local differences that are usually recognised as being matters 'of custom and practice' rather than formal, written agreement. In the late 1980s some companies have been concerned at increased regional disparities in living (especially housing) costs and have sought to widen regional pay differentials and, in some cases, to return to more localised negotiations on all aspects of pay and working conditions. This has been resisted by unions which have been able to use company problems in the high-employment and high-cost areas to win concessions that have then been applied nationally.

Bargaining at the Local Level

Industry and national company arrangements are often subject to supplements reached at establishment or small company level by bargaining between establishment managers and full-time local district union officials or, commonly, with part-time union shop stewards employed by the firm.

Some local variation in the terms of wider agreements is always likely for a number of reasons, including:

(a) Different historical customs and practices, especially when a branch establishment was formerly an independent company merged into a large group.
(b) Special conditions in local labour markets.
(c) Special relationships that may have developed with specific unions or union officials.

Current Trends in the Pattern of Bargaining

Apparently conflicting pressures between national and local bargaining have already been noted. Industrial relations observers are not in full agreement concerning current trends. There is some conflicting evidence and this can lead to different interpretations of available evidence.

(a) Brown and Terry (1978) noted a withdrawal of numerous multi-plant companies from the machinery for industry-level bargaining, preferring national company-level bargaining. They believed that this would then lead to a decline in local bargaining. This view has been supported by evidence of the increased use of job evaluation techniques across multi-plant companies to establish common wage levels.
(b) Elliot and Steele (1976) and Elliot (1981) noted the increase in the number of companies associated with industry-level bargaining processes and took this as evidence of the increasing significance of this form of bargaining at the expense of company negotiation. This view appeared to be reinforced by evidence of a decline in payment by results schemes as companies came to accept the safety net provided by basic industry agreements which they could supplement with local arrangements.

It is possible to reconcile, to some extent, these two approaches. Their observations relate mainly to specific companies so that there could be an increase in the number of companies involved in industry-level negotiations despite an increase in the proportion of workers who are covered by national company agreements.

Questions for Discussion and Review

4 One cause of industrial disputes in the late-1980s was the attempt by some private and public sector organisations, e.g. the Ford Motor Company and the Post Office, which had previously observed national agreements giving standardised conditions throughout the organisation, to introduce greater regional variations into their labour contracts. Explain:

(a) why trade unions were concerned at this tendency,

(b) why employers sought greater local and regional flexibility, and

(c) the economic case for and against greater local and regional flexibility.

5 Discuss the economic case for encouraging greater local and regional flexibility in public sector labour contract negotiations.

Economic Models of Trade Union–Company Negotiation
The Basic Model

Economists have tried to establish theoretical models to explain the effect of unions of labour markets. The basic theoretical model is very similar to the two-sector model for a minimum wage examined in Chapter 15. There are, however, more options available to workers and their employers. Consequently, the results of introducing a trade union to a labour market are less certain and potentially more diverse than the results of minimum wage legislation.

The model shown in Figure 16.1 assumes that a particular labour market contains two employers, the competitive firms A and B. Each requires labour of identical skills, human capital investment, etc. In all ways the labour employed by both firms is homogeneous and interchangeable. Initially neither firm is unionised. In firm A the interaction of labour supply and demand implies an equilibrium wage W_0 and employment E_u. In firm B the identical wage W_0 prevails and employment is E_n. Wage levels are the same in the two firms.

Workers in firm A then form or join a trade union so that wages and working conditions become subject to union–employer negotiation. As a result of this bargaining a new wage level is established at W_u, above the previous level W_0. The new wage level intersects the firm's demand for labour, indicated by the demand curve D_uD_u, at point X, implying a labour demand of E_{u1}. At this new wage level additional workers would desire to join firm A and the supply of labour, indicated by the curve S_uS_u, becomes E_{u2}. The wage level is prevented by union–employer agreements from adjusting downwards from W_u to W_0, which would have restored the original equilibrium. Consequently, at the new age W_u potential labour supply E_{u2} exceeds actual labour demand E_{u1}. The new equilibrium for firm A resulting from the introduction of trade union bargaining is the wage W_u and employment level E_{u1}. The higher wage has caused employment in firm A to fall by $E_u - E_{u1}$.

Given that labour in both firms is homogeneous and mobile, one option, as in the minimum wage case, is for labour that has become unemployed in firm A to move to the non-union firm B. Should that occur then a new supply curve $(S_{n2}S_{n2})$ for firm B will be generated to the right of the original $(S_{n1}S_{n1})$. Equilibrium, arising from the interaction of the existing demand curve D_nD_n and the new labour supply curve $S_{n2}S_{n2}$, is at point Z. This implies a new wage level, W_n, in the non-union firm and an increase in employment from E_n to E_{n1}.

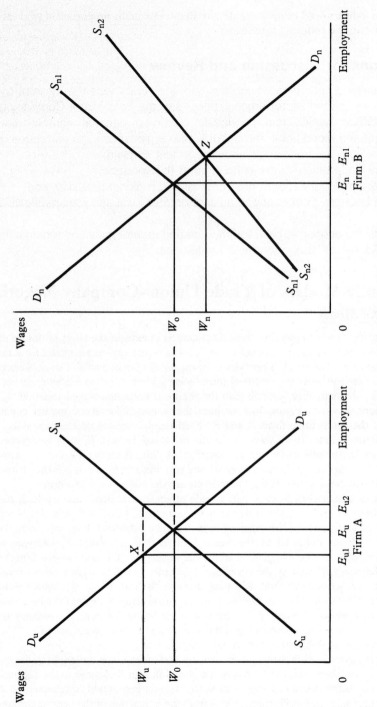

Figure 16.1 *Impact of labour organisations upon one firm (firm A) within a competitive market*

If it is assumed that all workers losing their employment in firm A switch to employment in firm B, then the value of $E_{n1} - E_n$ equals the value of $E_u - E_{u1}$, and the wage level in firm B moves downwards to permit this employment level to be achieved.

Initially, the wage levels in firms A and B were the same. The entry of a union to one firm in the market has brought about the following wage movements:

(a) In firm A wages rise from W_0 to W_u.
(b) In firm B wages fall from W_0 to W_n.

Those newly unionised workers in firm A who have kept their jobs have enjoyed a wage rise of $W_u - W_0$. All other workers in the market suffer a wage fall, $W_0 - W_n$, and some have undergone the personal upheaval of changing employer.

Wider Implications of the Basic Model

At the same time it is necessary to consider the wider implications of the wage changes brought about by the intervention of the trade union. These have resulted in the employees of one firm being paid higher wages than employees in the other. This wage difference is known as the 'union differential'. However, the prospect of different wages for the same work in the same market is likely to have further effects.

(a) The manager of firm B will be conscious that their own workers are being paid less than workers in the unionised firm (A) and will anticipate that their own workers may wish to try and restore wage equality by also joining the trade union. A possible consequence of this recognition is illustrated in Figure 16.2. In this model the non-union firm (B) which seeks to avoid the unionisation of its workforce raises the wages of its workers by an amount a little less than the union differential. It does this in the hope that it will retain some cost advantage from remaining non-union but reduces the incentive for workers to seek union representation. The increased wage is thus above the original market equilibrium W_0 but below the union-negotiated wage W_u. At this higher wage level the quantity of labour employed falls (from E_n to E_{u1}), but not as much as in the unionised firm. This action reduces the union differential to $W_u - W_n$. The total reduction in employment is increased by those displaced in the non-union firm.
(b) Workers obliged to leave − or unable to join − the non-union firm have a number of options. They may:
   1 Seek employment in the union firm at the higher wage rate where, however, they will be competing with other workers and their chances of gaining a job may be small.
   2 Choose to retire from the labour force. This is an option that the government may wish to encourage by making special payments to workers or their employers when this option is taken.
   3 Remain unemployed in the hope that an expansion of product demand will expand the total labour market and that employment opportunities may reappear in firm A. The government may try to discourage this by reducing welfare payments or by putting pressure on workers to retrain or seek employment in different labour markets where demand for labour is higher.
   4 Make a personal investment in human capital through further education and/or training in the hope of re-entering the labour market at a higher or more secure wage level.
   5 Seek employment or self-employment in another labour market, probably at the old or a lower wage level.
   Different individuals will, of course, make different choices depending on their attitudes

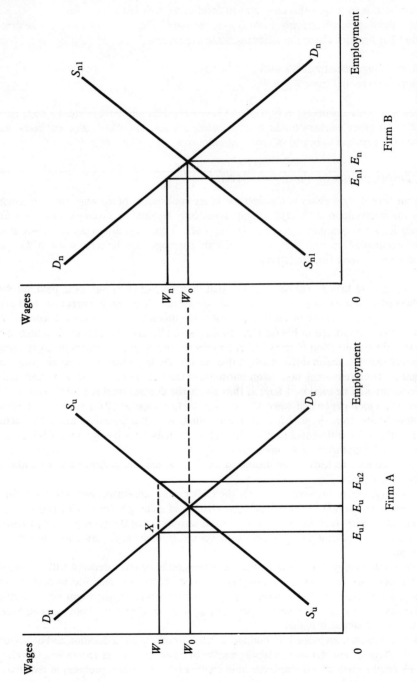

Figure 16.2 *Impact of labour organisations upon one firm (firm A) within a competitive labour market, and the defensive response of a competitive firm (firm B)*

and personal circumstances including age, earlier educational experience, and family circumstances. A worker with very young children is likely to be in a different position from one whose children are financially independent and whose spouse has a secure, reasonably well-paid job.

The model illustrated in Figure 16.2 assumed that the non-union firm would still seek to keep the wage level below that negotiated by the union. Some firms, however, believe that the long-term advantages of avoiding unionisation are worth a wage premium, and these take care to ensure that their wage levels are a little higher than those negotiated by unions. Such firms have to observe what is happening to wages and working conditions in unionised firms very carefully and they have to match any significant change negotiated by the union.

Whether or not the non-union firms aim to keep wage levels and other working conditions slightly worse or better (from the workers' point of view) than those in unionised firms, the union can justly claim that its efforts are bringing benefits to workers who are not members of the union and not contributing to its costs. The union can be expected to make considerable efforts to recruit these people, who will be seen as 'free-riders'. By 1988 it was clear to unions that they could not rely on traditional working class loyalties to support their efforts to attract new members but needed to offer benefits in addition to the normal union services of negotiating pay and working conditions. They could be seen as service organisations, selling in a competitive market—a change having some important social and political as well as economic implications.

There are, therefore, a number of models to explain possible consequences for labour markets following the entry of a trade union. All assume that a proportion of the workforce gains increased wages as a result of union activity. They also imply that some workers are likely to lose their jobs as employers seek to employ fewer workers at the higher wage. The extent and speed of employer reaction will depend on the ease with which employers can change their production processes and substitute capital for labour, and on the cost of capital, the level of technology, and any current changes in the productivity of labour and capital, i.e. on the price elasticity of supply of the product of labour and the wage elasticity of demand for labour. As a general rule, both these elasticities are likely to be lower in the public than in the private sector, so that public sector unions are more likely to believe that they can achieve wage increases without significant job losses. They anticipate that increased wage costs can be paid for by increases in product prices and/or charges against taxation without major changes in labour practices or production method. How far similar assumptions can be carried into privatised public utilities is uncertain.

Questions for Discussion and Review

6 Discuss possible reasons why a firm might be willing to pay wages above those negotiated by unions in other, similar firms in order to discourage its employees from joining trade unions.

7 'A trade union represents its members who have jobs and its leaders are elected by these members. Union leaders may make public statements that are full of sympathy for the unemployed but they will still pursue policies likely to bring benefits to working unionists regardless of their effect on the extent of unemployment.'
Discuss this statement.

Measuring the Union Differential

Formal Expression of the Union Differential

The existence of the union differential as defined in the previous section is now an accepted fact of economic life following the initial work undertaken in the USA by Lewis (1963). Subsequent empirical work in both the USA and Britain has, therefore, sought to establish the relative size of the differential, which was assumed to be positive, i.e. that unionisation results in wages higher than would be obtained by the same workers if they were not organised in unions. Some more recent studies in the USA, however, including that by Johnson (1977), which have taken account of the concentration of trade union membership in the older, declining sectors of the US industry, suggest the differential may now be negative, i.e. that unionisation may keep wage levels lower than those likely if workers were not organised in unions.

Trade unions have existed in market economies for differing periods, but the fact that they do exist makes it impossible to measure the absolute effect on wages when trade unions come into existence. Consequently, the studies undertaken in the USA, where single-union company bargaining is common practice, have sought to measure the impact of trade unions by identifying the relative size of the union differential. These studies have, therefore, sought to establish the relative difference in the wage levels established by trade unions compared with the assumed market equilibrium that would exist if there were no trade unions. Efforts are made to compare an actual company–union wage level with a theoretical wage level and to ignore possible spill-over effects arising from the mere existence of trade unions.

The actual measurement of the union differential, which has evolved from the work of Lewis (1963), is developed from the following identity:

Average Wage $(W_i) = T_i W_{iu} + W_{in} (1 - T_i)$

> where subscript i represents an industry or occupation
> and T_i = the union density of the industry, it being assumed that only union members benefit from the trade union's bargaining
> W_{iu} = the wage paid to trade union members in the industry
> W_{in} = the wage paid in the absence of a trade union

This is just a formal way of saying that the average wage in an industry is the sum of the wage paid to union members multiplied by the proportion of workers in the union plus the wage paid to non-union workers multiplied by the proportion of workers not in the union. Rearranging the expression gives:

$$W_i = W_{in} + T_i(W_{iu} - W_{in})$$

which simply says that the average wage in an industry is the wage of non-union members plus the difference between the union and the non-union wage multiplied by the proportion of workers who are union members. The difference between the union and the non-union wage $(W_{iu} - W_{in})$ is the union differential.

This formal expression can be useful for analysis and for making comparisons but, in itself, tells us nothing about how the union differential in a given industry originates or why a union differential in one industry is greater or less than that in another.

The Union Differential in US Labour Markets

Early studies in the USA endeavoured to make direct comparison between union and non-union employment sectors in order to identify and measure the union differential. Many of these studies, however, were suspect, as the groups chosen were not strictly comparable. One, for example, compared the wages of workers in a vehicle assembly factory with those of garage mechanics. More recent US studies have made extensive use of regression analysis and have sought to estimate non-union wages where these have not been present in an industry.

The union differential, estimated from studies of the US economy, has been found to vary from 0–50%. In spite of this apparently wide variation there is a fairly general consensus in the views presented in relation to the impact of trade unions on labour markets in the USA.

(a) Trade unions have obtained higher wages for their members than might otherwise have been expected.
(b) The magnitude of the union differential varied considerably between the different studies but this reflected:
   1 Differing levels of aggregation in the studies of different industries and occupations.
   2 The use of different variables, including human capital investment, skills, concentration ratios, gender, and race.
   3 Differing industries and/or occupations with differing rates of union membership, relative union–employer bargaining strength and price elasticities of product demand and supply and wage elasticities of demand and supply.
(c) Differentials appeared to change from time to time so that studies made at different times could give different results, for example:
   1 In periods of inflation—an indication of rising labour demand—the relative size of the union differential appeared to decline, suggesting that non-union members gained most from high demand by employers.
   2 In periods of deflation—an indication of falling labour demand—the relative size of the union differential appeared to increase, suggesting that trade unions were able to achieve a greater degree of wage stability in the face of fluctuating labour demand.

The Wage Differential in Britain

British studies of union wage differentials have been less extensive and intensive than those in the USA. This reflects differences in the quantity and quality of the information available for analysis. Nevertheless, Blanchflower (1984) provided details of thirteen different studies published in the ten-year period 1974–83 which estimated the impact of trade unions on relative wages in Britain. These gave variable estimates of the relative value of the union differential. Wabe and Leech (1978) estimated that it had a possible value of − 6%, whereas Minford (1981) suggested a value of + 74%.

There have been relatively few British studies that have followed the US pattern of comparing wages of union members with those of non-union members. Those which have done so include Pencavel (1974), Minford (1981), and Stewart (1983). British studies have more usually examined the terms and conditions of employment specified in collective agreements which often apply as much to non-union as to union members. Millward and Stevens (1988) provided data indicating that, in 1984, while 58% of employees were in trade unions, collective agreements actually regulated the employment conditions of 69% of employees. Thus the British approach has been to compare those sectors covered by union agreements with those sectors which are not so covered.

Of the thirteen studies noted by Blanchflower, the majority were based on detailed data relating to collective agreements as reported in the New Earnings Survey, 1973. The researchers did not always use the complete set of data and in certain instances supplemented this with other material. Consequently there was a wide disparity in the resulting conclusions concerning union wage differentials as shown by the following summary.

Study	Differential
Mulvey (1976)	26–35%
Mulvey and Foster (1976)	22–36%
Layard *et al.* (1978a)	25%
Mulvey and Abowd (1980)	4– 8%
Treble (1981)	8–40%
Geroski and Stewart (1982)	10–16%
Nickell and Andrews (1983)	7–32%

One significant point to emerge from these studies was the importance in Britain of the two-tier bargaining arrangements previously outlined. In the private sector this resulted in the modification of industry-level agreements by company and local area or establishment agreements. Pencavel (1974), whose work was not primarily concerned with analysing agreements, also noted the significance of the two-tier bargaining arrangements. He suggested that local bargains between trade unions and employers might be the most significant ones.

It is possible that, in Britain, industry-level agreements may reflect macroeconomic features in the economy at the time they are reached. National economic conditions may establish a basic pattern, especially in comparison with previous periods and agreements. For example, more difficult economic conditions could produce a general wage increase of, say, 4% as opposed to increases in previous years of 7–10%. A similar situation exists in the West German labour markets.

Nevertheless, an industry-level agreement may establish a wage level above that of the market. In the light of US studies, the British industry-wide agreements probably keep wage levels above the competitive market rate in recessionary periods but such agreements maintain wage rates below the market competitive level during periods of expansion. However, this latter effect is probably explained by individual company and local agreements. It appears, therefore, that industry-level agreements are not the most important mechanism for establishing the union wage differential, which depends rather on company and local arrangements. These are more likely to take into account the needs of individual employers and the degree of trade union strength at particular firms and establishments.

Questions for Discussion and Review

8 Discuss the proposition that 'the popular image of trade unions forcing up wages is very far from reality'.

9 'Without trade unions, wages would fluctuate more in line with movements of supply and demand in labour markets, but the long-run level of wages in most occupations would not change very much'. Discuss this statement.

Trade Unions and Inflation

Early Attitudes to Wages and Inflation

The possibility that trade unions might have an inflationary influence on the national economy only started to interest economists in the 1960s, when it became evident that the demand management policies based on earlier Keynesian models of the economy were not sufficient to curb the inflationary tendencies which increasingly concerned governments.

Pre-Keynesian classical economics had seen trade unions as a barrier to the smooth operation of economic markets where wages, as the price of the production factor of labour, depended on movements of labour demand and supply. Labour demand was derived from product demand and prices. Union resistance to wage reductions in the 1920s had been blamed for the failure of labour markets to reach full employment equilibrium and, consequently, for rising unemployment. Indeed, the British so-called General Strike of 1926 had its origins in resistance to a wage reduction imposed by the coal owners.

The Keynesian economic models of the 1950s accepted that organisational structures in labour markets would prevent wages falling to levels low enough to achieve full-employment equilibrium. There was an implied assumption, fully acceptable to all the major political party leaders who had witnessed the suffering caused by large-scale unemployment in the early 1930s, that trade unions were a force for social good among industrial workers. Keynesian economic policies assumed that the major government objective was to achieve and maintain full employment, and it is now recognised that the Keynesian analysis of inflation was rather weak. The concept of an 'inflationary gap', in which aggregate demand exceeded aggregate supply, concentrated mainly on income levels and expenditure demand. It did not take sufficient account of wage levels and union influences on wages and labour productivity.

When rising inflation started to replace unemployment as the main economic problem of governments, another Keynesian assumption, that consumer demand was a function of income, began to turn attention to influences on income levels and to the possibility that there could be an interaction between price movements in product markets and the forces affecting wages and employment in labour markets.

The Phillips Relationship

Evidence that there was a strong statistical relationship between the annual rate of price rises and annual unemployment rates was provided by Phillips (1958), who nevertheless warned that this should not be used as a basis for government policies aimed at directly influencing employment and wages in labour markets. However, the findings of Phillips, supported by evidence provided by other economists, e.g. Lipsey (1960), relating to the years following the period of his study, was used to help justify nearly two decades of direct government intervention in labour markets, including the imposition on several occasions of statutory controls over wages.

The Phillips relationship indicated that a higher inflation rate was associated with a lower unemployment rate. This implied that there was a trade-off between inflation and unemployment, and low rates of unemployment could only be maintained if prices and wages could be kept from rising. The Phillips relationship became widely known through the Phillips curve, shown in Figure 16.3, which appeared to suggest that inflation would be zero at an unemployment level of 2.5%.

The general argument appeared to be that the rate of increase in product prices (price inflation) reflected conditions in product markets and hence the level of labour demand derived from these. When prices and the demand for labour were rising, unemployment would be

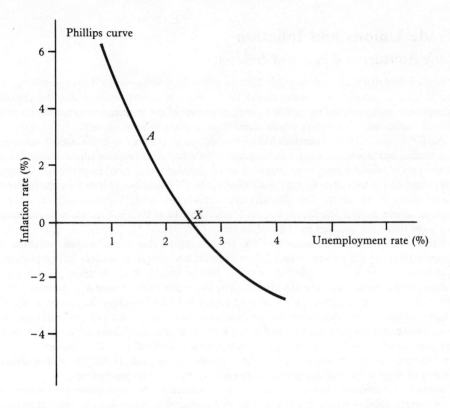

Figure 16.3 *The Phillips curve*
Note: The Phillips curve shows the trade-off between higher inflation and lower employment. At unemployment rate X, believed in the 1960s to be about 2.5%, labour demand in aggregate = aggregate supply and there is no pressure for wage or price inflation. X can be regarded as the natural rate of unemployment.

falling and wages would also be rising. Wages, however, were a production cost to employers. In a period when product demand and prices were rising, firms would be able to pass on wage increases to buyers through further price rises. This produced the wage–price spiral that government intervention sought to check, largely through controlling both price and wage increases.

This argument does not blame unions for causing wage or price inflation but suggests that co-operation of government, employers, and unions could intervene to regulate labour and product markets so that low rates of unemployment could be accompanied by low rates of price and wage inflation. Institutional co-operation might thus avoid the undesirable economic and social consequences of unregulated market forces.

Wages and Prices

Studies of price and unemployment rate links have been criticised for concentrating on absolute monetary figures without considering the purchasing power of money. Changes in the value of what can be bought for a given sum of money affect the purchasing value of wages, and changes have to be made to monetary wages to take these into account and so arrive at what economists call 'real wages'.

Changes in monetary wages, as Phillips showed, can respond to changes in the demand for labour, but they can also respond to changes in product prices. During inflationary periods, whether unemployment is high or low, workers may seek to increase their money wges in order to maintain their living standards. This aspect was recognised by Friedman (1968) and others, who nevertheless took a rather different view of the chain of cause and effect. They saw money wages as responding to the quantity of money in an economy, it velocity, and trends in prices. Money wage inflation was thus regarded as a response by workers, and their trade unions, to declining real incomes. This approach denied the existence of a relationship between changes in money wages and unemployment levels, the latter being considered to be a consequence of labour market imperfections.

There exist, therefore, two clear and distinct views of the cause of money wage inflation. It may or it may not reflect what is occurring to labour demand. Each of these conflicting economic analytical models is supported by substantial empirical evidence.

In his original analysis Phillips' objective was to try and identify certain statistical relationships within the economy, not to explain them. It is possible, however, that reference to trade unions might have provided one of the missing links in this analysis. It can be argued that labour market institutions, and in particular trade unions, provide the mechanism which turns excess labour demand in the economy into money wage inflation.

(a) A trade union's ability to achieve its objectives will be partly dependent upon its strength relative to that of employers at the time of negotiations. The last resort for a trade union is to instruct its members to strike. Similarly, the last resort of an employer is either to 'lock out' its employees or to dismiss them. In purely legal terms a worker who strikes, i.e. refuses to work or to obey management instructions, may be deemed to have broken his or her contract of employment and may be fairly dismissed by the employer.

If it is assumed that the demand for labour is high when an economy is buoyant then this will be the time employers will least wish to see their productive activities disrupted by trade union action. Thus, in periods of excess labour demand, the strength of a trade union increases relative to that of the employer. In such circumstances trade unions may be able to negotiate money wage increases higher than would be possible under less favourable economic conditions.

(b) Hines (1964) identified what he termed 'union pushfulness'. He questioned the concept of the Phillips trade-off approach, believing that there was a different explanation as to why there were periods of rapid money wage increases. He believed that there were historical periods when trade unions increased their level of militancy by seeking high wages for their existing members and by recruiting new members. He was able to offer statistical evidence to confirm that, in periods when an increasing percentage of the labour force was joining trade unions, there was likely to be money wage inflation. Hines believed that there were periods when trade unions would seek increased membership and thus pushed for higher money wages. He did not consider that the question of unemployment entered the thinking of trade unions and thought that any correlation between periods of high trade union militancy and excess labour demand was pure coincidence.

The Expectations-augmented Phillips Curve

There is a further way in which trade unions may become the instrument for putting into effect the natural reactions of workers during a period of price inflation. Workers and their unions realise that any level of negotiated wage rise is going to be eroded by future price rises. Since workers desire any wage rise to be a real rise leading to a real increase in living standards, unions inflate their wage claim by an amount expected to provide compensation for the anticipated price increases. Consequently, the rate of inflation associated with each rate of unemployment tends to rise, so that the Phillips curve moves outwards (as shown in Figure 16.4) and the natural rate of unemployment at which aggregate labour demand equals aggregate labour supply and there is no inflationary pressure also moves up (from X to X_2 in Figure 16.4). In the late 1960s and early 1970s this tendency, institutionalised by the agencies of collective bargaining, was frequently used to account for 'stagflation', the term applied to rising inflation accompanied by rising unemployment.

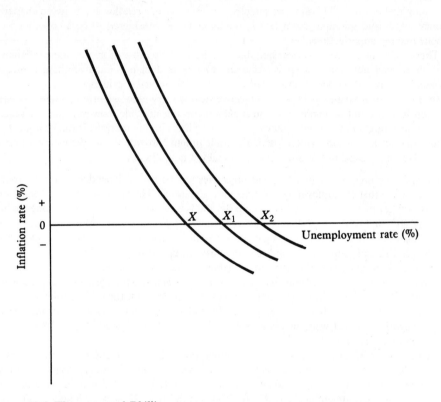

Figure 16.4 *The augmented Phillips curve*
Note: In a period of prolonged price inflation, workers and union anticipate an erosion in the purchasing power of money wage and each successive wage demand takes the anticipated erosion into account. The natural rate of unemployment therefore rises as does the rate associated with each level of price rises. There is thus both rising prices and rising unemployment.

There are two main groups of models used to explain the relationship between trade unions and price rises. One, associated with the basic assumptions of Keynesian macroeconomic analysis and accepting the existence of a general tendency for a Phillips-type relationship between inflation and unemployment, sees unions simply as institutional forces which give expression to worker reactions, aspirations, and expectations following changes in aggregate demand and supply in product and labour markets. There may be an associated belief that these worker attitudes can be modified by government-inspired policies on prices and incomes if these are supported by trade unions and implemented as part of a general package of measures involving employers as well as unions and the government itself.

In conflict with this general view are other models which follow the broad beliefs of Friedman that price and wage inflation are caused by forces ouside both labour and product markets. They are not directly associated with unemployment, which chiefly results from imperfections within labour markets. A particularly damaging imperfection is thought to be the trade union, so that governments, far from negotiating with and strengthening trade unions and trying to intervene in labour markets, should seek to restore unregulated markets and weaken institutional imperfections such as trade unions.

This book is not concerned to analyse and evaluate these conflicting views, but to show that they exist or have existed in the past and that they have influenced government policies and public attitudes towards unions and wage negotiations. Our concern here is not to decide whether or not the Phillips trade-off between inflation and unemployment exists, but to show that belief that it did exist helped to bring about certain government policies which, in turn, have affected the structure and operation of labour markets and institutions. Similarly, later rejection of the Phillips curve, combined with belief that trade unions were a major factor in causing labour markets to be inefficient and a cause of skill shortages and unemployment, led to the employment legislation of the 1980s.

Questions for Discussion and Review

10 Explain what is meant by the phrase 'the wage–price spiral of inflation'. On what grounds has it been argued that trade unions have played a part in bringing about this spiral?

11 Examine movements in prices and unemployment in Britain since 1986. Do these movements appear to support the view that the Phillips relationship, thought to have broken down in the 1970s, reappeared in the second half of the 1980s?

Further Aspects of Trade Unions and Inflation

Although there is no general agreement about the contribution, if any, of trade unions to the price and wage inflation of the 1960s and 1970s, there is a possibility that unions may have contributed to this.

The Inter-firm Comparative Approach

The establishment of wage levels in each firm is a complex process and dependent upon a number of economic and social considerations. Wage determination in firms cannot be solely explained in terms of the interaction of labour demand and supply.

For a high proportion of employees, wage levels incorporating a complex set of differentials are established by rules determined jointly by the firm's managers and the trade unions. In many firms, especially those with developed internal labour markets, these rules take the form of job-evaluated payment systems. While a proportion of the jobs within the firm are linked directly with the external labour market and are, therefore, subject to supply and demand influences, the remainder are not directly affected by these pressures, at least in the short term. Organisations in the public sector and many in the private sector negotiate with trade unions against the background of their perception of wages in other organisations which are felt to be comparable. Brown and Sissons (1975) show how this comparison is made.

One major company may increase its wage rates in response to a shift in the labour market in which it operates. This increase may then be transferred to other comparable companies even though they are not subject to quite the same market pressures. This kind of spill-over effect takes place even if only one type of worker is initially involved. Other companies follow the wage rate increase for this type of worker but, because of the institutional pressure to restore the former pattern of differentials and to preserve the wage pattern established under job evaluation, other workers in the firm also receive increases.

Relative Deprivation

This argument suggests that occupational and company labour groups tend to compare their pay levels to other groups and expect a particular standard of comparison to be maintained. Thus if teachers, for example, observe that policemen have received a significant increase in pay, then the teachers feel that they are a deprived and less-favoured group and they start to exert pressure through their unions to obtain a similar pay increase to overcome their feeling of deprivation.

Should a work group feel deprived, one probable consequence is a decline in morale with an associated fall in productivity and rise in the rate of labour turnover. Faced with this unwelcome development with its threat to profits, employers are likely to respond with a rise in wages. Regardless of whether the original pay rise was justified or not, this spills over to other groups where no such justification can be claimed. In this process the unions are the institutional means for turning worker attitudes into action.

Union Politics

This hypothesis represents a development on the approach of Ross (1948) to the leadership aspirations of those who run trade unions. Ross viewed trade union leaders as essentially 'politicians' eager for power and seeking it by obtaining higher wages for their members. Failure to do so may ultimately lead to the loss of the leadership role and personal career failure.

Consequently, when the leadership of trade union A achieves a wage increase for its members, all other trade union leaders seek to do the same. This is another force for ensuring that an initial wage increase which may have been justified by market circumstances spills over into other employment sectors. This suggests that the existence of the institution (the trade union) through the ambitions of its leaders provides the mechanism for constant pressure to increase money wages regardless of conditions within labour markets and of the inflationary and possible unemployment consequences for workers. Cynics might point out that those who lose their jobs usually cease to be members of the union and so lose their right to vote at leadership elections. Those who keep their jobs and gain the higher pay retain their union membership and votes. This attitude may not only affect the policies and actions of full-time leaders at national level but also those at local level who aspire to climbing the union promotion ladder and to part-time union activists, the more active and committed shop stewards at the work place, many of whom have ambitions for local leaderhip or for becoming full-time union officials.

Wage Leadership

Industrial economists are familiar with the idea that product prices in a particular industry tend to follow those set by a particular firm in that industry. Others follow not necessarily because they have any formal agreement to do so but because they believe that it is in all their best interests to keep prices in line with those set by the 'price leader'. Much the same attitude exists over wages, where agreements made between unions and one or two firms regarded as leaders in the industry are taken as the model, or 'key bargain', on which all other negotiations in the industry are based. This system of pattern bargaining was identified by Levington (1960). With wages, of course, communication links are probably swifter and clearer than with prices. The union provides one channel of communications; personal contacts between personnel officers provides another. Moreover, it is in the wage leader's interests to co-operate in the communication process because this helps to ensure that the additional wage cost is quickly matched by similar extra costs to competitor firms.

As in the other explanations, the key bargain may or may not be appropriate to the economic conditions faced by the firm making it, but the spreading of the terms agreed to other firms takes place with little regard to the product and labour market conditions in the remainder of the industry. The union is also likely to be selective in promoting bargains made by several of the industrial leaders. To take an extreme example, the basic wage rate in company A may be the highest but company B may offer the most generous terms for paid holidays. The union will try to persuade other firms to match both A's basic pay and B's holiday terms.

Productivity Growth

The rate of productivity growth varies between sectors of the economy. At any given time some sectors are likely to be growing faster than others and some will be declining. The swiftly expanding sectors are likely to want to attract labour and the most obvious method of attraction is to offer high wages. Firms in these sectors are likely to be making above-average profits, be achieving high labour productivity, and be able to justify and afford high wages.

Trade unions, however, tend to put pressure on firms in other sectors to follow these increased wages and managers may be willing to do so because they may have started to lose some labour to the expanding firms and believe that they must increase wages in order to retain their remaining workers and to attract replacements for those who have left. These increased wages will be paid even though there are no increases in labour productivity to justify them in economic terms. This process was experienced in the West Midlands in the late 1950s and early 1960s when the motor industry was expanding rapidly. Unskilled workers could earn high wages on the vehicle assembly tracks and recruits were gained from a wide range of local firms as well as from workers moving from less prosperous areas. Within a short time other industries in the West Midlands had to match wages on the assembly lines and wages in other regions also moved up. There were similar experiences during the period of legally controlled incomes policies some years later. One firm would make a genuine productivity agreement that gained the approval of the then Department of Employment and Productivity. Other firms in the same industry and/or area quickly faced demands from their workers for similar wages and were threatened with industrial disruption and loss of key workers if they resisted. There was more than one case where local union leaders sat down with managers and local Department of Employment officials to put together a document that would satisfy the civil servants and politicians in London that the law relating to productivity-based wage rises was being observed. In fact the increases were fed through the industry with very little attempt to copy the productivity gains made by the original firm, whose workers and union representatives quickly discovered what had happened and consequently felt under no obligation to keep to the productivity agreements that had been negotiated.

The Regular Wage Round

There is evidence that wage negotiation is not the one-off event an individual industry or firm may wish to believe but is more of a continuous process through the economy, as suggested by Ashenfelter and Pancavel (1975). Nevertheless, this does not necessarily mean that all wage bargains are the same in any one year. Indeed, there is considerable evidence to the contrary. In any given year Phelps Brown and Browne (1962) found that each industry would negotiate a wage increase for its employees, and in each industry those wage increases appeared relevant to the industry's product market, profit levels, labour market condition, etc. In some years certain industries would lead the round, either in terms of timing or size of settlements, while in other years there would be different industries leading the way. For each year the negotiated wage increases appeared 'appropriate'. In each year, while some industries appeared to gain in relation to other industries, others lost. No apparent pattern appeared to exist. However, when a longer period of ten years was considered the original pattern of wage relationships had re-established itself almost completely. Not only had all the industries increased their wage levels but, over this period, they had done so by the same percentage figure, a feature that had not been obvious when year to year figures were compared. Over the period, the different industries would have experienced different productivity trends and different supply and demand conditions in product and labour markets. Consequently, Phelps Brown and Browne believed that the explanation lay in a spill-over process.

The Institutional Mechanism

The different institutional explanations offered for wage rises in the economy cannot be used to form a single all-embracing theoretical model to determine their relative strengths and importance. Evidence of each has emerged at particular times, and it seems probable that influences important in certain periods are hardly present at all in others.

It has to be recognised that the strength and strategies of institutions depends as much on social and political influences as on economic forces. Trade union strategy and behaviour in a period of economic growth and high inflation which a government is attempting to control through a statutory wages policy are likely to be rather different from those adopted during a period of low or negative growth and high unemployment. In these circumstances it might be that attempts to formulate a single model to explain the relationship between trade unions and wage inflation are likely to be as fruitful as searching for the philosopher's stone. On the other hand, although no alchemist succeeded in turning base metal into gold, many did make some interesting and eventually valuable scientific discoveries in the course of their research. Labour economists may hope to do the same.

All the explanations offered in this section have one feature in common: they all suggest a mechanism whereby a wage increase which is justified in economic terms, as a result, say, of increased productivity, spills over into other firms, regions, or industries where it has little or no economic justification. Nor should it be assumed that the activities of trade unions and company managers render the economic theory of wage determination irrelevant to modern economies. Indeed, the reverse is true. What the institutional explanations suggest is that supply and demand within the labour market are of considerable relevance for certain firms, occupations, or industries at specific times. The labour market conditions establish certain wage levels appropriate to those conditions. The institutional explanations suggest that these wage levels are then spread to other groups in the aggregate labour market and these then receive money wage increases which are out of line with productivity trends in their sectors. Increases in money wages unrelated to changes in the real production of goods and services are likely under many conditions to produce inflationary wage and price tendencies.

Questions for Discussion and Review

12 Discuss the view that trade unions only provide a channel for wage movements and do not actually change the pattern of wages that would exist if unions did not exist.

13 Discuss the case that a national prices and incomes policy is essential because this is the only way to control the inflationary pressures applied by trade unions.

Suggestions for Written Assignments

1 Choose one industry or sector of activity which is strongly unionised and one which is not. Examine the movements of wages in each over the previous three years and write a report outlining why your findings either support or refute the view that trade unions tend to push up wage levels.

2 Interview one local trade union leader and one local personnel officer or small business employer. On the basis of the comments made by each, prepare a report on the attitudes of each to the effect of trade union activity on wages. Before each interview, take care to prepare an outline questionnaire and seek advice from your tutor on the questions you should ask.

3 With the help of available textbooks on macroeconomics draw and explain the meaning of the Phillips curve. In the light of movements in prices and unemployment in the previous five years, state whether you think that these provide evidence supporting or refuting the existence of the Phillips relationship.

4 Many times from the early 1960s onwards British Governments have declared an objective of keeping wage increases in line with increases in labour productivity. Discuss the argument that 'this is an impossible dream'.

Suggestions for Further Reading

A general background to the nature of British trade unions and industrial relations can be found in both Clegg (1979) and Bain (1983). Each of these books provides a detailed, but sometimes perhaps lengthy, explanation. Your librarian or tutor should also be able to suggest a text specific to your immediate needs.

For the impact of trade unions on the labour market and, particularly, on wage levels, there are three review essays: Parsley (1980), Lewis (1983), and Carline (1985). This last essay, although not exclusively concerned with Britain, is more biased towards it than the other two.

More extensive studies of the economic impact of trade unions have been provided by Mulvey (1978), Freeman and Medoff (1984), and Hirsh and Addison (1986). Each of these develops models relating to the assumed impact of trade unions and considers the empirical findings as they relate to union effects.

17
Labour Markets Today and in the Future

Major Contemporary Issues

Labour markets in industrial economies are constantly changing, but there remain major issues which in many countries, including Britain, pose severe economic and social problems.

Unregulated Markets and State Intervention

The underlying theme of this book has been the operation of the neo-classical model of the market within which there is interaction to produce equilibrium between the forces of supply and demand. No one disputes the fundamental laws of the market place, but unfortunately there can never be any guarantee that the consequences of market operations will be acceptable to current social attitudes and beliefs. There is a natural reluctance to see human beings as 'factors of production' and an even greater reluctance to believe that the maximisation of self-interest is an acceptable basis for maintaining a social system. Opponents of neo-classical economies argue that too often free markets become the agencies of human greed and the means whereby the economically weak are exploited in the interests of profits accumulated by the economically strong.

Today, when there appears to be a world movement in favour of a return to market economies and a readiness to applaud the virtues of Adam Smith, it is perhaps desirable to remind ourselves of the economic and social evils, the mass of human misery, that led to social and political change and the rise of new models based on the belief that human societies could manage their affairs to produce a more just, fair, and humane economic system.

We have to remember that unregulated product markets can only function effectively if all the production factors also operate in unregulated markets. If prices are to be freed to move down as well as up then factor prices and quantity levels must have a similar freedom. In labour market terms this means that wages must be able to move down as well as up and that no one can have the luxury of a secure job. A further consequence of this is that living standards must also be flexible for a great many people. In such a system no one can be sure that next week's spending will be at the same level as last week's.

When the current political scene is surveyed we may note that the very groups of people who argue most strongly for a return to unregulated markets at the same time encourage the spread of property ownership, although this is based on long-term borrowing which can only flourish under conditions of income stability. These same groups also encourage State aid for home ownership and the protection of land for 'environmental purposes'. Consequently, the main single item in people's spending and standard of living—housing—depends on a highly regulated and distorted market. There seems to be a very strange reluctance to accept the full implications of what a return to unregulated markets really involves.

There is, perhaps, a more general awareness of the dangers of limited intervention in markets. Keynesian models of demand management fostered the dream that there could be a 'middle way' between the extremes of classical market models and the total control of Marxism. As the instruments of intervention became more complicated and contradictory, so governments were led to intervene increasingly in the market mechanism until business managers found they were unable to take the most basic decisions on product prices and employee wages without reference to civil servants. As most first-year students of economics could have warned, an attempt to regulate a market by price alone led to gross distortions. Few supporters of prices and incomes controls seem prepared to face the logic of their analysis and accept that market control has to involve control over the forces of supply and demand. In labour markets this can only mean full direction of labour and control over the use of labour, over what is to be produced and how, i.e. to the ideal of full socialism, or the prison state, depending on one's point of view.

If both extremes lead to unacceptable social consequences and if leaning on one side or the other inevitably leads towards one of these extremes, what solution does the economist propose? Here we have to admit human fallibility. It is difficult to see any complete solution to the problem. Probably the best contribution that the economist can make is to warn that there are no simple solutions. Every benefit involves an economic cost. Any economic structure produces casualties and social structures should perhaps concentrate on healing the wounds and accept that the ideal economic system is not going to be found this side of paradise.

Problem Areas for Further Thought and Discussion

If you have worked carefully through this book you will now be equipped with a set of economic concepts and some useful analytical techniques to enable you to understand the issues surrounding some of the major problems of contemporary labour markets and to examine critically possible remedies to these problems. In this section we identify the major issues as we see them and suggest that you apply the knowledge you have gained to analysing and discussing these. In particular you should be aware how logical economic solutions might have social or political implications that make them undesirable or impractical.

1 What do you think is the economic role of government today? Make one list of those sectors of economic activity which you think should always be in the public, State-controlled and -financed sector, and a second list which you think might be shared between the public and private sectors.

   What effects do you think advances in technology have had on these sectors in the past quarter century and what further advances are likely in the future?

   What are the consequences of your decisions for management and employment in both the public and the private sectors of the economy?

2 What do you consider to be the role and functions of trade unions in modern labour markets in both the private and the public sectors of the economy? Do you think unions are primarily economic or political institutions? Is there any conflict between these two aspects?

   Is trade union activity an imperfection impeding the efficient operation of the labour market or is it an indication within an imperfect market that there is a serious imbalance between labour demand and supply?

How do you think trade unions should react to trends which
(a) provide increased legal rights to individual workers, and
(b) seek to reduce the extent of State intervention in product and labour markets?

3 What are the difficulties in achieving full employment without also introducing strong inflationary tendencies into the economy? How far are present trends towards restoring free market forces likely to assist in overcoming these difficulties?

4 Discuss the economic case for increasing labour mobility. What are the main economic, social, and political barriers to this mobility and what actions do you think a government should take if it were determined to increase labour mobility?

5 Discuss the difference between general and job-specific post-school education and training. Assuming that it is possible to distinguish between these two types of investment in human capital, how far and on what grounds do you think there is an economic case for requiring individuals to contribute to the cost of providing either or both of these forms of personal development. Is there a case for modifying any of your arguments on social grounds?

Significant Trends of Change

It has frequently been observed that the developments in microelectronics since about the early 1970s have made such profound changes to both products and production methods that the world has really been undergoing a second industrial revolution with consequences for work, society, and general patterns of living as significant as those that followed from the first industrial revolution between, say, 1750 and 1850.

There are some similarities between the two 'revolutions'. In each case work previously carried out by people was now done by machines. New technology created many new activities and economic opportunities. It changed the social and political as well as the economic structure not only within communities but also between the various nations of the world.

There are, however, some important differences in the direction and the speed of these changes. The first industrial revolution developed over a period of a century or even a century and a half. It transferred work from the home to the factory and office. It encouraged the growth of large, tightly structured business organisations within which almost every detail of work became subject to strict managerial supervision and control. It also, of course, changed the role of government in its relationships towards business, work, and the workers.

We are still living through the second industrial revolution and no one can predict the future with certainty. However, so swift is the pace of change that a number of trends have already become clear and any predictions that we might wish to make are likely to have become realities—or been disproved—by the time you have read this book. Among the more significant trends that are clearly evident are the revival of small firms, especially those with owners able to make use of modern technology to provide products and services that previously required large organisations, and the growing volume of work that is now moving back to the home, again much of it making use of modern information technology. These trends present enormous challenges and probably require changes in attitudes as great as the skill changes involved. As in the previous section we ask you to examine a number of issues and consider their implications for the future.

1 A great deal of production can now be carried out by small firms. On the other hand, knowing what to produce and marketing the product still often requires the resources of large firms.

   Discuss the implications of this situation for the future structures of (a) business organisations and (b) employment.

2 Much work now performed in offices can be efficiently carried out in workers' homes.

   Discuss the implications of a possible transfer of work to employee's homes for
   (a) the functions and skills of business managers,
   (b) payment systems, and
   (c) the education and training of an adequately skilled labour force.

3 Future workers operating from home may be able to choose to work for themselves, for a single employer, for several employers, or for a combination of these options.

   Discuss the implications of this development for payment systems and taxation, including National Insurance contributions.

4 Continuing developments in information technology are making it feasible for workers to live and work in one country even though, to a large extent, their work is organised by and carried out under the control and direction of managers situated in another.

   Discuss the effects of such a development on labour markets, payment systems, and relationships between governments, businesses, and workers.

We have identified some issues arising out of changes in contemporary technology and labour markets. You may well think of others. We hope that your understanding of these will have benefited from the knowledge and skills gained from your reading of this book.

Bibliography

Adamson, A.B., Reid, T.M., (1980), "The rate of return to post-compulsory education during the 1970s: an empirical study for Great Britain", Department of Education and Science (mimeo), London.

Addison, J.T., (1976), "The composition of manual worker wage earnings", *British Journal of Industrial Relations*, Vol. 14, pp. 56–69.

Addison, J.T., Siebert, W.S., (1979), 'The Market For Labor: An Analytical Treatment', Goodyear Publishing, Santa Monica, California.

Altonji, J.G., Paxon, C.H., (1986), "Job characteristics and hours of work", in Ehrenberg, R.G., (1986).

Armstrong, E.G.A., (1966), "Minimum wages in a fully employed city", *British Journal of Industrial Relations*, Vol. 4, pp. 22–38.

Arrow, K., (1973), "Higher education as a filter", *Journal of Public Economics*, Vol. 2, pp. 193–216.

Ashenfelter, O., Pencavel, J.H., (1975), "Wage changes and the frequency of wage settlements", *Economica*, Vol. 42, pp. 162–170.

Ashenfelter, O., Layard, R., eds., (1986), 'A Handbook of Labour Economics, Volume 1', North Holland Publishing, Amsterdam.

Atkinson, A.B., (1983), 'The Economics of Inequality', 2nd edn, Oxford University Press, Oxford.

Atkinson, G.B.J., (1988), 'Developments in Economics: An Annual Review, Volume 4', Causeway Press, Ormskirk, Lancashire.

Atrostic, B.K., (1982), "The demand for leisure and non-pecuniary job characteristics", *American Economic Review*, Vol. 72, pp. 428–440.

Azariadis, C., (1975), "Implicit contracts and underemployment equilibria", *Journal of Political Economy*, Vol. 83, pp. 1183–1202.

Bain, G.S., ed., (1983), Industrial Relations in Britain, Blackwell, Oxford.

Bain, G.S., Price, R., (1983), "Union growth: dimensions, determinants and destiny", in Bain, G.S., (1983)

Baxter, J.L., McCormick, B.J., (1984), "Seventy percent of our future: the education, training and employment of young people", *National Westminster Bank Quarterly Review*, August, pp. 36–44.

Beacham, R.H., (1979). 'Pay Systems: Principles and Techniques', Heinemann, London.

Becker, G., (1957), 'The Economics of Discrimination', University of Chicago Press, Chicago.

Becker, G.S., (1962), "Investment in human capital: a theoretical analysis", *Journal of Political Economy*, Vol. 70 [Supplement], pp. 9–49.

Becker, G.S., (1975), 'Human Capital: A Theoretical and Empirical Analysis with Special Reference to Education', University of Chicago Press, Chicago.

Blackaby, D..H., Manning, D.N., (1987), "Regional earnings revisited", *Manchester School of Economics and Social Sciences*, Vol. 55, pp. 158–183.

Blanchflower, D., (1984), "Union relative wage effects: a cross section analysis using establishment data", *British Journal of Industrial Relations*, Vol. 22, pp. 311–332.

Blanchflower, D., (1986), "Wages and concentration in British manufacturing", *Applied Economics*, Vol. 18, pp. 1025–1038.

Blight, D.B., Shafto, T.A.C., (1989), 'Microeconomics', Hutchinson, London.

Blundell, R., Ham, J., Meghir, C., (1987), "Unemployment and female labour supply", *Economic Journal*, Vol. 97 [Supplement], pp. 44–63.

Blyton, P., Hill, S., (1981), "The economics of work-sharing", *National Westminster Bank Quarterly Review*, November, pp. 37–45.

Bosanquet, N., Doeringer, P.B., (1973), "Is there a dual labour market in Great Britain?", *Economic Journal*, Vol. 83, pp. 421–435.

Bosworth, D.L., Dawkins, P.J., (1980), "Compensation for workers' disutility: time of day, length of shift and other features of work patterns", *Scottish Journal of Political Economy*, Vol. 27, pp. 80–96.

Bowen, W.G., Finegan, T.A., (1966), "Educational attainment and labor force participation", *American Economic Review*, Vol. 56 [Supplement] pp. 567–582

Bowers, J., Deaton, D.R., (1982), 'Labour Hoarding in British Industry', Blackwell, Oxford.

Bowley, A.M., (1969), "Labour stability curves and a labour stability index", *British Journal of Industrial Relations*, Vol. 7, pp. 71–83.

Bowley, A., (1980), "Coming to terms with comparability", *Personnel Management*, Vol. 12, No. 2, pp. 28–33.

Bowley, A., ed., (1975), 'Handbook of Salary and Wage systems', Gower, London.

Bramham, J., (1988), 'Practical Manpower Planning', 4th edn, Institute of Personnel Management, London.

Briggs, V.M., (1987), "Human resource development and the formation of national economic policy", *Journal of Economic Issues*, Vol. 21, pp. 1207–1240.

Bronfenbrenner, M., Mossin, J., (1967), "The shorter work week and labor supply", *Southern Economic Journal*, Vol. 33, pp. 322–331.

Brown, A.J., (1972), 'The Framework of Regional Economics in the United Kingdom', Cambridge University Press, Cambridge.

Brown, C., Gilroy, C., Kohen, A., (1982), "The effect of the minimum wage on employment and unemployment", *Journal of Economic Literature*, Vol. 20, pp. 487–528.

Brown, W., (1976), "Incomes policy and pay differentials", *Oxford Bulletin of Economics and Statistics*, Vol. 38, pp. 27–51.

Brown, W., Sisson, K., (1975), "The use of comparisons in workplace wage determination", *British Journal of Industrial Relations*, Vol. 13, pp. 23–53.

Brown, W., Terry, M., (1978), "The changing nature of national wage agreements", *Scottish Journal of Political Economy*, Vol. 25, pp. 119–133.

Cain, G.G., (1975), "The challenge of dual and radical theories of the labor market to orthodox theory", *American Economic Review*, Vol. 65 [Supplement], pp. 16–22.

Cain, G.G., (1976), "The challenge of segmented labor market theories to orthodox theory: a survey", *Journal of Economic Literature*, Vol. 14, pp. 1215–1257.

Cairnes, J.E., (1974), 'Political Economy', Harper, New York.

Campbell, C.B., Campbell, R.G., (1969), "State minimum wage laws as a cause of unemployment", *Southern Economic Journal*, Vol. 35, pp. 323–332.

Carline, D., (1985), "Trade unions and wages", in Carline, D., *et al.*, (1985).

Carline, D., Pissarides, C.A., Siebert, W.S., Sloane, P.J., (1985), 'Surveys in Economics: Labour Economics', Longman, London.

Carnoy, M., Marenbach, D., (1975), "The return on schooling in the US: 1939–1969", *Journal of Human Resources*, Vol. 10, pp. 312–331.

Cartter, A.M., (1959), 'Theory of Wages and Employment', Irwin, Homewood, Illinois.

Cartter, A.M., (1967), 'Labor Economics', Irwin, Homewood, Illinois.

Charter, R.E.J., Dean, A., Elliot, R.F., eds., (1981), 'Incomes Policy', Clarendon Press, Oxford.

Chiplin, B., Sloane, P.J., (1974), "Sexual discrimination in the labour market", *British Journal of Industrial Relations*, Vol. 12, pp. 371–402.

Clark, C., (1960), 'The Conditions of Economic Progress', 3rd edn, Macmillan, London.

Clegg, H.A., (1971), 'How to Run an Incomes Policy and Why We Made Such a Mess of the Last One', Heinemann, London.

Clegg, H.A., (1979), 'The Changing System of Industrial Relations in Great Britain', Blackwell, Oxford.

Clegg, H.A., [chairman], (1980), Standing Commission on Pay Comparability, Report No. 7: Teachers, HMSO (Cmnd 7880), London.

Collier, P., Knight, J.B., (1985), "Seniority payments, quit rates and internal labour markets in Britain and Japan", *Oxford Bulletin of Economics and Statistics*, Vol. 47, pp. 19–32.

Collier, P., Knight, J.B., (1986), "Wage structure and labour turnover", *Oxford Economic Papers*, Vol. 38, pp. 77–93.

Corry, B.A., Roberts, J.A., (1970), "Activity rates and unemployment: the experience of the United Kingdom 1951–66", *Applied Economics*, Vol. 2, pp. 179–201.

Corry, B.A., Roberts, J.A., (1974), "Activity rates and unemployment: the United Kingdom experience, some further results", *Applied Economics*, Vol. 6, pp. 1–21.

Courtney, G., Hedges, B., (1977), 'A Survey of Employers' Recruitment Practices', Social and Community Planning Research, London.

Cowling, K., Metcalf, D., (1967), "Wage unemployment relationships: a regional analysis for the United Kingdom 1960–65", *Bulletin of the Oxford University Institute of Economics and Statistics*, Vol. 29, pp. 31–39.

Creedy, J., ed., (1981), 'The Economics of Unemployment in Britain', Butterworths, London.

Creedy, J., Hart, P.E., (1979), "Age and the distribution of earnings", *Economic Journal*, Vol. 89, pp. 280–293.

Creedy, J., Thomas, B., ed., (1982), 'The Economics of Labour', Butterworth Scientific, London.

Crossley, J.R., (1966), "Collective bargaining, wage structure and the labour market in the United Kingdom", in Hugh-Jones, E.M., (1966)

Culyer, A.J., (1980), 'The Political Economy of Social Policy', Martin Robertson, Oxford.

Cullen, D.E., (1956), "The inter-industry wage structure 1899–1950", *American Economic Review*, Vol. 46, pp. 353–369.

Cyert, R.M., March, J.C., (1963), 'A Behavioral Theory of the Firm', Prentice-Hall, New Jersey.

Denison, E.F., (1967), 'Why Growth Rates Differ: Postwar Experience in Nine Western Countries', Brookings Institution, Washington.

de Wolff, P., (1965), 'Wages and Labour Mobility', OECD, Paris.

Dow, J.R.C., Dicks-Mireaux, L.A., (1958), "The excess demand for labour: a study of conditions in Great Britain, 1946–1956", *Oxford Economic Papers*, Vol. 10, pp. 1–33.

Doeringer, P.B., Piore, M.J., (1971), 'Internal Labor Markets and Manpower Analysis', Heath Lexington Books, Lexington, Massachusetts.

Donaldson, J., Philby, P., (1984), 'Pay Differentials', Gower, London.

Dunlop, J.T., (1964), "The task of contemporary wage theory", in Dunlop, J.T., ed., (1964)

Dunlop, J.T., ed., (1964), 'The Theory of Wage Determination', Macmillan, London.

Ehrenberg, R.G., (1970), "Absenteeism and the overtime question", *American Economic Review*, Vol. 60, pp. 352–357.

Ehrenberg, R.G., ed., (1977), 'Research in Labor Economics: A Research Annual, Volume 1', Jai Press, Greenwich, Connecticut.

Ehrenberg, R.G., ed., (1981), 'Research in Labor Economics: A Research Annual, Volume 4, Jai Press, Greenwich, Connecticut.

Ehrenberg, R.G., ed., (1982), 'Research in Labor Economics: A Research Annual, Volume 5, Jai Press, Greenwich, Connecticut.

Ehrenberg, R.G., ed., (1986), 'Research in Labor Economics: A Research Annual, Volume 8 (Part A), Jai Press, Greenwich, Connecticut.

Elliot, R.F., (1977), "The growth of white collar employment in Great Britain: 1951–1971", *British Journal of Industrial Relations*, Vol. 15, pp. 39–44.

Elliot, R.F., (1981), "Some further thoughts on the importance of national wage agreements", *British Journal of Industrial Relations*, Vol. 19, pp. 370–375.

Elliot, R.F., Fallick, J.L., (1981). 'Pay in the Public Sector', Macmillan, London.

Elliot, R.F., Steele, R., (1976), "The importance of national wage agreements", *British Journal of Industrial Relations*, Vol. 14, pp. 43–55.

Field, F., ed., (1973), 'Low Pay', Arrow Books, London.

Field, F., (1984), 'The Minimum Wage: Potential and Dangers', Heinemann, London.

Flanagan, R.J., (1973), "Segmented market theories and racial discrimination", *Industrial Relations*, Vol. 12, pp. 253–273.

Flanders, A., (1970), 'Management and Unions', Faber & Faber, London.

Fogarty, M.P., (1961), 'The Just Wage', Chapman & Hall, London.

Frank, R.F., (1984), "Are workers paid their marginal product?", *American Economic Review*, Vol. 74, pp. 549–571.

Freeman, R.B., Medoff, J.L., (1984), 'What Unions Do', Basic Books, New York.

Friedman, M., (1968), "The role of monetary policy", *American Economic Review*, Vol. 58, pp. 1–17.

Fuchs, V.R., (1967), "Hourly earnings differentials by region and size of city", *Monthly Labor Review*, January, pp. 22–26.

Galambos, P., (1967), "Activity rates of the population of Great Britain", *Scottish Journal of Political Economy*, Vol. 14, pp. 48–69.

Garbarino, J.W., (1950), "A theory of inter-industry wage structure variation", *Quarterly Journal of Economics*, Vol. 64, pp. 282–305.

George, K.D., Shorey, J., (1985), "Manual workers, good jobs and structured internal labour markets", *British Journal of Industrial Relations*, Vol. 23, pp. 425–447.

Geroski, P., Stewart, M., (1982), "Trade union differentials in the United Kingdom: a strange and sad story", Queen Mary College, University of London (mimeo).

Gershuny, J., (1978), 'After Industrial Society: The Emerging Self Service Economy', Macmillan, London.

Gleave, D., Palmer, D., (1980), "Spatial variation in unemployment problems: a typology", Papers of the Regional Science Association, Vol. 44, pp. 57–71.

Goetschin, P., (1987), "Re-shaping work for an older population", *Personnel Management*, June, pp. 39–41.

Goodman, J.F.B., (1970), "The definition and analysis of local labour markets: some empirical problems", *British Journal of Industrial Relations*, Vol. 8, pp. 179–196.

Gramm, W.L., (1974), "The demand for wives' non-market time", *Southern Economic Journal*, Vol. 41, pp. 124–133.

Greenhalgh, C., (1977), "A labour supply function for married women in Great Britain", *Economica*, Vol. 44, pp. 249–265.

Greenhalgh, C., (1979), "Male labour force participation in Great Britain", *Scottish Journal of Political Economy*, Vol. 26, pp. 275–285.

Greenhalgh, C., (1980a), "Male–female wage differentials in Great Britain: is marriage an equal opportunity", *Economic Journal*, Vol. 90, pp. 751–775.

Greenhalgh, C., (1980b), "Participation and hours of work for married women in Great Britain", *Oxford Economic Papers*, Vol. 32, pp. 296–318.

Greenhalgh, C., Layard, R.G.D., Oswald, A.J., ed., (1983), 'The Causes of Unemployment', Oxford University Press, Oxford.

Greenhalgh, C., Stewart, M.B., (1985), "The occupational status and mobility of men and women", *Oxford Economic Papers*, Vol. 37, pp. 40–71.

Greenhalgh, C., Stewart, M., (1987), "The effects and determinants of training", *Oxford Bulletin of Economics and Statistics*, Vol. 49, pp. 171–190.

Gujarat, D., (1972), "The behaviour of unemployment and unfilled vacancies", *Economic Journal*, Vol. 82, pp. 195–204.

Hakim, C., (1979), "Occupational segregation", Research Paper No. 9, Department of Employment, London.

Hakim, C., (1987), "Trends in the flexible workforce", *Employment Gazette*, Vol. 95, pp. 549–560.

Hamermesh, D.S., (1980), "Unemployment insurance and labor supply", *International Economic Review*, Vol. 21, pp. 517–527.

Hamermesh, D.S., Rees, A., (1984), 'The Economics of Work and Pay', 3rd edn, Harper and Row, New York.

Harbison, F.H., (1973), 'Human Resources as the Wealth of Nations', Oxford University Press, Oxford.

Harris, A.I., (1968), "Labour mobility in Great Britain: 1953–63", Report No. 333, Government Social Survey, HMSO, London.

Harris, M., (1964), "The social aspects of labour turnover in the USSR", *British Journal of Industrial Relations*, Vol. 2, pp. 398–417.

Hart, R.A., MacKay, D.I., (1975), "Engineering earnings in Britain: 1914–68", *Journal of the Royal Statistical Society*, Series A, Vol. 138, pp. 32–50.

Hartley, K., (1985), "Youth training", *Economic review*, Vol. 2, No. 5, pp. 9–14.

Hashimoto, M., (1982), "Minimum wage effects on training on the job", *American Economic Review*, Vol. 72, pp. 1070–1087.

Hasluck, C., (1987), 'Urban Unemployment: Local Labour Markets and Employment Initiatives', Longman, London.

Hawkesworth, R.I., (1978), "The movement of skill differentials in the United Kingdom engineering industry", *British Journal of Industrial Relations*, Vol. 16, pp. 277–286.

Hawkins, K., (1987), 'Unemployment', 3rd edn, Penguin Books, London.

Hedges, B., (1982), 'Survey of Employers' Recruitment Practices', Social and Community Planning Research, London.

Hicks, J.R., (1964), 'The Theory of Wages', Macmillan, London.

Hines, A.G., (1964), "Wage inflation in the United Kingdom: 1893–1961", *Review of Economic Statistics*, Vol. 31, pp. 221–252.

Hirch, B.T., Addison, J.T., (1986), 'The Economic Analysis of Unions: New Approaches and Evidence', Unwin Hyman, London.

Hood, W., Rees, R.D., (1974), "Inter-industry wage levels in United Kingdom manufacturing", *Manchester School of Economics and Social Science*, Vol. 42, pp. 171–185.

Houghton, Lord, [chairman], (1975), Report of the Committee of Inquiry: Pay of Non-university Teachers, HMSO (Cmnd 5848), London.

Hughes, J.J., Perlman, R., (1984), 'The Economics of Unemployment: A Comparative Analysis of Britain and the United States', Wheatsheaf Books, Brighton.

Hugh-Jones, E.M., ed., (1966), 'Wage Structure in Theory and Practice', North Holland, Amsterdam.

Hunter, L.C., with P.B. Beaumont, (1978), "Labour shortages and manpower policy", MSC Manpower Studies No. 19782, HMSO, London.

Hyman, R., (1983), "Trade unions: policies and politics", in Bain, G.S., (1983).

Institute of Manpower Studies, (1986), 'Changing Working Patterns', NEDO Books, London.

Johnson, G.E., (1966), "Wage theory and inter-regional variation", *Industrial Relations*, Vol. 6, pp. 321–338.

Johnson, G.E., (1977), "The determination of wages in the union and non-union sectors", *British Journal of Industrial Relations*, Vol. 15, pp. 211–225.

Johnson, R., (1984a), "Youth training in Europe", *Personnel Management*, July, pp. 24–26 and 37.

Johnson, R., (1984b), "Adult training in Europe", *Personnel Management*, August, pp. 24–27.

Jones, D.R., Martin, R.L., (1986), "Voluntary and involuntary turnover in the labour force", *Scottish Journal of Political Economy*, Vol. 33, pp. 124–144.

Jones, R.M., (1969), "A case study of labour mobility", *Manchester School of Economics and Social Sciences*, Vol. 37, pp. 169–174.

Joshi, H.E., (1981), "Secondary workers in the employment cycle in Great Britain", *Economica*, Vol. 48, pp. 29–44.

Joshi, H.E., Layard, R., Owen, S.J., (1985), "Why are more women working in Britain?", *Journal of Labor Economics*, Vol. 3, No. 1, Part 2, pp. S147–S176.

Kamerschen, D.R., (1967), "Inter-industry earnings differentials, productivity, size and concentration", *Journal of Industrial Relations*, Vol. 9, pp. 52–67.

Keeley, M., (1981), 'Labor Supply and Public Policy', Academic Press, New York.

Kerr, C., (1950), "Labor markets: their character and consequences", *American Economic Review*, Vol. 40 pp. 278–291.

Khan, H.R., (1956), "The distinction between wages and salaries", *Scottish Journal of Political Economy*, Vol. 3, pp. 126–145.

Killingsworth, M., (1981), "A survey of labor supply models: theoretical analysis and first generation empirical results", in Ehrenberg, R.G., (1981).

Killingsworth, M.R., (1983), 'Labour Supply', Cambridge University Press, Cambridge.

Killingsworth, M.R., Heckman, J.T., (1986), "Female labour supply: a survey", in Ashenfelter, O., and Layard, R., (1986).

Koutsoyannis, A., (1981), 'Modern Microeconomics', 2nd edn, Macmillan, London.

Lawson, T., (1982), "On the stability of the inter-industry structure of earnings in the United Kingdom, 1954–78", *Cambridge Journal of Economics*, Vol. 6, pp. 249–268.

Layard, P.R.G., Barton, M., Zabalza, A., (1980), "Married women's participation and hours", *Economica*, Vol. 47, pp. 51–72.

Layard, R., Metcalf, D., Nickell, S. (1978a), "The effect of collective bargaining on relative and absolute wages", *British Journal of Industrial Relations*, Vol. 16, pp. 287–302.

Layard, R., Piachaud, D., Stewart, M., (1978b), "The causes of poverty", Background paper No. 5, Royal Commission on the Distribution of Income and Wealth, HMSO, London.

Lazear, E.P., (1986), "Raids and other matching", in Ehrenberg, R.G., (1986).

Lees, D., Chiplin, B., (1970), "The economics of industrial training", *Lloyds Bank Review*, No. 96, pp. 29–41.

Lester, R., (1946), "Shortcomings of marginal analysis for wage employment problems", *American Economic Review*, Vol. 36, pp. 63–82.

Lester, R., (1967), "Pay differentials by size of establishment", *Industrial Relations*, Vol. 7, pp. 57–67.

Levinson, H.M., (1960), "Pattern bargaining: a case study of the automobile industry", *Quarterly Journal of Economics*, Vol. 74, pp. 296–317.

Lewis, H.G., (1963), 'Unionism and Relative Wages in the United States: An Empirical Enquiry', University of Chicago Press, Chicago.

Lewis, H.G., (1983), "Union relative wage effects: a survey of the macro estimates", *Journal of Labor Economics*, Vol. 1, pp. 1–27.

Lianos, T., (1976), "A note on discrimination in the labor market", *Southern Economic Journal*, Vol. 43, pp. 1177–1180.

Lindley, R.M., (1976), "Inter-industry mobility of male employees in Great Britain, 1959–68", *Journal of the Royal Statistical Society*, Series A, Vol. 139, pp. 56–77.

Lindley, R.M., (1982), "Occupational choice and investment in human capital", in Creedy, J., Thomas, B., (1982).

Lipsey, R.G., (1960), "The relation between unemployment and the rate of change of money wage rates in the United Kingdom", *Economica*, Vol. 27, pp. 1–31.

Loveridge, R., Mok, A., (1979), 'Theories of Labour Market Segmentation', Martinus Nijhoff, The Hague.

Lupton, T., ed., (1972), 'Payment Systems', Penguin, London.

Lynch, L.M., (1983), "Job search and unemployment", *Oxford Economic Papers*, Vol. 35 [Supplement], pp. 595–606.

McCall, J.J., (1970), "Economics of information and job search", *Quarterly Journal of Economics*, Vol. 84, pp. 113–126.

McCormick, B.J., (1977), "Methods of wage payment, wages structures and the influence of factor and product markets", *British Journal of Industrial Relations*, Vol. 15, pp. 246–264.

McCormick, B., (1988), "Quit rates over time in a job rationed labour market: the British manufacturing sector: 1971–1983", *Economica*, Vol. 55, pp. 81–94.

Mace, J.D., Wilkinson, G.C.G., (1977), "Are labour markets competitive?—a case study of engineers", *British Journal of Industrial Relations*, Vol. 15, pp. 1–17.

McElroy, M.B., (1981), "Empirical results from estimates of joint labor supply functions of husbands and wives", in Ehrenberg, R.G., (1981).

Machlup, F., (1946), "Marginal analysis and empirical research", *American Economic Review*, Vol. 36, pp. 519–541.

Machlup, F., (1967), "Theories of the firm: marginalist, behavioral, managerial", *American Economic Review*, Vol. 57, pp. 1–33.

MacKay, D.I., Boddy, D., Brack, J., Diack, J.A., Jones, N., (1971), 'Labour Markets Under Different Employment Conditions', Allen and Unwin, London.

McNabb, R., (1987), "Testing for labour market segmentation in Britain", *Manchester School of Economics and Social Science*, Vol. 55, pp. 257–273.

Madden, J.F., (1981), "Why women work closer to home", *Urban Studies*, Vol. 18, pp. 181–194.

Main, B.G.M., (1982), "The length of a job in Great Britain", *Economica*, Vol. 49, pp. 325–333.

Maizels, J., (1965), "The entry of school leavers into employment", *British Journal of Industrial Relations*, Vol. 3, pp. 77–89.

Maki, D., Spindler, Z.A., (1975), "The effect of unemployment compensation on the rate of unemployment", *Oxford Economic Papers*, Vol. 27, pp. 440–454.

Mallier, A.T., Rosser, M.J., (1987), "Changes in the industrial distribution of female employment in Great Britain, 1951–81", *Work Employment and Society*, Vol. 1, pp. 463–486.

Manpower Services Commission, (1978), 'People and their Work', MSC, London.

Manwaring, T., (1984), "The extended internal labour market", *Cambridge Journal of Economics*, Vol. 8, pp. 161–187.

Marin, A., Psacharopoulos, G., (1982), "The reward for risk in the labor market: evidence from the United Kingdom and a reconciliation with other studies", *Journal of Political Economy*, Vol. 90, pp. 827–851.

Marquand, J., (1967), "Which are the lower paid workers?", *British Journal of Industrial Relations*, Vol. 5, pp. 359–374.

Marriot, R. (1968), 'Incentive Payment Systems', Staples Press, London.

Martin, J., Roberts, C., (1984), 'Women and Employment: A Lifetime Perspective', HMSO, London.

Masters, S.H., (1969), "An inter-industry analysis of wages and plant size", *Review of Economics and Statistics*, Vol. 51, pp. 341–345.

Mayhew, K., (1975), "The reversal of skill differentials under payment by results systems: the case of engineering", *Oxford Bulletin of Economics and Statistics*, Vol. 37, pp. 251–268.

Mayhew, K., (1976a), "Regional variations of manual earnings in engineering", *Oxford Bulletin of Economics and Statistics*, Vol. 38, pp. 11–26.

Mayhew, K., (1976b), "Plant size and the earnings of manual workers in engineering", *Oxford Bulletin of Economics and Statistics*, Vol. 38, pp. 149–160.

Mayhew, K., Rosewell, B., (1979), "Labour market segmentation in Britain", *Oxford Bulletin of Economics and Statistics*, Vol. 41, pp. 81–116.

Mayhew, K., Rosewell, B., (1981), "Occupational Mobility in Britain", *Oxford Bulletin of Economics and Statistics*, Vol. 43, pp. 225–255.

Meredeen, S., (1988), 'Managing Industrial Conflict', Hutchinson, London.

Metcalf, D., Nickell, S., (1982), "Occupational mobility in Great Britain", in Ehrenberg, R.G., (1982).

Mill, J.S., (1895), 'Principles of Political Economy", Routledge and Sons, London.

Miller, E.M., (1977), "The extent of economies of scale: the effects of firm size on labor productivity and wage rates", *Southern Economic Journal*, Vol. 44, pp. 470–487.

Millward, N., Stevens, M., (1988), "Union density in the regions", *Employment Gazette*, Vol. 96, pp. 286–295.

Minford, P., (1981), "Labour market equilibrium in an open economy", Conference on Unemployment, Newnham College, Cambridge.

Mitchell, J., (1972), 'The National Board of Prices and Incomes', Secker Warburg, London.

Molho, I., (1984), "A dynamic model of interregional migration flows in Great Britain", *Journal of Regional Science*, Vol. 24, pp. 317–334.

Molle, W., van Mourik, A., (1988). "International movement of labour under conditions of economic integration: the case of Western Europe", Journal of Common Market Studies, Vol. 26, pp. 317–339.

Mulvey, C., (1976), "Collective agreements and relative earnings in United Kingdom manufacturing in 1973", *Economica*, Vol. 43, pp. 419–427.

Mulvey, C., (1978), 'The Economic Analysis of Trade Unions', Martin Robertson, Oxford.

Mulvey, C., Abowd, J.M., (1980), "Estimating the union/non-union wage differential: a statistical issue", *Economica*, Vol. 47, pp. 73–79.

Mulvey, C., Foster, J.L., (1976), "Occupational earnings in the United Kingdom and the effects of collective agreements", *Manchester School of Economics and Social Sciences*, Vol. 44, pp. 258–275.

National Board of Prices and Incomes Report No. 65, (1968), Payment by Results Systems, HMSO (Cmnd 3627), London.

National Board of Prices and Incomes Report No. 83, (1968), Job Evaluation, HMSO (Cmnd 3772), London.

National Board of Prices and Incomes Report No. 169, (1971), General Problems of Low Pay, HMSO (Cmnd 4648), London.

Nicholson, N., West, M., (1987), 'Managerial Job Change', Cambridge University Press, Cambridge.

Nickell, S., Andrews, M., (1983), "Unions, real wages and employment in Britain: 1951–1979", *Oxford Economic Papers*, Vol. 35, pp. 508–530.

Nixson, F., (1988), "Population", in Atkinson, G.B.J., (1988).

Nowak, M.J., Crockett, G.V., (1983), "The operation of the internal labour market: three case studies", *Journal of Industrial Relations*, Vol. 25, pp. 445–464.

Oatey, M., (1970), "The economics of training with respect to the firm", *British Journal of Industrial Relations*, Vol. 8, pp. 1–21.

O'Donnell, C., (1984), "Major theories of the labour market and women's place within it", *Journal of Industrial Relations*, Vol. 26, pp. 147–165.

Old, J., Shafto, T.A.C., (1989), 'Introduction to Business Economics', Hutchinson, London.

Office of Manpower Economics, (1973), 'Incremental Payment Systems', HMSO, London.

Office of Manpower Economics, (1973), 'Measured Daywork', HMSO, London.

Oi, W., (1962), "Labor as a quasi-fixed factor", *Journal of Political Economy*, Vol. 70 [Supplement], pp. 538–555.

Organization for Economic Co-operation and Development, (1986), 'Flexibility in the Labour Market: The Current Debate', OECD, Paris.

Osterman, P., (1975), "An empirical study of labor market segmentation", *Industrial and Labor Relations Review*, Vol. 28, pp. 508–521.

Oswald, A.J., (1981), "The theory of internal wage and employment structure", *Bell Journal of Economics*, Vol. 12, pp. 263–271.

Owen, S.J., Joshi, H.E., (1987), "Does elastic retract: the effect of the recession on women's labour force participation", *British Journal of Industrial Relations*, Vol. 25, pp. 125–144.

Parsley, C.J., (1980), "Labor unions and wages: a survey", *Journal of Economic Literature*, Vol. 18, pp. 1–31.

Parsons, D.O., (1972), "Specific human capital: an application to quit rates and layoff rates", *Journal of Political Economy*, Vol. 80, pp. 1120–1143.

Parsons, D.O., (1977), "Models of labor market turnover: a theoretical and empirical survey", in Ehrenberg, R.G., (1977).

Parsons, D.O., (1980), "The decline of male labor force participation", *Journal of Political Economy*, Vol. 88, pp. 117–134.

Parsons, D.O., (1982), "Male labour force participation decision: health, reported health, and economic incentives", *Economica*, Vol. 49, pp. 81–91.

Paukert, L., (1984), 'The Employment and Unemployment of Women in OECD Countries', OECD, Paris.

Pencavel, J.H., (1974), "Relative wages and trade unions in the United Kingdom", *Economica*, Vol. 41, pp. 194–210.

Pencavel, J.H., (1977), "Work effort, on-the-job screening, and alternative methods of remuneration", in Ehrenberg, R.G., (1977).

Pencavel, J.H., (1986), "Labour supply of men: a survey", in Ashenfelter, O. and Layard, R., (1986).

Perlman, R., (1960), "Observations on overtime and moon-lighting", *Southern Economic Journal*, Vol. 33, pp. 237–244.

Perlman, R., (1969), 'Labor theory', John Wiley & Sons, New York.

Peterson, J.M., (1962), "Research needs in minimum wage theory", *Southern Economic Journal*, Vol. 29, pp. 1–9.

Pettman, B.O., ed., (1975), 'Labour Turnover and Retention', Gower Press, London.

Phelps Brown, E.H., (1962), 'The Economics of Labor', Yale University Press, London.

Phelps Brown, E.H., (1977), 'The Inequality of Pay', Oxford University Press, Oxford.

Phelps Brown, E.H., Browne, M.H., (1962), "Earnings in industries of the United Kingdom: 1948–1959", *Economic Journal*, Vol. 72, pp. 517–549.

Phelps Brown, E.H., Hopkins, S., (1955), "Seven centuries of building wages", *Economica*, Vol. 22, pp. 349–354.

Phelps Brown, E.H., Hopkins, S., (1956), "Seven centuries of the price of consumerables compared with builders' wage rates", *Economica*, Vol. 23, pp. 296–314.

Phelps Brown, E.H., Hopkins, S., (1961), "Seven centuries of wages and prices: some earlier estimates", *Economica*, Vol. 28, pp. 30–36.

Phillips, A.W., (1958), "The relation between unemployment and the rate of change in money wage rates in the United Kingdom: 1861–1957", *Economica*, Vol. 25, pp. 283–299.

Pigou, A.C., (1932), 'The Economics of Welfare', 4th edn, Macmillan, London.

Pissarides, C.A., (1981), "Staying on at school in England and Wales", *Economica*, Vol. 48, pp. 345–363.

Pissaridies, C.A., (1982a), "From school to university: the demand for post-compulsory education in Britain", *Economic Journal*, Vol. 92, pp. 654–667.

Pissarides, C.A., (1982b), "Job search and the duration of layoff unemployment", *Quarterly Journal of Economics*, Vol. 97, pp. 595–612.

Pissarides, C.A., (1985), "Job search and the functioning of labour markets", in Carline, D., *et al.*, (1985).

Psacharopoulos, G., Layard, P.R.G., (1979), "Human capital and earnings: British evidence and a critique", *Review of Economic Studies*, Vol. 46, pp. 485–503.

Rajan, A., Pearson, R., ed., (1986), 'UK Occupational and Employment Trends to 1990', Butterworths, London.

Reddaway, W.B., (1977), "The economic consequences of zero population growth", *Lloyds Bank Review*, No. 124, pp. 14–30.

Reder, M.W., (1955), "The theory of occupational wage differentials", *American Economic Review*, Vol. 45, pp. 834–840.

Reder, M.W., (1969), "The theory of frictional unemployment", *Economica*, Vol. 36, pp. 1–28.

Rees, A., (1966), "Information networks in labour markets", *American Economic Review*, Vol. 56 [Supplement], pp. 559–566.

Reich, M., Gordon, D.M., Edwards, R.C., (1973), "A theory of labor market segmentation", *American Economic Review*, Vol. 63 [Supplement], pp. 359–365.

Reid, G.L., (1972), "Job search and the effectiveness of job-finding methods", *Industrial and Labor Relations Review*, Vol. 25, pp. 479–495.

Richardson, R., Robinson, C., Smith, J., (1977), "Quit rates and manpower policy", *Department of Employment Gazette*, Vol. 85, pp. 14–18.

Roberts, B.C., Smith, J.H., ed., (1966), 'Manpower Policy and Employment Trends', Bell, London.

Robinson, D., (1968), 'Wage Drift, Fringe Benefits and Manpower Distribution', OECD, Paris.

Robinson, D., ed., (1970), 'Local Labour Markets and Wage Structures', Gower, London.

Robinson, O., (1979), "The changing labour market: the phenomenon of part-time employment", *National Westminster Bank Quarterly Review*, November, pp. 19–29.

Rolfe, P.H., (1981), "The causes of inter-regional labour force migration in Great Britain", *Bulletin of Economic Research*, Vol. 33, pp. 74–81.

Roper, S., (1988), "Recruitment methods and vacancy duration", *Scottish Journal of Political Economy*, Vol. 35, pp. 51–64.

Rosen, S., (1977), "Human capital: a survey of the empirical research", in Ehrenberg, R.G., (1977).

Rosewell, B., Robinson, D., (1980), "The reliability of vacancy statistics", *Oxford Bulletin of Economics and Statistics*, Vol. 42, pp. 1–15.

Ross, A.M., (1948), 'Trade union wage policy', University of California Press, California.

Ross, A.M., Goldner, W., (1950), "Forces affecting inter-industry wage structure", *Quarterly Journal of Economics*, Vol. 64, pp. 254–281.

Rottenberg, S., (1956), "On choice in labor markets", *Industrial and Labor Relations Review*, Vol. 9, pp. 183–199.

Routh, G., (1980), 'Occupation and Pay in Great Britain: 1906–1979', 2nd edn, Macmillan, London.

Royal Commission on the Distribution of Income and Wealth, (1980), 'An A to Z of Wealth and Income', HMSO, London.

Salop, J., Salop, S., (1976), "Self-selection and turnover in the labor market", *Quarterly Journal of Economics*, Vol. 90, pp. 619–627.

Salop, S.C., (1973), "Systematic job search and unemployment", *Review of Economic Studies*, Vol. 40, pp. 191–201.

Schultz, T.W., (1961), "Investment in human capital", *American Economic Review*, Vol. 51, pp. 1–17.

Selby Smith, C., (1970), "Costs and benefits in further education: some evidence of a pilot study", *Economic Journal*, Vol. 80, pp. 583–604.

Shah, A., (1985), "Does education act as a screening device for certain British occupations", *Oxford Economic Papers*, Vol. 37, pp. 118–124.

Sheldlake, J., Vickerstaff, S., (1987), 'The History of Industrial Training in Britain', Gower Press, London.

Shipiro, D., Shaw, L.B., (1983), "Growth in labor force attachment of married women: accounting for the changes in the 1970s", *Southern Economic Journal*, , Vol. 50, pp. 461–473.

Shishko, R., Rostker, B., (1976), "The economics of multiple job holding", *American Economic Review*, Vol. 66, pp. 298–308.

Siebert, W.S., (1985), "Development in the economics of human capital", in Carline, D., *et al.*, (1985).

Simon, H., (1979), "Rational decision making in business organizations", *American Economic Review*, Vol. 69, pp. 493–513.

Simon, H.A., (1957), 'Administrative Behaviour: A Study of Decision-making Processes in Administrative Organizations', Macmillan, London.

Singh, A., (1977), "United Kingdom industry and the world economy: a case of de-industralization", *Cambridge Journal of Economics*, Vol. 1, pp. 113–136.

Sjaastad, L.A., (1962), "The costs and returns of human migration", *Journal of Political Economy*, Vol. 70 [Supplement], pp. 60–93.

Sleeper, R.D., (1972), "SET and the shake out: a note on the productivity effects of the Selective Employment Tax", *Oxford Economic Papers*, Vol. 24, pp. 197–211.

Sloane, P.J., (1985), "Discrimination in the labour market", in Carline, D., *et al.*, (1985).

Smart, M.W., (1974), "Labour market areas: uses and definition", *Progress in Planning*, Vol. 2, Part 4, monograph edition.

Smith, A., (1961), "The Wealth of Nations", University Paperbacks, London.

Smith, E., (1988), "Vacancies and recruitment in Great Britain", *Employment Gazette*, Vol. 96, pp. 211–213.

Smith, I., (1983), 'The Management of Remuneration', Institute of Personnel Management, London.

Smith, J.H., (1966), "The analysis of labour mobility", in Roberts, B.C. and Smith, J.H., (1966).

Smith, R.S., (1979), "Wage differentials and public policy: a review", *Industrial and Labor Relations Review*, Vol. 32, pp. 339–352.

Spence, M., (1973), "Job market signalling", *Quarterly Journal of Economics*, Vol. 87, pp. 355–374.

Stewart, M., (1983), "Relative earnings and individual union membership in the United Kingdom", *Economica*, Vol. 50, pp. 111–125.

Stigler, G.J., (1946), "The economics of minimum wage legislation", *American Economic Review*, Vol. 36, pp. 358–367.

Stigler, G.J., (1962), "Information in the labor market", *Journal of Political Economy*, Vol. 70 [Supplement], pp. 94–105.

Summerfield, P., (1984), 'Women Workers in the 2nd World War', Croom Helm, London.

Symonds, J.S.V., (1985), "Relative prices and the demand for labour in British manufacturing", *Economica*, Vol. 52, pp. 37–49.

Symonds, J.S.V., Layard, R., (1984), "Neoclassical demand for labour functions for six major economies", *Economic Journal*, Vol. 94, pp. 788–799.

Tarling, R., Wilkinson, F., (1982), "Changes in the inter-industry structure of earnings in the post-war period", *Cambridge Journal of Economics*, Vol. 6, pp. 231–248.

Taubman, P., (1976), "Earnings, education, genetics and environment", *Journal of Human Resources*, Vol. 11, pp. 447–461.

Thirwell, A.P., (1970), "Regional Phillips curves", *Bulletin of the Oxford University Institute of Economics and Statistics*, Vol. 32, pp. 19–32.

Thirwell, A.P., (1982), "De-industrialization in the United Kingdom", *Lloyds Bank Review*, No. 144, pp. 22–37.

Thomas, B., Moxham, J., Jones, J.A.G., (1969), "A cost–benefit analysis of industrial training", *British Journal of Industrial Relations*, Vol. 7, pp. 231–264.

Thomas, R.B., (1973), "On the definition of 'shortages' in administered labour markets", *Manchester School of Economics and Social Sciences*, Vol. 41, pp. 169–186.

Thomas, R.B., Deaton, D., (1977), 'Labour Shortage and Economic Analysis', Heinemann Educational Books for Blackwell, Oxford.

Thomason, G., (1985), 'Job Evaluation: Objectives and Methods', Institute of Personnel Management, London.

Thurlow, L., (1975), 'Generating Inequality', Basic Books, New York.

Treasury White Paper, (1967), 'Nationalised Industries: A Review of Economic and Financial Objectives', HMSO (Cmnd 3437), London.

Treble, J.G., (1981), "A critique of the Lewis method for estimating the union/non-union wage differential", Research Paper No. 78, University of Hull, Hull.

Turner, H.A., (1964), "Inflation and wage differentials", in Dunlop, J.T. (1964).

Tylecote, A.B., (1975), "Determinants of changes in the wage hierarchy in United Kingdom manufacturing industry 1954–70: a test of a new theory of wage determination under collective bargaining", *British Journal of Industrial Relations*, Vol. 13, pp. 65–77.

Wabe, S., Leech, D., (1978), "Relative earnings in United Kingdom manufacturing: a reconsideration of the evidence", *Economic Journal*, Vol. 88, pp. 296–313.

Wachter, M.L., (1974), "Primary and secondary labor markets: a critique of the dual approach", *Brooking's Papers on Economic Activity*, Vol. 3, pp. 637–693.

Wales, T.J., Woodland, A.D., (1976), "The estimation of household utility functions and labor supply response", *International Economic Review*, Vol. 17, pp. 397–410.

Walsh, W.D., (1977), "The short-run behaviour of skilled wage differentials", *Industrial and Labor Relations Review*, Vol. 30, pp. 302–313.

Walton, R.E., McKersie, R.B., (1965), 'Behavioral Theory of Labour Negotiations', McGraw-Hill, London.

Weiss, L.W., (1966), "Concentration and labor earnings", *American Economic Journal*, Vol. 56, pp. 96–117.

Weisskoff, F.B., (1972), "Women's place in the labour market", *American Economic Review*, Vol. 62 [Supplement], pp. 161–166.

Werneke, D., (1978), "Economic slowdown and women's employment opportunities", *International Labour Review*, Vol. 117, pp. 37–52.

White, S., (1968), "The process of occupational choice", *British Journal of Industrial Relations*, Vol. 6, pp. 166–184.

Whitfield, K., (1982), "Professional labour markets", in Creedy, J., Thomas, B. (1982).

Whitley, J.D., Wilson, R.A., (1986), "The impact on employment of a reduction in the length of the working week", *Cambridge Journal of Economics*, Vol. 10, pp. 43–59.

Wilkinson, G.C.G., Mace J.D., (1973), "Shortage or surplus of engineers: a review of recent UK evidence", *British Journal of Industrial Relations*, Vol. 11, pp. 105–123.

Williams, W.M., ed., (1974), 'Occupational Choice', Allen and Unwin, London.

Williamson, D.E., (1970), 'Corporate Control and Business Behaviour', Prentice Hall, London.

Wood, A., (1978), 'A Theory of Pay', Cambridge University Press, Cambridge.

Woodhall, M., (1974), "Investment in industrial training: an assessment of the effects of the Industrial Training Act on the volume and costs of training", *British Journal of Industrial Relations*, Vol. 12, pp. 71–90.

Wootton, B., (1962), 'Social Foundations of Wages Policy: A Study of the Contemporary British Wage and Salary Structure', 2nd edn, Allen and Unwin, London.

Wright Bakke, E., (1954), 'Labor Mobility and Economic Opportunity', The M.I.T. Press, Cambridge, Massachusetts.

Ziderman, A., (1973), "Does it pay to take a degree", *Oxford Economic Papers*, Vol. 25, pp. 262–274.

Ziderman, A., (1978), 'Manpower Training: Theory and Policy', Macmillan, London.

Index